These Sought a Country

THESE SOUGHT A COUNTRY

A History of Israel in Old Testament Times

ROBERT L. CATE

BROADMAN PRESS
Nashville, Tennessee

© Copyright 1985 • Broadman Press
All rights reserved
4212-32
ISBN: 0-8054-1232-8
Dewey Decimal Classification:
Subject Heading:
Library of Congress Catalog Card Number:
Printed in the United States of America

Abraham and Lot
© 1976, Convention Press

Moses Becomes Israel's Leader
© 1975, Convention Press

David at the threshing Floor
© 1983, Convention Press

Isaiah Writes God's Message
© 1984, Convention Press

Solomon Dedicates the Temple
© 1982, Convention Press

Scripture quotations are from the Revised Standard Version of the Bible, copyrighted 1946, 1952, © 1971, 1973.

Library of Congress Cataloging in Publication Data

Cate, Robert L.
  These sought a country.

  Bibliography: p.
  Includes index.
  1. Bible. O.T.—History of Biblical events.
2. Jews—History—To 70 A.D. I. Title.
BS1197.C34   1985   221.9′5   84-23909
ISBN 0-8054-1232-8

To Ruth,
who believes that to accomplish much,
one must attempt much
with the expectation of achieving

Contents

Preface	11
The Need for Such a Book	13
The Purposes of This Book	15
The Arrangement of the Book	17

Sources for the Study; Major Problems for Consideration; The Background of the Period; The History of the Period; The Significance of the Period

The Author's Presuppositions	21
1. Introduction to Old Testament History	23
Major Approaches to Old Testament History	23

The "Noncritical Approach"; The "Literary-Critical Approach"; The "Tradition-Historical Approach"; The "Critical, Biblical Archaelogical Approach"; The "Historical, Archaeological Biblicism Approach"; The "Sociological Approach"

The Approach of This Book	30
Preliminary Considerations	33

Israel's Approach to History; Israel's Time Consciousness; The Nature of Old Testament Chronological Data; Establishing an Absolute Chronology

2. Israel's Prehistory: The Patriarchal Period	43
Sources for the Study	44
Major Problems for Consideration	45

The Nature of the Biblical Narratives; The Chronology of the Period; The Relationship to the Habiru'

The Background of the Period	55

The Patriarchal Wanderings; The Patriarchal Vocations; The Patriarchal Customs; The Patriarchal Names

The History of the Period	60

Abraham; Isaac; Jacob/Israel; Joseph

	The Significance of the Period	85
3.	Israel's Birth: The Exodus and Wilderness Wanderings	88
	Sources for the Study	89
	Major Problems for Consideration	90

      The Silence of Egyptian Records; The Date of the Exodus; The Numbers Involved in the Exodus; The Location of Sinai; The Nature of the Covenant at Sinai

    The Background of the Period 101

      The Hyksos; The Amarna Letters; The Akhenaten Heresy; Building Programs; Law in the Ancient World

    The History of the Period 105

      The Sojourn in Egypt; The Oppression of Israel; The Early Days of Moses; The Deliverance from Egypt; The Journey from Egypt to Sinai; Israel Before the Mount; The Rebellion at Kadesh; From Kadesh to the Plains of Moab

    The Significance of the Period 127

      The Concept of God; The Concept of Rebellion and Forgiveness; The Concept of the Chosen People; The Basis of Hebrew Prophetism

4.	Israel's Land: The Conquest and Settlement	132
	Sources for the Study	132
	Major Problems for Consideration	135

      The Geography of Palestine; The Nature of the Conquest; The Chronology of the Conquest; The Nature of the Oppressions; The Chronology of the Oppressions; The Nature of a Judge

    The Background of the Period 149

      The Major Powers; The Canaanites; The Philistines; The Tranjordan Peoples: Edom, Ammon, and Moab; The Midianites and Amalekites

    The History of the Period 159

      The Work of Joshua; The Period of the Judges

    The Significance of the Period 185

      A Time of Transition; The Land as God's Gift; The Concept of "Called" Leaders; The Cyclical View of History; The Need for Human Government; God's Sovereignty

5.	The Hebrew Kingdom: Union and Division	191
	Sources for the Study	191
	Major Problems for Consideration	194

      The Nature of the Biblical Sources; The Chronology; The Nature of the Kingship; The Nature of the Tribal Union

    The Background of the Period 203
        International Weaknesses; International Pressures; The
        Nature of Warfare; International Developments; Internal
        Developments in Israel
    The History of the Period 210
        Samuel and Saul: An Opportunity for Greatness; Saul and
        David: Hostility and Dissolution; David's Kingship: The
        Best and the Worst; Solomon's Kingship: Days of Success
        and Failure
    The Significance of the Period 236
        The Concept of Kingship; Change in the Concept of Nationhood; The Awareness of Responsibility Before God; The Nature of the Hebrew Prophetic Movement; The Future of the Hebrew Messianic Hope

6. Division and Destruction: Judah and Israel to the Fall of
    Samaria 241
    Sources for the Study 242
    Major Problems for Consideration 244
        The Chronological Data; The Nature of Baalism; The
        Geographical Influences
    The Background of the Period 254
        The Aramaean Kingdoms; Assyria; Egypt; Other Peoples
        of Significance
    The History of the Period 261
        The Time of Separation and Conflict; The Time of Israelite Supremacy; The Prophetic Revolution; Israel's Revival as a World Power; Israel's Ultimate Downfall
    The Significance of the Period 294
        The Insecurity of Faithlessness; The Flowering of Hebrew Prophecy; The Developing Concept of Judgment; The Developing Concept of Mercy; The Growing Sense of God's Sovereignty

7. The Road to Judgment: Judah to the Fall of Jerusalem 302
    Sources for the Study 303
    Major Problems for Consideration 305
        The Chronological Difficulties; The Scythians, Imaginary
        or Real?; Josiah's Reform, Deuteronomy, and Jeremiah
    The Background of the Period 309
        The Assyrians; The Egyptians; The Scythians; The
        Babylonians

    The History of the Period 316
        The Period of Assyrian Domination; The Great Reform;
        Judah's Last Days
    The Significance of the Period 336
        An Enlarged Understanding of God; A New Hope

8. From the Fall of Jerusalem to Alexander's Conquest 339
    Sources for the Study 339
    Major Problems for Consideration 341
        Chronology; Problems Due to Geographical Location; The
        Last King of Babylon: A Nonproblem; The Nature of the
        Fall of Babylon; The Sequence of Ezra and Nehemiah; The
        Ten "Lost" Tribes; The Effect of Foreign Religions; The
        Rise of Judaism
    The Background of the Period 351
        The Babylonians; The Persians
    The History of the Period 357
        The Era of the Babylonian Captivity; The Return from
        Exile and the Rebuilding of the Temple; The Period of
        Ezra and Nehemiah
    The Significance of the Period 374
        A Theology of Suffering; The Decline of Prophecy; The
        Rise of Judaism; The Beginning of Canonization; The
        Samaritan Schism

9. The Message of Israel's History 379
    The Sovereignty of God 381
    The Mission of Redemption 383
    The Relationship Between Faith and History 385
    The Inadequacy of Empty Ritual 387
    The Demand for Practical Righteousness 390
    The Covenant Community 392
    The Expectation of Committed Leadership 394
    The Legacy of a Dynamic Faith 395
    Setting the Stage for the New Testament 396
Appendix: Chronological Table 399
Annoted Bibliography 402
Scripture Index 405

Preface

"Why?"

"Why do we Christians use the Old Testament anyway? The New Testament is the basis for our faith."

"Why should I know anything about the Old Testament, its history, or its message?"

These questions and countless others like them expose the perplexity which most Christians feel about the Old Testament and its message. Among contemporary Christians, I find several different attitudes toward the Old Testament and its study. Perhaps you can identify with one or more of these.

First, there are those who simply believe that since we are New Testament Christians, we have absolutely no need to study the Old Testament at all. Such persons are content to devote all of their study of the Bible to the New Testament. Unfortunately, they frequently forget that the New Testament is the flower which grew from the Old Testament root. All the early followers of Jesus were Jews, and He Himself was a Jew. Paul was a rabbi. The Old Testament was their Bible. Trying to understand the mission and message of Jesus without some knowledge of the Old Testament is like trying to understand a house by looking at the roof, without examining the walls and foundations which support it.

Second, there are other Christians who think that a knowledge of the Old Testament is important for its antiquarian interest. These Christians study the Old Testament as a history book. They either are seeking to understand the background of Christianity or are just trying to learn something of ancient history. For either reason, a study of the history of the Old Testament is important. Although the reasons of these two groups are different, their desires are essentially the same.

Third, some Christians approach the Old Testament on the same plane as the New Testament. They see both Old and New Testaments as a part of their Bibles. Thus, the Old Testament is sacred Scripture. But they approach the Old Testament without any understanding of its history or the times in which it was written. For these people, all Scripture is viewed upon the same level. Any word from the Old Testament, they believe, is to be taken just as we would take any word from the New Testament. When such an approach leads to a difficult passage, those who make this approach often just ignore the problem.

Fourth, there are those who realize that if the Old Testament is the root from which the New Testament grew, we have an obligation to master it in order to understand our faith more fully. But they also realize that if the Old Testament is to be understood, it must be understood as a part of the revelatory processes of God. If this is true, then studying the New Testament without studying the Old is like reading the last chapter in a murder mystery without reading the whole book. But there is a difference. Reading the mystery is for my entertainment. Studying the Bible is for my life or death. I can misunderstand a mystery, and I have simply lost a bit of entertainment. If I misunderstand the Bible, I may miss out on my eternal relationship with God. Further, even if that does not happen, by misunderstanding the Bible, I may cause others to miss out on their relationship to God. Thus, the better part of wisdom calls me to a mastery of the Old Testament.

For the Christian, there is yet another reason for studying the Old Testament. From a pietistic standpoint, it is easy to say that we have the Old Testament because God inspired and preserved it; therefore, we ought to study it. But from a human standpoint, we Christians have the Old Testament because the early Christians preserved it. It was the only Bible they had. Even more important, they saw Jesus as its fulfillment. It had led them to Him. Most important, however, Jesus Himself set an example for us by using and commending it. In fact, Jesus said: "Think not that I have come to abolish the law and the prophets; I have come not to abolish them but to fulfil them. For truly, I say to you, till heaven and earth pass away, not an iota, not a dot, will pass from the law until all is accomplished" (Matt. 5:17-18). Here, then, is our basic reason for giving serious study to the Old Testament. It should be sufficient.

The Need for Such a Book

This viewpoint, however, brings us to another question. Granted that we Christians should study the Old Testament, why should we study Old Testament history? The answer to this question is more obvious. The Old Testament itself deals with a faith which was born and developed over a long period of history. The period from Abraham to the beginning of the New Testament covers at least eighteen to twenty centuries. It involved nations and peoples which are wholly foreign to us, such as Babylon, Assyria, Phoenicia, Philistia, Egypt, Moab, Edom, and others. It involved people with strange names and stranger customs. Who among us is not startled to read Ezekiel's words about Nebuchadnezzar? "For the king of Babylon stands at the parting of the way, . . . he shakes the arrows, he consults the teraphim, he looks at the liver" (Ezek. 21:21). Furthermore, many of the messages of the prophets are relatively meaningless if we do not know the historical background against which they were proclaimed. Thus, if we are going to deal seriously with the message of the Old Testament, we must deal with the history of the world from which it came and in which it was written.

At precisely this point, many of us throw up our hands in surrender. We know little of Israel's history and less of that of the nations round about it. We have heard stories about David, Abraham, Moses, Isaiah, Daniel, and Samson, but we seldom know much about how they are related to one another. These are the things which we must know if we are going to be good stewards of God's revelation to us. So we must study the history of the Old Testament if we are going to be students of the Bible and followers of God. It is that simple.

On the other hand, perhaps we need to hear the words of an Old Testament preacher who said, "Of making many books there is no end, and much study is a weariness of the flesh" (Eccl. 12:12). As we look upon the shelves of the book stores and of our libraries, we discover that a large number of Old Testament history books are already in existence. Is there any real justification for another? As noted in chapter 1, "Introduction to Old Testament History," there are several different approaches made to Old Testament history. Many of these have presuppositions with which I do not agree and which, therefore, appear to weaken their study. But that is not the main reason for another book as I see it.

Books which deal with Old Testament history fall mainly into two categories. Many books are well written and quite thorough in their survey of Old Testament history. That is precisely the problem. These books get so technical that the busy, volunteer worker in a church has neither the time nor the background to deal with them adequately. Given such a book, most lay Bible teachers get bogged down quite early and never finish the study. This may leave you worse off than before you started because to confusion has been added discouragement. You begin to feel that the subject just cannot be mastered by a nonspecialist.

On the other hand, other Old Testament histories are written from a nontechnical standpoint, giving a hurried survey of the subject. Unfortunately, these books frequently give a very simplistic treatment to Old Testament history and do not grapple with some of the very real problems which are there. Such treatments almost leave you feeling guilty for raising a question which some authors do not even identify.

My intent was to try to write in the area between these two extremes. I wrote primarily (though not exclusively) for volunteer teachers of Christian Bible study groups. It matters not whether such teachers work in a traditional

PREFACE

Sunday School or in some nontraditional weekday Bible study group. There is a need for help here which generally has not been met by most of the books on Old Testament history that are currently on the market.

The Purposes of This Book

Given the particular target group and the need which I have identified, my writing of this book is governed by several distinct purposes.

The basic purpose of the book is set forth in as concise a form as possible, the history of the Old Testament era. In doing this, I intend to deal in a fairly comprehensive manner with the history of the Hebrew people from the time of the call of Abraham to the fall of the Persian empire before the forces of Alexander the Great. These two extremes will set the temporal boundaries. However, the people of God did not live in a vacuum. Many of the nations of the ancient Near East came in contact with the Hebrews, and their histories significantly affected each other. So we shall deal with the contemporary history of the nations around Israel, as well as those peoples who never achieved nationhood, as they came in contact with and affected the history of the people of the Old Testament. This book, then, is a survey of ancient Near Eastern history as it relates to the people of God.

In addition, since history in the modern sense is quite different from history in the ancient sense, I have sought to help modern readers bridge this gap. We need to come to an understanding of the way the ancient Hebrews wrote history. It is important for us to recognize that what the biblical writers were recording was not really a history of Israel. They were recording the acts of God with, through, and to Israel. Thus, their primary concern was not just an event but the meaning of that event. Because of this, I have tried to help readers see not merely what was happening to the peoples of the Old Testament but also what it meant to them and to God.

Furthermore, I am hoping to provide here a historical framework upon which the serious Bible student can place other parts of the Old Testament in order to better understand them. The framework will serve as the basis for your future study of the prophets, Israel's worship, and the religion and theology of the Old Testament. In addition, by tracing the historical workings of God with Israel in the Old Testament, we shall find a basis for understanding His workings with us. God is still the God who works through history. The patterns of His past actions cast a shadow by which we can grasp something of His present acts.

Every student of the Bible needs a reference book of biblical history to which he or she can turn when dealing with the historical background of passages. I intend for this book to furnish that kind of future reference for your study of the Old Testament. I would hope that you would find this book more valuable as you turn to it again and again over the passing years. Admittedly, parts of it may become outdated with new discoveries in the biblical world. Essentially, I have focused upon the more assured results of biblical historical scholarship.

Related to this, I have sought to bring to this study the results of the best in contemporary scholarship. The best works of the biblical historians have been surveyed and are reflected in my treatments. Further, the results of the archaeology of the biblical world have also been brought to bear. This, of course, includes the historical records of the surrounding nations as such records are available. At the same time, keeping my target audience in mind, I have not burdened the book with footnotes. Anyone who reads more widely either in books identified in the annotated bibliography or in other books will recognize my indebtedness to all who have gone before.

This brings me to the final purpose of this book. It is my hope and prayer that this study will be exciting. The history of the people of God was exciting. If it becomes dull, it is my fault as a historian, not the history itself. If you become excited in reading about the ways of God with His people, perhaps you will continue your study beyond this book. Furthermore, if you are excited by the study, it will be easier for you to get others excited about it. The end result of that kind of chain reaction will be more people studying the Bible.

In no way is this book intended to be a substitute for your study of the Old Testament. Rather, I want to lead you to a deeper and more thorough study of the Old Testament, to the end that you will hear God speak to you through its pages. This is a guidebook to the twisting and turnings of Israel's history. Use it together with your Bible, and you will find it far more profitable. In order to facilitate this, you will find two things in the back of the book which will be helpful. The "Chronological Tables" bring together in one place a survey of the basic dates of significance for the study of the Old Testament. The "Scripture Index" will help you locate any biblical passage to which reference is made within the book.

The Arrangement of the Book

A quick glance at the "Contents" will show that, with the exception of the introductory and the concluding chapters, each of the remaining chapters has the same basic outline. This is quite deliberate and is intended to aid you in your study. Chapter 1, "Introduction to Old Testament History," does precisely what it says. You will find there the basic items of information which you need to understand in order fully to appreciate the nature of the Old Testament history. You will discover the basic approaches made by modern scholarship to this study, as well as my reasons for the approach which I have taken. More important, you will be able to see the differences between the way a modern writer and an ancient writer recorded history. This will enable you to better understand the task and the problems of understanding biblical history. It will also help you to appreciate the creative genius of those ancient biblical historians who were moved by God to write.

The concluding chapter, "The Message of Israel's History," brings together in summary fashion the meaning of the events we will have studied. This is not intended as a theological survey as such. Rather, it is intended to be seen as the proclamation of Israel's history writers.

The intervening chapters may surprise you by the identical outlines used for each. The reasons for this are all based upon a desire to make the book more useful for you. Consider each of the sections.

Sources for the Study

Anyone seeking to study the history of any particular era in the Old Testament world needs to know the primary sources which are available for use. Furthermore, as you seek to evaluate my work or to check the ways by which I have arrived at my conclusions, you need to know which primary historical sources I have used.

In addition to the primary sources which come from the ancient world itself, you also need to know those scholars whose works have been most influential in the field and upon my own thinking. This kind of material will serve as an aid to you if you desire to do further study in this particular period of ancient history. (Those who are specialists in the field will quickly recognize that my listings of secondary sources in the field is not intended to be exhaustive. I am only attempting to suggest places where the reader can go for further study.)

Furthermore, if you are merely seeking to get an overview of the history of any particular period of Hebrew history, the source section of each chapter can be omitted without serious harm. If, at the moment, you are only interested in the ongoing story of the period, this section should be skipped. It is included with each chapter for the person who is interested in help for making a broader and deeper study of the particular period.

Major Problems for Consideration

The study of any period of history is almost always confronted with a long list of problems which must be considered and about which conclusions must be drawn. Studying history is never easy, for the historian must always be selective. We cannot deal with everything which happened in any particular era. Furthermore, we must face the fact that those who have written history or recorded events have already been selective on the basis of their own purposes and biases. For example, there was a great deal going on in the time of Ahab and Jezebel besides their confrontations with Elijah. People were being born, others were dying, wars were being fought, and the like. But almost all of these events were not of interest to the biblical historian. On the other hand, some of these events were recorded by other, nonbiblical historians. We have to try to reconcile these events and then decide how to deal with them, or even whether to deal with them at all.

Furthermore, we sometimes have records within the Bible itself which give us real problems in interpretation. These, too, must be considered and evaluated. For anyone who seeks to grapple with Old Testament history, a knowledge of these basic problems is essential. You need to know how I have dealt with them. But if all you are interested in at the moment is a survey of the actual story of Israel's history, this section, too, can be skipped. On the other hand, you may already be familiar with the story of the period. If what you are looking for is help in grappling with these historical problems, then this section becomes of major significance. How, or whether, you use this section will depend upon your needs at the moment.

The Background of the Period

In each chapter is included a section which seeks to give a brief, broad background of the period under study. Here I have set forth the *basic* and *significant* features of what was going on in the world in the era with which the chapter deals. For example, in the time of the Exodus, a great deal was going on in the Mesopotamian Valley. But these events were of no significance for an understanding of what was happening to the Hebrews. However, what went on in that geographical area is of extreme significance for understanding the final days of the kingdom of Judah. Thus in the earlier chapter, we have no need to consider this as a part of the background while in the latter we do.

Significant geographical features are frequently quite important in understanding various periods of history.

The location of the major north-south highways is important for understanding some of the differences between the histories of the Northern Kingdom and the Southern Kingdom. Other geographical features are important for understanding the period of the patriarchs. Where these appear to me to be important, I have pointed them out, in order to help you get a better understanding of why some things happened the way they did.

The History of the Period

This section of each chapter is obviously the main feature. Here I set forth the basic story of what was going on at the time. If all you wish at the moment is to get a survey of the history of the period, this is the only section of the chapter which you need to read. If, on the other hand, you want a survey of the history of the entire Old Testament era, then you should read this section in each chapter. For a more serious survey of the history, either of a particular period or of the whole Old Testament, you will need to deal with the other sections of each chapter.

The Significance of the Period

The final section of each chapter is my attempt to point out what I consider to be the basic significance of each period. We must remember that we are dealing with more than history, we are dealing with divine revelation. The Hebrews themselves identified the Books of Joshua, Judges, 1 and 2 Samuel, and 1 and 2 Kings as a part of their canon of the prophets. They were called "The Former Prophets." This classification clearly indicates that they were preserved because they proclaimed a message. We will have abused our study of their history if we do not seek to understand what it is that this material proclaimed and still teaches us.

Again, if all you are interested in at a particular time is a survey of the history, then you can ignore this final section of each chapter. If, on the other hand, your primary interest rests with seeing the development of the Hebrews' basic faith, you can place primary attention upon this section along with the summary in the final chapter of the book, "The Message of Israel's History."

My intent through the planning, preparation, and writing of this book has been to make it as useful and as flexible as possible. I pray that you will find it to be so.

The Author's Presuppositions

In reading any book, it is important to know the author's presuppositions, for that is the basis upon which he makes his judgments concerning the available evidence. It is also the basis by which he determines the emphases he makes in his presentation. More often than not, authors do not set forth their presuppositions and you are left to try to deduce them from the book itself. In order to help you at this point, I am stating my basic presuppositions as I approached the task of writing.

First, my fundamental presuppositions have to do with God. I believe that God is. I believe that He is the Creator, the sovereign Lord of the universe. I further believe that He is not some unmoved mover, nor is He a grandfatherly type who holds Himself aloof from the real issues of life and death. It is my belief that God is intimately involved in the affairs of life and that He is concerned with you and me, His creatures.

Second, I also have some presuppositions concerning humanity in general, and you and me in particular. I have sinned. So have you. Furthermore, our sin was not just a slip into disobedience; it was a willful rebellion on our part. We have known what God intended for us and have stubbornly refused to do His will or to follow His leadership. By our sin, we have alienated ourselves from God because His awesome holiness and righteousness cannot condone or put up with sinfulness. In addition, struggle as I might, there is no way by which I can make myself fit for God's presence again. The stain of my sin is indelibly marked upon my life.

Third, I have some presuppositions regarding what has been done for you and me in our predicament of alienation. God, while awesome in His holiness, is also loving. Recognizing our helplessness, He has acted in His love to effect a way of redemption for us. He has come into the world in a special way through the presence of His only Son, Jesus Christ. Through the death and resurrection of Jesus, He has Himself borne the punishment for our sin and offered us new life through Christ Jesus. This new life springs out of the overabundant love of God and is made available to all sinful people through their own faith and trust in what He has done.

Fourth, I also presuppose that God has not left Himself in this world without witness. Aside from seeing His presence in the world of nature, you and I have been left with the Bible, God's revelation, and His Holy Spirit, who will guide us into all truth. The events which the Bible records were a historical statement of the historical faith of God's people. As such, it can best be understood against the historical background from which it sprang. It is this, then, which makes our dealing with the history of God's people in the Old Testament of primary importance. If, as I believe, God has spoken through that history, then I should try to know that history to be better able to hear Him speak. In relation to this, I have a negative presupposition. The Bible is not primarily a history Book. It is a Book of revelation, a Book of faith. If we deal with it only, or even primarily, as a history book, we shall misunderstand it entirely.

Finally, as I come to grips with how God dealt with His people in the ancient world, I will be better able to see and to understand His work in this present age. I study biblical history in general, and Old Testament history in particular, to hear God speak to me through that study and to enable me to interpret His works in our world today. If I am going to be the best servant I can be, there is no other way.

I am a committed Christian, nurtured in the faith of our fathers. I have been called to minister to God's people through the study and proclamation of His Word. Unashamedly, it is from this standpoint that I present to you this survey of Old Testament history.

1
Introduction to Old Testament History

The study of Old Testament history really does not need a defense. For any serious student of the Bible, the pressing need for such a study is immediately obvious. The Old Testament cannot be understood apart from the history of its people. On the other hand, it should be equally as obvious, but seldom appears to be so, that the study of Old Testament history is no substitute for the study of the Old Testament itself. Rather, our study of Israel's history should arise from the study of the Old Testament. It should also guide us back to the study of the Old Testament with renewed vigor and enthusiasm.

Major Approaches to Old Testament History

In any survey of Old Testament history, we need to arrive at a definition of precisely what we intend to cover. Various historians disagree as to precisely when Israel became a nation or even when we can truly say that we are dealing with the history of Israel. Some begin with Abraham and the patriarchs, others begin with Moses and the Exodus experience, a third group begins with settlement in the land of Canaan, and still others begin with the rise of the Hebrew monarchy under Saul. Not only is the beginning point difficult to define, so is the ending point. We may end with the fall of Judah to the Babylonians, we may end with the conclusion of the Persian period, or we might not end until we actually get to the time of the New Testament or even beyond. This kind of difference is not what I will deal with as we consider the major approaches to Old Testament history. These boundaries, while very important, are merely a matter of an author's definition.

What I am concerned with at this point is not the delineation of our time boundaries but the determination of the basic philosophical and theological approaches made to the subject. To these we must first direct our thought and attention.

While there are many variations upon the approaches to Old Testament history, it appears to me that six basic approaches have been made to the subject. No one is as aware as I that these cannot be as precisely separated as I am doing here. At the same time, I am seeking to identify what appears to me to be the basic principle(s) behind the interpretation and presentaiton of the subject matter in each. I will also list what appears to me to be the best example of each of these approaches.

It ought to be obvious, but may not be, that any approach to Old Testament history takes as its basic beginning point the Old Testament itself. However, the ways by which the Old Testament's information is handled differs rather widely.

Before we actually consider these different approaches to the study of Old Testament history, there is one definition which we must get before us. You need to know what I mean by the phrase, "the critical study of the Old Testament." To some persons, the idea of criticism carries a negative connotation. While that may be understandable, it is not really correct. When you and I engage in critical study of the Bible, we are not opposed to the Bible or trying to tear it down. What we are doing is giving a serious consideration to all the evidence on any issue and seeking to reach a conclusion based upon our evaluation of that evidence.

You may go to a doctor complaining of a series of nagging headaches which aspirin do not seem to ease. He might hurriedly examine you, remember that the last patient he faced with similar complaints had a brain tumor, and decide to operate. But he might (and hopefully would) give more serious thought to your case, evaluate X rays and brain scans, check you over thoroughly, and decide rather that you were wearing shirt collars which were too tight. It would be tragic to go to a doctor who did not think critically about your problem. It can be just as tragic to deal with the Old Testament without thinking critically about all of the evidence which can be gathered concerning any issue. Since the Bible is concerned with matters of eternal significance, we must give its study our best attention, our very best thought. Anything less can be death dealing.

Let us clearly understand as we approach our study of the history of the Old Testament that *the Christian does not have anything to fear from truth.* Our obligation is rather to determine what is truth and then to act upon it. With this background, we shall now consider the basic approaches which have been made to the study of Old Testament history.

The "Noncritical Approach"

This approach is usually characterized by beginning with the evidence of the historical material of the Old Testament, taking it simply at face value, and making little or no enquiry into archaeology or other ancient records. This approach is usually characterized by a verse-by-verse or paragraph-by-paragraph study and neither sees nor considers apparent discrepancies or difficulties. Typical of this approach is that of H. I. Hester, *The Heart of Hebrew History.* Books based upon this approach are sometimes superficial, seldom acknowledging the real problems which are present and the gaps which are left in any reconstruction of this history. For a hurried survey of the biblical material, this approach may be adequate. For a real understanding of Old Testament history, it leaves a great deal to be desired.

The "Literary-Critical Approach"

Far to the extreme other end of the spectrum of Old Testament histories are those which I characterize as the "literary-critical approach." Those who are familiar with Old Testament studies will be quite familiar with what I mean by "literary-critical." For the reader who is not familiar with the approach, it is the outgrowth of a long period of development which reached its zenith with the work of Julius Wellhausen. The approach assumes that the Old Testament came into being as a series of literary compositions which primarily reflect the times in which they were written and may be grossly inaccurate with regard to the actual information which they claim to record.

Although these views were later modified to some extent, the basic consequence of such an approach to the study of the Old Testament is that the author approaches his subject with a preconceived philosophy as to how the history and theology or faith of Israel developed. Anything which does not fit is usually cast aside as some kind of late addition. Basically, such an approach to the study of Old Testament history results in the elimination of biblical evidence in favor of other evidence or in favor of the author's own predetermined concept of history. Perhaps the best example of this kind of approach is that made by T. H. Robinson and W. O. E. Oesterley in their two-volume work *A History of Israel.* Although quite well done, its basic approach leaves a great deal to be desired by those who believe that biblical evidence should not be so quickly abandoned.

The "Tradition-Historical Approach"

Growing out of the literary-critical school of Old Testament studies, but reacting to a too glib abandonment of biblical evidence, came a methodology which is generally classified as the "tradition-historical approach." This approach recognizes that the Old Testament materials did take their final form through a series of distinct developments but that, prior to the actual writing of the materials, there was a long prehistory of their transmission. We find it difficult to understand since our culture is based so much upon the printed page; but once ancient oral traditions took a fixed form, they could be passed down relatively unchanged for generations. (This is still true in all societies where writing is either unknown or is the province of the very few who are scribes.)

This approach to Old Testament history seeks to study the collection and preservation of Israel's historical traditions, trying to write as much of a history of traditions as anything else. At the same time, this approach usually seeks to integrate Israel's traditions into those of other ancient Near Eastern countries. This approach also asks Why? of the material which isn't there. Unfortunately, sometimes the answers to these questions may be accorded the same weight as the material which is present. The best example of this kind of approach is that by Martin Noth, *The History of Israel*. Unfortunately, his work seems to give less attention to archaeological evidence than it merits. He also, it appears to me, works harder to prove his own theories than to evaluate all of the evidence which was available. Perhaps the most unusual dimension of Noth's work is found in the era of the conquest and settlement. We shall consider it again at that point of our study. His greatest contribution was in his recognition that the material in Joshua, Judges, 1 and 2 Samuel, and 1 and 2 Kings all share a common tradition which appears to be quite similar in outlook to Deuteronomy. Siegfried Hermann's more recent book *A History of Israel* carries on beyond Noth's work but focuses primarily upon issues which are presently being debated in Germany and are of little interest to the nonspecialist student of Old Testament history.

The "Critical, Biblical Archaeological Approach"

In reaction to the approaches which we have already considered, yet another approach has been made which I term the "critical, biblical archaeological approach." The best example of this is John Bright's *A History of Israel*. This approach seeks to take the biblical narrative quite seriously but interprets it in the light of archaeological and ancient historical evidence. Since this approach begins with a bias toward the results of biblical archaeology, it has frequently been characterized by a need to reinterpret old evidence as new evidence is brought to light. Admittedly, if we wait to interpret until all possible questions are answered, we shall never interpret. But there is a tendency to draw conclusions before there is really sufficient evidence to do so. However, this approach does give a much more rational approach to the biblical evidence with less objectionable presuppositions. However, where there is either a real or a potential discrepancy between archaeological evidence and biblical evidence, supporters of this approach will unquestionably come down on the side of archaeology, even when experience has shown that many archaeological conclusions are not always certain.

The "Historical, Archaeological Biblicism Approach"

Many biblical historians have reacted with dismay to all of the above approaches. The debate between these will go on, for there is no consensus in sight. However, a new approach to Old Testament history has been made since World War II which I call a "historical, archaeological biblicism." Its primary focus, to this time, has been upon the period of the separate monarchies of Israel and Judah. The basic assumptions of this approach have been: (1) there are obvious problems in interpreting the actual data given to us in the Books of 1 and 2 Kings, much less including 1 and 2 Chronicles; and (2) there are equally as obvious problems in reconciling this data with that of archaeology and other historical records of ancient Near Eastern nations. This approach, however, does not blindly decide to accept one piece of evidence at the expense of another. Rather, it has assumed that the basic problem is not one of evidence not agreeing but of our failure to understand the evidence which we have. In other words, the basic presupposition of this approach is that a primary consideration in dealing with such ancient materials is our own ignorance.

The best example of this approach is found in Edwin R. Thiele's book *The Mysterious Numbers of the Hebrew Kings* and in his less technical work *A Chronology of the Hebrew Kings.* It is immediately obvious that this approach has not been made to the entire period of Old Testament history. On the one hand, that is a severe limitation. On the other, Thiele has grappled with apparent success with what is the major problem of Old Testament chronology, that of the Hebrew kingdoms.

Instead of simply reconstructing the history of Israel and Judah by ignoring Old Testament chronological data and instead of history-of-tradition criteria, Thiele sought to bring to bear the actual chronological systems used by ancient Near Eastern scribes in recording the histories of their own nations. Furthermore, instead of noncriticaly dealing with the biblical narratives while ignoring the proven results of modern scholarship, he sought to incorporate both. Finally, in carrying out his work, Thiele has not lost sight of the fact that the biblical historian is dealing both with theories and facts. Theories are human attempts to explain facts; they are never more than this. Facts do not change; theories will change as new facts are added for our consideration. The problems arise when we begin to confuse our theories with facts, whether we are dealing with science, religion, or history.

The results of Thiele's work do not differ significantly from the results of Bright's. But their basic approaches are radically different.

The "Sociological Approach"

The most recent methodology applied to the study of Old Testament history can be classified as the "sociological approach." Basically, this approach is characterized by a presupposition that the history of the Old Testament era is nothing more or less than a natural, predictable result of the sociological dynamics of the period. This approach wholly does away with any idea of Israel's religion as being revelatory. The developing idea of God is seen as nothing more than the normal development of current sociological dynamics. The best, or worst, example of this approach is Norman Gottwald's *The Tribes of Yahweh*. The study is basically limited to the period covered by the Books of Joshua and Judges. The approach certainly calls our attention to the fact that the Old Testament historian cannot ignore the sociological features of Israel's history. To try to reconstruct that history wholly upon this foundation, however, essentially destroys the mainstream of faith in both Judaism and Christianity.

As I indicated, no one book on Old Testament history wholly fits into any of these categories which I have identified. Further, my description of each of these categories is too brief and too general to be fully accurate. However, I do not think that I have been unfair either in my basic description or in my categorizations. We could devote an entire book to the subject of approaches to Old Testament history, but that is not my purpose here. What I have done is to show that students of Old Testament history are hard at work but have not yet spoken the final word. I do not propose to say the final word here, nor even to speak a new one. What I do propose is to bring the best of serious Old Testament historical scholarship to bear in presenting an Old Testament history for non-technical students.

The Approach of This Book

In approaching the study of Old Testament history, there are certain basic guidelines which will control my presentation. You need to know what these are in order to fully understand my presentation.

First, I begin with the biblical text. This means that all of the discipline of Old Testament textual criticism must be applied to the biblical text. It does little good to grapple with any passage until we are first as sure as we reasonably can be what was originally said in that text. Over the years of copying ancient manuscripts, scribal mistakes have gotten into biblical texts. The discipline of textual criticism seeks to get as close as possible to what the text originally had in it.

Yet beginning with the text is not enough. There are many gaps in the narratives which a historian wishes to fill. There are also many difficulties of understanding with which we must grapple. There are numerous problems in understanding biblical chronology which the historian must try to solve. This all necessitates additional steps.

The second step in developing the history of the Old Testament is to apply a thorough use of the basic critical methods used by Old Testament scholars. Some people wish to argue with the conclusions reached by biblical critics on the basis of theology. The only way we can adequately deal with conclusions with which we are unhappy is not by our theology but by a more searching, more thorough study of the biblical material itself. We must thoroughly examine the biblical evidence. There is no other way.

In dealing with the biblical evidence to reconstruct an Old Testament history, we must recognize that there is always a difference between a historical fact and its interpretation. For example, the Exodus narrative says that "the Lord drove the sea back by a strong east wind all night, and made the sea dry land" (Ex. 14:21). That enabled the Israelites to finally escape from Egypt. The event is presented as a fact of history. But the eyes of faith see that it was done by "the Lord." A bystander might have said simply that the wind blew the waters back. Thus, in reconstructing the history we must seek to recognize and understand the difference between an event and its interpretation. While the theological statement was the primary purpose of recording the events, in writing a history we must seek to differentiate between theology and history.

Third, I will illuminate, fill in the gaps, and add depth to the historical narrative with those countless historical records from the ancient Near East which we now have available. Where there are disagreements, we shall deal with them and see how they should be understood. The ancient records are primarily official records of ancient kingdoms or inscriptions upon monuments. Ancient religious records will help us get a feel for the world of faith in which Israel grew up. In addition, a few documents come from the arena of business or military activities. The greatest amount of historical evidence comes from national archives. Here again, the historian must be careful to try to separate events from their interpretation. But from these records, we can add many details to the history of the Old Testament.

Fourth, I will also add to the narrative those details from the investigations of archaeology in this region of the ancient Near East.

In general, the results of archaeology give us more of a feel for daily life and for the conditions of the common people. Ancient written records usually give a view of life from the standpoint of the rich, the powerful, and the victorious. The results of archaeological investigation allow us also to get a glimpse of what ordinary life was like. This adds depth to our study. Let us clearly understand that archaeology does not "prove" the Bible. That is a matter of faith. Rather, archaeology illuminates the biblical narrative, allowing us to see the Old Testament more clearly as a product of its times and against its own temporal background.

Fifth, in presenting my history of the Old Testament, I am forced to set both temporal and geographical limits. Although the Old Testament begins with the story of creation, any quick reading of the material of Genesis reveals that beginning with Genesis 12 the narrative takes on a wholly different tone. Further, the story of the Hebrew people cannot be carried back any earlier than the time of the patriarchs. So I will begin my survey of this history with the patriarchal period, beginning with Abraham. The other end of Old Testament history is much more difficult to define. Israel actually went on as a nation into and perhaps beyond the close of the New Testament. But there was a major turning point at the time of the Greek conquest of Persia in 333 BC. Although the Old Testament canon was not yet completed, this date affords a reasonable termination for the history of the Old Testament itself. It is at that point of time that I will conclude my study of Old Testament history.

The geographical boundaries of our study will be less precisely defined. I am, of course, primarily concerned with the Land of Canaan, what the Old Testament more normally identifies as the Land of Promise. However, we must be concerned with the other nations of Israel's world which came in contact with them and with which they came in contact. Thus, where it is helpful to our understanding of what was happening to Israel, we deal with the history of the ancient Near East from Egypt to Babylon, from the Nile Valley to the Mesopotamian Valley.

Admittedly, this means that I will be forced to make judgments as to whether events in external regions are significant enough to be included. But that cannot be avoided. I will make that kind of judgment about every event I record, biblical or otherwise.

My approach then is shaped by the biblical material, focused by serious critical studies, illuminated and enlarged by historical and archaeological records, and controlled both by my purpose and my presuppositions (as set forth in the preface).

Preliminary Considerations

Israel was not a philosophical people. Even a very cursory reading of the Old Testament reveals that they were not very concerned with thoughts or ideas about God. Their primary concern was with what God had done, not with what men thought about Him. This basic outlook colored both their understanding of God and their understanding of history. A person writing from a Greek background could say, "God is love." But someone writing from the Hebrew background would have said, "God loves us."

God is love is a quite general statement and very nonspecific. On the other hand, to say that God loves us requires a description of the events through which and by which God demonstrates that love.

In order to help us better to understand the nature of Old Testament history and Israel's understanding of it, we must understand four general considerations. These will help us to bridge the gap between our time and the Hebrews', and between their thought patterns and ours.

Israel's Approach to History

The basic approach to history which we find in the Old Testament would be called nonhistorical by contemporary standards of what history is or ought to be. Israel does not seem to have recorded events simply as a recitation of what had happened. To the contrary, Israel recorded events because of their meaning.

An ancient Egyptian historian might have told how a

group of wandering Hebrews migrated into Egypt at a time of famine. Later, they multiplied in number and were forced into slave labor by their Egyptian taskmasters. They were organized by a leader from among the slaves and took advantage of a series of catastrophes to flee the land, finally escaping through the waters of the sea when a strong wind parted them opportunistically. The chariots of the pursuing Egyptians got bogged down in the mud, and they were drowned when the wind stopped and the waters came rolling back.

However, the story was told quite differently by the ancient Hebrew. His eyes of faith saw the hand of God at work in all of these events. Thus he recorded the events as a series of acts of God.

A modern history writer does not, in fact cannot, sit in judgment upon the faith statement. What the modern history writer looks for is a story of what happened. The faith interpretation of what happened is the province of the theologian, not of the historian. What we are seeking to do here is to find out what happened. In doing that, we dare not forget that this is directly opposite to what the Hebrew was recording. Thus we must seek to probe behind the meaning of the event which the Old Testament records and come to grips with the events themselves.

Furthermore, we must recognize that the history recorded in the Old Testament is never merely the record of history as such but of significant history. Consider for example the reigns of two kings of Israel, Omri and his son Ahab, as recorded in 1 Kings 16:21-28 and in 1 Kings 16:29 to 22:40. The reign of Ahab would appear to be much more important since 209 verses are devoted to it while only eight verses were devoted to the reign of his father. However, the reign of Omri was so important that the Assyrian empire never forgot him, regularly referring to Israel in later years as "the land of Omri." Ahab certainly made a lesser impact upon his world. The question arises as to how to explain the difference in evaluating the reigns of these two men.

Our answer to this question must be found not in the relative importance of the two men but in what Israel saw

God doing in the kings' reigns. During the time of Ahab, Elijah prophesied. Thus the significance placed upon the two reigns did not rest in the importance of the kings but in the understanding of faith regarding what the God of Israel was doing. In a very real sense, the Old Testament is not so much a history of Israel as it is a history of the God of Israel as seen through the eyes of faith.

Israel's approach to history, then, was that it was first of all a record of significant history. It was the story of revelation, not the record of events. If we ever forget that, our approach to the history of the Old Testament history is likely to be flawed.

A second dimension to Israel's approach to history must be considered. Granted that the Hebrew historian's basic approach was a statement of what *God* had done, it was also a record of what God had *done*. Events were important. Since God was known through His historical acts, it was important to see those acts as historical events set against a specific historical background. If we are going to understand Israel's theology, we must first of all understand their history.

What we have in the Old Testament is not presented as a figment of someone's imagination, trying to make God believable. Rather, the Hebrew understanding of God took on new depth precisely because God was seen as acting in real history. The messages of Jeremiah take on a real urgency when we read them in light of the chaotic days of the defeat, destruction, and captivity of Judah before the Babylonian onslaught. The preaching of Isaiah becomes situation-specific when seen against the background of the defeat of the Northern Kingdom while the Southern Kingdom struggled to survive in a world dominated by Assyrian might. Thus, while the Old Testament is not primarily a history book, it certainly is set against a historical background, rooted and grounded in real events involving real people. Its heroes and heroines were no plaster saints but were real people trying to serve their God in real events. They faced real temptations, made real compromises, fell into real sin, and experienced real judgments and real mercy. In our study, we must seek to reconstruct the outline of the real events through which they lived.

The third dimension of Israel's approach to history is the fact that history was, for them, a process en route to a goal. Examined briefly, there was a cyclical view of history. The day repeats itself with sunset and sunrise. The year repeats itself with a progression of the seasons. History was seen to repeat itself over brief periods. At the same time, there was a meaningful process at work in their history since they saw it as the outgrowth of God's activities with them. Everything was seen to be an example of God's sovereignty and His control of their destiny. In no other nation of the ancient world was this true.

In the ancient world, when a nation was defeated, it was universally understood to be a defeat of the gods of that nation. Only in Israel did the people develop an understanding that God could use their defeats and might have caused them as temporal judgment. Again, this is primarily a matter of faith. For our purposes, however, because of this faith, Israel had a place in their history for the recording of defeat. Other ancient nations did not. In Assyria or in Egypt, defeats were recorded as great victories. Only as we correlate the records do we see where an Assyrian "victory" was followed by "a strategic advance to the rear" followed by a period of rebuilding the army. At the same battle, the Egyptians also recorded a victory, but it was accompanied by military advance and the occupation of new territory. Ancient nations just could not face reversals in their history. Israel had a faith which could do so. They saw all history as having meaning and being under God's control. Their task was to find out what God was doing. Our task, as history students, is to find out what was happening.

Israel's Time Consciousness

To the ancient Hebrew, time was important, for it was the arena of history. If history became important because of what God did, time was important because that was where God did it. However, it was also the sphere of human decision and action. The modern world is concerned with hours and minutes, with months and years, and thus with watches and calendars. To the ancient Hebrew, time was important not because it had passed but because of what had happened in it. As a result, we frequently are given far less chronological data than we would wish. Furthermore, we sometimes fail to fully understand the data we are given because we fail to understand what time meant to the Hebrews.

The basic word for time (*'eth*) actually seems to have meant "that which we meet or encounter." Their months were named by what happened in them. Thus there was "barley harvest," "flax harvest," "early planting," and such. Perhaps the best example of their understanding of time is seen in the summary of Ecclesiastes,

> For everything there is a season,
>   and a time for every matter under heaven:
> a time to be born, and a time to die;
> a time to plant, and a time to pluch up what is planted;
> ....
> a time to love, and a time to hate;
> a time for war, and a time for peace (Eccl. 3:1-8).

Time was important only because of what happened. It is that simple.

The second key word in Hebrew time vocabulary is *day*. It was not used with any greater precision by the Hebrews than we use it now. Thus it could refer to a twenty-four hour period. But it could also refer to an indefinite period, such as "in George Washington's day." They used it in referring to some indefinite period either in the past or in the future. "The day of the Lord" frequently is used in this sense.

But when used chronologically, the day was governed by the sun. It extended from sunset to the following sunset. The month was governed by the moon, extending from one new moon to the next. In fact, the basic word for month meant "the new one." The year was governed both by sun and moon and was measured by the steady passage of the seasons. In each of these, it is obvious that time was no abstraction; it was a series of events.

Although not important for our study of history, the Hebrew understanding of eternity is far different from the Greek understanding of it. For the Hebrews, there was no idea of a timeless eternity. Two basic Hebrew words for eternity describe the "dim unknown"—the very edge of time—and "stretched-out days," still within the boundaries of time as they understood it. This, too, is readily understandable, for history and time were where God acted. Wherever they saw God acting, either in the past or in the future, it involved the Hebrews' understanding of time.

Yet, in recognizing the Hebrews' understanding of time, we must confront the fact that when the Hebrews recited God's actions, they could easily slide over periods when there was nothing visible of His actions. Further, periods where the acts of God were readily seen could be blown out of proportion insofar as the historian may be concerned. Thus to understand Israel's history writing, we must understand her time consciousness.

The Nature of Old Testament Chronological Data

Israel's chronological data must be interpreted against the background of her time consciousness. It must also be interpreted against the background of her use of numbers. For example, some numbers were of particular significance to the Old Testament writers. Among these are *seven, ten, twelve,* and *forty.*

Forty is sometimes used to express a long but indefinite period of time. It occasionally appears to refer to a generation when used with years. *Twelve* apparently attained significance due to the twelve tribes. Thus it symbolized completeness, fullness, wholeness. *Seven* apparently rose from the days of the week and came to refer to fullness or sacredness (possibly because the seventh day was sacred). *Ten* was a particularly rounded number and also indicated a sense of real completeness.

When any of these numbers which had a symbolic meaning are used in given chronological data, the interpreter must ask whether they are being used literally or symbolically. They are apparently used in both ways.

INTRODUCTION TO OLD TESTAMENT HISTORY   39

Furthermore, rounded off numbers were used in both ancient and modern times as an approximation of time rather than as specific time. Thus, rounded numbers must be queried as to whether or not they are approximations.

Different systems of counting years were used by different nations in ancient Near East. Sometimes a particular system was changed due to outside influences. Thus, if a king died in the middle of one year and another king began to reign in the same year, each of them sometimes had the same year counted in their length of reign. In the case of some brief reigns of less than a year, it was possible for three different kings to have the same year credited to their total. In these instances, the problem arises as to how we recognize such usages. The answer is that we recognize this kind of usage by the fact that applying simple addition leaves us far afield in understanding the data.

Furthermore, a king frequently associated his son on the throne with him in a coregency. Thus, for a period of time, a nation was left with a joint kingship. Unfortunately, the official chronicles of the kings' reigns would count the period of coregency to both kings. In this and the previous case, our problem is not one of not having data but of understanding the data which we have.

An additional problem arises in understanding Old Testament chronological data due to the fact that sometimes we have less data than we would care to have, or it might be unclear in its reference. For example, Amos's ministry is dated rather precisely to a time "two years before the earthquake." However, in trying to assign a precise date for his ministry, we are suddenly confronted by the fact that we do not know when the earthquake occurred. Thus we have data which appears to be adequate only to discover that we are still left with a lack of adequate information, so we have to make an educated guess.

This discussion could be carried on in much greater detail. However, for our purposes here, the point is that while we have data, much of it still leaves us with uncertainties. Dealing with the chronological data of the Old

Testament is a task for a highly specialized technician. As long as we who are not such technicians recognize the magnitude of the problem, we are better able to understand the differences in the chronological systems of the scholars who seek to understand the data. Basically, the differences are minor. Our reconstruction of the chronology of Israel's history is on much firmer footing than we should expect, considering how far removed we are from those events.

Establishing an Absolute Chronology

For any student of ancient history, a fundamental problem is the establishment of an absolute chronology. The Old Testament in the Books of 1 and 2 Samuel, 1 and 2 Kings, and 1 and 2 Chronicles gives us a relative chronology of the period of the Hebrew kingdoms. Any student who grapples with these quickly discovers that there are immediate difficulties in understanding the data. (We shall deal with these difficulties in the chapters dealing with the history of the Hebrew monarchies.) But, even if we assume that there is no problem in understanding the chronological data of the period of the kingdom, we are confronted by the fact that every date we have given is relative. The dates of both the Southern and the Northern Kingdoms are related to one another by synchonisms. They are also given in terms of the years each king's scribes claimed for his master. Further, there are events in the Old Testament which relate to battles or to reigns of kings of Egypt, Assyria, and Babylon. Search as we might, there is not one single absolute date given.

We might say the same kinds of things for the historical records of Egypt, Assyria, and Babylonia. We have Assyrian records which give us a very detailed history of Assyria for considerably more than a thousand years, Babylonian records which cover more than five centuries, and Egyptian records which give a detailed history of almost three thousand years. All of these overlap with one another and with the history of the Hebrew monarchies. By checking and cross-checking, we can establish a very accurate relative chronology between these three empires and Israel. Or, at least, so it seems. But if this were all we had, we still would not have an exact chronology of the period of Old Testament history. Fortunately for us, we have more information.

From Egypt, Assyria, and Babylon, we have astronomical references which allow us to establish a scheme of exact dates for these ancient records. The Assyrian records list an eclipse of the sun as a significant event in one year. The only eclipse of the sun which occurred anywhere near the appropriate place and time occurred in 763 BC. Thus we have a peg on which to hang the Assyrian records. We can calculate both backward and forward and arrive at a system of absolute dates for Assyria. The Babylonian records can be given absolute dates based upon a chart which they drew of the movements of the planet Venus. The Egyptian records list an astronomical event which occurred every 1,461 Egyptian years. One such cycle ended in the second century AD. This allows us to begin to establish an absolute chronology for Egypt.

With the apparent establishment of an absolute chronology of each of these empires, we are able to check them against one another where these nations came in contact in common battles and such. While there are still discrepancies between these synchronisms from one kingdom to the other, we can state with great assurance that we are now very close to an absolute chronology for the ancient Near East.

We must still translate these ancient Near Eastern dates into an absolute chronology for the Hebrew monarchies. There are numerous events where this can be done. King Ahab of Israel is listed in the Assyrian records as having fought at the Battle of Qarqar in 853 BC. Although this is not mentioned in the Old Testament, Ahab obviously had to be king at this time. King Jehu of Israel is depicted as paying tribute in 842 BC to Shalmaneser III of Assyria. This is depicted in a relief on the famous black obelisk. Again, this event is not mentioned in the Bible, but Jehu obviously had to be king. King Josiah of Judah was killed in the Battle of Megiddo in 609 BC by Pharaoh Neco II of Egypt. This is recorded in 2 Kings 23:29 and in 2

Chronicles 35:20-24. There are further correlations with the fall of Samaria in 722/21 BC and the fall of Jerusalem in 587 BC (2 Kings 17:6; 25:1-7).

By using these dates, we can then calculate backward and forward to establish other dates for the history of the Old Testament. As in the case of the other kingdoms, there are still some problems which have yet to be solved. At the same time, we can be quite certain that we are now very close to the absolute dates for the period of the Hebrew kingdoms. As we move further back in time from this period, our degree of certainty lessens.

Now it goes without saying that there is only one correct chronology. Every event happened at some specific point in time. However, given the kinds of records that were kept and the number of gaps which we have in the information which we would like to possess, we can surely rejoice that we are as close as we now are to the actual dates of events which occurred so long ago.

2
Israel's Prehistory: The Patriarchal Period

Israel did not become a nation until the time of the monarchy. With the reign of the first king, the people of Israel clearly began to develop a national existence. Prior to this, the people of Israel had been a more or less loosely organized group of tribes living in the land of Canaan. During the period of the conquest and settlement of the land, Israel could certainly be called a people but could hardly be called a nation. However, even with this noncentralized, nongovernmental national life, we can perhaps say that they had a national history during this period. Their national life may even be said to have begun when they entered into a covenant with God at Sinai (Ex. 19:1-6).

Prior to the experience at Sinai, however, it can hardly be said that Israel had any sort of national existence. In the latter part of their sojourn in Egypt, they were oppressed slaves but do not seem to have had any sort of national identity. Certainly there was no national identity in the time of the patriarchs. With Abraham, Isaac, and Jacob, we are dealing with individuals and with their families or clans, not with a nation.

Nevertheless, even though we cannot classify the period of the patriarchs as a part of the history of the *nation* of Israel, it most certainly is a part of the history of the Old Testament era. While families do not keep historical records as kingdoms do, they certainly preserve their family traditions. Their lives are lived out in history and against a historical background. Thus we can identify this period as a part of the nation's prehistory, while at the same time treating it as a part of Old Testament history.

Sources for the Study

The first source to which we must turn in order to reconstruct the history of the patriarchal period is the biblical material which is found essentially in Genesis 12—50. There are a few minor references to these early narratives scattered through the rest of the Bible, but they do not really add anything to what the Genesis material contains.

In addition to the biblical material, some other ancient historical records help us understand the world in which the patriarchs of Israel lived. At least five documents or collections of documents of such ancient materials can be identified with the general period in which the patriarchs lived.

The law code of Hammurabi, the sixth king of the Amorite dynasty of Babylon, gives a detailed picture of the legal basis for society in this period. In addition to this, we have numerous tablets from ancient Mari, a city on the upper Euphrates, and from Ugarit (modern Ras Shamra), a city in western Syria. These two collections of documents reflect numerous customs of that period which help us understand many of the patriarchal practices. Furthermore, from Egypt comes a story called "the Tale of Sinuhe" which tells the adventures of an Egyptian official who fled from Egypt and settled in a place which sounds very much like ancient Syria. There he met a tribal chieftain who lived much like the patriarchs did. We find countless patriarchal customs being practiced. The most recent written materials which have been discovered in this area which seem to reflect this period are known as the Ebla materials. They were found at Tel Mardikh, in northern Syria. Although they have not been fully published yet, there have been claims that these, too, will add depth to our understanding of the patriarchal era.

All of these written materials help us understand that the patriarchs were very much people of their times. We find names in these documents which are similar to many of the biblical names. These are most likely not to be identified with the patriarchs, but they do indicate that even the names of the patriarchs were common in their day.

In addition to the documentary evidence, there are other helps for understanding this period which have been found throughout the ancient Near East. There is a famous Egyptian relief found in a tomb at Beni-hasan, which portrays a family of Semitic seminomads entering Egypt. The panel is to be dated about 1900 BC and very likely represents the way the families Abraham, Isaac, and Jacob were seen as they entered Egypt.

Surface explorations and excavations have shown that during the period of the patriarchs, the central highlands of the land of Canaan were very sparsely populated. This explains why the migrations of the patriarchs were generally located in these regions. Those rugged hills were relatively unsettled, so the entrance of the patriarchs into that region presented no major threat to people already there. That allowed them to move about in peace.

Finally, other excavations reveal many characteristics of the daily life of people who lived in this period. We are able to find help in viewing the patriarchs as people of their times, rather than seeing them as mere characters in a story.

The study of the ancient sources gives to us an understanding of the patriarchs as real people. As we see them against the background of the early second millennium BC, we begin to feel that we know them. Furthermore, even though many of their practices are totally foreign to us, the ancient sources which we have in addition to the Bible help us to make the attempt to bridge both the temporal and the cultural gaps.

Major Problems for Consideration

In any detailed study of the patriarchal period and of the patriarchal narratives in Genesis, we can readily identify three major problems with which we must deal. Before we can seriously begin any description of the history of the period, we must come to some conclusions concerning these issues. These are the basic issues which are raised by the majority of the books which deal with this era and which we must attempt to bring to some satisfactory conclusion.

The Nature of the Biblical Narratives

To a serious student of the Bible, it is immediately obvious that the material in Genesis 12—50 (the patriarchal narratives) is significantly different from that contained in the books generally classified as histories, such as Kings or Chronicles. To illustrate, think of the stories with which you are most familiar. Most Christians are familiar with the call of Abraham (Gen. 12:1-9; although he was known as Abram in the early narratives, I shall consistently use Abraham as the name of the founding patriarch). They are far more familiar with the destruction of Sodom and Gomorrah (Gen. 18:16 to 19:29), Jacob's stealing Isaac's birthright (Gen. 27:1-40), and Joseph's being sold into slavery (Gen. 37:1-36) than with the conflicts of Rehoboam and Jeroboam (1 Kings 12:1-33) or with the reign of Manasseh (2 Kings 21:1-18). The reason for our familiarity with one block of material and our lack of familiarity with the other rests in the very nature of the material itself.

The patriarchal narratives are just that; they are stories. They are told in the form by which stories have been told throughout all history. These narratives are entertaining and could easily have been told around ancient campfires in order to help entertain as well as to communicate the tribal and national heritage.

Contemporary studies of this biblical material have left us with two conclusions which are almost certain. First, these ancient patriarchal stories were told orally for a long period of time before they were ever written down. Being told orally, they were put into a form which would make it easy to listen to them and to remember them. Thus, there is always a dimension of action and entertainment in them. Second, even though to the modern mind things which are not written are considered to be suspect as far as accuracy goes, this is not true of ancient materials. When few people could read and write, the only way of communicating the truth to large numbers of people was orally. What we now know of these processes give us a significant assurance that such oral traditions were passed on with an accuracy equal to that of writing.

However, oral narratives were passed on without the amount or the kinds of historical detail which is found in the official records of a king's court. This kind of detail is what allows us to place historical records in their proper context. The absence of such detail serves as a significant hindrance to the proper placement of these stories.

In dealing with this material, we must also face the fact that these stories were not told as history but as stories. We know that in the ancient Near East stories were frequently told about tribes or clans but were told in terms of the individuals who were the head of that tribe or clan. Is it possible that some of the stories of the problems between the sons of Jacob also reflect tribal relationships? Even though this is not the way we tell stories today, it was certainly the way that ancient peoples told stories and must not be discounted.

Regardless of how we deal with the actual content of the patriarchal narratives, two things stand out. We are not dealing with historical records of the same kind which we have in the so-called histories of the Old Testament. Neither are we given the kinds of material which will allow us to place the patriarchal narratives in their historical context with the same degree of precision as we can do with the material coming from the Hebrew monarchies.

The Chronology of the Period

There is no such thing as an almost accurate chronology. Chronology is either correct or it is not. But when we are dealing with events which happened so many centuries ago and when we are dealing with chronological data with which we are not at all familiar, we must be content with assigning dates to these ancient events which are approximately correct. At the same time, we must recognize that the dates which we assign to these ancient people are in the final analysis only the best approximations which we can give with the present limitations of our knowledge.

In trying to establish an absolute chronology for the patriarchs, two approaches might at first glance appear to be profitable. The first is that of simply dealing with the chronological data of the biblical narratives. The second is trying to identify some event recorded of the patriarchs with an event recorded about the other ancient Near Eastern histories of the era.

There is not a great deal of chronological data concerning the patriarchs given in Genesis. (1) Abraham is said to have been 100 years old and Sarah 90 when they are told of the forthcoming birth of Isaac (Gen. 17:17). At the same time, Abraham is said to have been fearful that Abimelech, king of Gerar, might kill him in order to add Sarah to his harem (Gen. 20:2,11). (2) Abraham was still 100 years old when Isaac was born (Gen. 21:5). (3) Sarah is said to have lived 127 years, and Abraham is said to have lived 175 years (Gen. 23:1; 25:7-8). (4) Isaac is said to have been 40 years old when he married Rebekah and to have been 60 when she gave birth to Jacob and Esau (Gen. 25:20,26). (5) Isaac is said to have been 180 years old at his death (Gen. 35:28-29). (6) While we are not given the age of Jacob at Joseph's birth, it occurred between the seventh year of his sojourn with Laban, when he had married Rachel following his marriage to Leah, and his twentieth year, when he fled to Canaan (Gen. 29:15-30; 30:22-24; 31:17-21). (7) Joseph is said to have been 17 years old when his brothers sold him into slavery (Gen. 37:2-36). (8) Joseph's age when he was made prime minister of Egypt was 30 (Gen. 41:39-41,46). (9) Between 7 and 14 years later, Joseph's brothers and his father came into Egypt as Pharaoh's guests (Gen. 41:47-49,53-57; 42:1-2; 45:16-20). (10) Jacob is said to have been 130 years old when he moved into Egypt, and he died there 17 years later (Gen. 47:9, 28). (11) Joseph is said to have been 110 when he died in Egypt (Gen. 50:26).

Given this information, it would appear that we could establish a chronology of the patriarchs. This is an absolute chronology, based only upon the biblical data. (In establishing these dates, we set the date of Abraham's birth at year 0. We also assume Joseph's birth to be about the fourteenth year after Jacob's flight to his Uncle Laban in Haran, and we assume that Jacob and his sons descended into Egypt about the third year of famine.)

Year	Event
0	Abraham's birth
10	Sarah's birth
100	Announcement of Isaac's birth; his birth
137	Sarah's death
140	Isaac's marriage
160	Jacob's birth
175	Abraham's death
ca. 236	Jacob fled to Haran
ca. 243	Jacob's marriage to Leah and then to Rachel one week later
ca. 250	Joseph's birth
ca. 256	Jacob and family returned to Canaan
ca. 267	Joseph sold into Egypt
280	Isaac's death
ca. 280	Joseph made prime minister of Egypt
ca. 290	Jacob and family entered Egypt
307	Jacob's death
ca. 360	Joseph's death

Aside from the basic assumptions which we have made, this at first glance appears quite straightforward. However, that is somewhat deceiving. Paul stated that the law (of Sinai) was given to Israel 430 years after the promises made to Abraham (Gal. 3:16-17). This is further complicated by the statement made to Abraham that his descendents would be oppressed in Egypt for four hundred years (Gen. 15:13). This would mean that the sojourn in Egypt would run from approximately 290 to 690 on my absolute system as established above. The statement of Paul just does not fit in well here, for the laws of Sinai would have to be given before the Exodus from Egypt. This is further complicated by the statement made to Abraham that the Exodus would occur four generations after the entrance into Egypt (Gen. 15:16).

We shall return to these problems later, but there are some others which we need to consider. First, the very "roundness" of some of the numbers will certainly make a historian wonder if we are dealing with estimates in some places rather than with an actual, detailed chronology. Second, the very long periods assigned to the life of these patriarchs might also cause us to raise questions as to whether we really know precisely how such chronological details were understood or intended. Given what we know today, it is quite unlikely that any Oriental ruler would have sought to add a ninety-year-old woman to his harem. This in no way is to say that God could not have granted such long life spans. He most certainly could have done so. But we must at least raise the question as to whether our ignorance of the way the Hebrews used chronology is not creating problems for us which were not problems for the people of Old Testament times. As noted earlier, the people of the Old Testament frequently used numbers as symbols rather than as data to be understood simply as chronology. It is possible that we are dealing with such here. For example, it appears probable that in Genesis 15:13, one hundred years was used as a symbol for a generation. This seems to lead us to the conclusion that while our table is accurate insofar as we can make it, it may also be suspect insofar as our understanding is concerned. (We will return to this biblical data later in this section.)

Since the superficial utilization of the biblical data may not have given us the kinds of results which we needed or wanted, we must turn to the second approach in trying to establish the chronology of the patriarchal era. In trying to establish the absolute chronology of the patriarchal period, let us try to connect an event or events recorded in the biblical material which can be identified with some event recorded in the extrabiblical sources.

The passage which it has been generally agreed offers the best opportunity for this kind of specific historical correlation is Genesis 14.

ISRAEL'S PREHISTORY

> In the days of Amraphel king of Shinar, Arioch king of Ellasar, Chedorlaomer king of Elam, and Tidal king of Goiim, these kings made war with Bera king of Sodom, Birsha king of Gomorrah, Shinab king of Admah, Shemeber king of Zeboiim and the king of Bela (that is Zoar) (Gen. 14:1-2).

In the course of that battle, Lot was captured, and Abraham was eventually involved. If we could identify any of the kings included in the attack, we might be able to date this specific event in Abraham's life.

Obviously, any records of the local Canaanite kings would have been destroyed in the cataclysm which later befell the cities of the plain (Gen. 19:24-25). If there is any hope, it must rest with the other four kings. The route which the four invading kings took led them down the King's Highway on the Transjordan Plateau, down into the Arabah south of the Dead Sea, and then back up into Canaan from the south. This would have served the double purpose of allowing them first to secure the ore deposits in the south and then make a surprise attack from the rear upon the kings of the cities of the plain. The strategy and the geography make sense. But we are still faced with the problem of identity. Who were these kings?

For a long time scholars have tried to identify "Amraphel king of Shinar" with Hammurabi king of Babylon. There is no question but that in the Bible Shinar and Babylon are to be identified (Gen. 10:10). However, in spite of the various ways by which Hammurabi is spelled in ancient documents, there is just no satisfactory way to explain the presence of the final *l*. Others have suggested that Amaphel might be identified with one Amut-piel of Katna. Even if this were possible, there is no way by which Katna in Syria can be identified with Shinar.

The second king, "Arioch of Ellasar" remains unidentified as a specific individual from ancient texts. The name appears in the Mari tablets as Arriwuk. It was thus a common name but is otherwise historically unidentifiable.

"Tidal king of Goiim" could be translated as "Tidal

king of the Gentiles." Goiim does not have to be identified as a specific nation. Tidal appears to be identical to "Tudhalias," a name of several kings of the Hittite empire. But there is no other detail given concerning any of these Hittite kings which would tie them into such a confederation as set forth in Genesis or which would tie any one of them into an attack on Canaan as is described here.

The fourth king, "Chedorlaomer king of Elam," offers a different kind of problem. The name can be identified with the name of an Elamite god, Kuder-lagomer. However, there are no records which would indicate which king of Elam was ever so identified or nicknamed. Further, although we have countless records from ancient Elam, we have no record of such an attack by the Elamites on Canaan, nor are there any records of an Elamite treaty which would have put their king at the head of a confederation of four kings, such as these, for any kind of military action in the region of Canaan.

All of this is negative evidence. All we can say regarding the events of Genesis 14:1-16 is that we do not have any way of tying this to a particular date in history by comparison with any contemporary records presently known. On the other hand, we can say that some of the personal names and many of the geographical names of the chapter are quite commonly attested in contemporary records of the early second millennium BC.

In addition to this, there are two other major considerations which may also point to this general period. First, there was a major Amorite migration from the region of Mesopotamia into the region of Syria-Palestine about 2000 BC. The patriarchal migration may be connected with this. While this is by no means certain, it would fit well into the world history of that era. Some might see this identification as being a denial of the fact that Abraham moved in obedience to a "call" from God. Not so. That he migrated is an historical statement. That he moved in obedience to God is a theological statement. We must keep the two separate.

As an illustration, I moved with my family from a

pastorate in South Carolina to a teaching position at Golden Gate Theological Seminary in late 1974. Many other people moved into California at the same time. I was one of a great movement from the East to the West. But I moved in response to my sense of a divine call. While I did the same thing which others were doing and at the same time, my reasons were different. Thus if Abraham were a part of the Amorite migrations, it does not undermine his reasons for the move. It just helps us get a handle on his historical background.

The other consideration which may put the patriarchs into the period under examination comes from the archaeological investigations into this era in the land of Palestine. For about two centuries at the beginning of the second millennium BC, the central highlands of Canaan were relatively uninhabited. The major centers of population during this period were in the lowlands and the foothills. Thus the very fact that the patriarchs could have moved back and forth through the land without running into major hostility or opposition fits better into this period than any other.

Given this background, although we cannot date the patriarchs with any precision, we can at least say that it appears that they entered the land of Canaan sometime during the early part of the second millennium BC. The earliest date we should probably assign to Abraham's entrance would be about 2000 BC, and the latest date would probably be about 1700 BC. As we gather more evidence later in our study, we may be able to be a bit more precise than this. Looking back at our earlier chart, if we assume its accuracy (which, for the reasons noted above, we may not be able to do) and if Abraham was about fifty when he entered Canaan, the Hebrews would have gone into Egypt about 240 years later. Certainly, then, the entire patriarchal period would fit into the first half of the second millennium BC. (While not all scholars would agree with this, it would appear to be the best interpretation of all of the evidence presently available.)

The Relationship to the Habiru'

Anyone who has done much reading in the area of Old Testament history and archaeology has been faced with some kind of discussion concerning the relationship between the Hebrews and the Habiru'. Throughout almost all of the second millennium BC (2000 to 1000 BC), there are numerous references from the regions, including Mesopotamia, Egypt, and Canaan, to a people variously identified as the Habiru', the Hapiru', or the 'Apiru'. Since some of these references from Canaan were pleading to Egypt for help in delivering them from invasions or incursions of these Habiru', numerous interpreters have sought to identify these people with the invading Hebrews under Joshua. The question arises as to whether this identification is valid.

The Old Testament word for *Hebrew* first shows up when Abraham is identified as "the Hebrew" (Gen. 14:13). Linguistically, a good case can be made for a similarity between the word *Hebrew* and *Habiru'*. But a similarity does not prove an identity, so we must go further.

If the only external evidence for the use of the term *Habiru'* came from the Amarna letters which tell of the problem the Canaanite city states were having from these people, we might conclude that there might be an identification between them and the Hebrews. But this is not the case. The multiplicity of the references to these people and the widespread use of the term both in chronology and in geography gives us much more evidence to consider.

The general picture of the Habiru' is that they were of many different nationalities and spoke a variety of languages. They were occasionally nomadic invaders from without and were sometimes revolutionaries from within. As more and more places turn up where the term was used, it appears to have generally referred more to a social status than to a race, a language, a tribe, or a nation. The Habiru' were generally of the lower social structure of any society and were usually involved in an attempt to overthrow the existing government.

Thus it might be possible to equate some or all of the Habiru' of the Amarna letters with the Hebrews, but it is not necessary. (We shall return to this issue in chapter 4, "Israel's Land: The Conquest and Settlement.") But it appears that there is no way by which we can positively identify the term *Hebrew* as applied to Abraham with the Hapiru' of the ancient Near East.

The Background of the Period

Once we have established the general era in which the patriarchs seem to have lived, we must seek to discover the nature of this period and how the patriarchal narratives fit into it. Here we must turn to the extrabiblical sources to seek evidence and must try to fit the patriarchal narratives from Genesis against that background as best we can. There are three major categories and one minor category which we need to investigate in order to deal appropriately with the issue.

The Patriarchal Wanderings

The biblical narratives begin with Abraham departing from "Ur of the Chaldeans" along with his father Terah and journeying to the region of Haran in northern Mesopotamia (Gen. 11:31). From this region of Syria (or Aram), the patriarchal wanderings led them into Canaan where they located in the region of the central hill country, with only occasional excursions out of it in times of famine.

The biblical picture of these wanderings fits in well with what is known of the region from the surface explorations, the archaeological digs, and the records from the Egyptian "execration texts." All of these indicate that the central hill country was quite sparsely populated at this time. Much of it appears to have been covered with the grasslands suitable for the pasturing of flocks. Further, insofar as they have been identified, the cities which are listed in the patriarchal wanderings were in existence during the first half of the second millennium BC.

The Patriarchal Vocations

The question has been frequently raised as to the actual vocation of the patriarchs when set against the background of this era. They have sometimes been called nomads, but this is hardly possible for the camel was not fully domesticated until near the end of the second millennium. Camels are occasionally mentioned in the patriarchal stories, but they were obviously not of major significance to them. This fits in well with the archaeological finds from the era where camel bones have been found in the early part of the period, but rather infrequently. They do not show up in any significant quantity until much later.

The importance of this rests in the fact that true nomads cannot exist without camels. They are the only animals who can exist for long periods in the desert, where both food and water are quite scarce. Without domesticated camels in large quantities, true nomadism cannot exist.

Some have sought to identify the patriarchs as seminomads. It would appear that we have to do a good bit of redefining of what we mean by nomad in order to get by with this kind of title. Either a people can live and move through the desert or they cannot. It is just impossible to be halfway able to do so. Further, the patriarchs are regularly described as having large flocks and herds which could not have survived in the deep deserts.

Perhaps the best description of the patriarchs' vocation is that of tenders of sheep, goats, and cattle. Such people have always abounded in the Near East, living more or less on the fringes of civilization. There were two basic regions which such people occupied. First, they lived on the border between the desert and the arable land. In times of drought when the grasslands receded, these peoples moved closer to civilization. In rainy seasons when the grass advanced, such peoples moved further from centers of civilization. Second, where there were regions of grassland which were uninhabited, these sheep and cattle tenders could live in the midst of the land, but away from the danger of civilized settlements. This fits in well with the biblical picture which we have of the patriarchs. In times of drought and famine, they moved into the civilized regions. Otherwise, they kept their distance.

We need to observe that people who kept flocks and herds did not normally move over large areas. Rather, their wanderings were usually quite localized, moving from one grassy place to another and settling down where both the water and the grass were adequate. Thus the long march of Abraham would normally have been quite out of character with such vocations. However, given the Amorite migrations which were going on at the time, his journey was made at a time when normal patterns were being broken by large numbers of people. Thus Abraham's movement at that time would not have been such as to attract undue attention to himself and his family.

Somewhere along the way, however, these sheep and cattle tenders appear to have begun to settle down to one particular region as they learned the benefits of growing crops and harvesting them. This also appears to have been what happened to the patriarchs. There seems to be no indication that Abraham ever became a husbandman. But Isaac is said at least once to have sowed and reaped (Gen. 26:12). Joseph's dreams of his sheaf of grain and those of his brothers make it plain that by that time Jacob was involved in agriculture (Gen. 37:5-7). Thus the movement from mere animal raisers to becoming full-fledged farmers fits in well with the period. Once agriculture became a way of life, the movement of flocks and herds had to be confined to regions near the place where the grain was raised. Again, the patriarchal vocations are seen to fit in well with what is known of the first half of the second millennium BC.

The Patriarchal Customs

There are several customs referred to in the patriarchal narratives which appear quite strange to any modern interpreter of this Old Testament material. We must investigate whether these were common practices in the historical period under examination. Although we could deal with several instances, let us consider four of these.

Adoption. Before the birth of Isaac, Abraham complained to God about his childless condition. Abraham said, "O Lord God, what wilt thou give me, for I continue childless, and the heir of my house is Eliezer of Damascus? . . . Behold, thou hast given me no offspring; and a slave born in my house will be my heir" (Gen. 15:2-3). From the Nuzi texts we discover that, during this period of history, their ancient law codes provided that a childless couple adopt a son who would serve them all of their lives and would inherit the estate at the death of the father. However, should a natural son be born, the adopted son had to yield his claim to the inheritance. This gives a vivid background for the concerns of Abraham and for Isaac's later inheritance of the tribal leadership.

Marriage. Marriage practices in the patriarchal narratives have also given us problems. The practice of a childless wife furnishing a substitute to her husband shows up both in the stories of Sarah and Abraham and of Rachel, Leah, and Jacob (Gen. 16:1-3; 30:1-4,9). The Nuzian laws state that a childless wife must furnish exactly this kind of substitute. Such practices are also recorded at Alalakh in northern Syria in the middle of the second millenium BC.

Furthermore, when such a substitute gave birth, she frequently did so actually sitting in the lap of the barren wife. The newborn child was considered in this latter instance to be the child of the barren wife. There is a clay statue of such a process from Cyprus at a somewhat later period. But the point is that these marriage practices, although foreign to us, were the accepted procedure in precisely the times with which we are dealing.

Household Gods. In the story of Jacob's departure from Laban, his father-in-law, Rachel stole her father's household gods (Gen. 31:19,30). Some translators use a transliteration of their Hebrew name calling them teraphim. At first glance, it appears to us that Rachel was seeking to continue her father's idol worship. But there is more than that to the story.

The Nuzi material provides another dimension to this story. In that ancient society, the teraphim were considered to be more than simply the idols which a particular family worshiped. They were also of more worth than the gold or silver from which they had been made or with which they were adorned. Teraphim were frequently little more than small clay statues. While there is some debate as to how the passages dealing with them in the Nuzi material are to be understood, the teraphim at least carried with them a legal claim to the headship of the family. They may also have carried title to the family property. That extrinsic value made Laban's household gods especially desirable to Rachel and made her father search so diligently for them.

Birthright. The right of the firstborn son in several ancient societies adds significance to several of the patriarchal narratives. The firstborn son had a claim to a double inheritance of the father's estate. He also apparently had the right of leadership for the family or tribe when the father died. But, depending upon the circumstances, a father could designate some other son as the inheritor of this right.

These customs help us to understand the Jacob-Esau conflict over the "birthright" (Gen. 25:29-34; 27:1-40). This also helps us understand some of what was going on when Joseph and his father Jacob disagreed over which of Joseph's sons should have this birthright (Gen. 48:17-20).

While I could further multiply this kind of illustration, space limitations prevent it. I am quite aware that not all of the ancient references are without ambiguity. On the other hand, the amassing of the data gives more and more substance to the conclusion that the patriarchs were truly men of their time. The customs reflected by the Genesis narratives, insofar as they are identifiable, make these men and their families become visible as living people and not as plaster saints or figures in a book.

The Patriarchal Names

The question is frequently asked as to whether we have any extrabiblical evidence to the actual existence of the patriarchs. The answer is an unqualified no. While the names of Abraham (in the form Abram) and Jacob do occur in ancient texts, they can in no way be identified with the patriarchal figures of the Old Tesatment. Even though Isaac and Joseph have not yet been found outside the Bible, their names are of a form which is quite common in the period. (It is possible that these two names may be attested in the Ebla material, but at the time of writing, this has not been verified.) Furthermore, numerous other names within the patriarchal families have been found applied both to persons and places in the early part of the second millennium BC. However, again there is no reference which can be identified with the patriarchs of Genesis.

We could easily multiply our examples of ancient materials which add to our understanding of the background of the patriarchal stories. The task is beyond the bounds of this book. What this material shows is that these people were people of their time and that time was the first half of the second millennium BC. We have not proved that the biblical narratives of the patriarchs are true. That is a matter of faith. This investigation demonstrates that the narratives do fit quite well into the era which they claim to describe. We are now ready to look at these narratives and the story which they tell.

The History of the Period

The first eleven chapters of Genesis set the stage for the divine drama of redemption. We are told of the creation of the universe and of people. But God's creation was spoiled by human sinful rebellion. In spite of a punishing flood, the sad details of humanity's degrading sin goes through the story of the tower of Babel. The stage is clearly described. The two main characters, God and man, have been introduced. The problem has been posed, what can be done about the sin, the rebellion and folly of humanity? Against that background, the biblical narrators began to tell the story of God's redemption. It is a theological story. It is also a historical story. The events of that story are set in history. It began in Ur of the Chaldeans (Gen. 11:31).

Abraham

Two forms of Abraham's name are known in the Old Testament. *Abram* is used essentially from his introduction (Gen. 11:27) until the name was changed to *Abraham* in Genesis 17:5. *Abram* apparently meant "Exalted Father" while *Abraham* is said to mean "Father of a Multitude."

Although Abraham followed his father Terah from Ur to Haran, he left Terah there and journeyed on into Canaan in response to God's call (Gen. 12:1-3). Although a simple reading of the narrative makes it appear that Abraham did not hear God's call until after the death of his father, the details which are given make it apparent that he actually left Haran some sixty years before Terah's death (Gen. 11:26, 32; 12:4). The very fact that he led his part of the clan to depart from his father indicates the utter seriousness with which he took the call from God. In patriarchal times, the family normally gave absolute allegiance to the father.

Such a departure from normal practice adds to the significance we must give to Abraham's response. It is also remarkable that Abraham made his journey without knowing his destination (Gen. 12:1). Such a response indicates a high degree of commitment to the God who had called him.

Abraham's journey of obedience led him to Canaan, where he received the promise that the land would one day belong to his descendants (Gen. 12:7a). The entire journey is described in terms of a pilgrimage and, when the destination had been reached, was culminated in worship at an altar which Abraham erected (Gen. 12:7b). To Abraham, the journey had not been so much of a migration as it had been a response of faith. Although Abraham moved through the sparsely populated central hill country, he did not settle there. Rather, he led his family on toward the Negeb (Gen. 12:9). The Negeb was an even more desolate region to the south of the central hill country. In such a region, Abraham was free from threat while he cared for his family and flocks.

The margin between adequate rainfall and inadequate rainfall in the Negeb was quite thin. It still is. When the rains fail, famine comes. At such a time, Abraham led his family on into nearby Egypt where the fruitful grasslands were not so dependent upon the rain (Gen. 12:10). There, Abraham let his fear overcome his love to Sarah, his wife, and passed her off as his sister (Gen. 12:11-13). It does not really ease the problem to point out that in ancient Nuzi men occasionally adopted their wives as sisters. At the very best, Abraham's treatment of Sarah shows an attitude of selfishness on his part. At the worst, he treated her as little more than a piece of property. In the entire story it is quite clear that the pharaoh of Egypt showed up in a better light than did Abraham (Gen. 12:15-20). The biblical writers never tried to hide the humanity of their heroes.

A problem is presented by the fact that Abraham is said to have pulled a similar trick on Abimelech, the king of Gerar (Gen. 20:1-18). The problem is further complicated by the fact that Isaac is said to have done an almost identical thing with Abimelech later (Gen. 26:1-11). Interpreters grappling with this problem have acknowledged the fact that it is difficult to conceive of the same trick being pulled twice on Abimelech. It is also difficult to conceive of Abraham descending to such a level twice. It has been suggested, given the oral nature of these early stories, that Abraham pulled the deception on Pharaoh and that later Isaac did the same thing with Abimelech. Then, later on these two stories got intertwined in the telling. This also leaves us with a problem concerning the very nature of the stories. Given the present state of our knowledge, it appears best to admit that we have a problem for which we do not have a solution that will satisfy all objections.

Suffice it to say whether Abraham pulled this stunt once or twice, he certainly does not tower as a giant of ethics or morality. He, too, had a sin problem which needed to be dealt with. It is probable that this is the primary message which the biblical author was communicating.

Sometime after Abraham's experience in Egypt, he returned to Canaan with his entire clan (Gen. 13:1-4). This return journey also appears to have been something of a religious pilgrimage, for he went back to the altar which he had earlier erected. Abraham's prosperity gave rise to a conflict between his servants and those of his nephew, Lot. Abraham sought to be a peacemaker, offering to Lot the choice of a region in which to settle and promising that he would go some other direction (Gen. 13:8-9). If the preceeding episode revealed Abraham's littleness, this one showed his greatness. As the patriarch of the clan, he had the authority to choose the best for himself and to assign a worse place to Lot. He could also have achieved peace by simply thrusting Lot from the family. That he did neither of these revealed a character of peace-loving generosity.

Lot, in greed, chose the best for himself (Gen. 13:10-11). This was the beginning of Lot's downfall. With consummate skill, the biblical writer traced the steps of Lot's ultimate loss. "Lot lifted up his eyes, and saw. . . . Lot . . . moved his tent as far as Sodom. . . . dwelt in Sodom, . . . Lot was sitting in the gate of Sodom" (Gen. 13:10,12; 14:12; 19:1). Although he never intended it, Lot's choice cost him his wife and his possessions.

Abraham moved back into the region of the Negeb, settling near Hebron (Gen. 13:18). His generosity had given him a less fertile place to live. But with God it was enough. There again, Abraham showed his religious devotion by establishing a worship center.

The biblical writer added another dimension to our picture of Abraham's character as he told of Abraham's response to the crisis when the coalition of foreign kings attacked the people of the plain (Gen. 14:1-11). Abraham moved his men-at-arms immediately to the attack. He pursued the kings far to the north. There he managed to free the captives and the captured goods and returned them to their homeland (Gen. 14:14-16). Again, Abraham is revealed as a man of faith in his worship following his victory (Gen. 14:18-20). He also further underscored his generosity by refusing to profit from his victory (Gen. 14:21-24).

From the standpoint of faith, perhaps the high point of Abraham's life is seen in his covenant experience with God (Gen. 15:7-18*a*). The practice of sealing a covenant by splitting sacrificial victims in half is well attested. The partners to such a covenant ceremony walked between the slain victims, apparently expressing the desire that such a fate would happen to them if they ever violated their commitments. Abraham seems to have dreamed that a flaming torch and a smoking fire pot passed between the pieces of the sacrifice (Gen. 15:17). In the Old Testament, fire is regularly used as a symbol for God (Ex. 19:18; 40:38).

A renewal of the covenant commitment is recorded later along with the change of Abraham's name and the institution of the rite of the circumcision (Gen. 17:1-14). A name in the ancient Near East was more than a title by which one was called. It was considered to reveal something of the nature of the person. Thus a changed name indicated a changed character. The one who changed the name had the authority to effect or to require the change in character. Further, the sign of circumcision became for the Hebrews a sign of their covenant relationship with God. From the standpoint of Hebrew faith, it is worth noting that God's covenant with Israel was based upon His choice alone. He chose them through Abraham; they did not choose Him. On the other hand, it is also worthy of note that the covenant demanded obedience on the part of Abraham. Unfortunately, Abraham's descendants regularly seem to have forgotten the demand for obedience.

In Israel's subsequent history, the covenant with Abraham was almost always seen as of lesser importance than the covenant with Moses and Israel at Sinai. However, the covenant with Abraham was an idea which was inherently more subject to misinterpretation than the later Sinai covenant. For, even in the time of Jesus, the pride of being Abraham's descendants led to a presumption of automatic blessing from God (Matt. 3:9; Luke 3:8; John 8:33).

The story of Abraham, much like our own life stories, seems to progress from high points to low points. God had promised Abraham and Sarah a son who would be the first of a multitude of descendants (Gen. 15:4-5). However, as time passed without such a son, they took matters into their own hands. Using a common practice of the time, Sarah furnished Hagar (her handmaid) to Abraham to produce an heir (Gen. 16:3). The sad story of the abuse of Hagar and the birth of Ishmael stand as a monument to Abraham's lack of faith. Tragically, some of the modern Arab-Israeli conflict has its roots in this experience, for some of the modern Arab states trace their heritage back to Ishmael. It is worthy of note that only the intervention of the "angel of the Lord" brought about the deliverance of Hagar (Gen. 16:7-9). In the Old Testament, the angel of the Lord is not a heavenly creature subordinate to God but in some way was always seen as an extension of God Himself. Whenever He appears, the Old Testament people recognized Him as a representation of God (Gen. 16:13).

Our next view of Abraham is couched in a story that is obviously quite hallowed by its traditional usages. Abraham received a revelation from God that the cities of the plain were about to be destroyed for their sinfulness. It is at this point that we are shown the greatness of Abraham as an intercessor. He pleaded with God for the people of Sodom and Gomorrah in one of the greatest examples of intercession which the Old Testament affords (Gen. 18:23-33). Unfortunately, the evil of Sodom was greater than Abraham imagined.

While it is not certain exactly what its limits were, the sins of Sodom were obviously sexual. Homosexuality appears to have been part of their problem if not the major portion (Gen. 19:5). The men of Sodom sought to "know" the guests who had come to stay with Lot in the city. That usage of the verb *know* is clearly sexual (see Gen. 4:1).

The real story of Abraham, however, followed a different path. The hope of Abraham and Sarah for a son had obviously fallen to a low ebb. However, at the statement that God's earlier promise was still going to come to pass and that they would yet have a son, "Sarah laughed" (Gen. 18:12). Such a note supplies the human interest detail of a laughter that expressed skepticism mingled with hope and hope mingled with skepticism. It is of interest that when the son was born, he was named Isaac which means "laughter" (Gen. 21:1-6). Thus did God give real joy to Sarah and Abraham in their old age.

The patriarchal historian was seeking to demonstrate in his narrative the power of a God who does not forget his promises. Human nature in Abraham and Sarah found it difficult to hold on to faith when everything in human experience seemed to point to its futility. It is worth noting that their lack of faith was not condemned. It did rob Sarah and Abraham of a long period of real laughter. God's promise was fulfilled anyway.

The greatest test of Abraham's faith was yet to come. He lived in a world where child sacrifice was regularly practiced. In particular, the firstborn son was considered to belong to the gods in a very special way. Against that background, we must set the story of Abraham's willingness to sacrifice Isaac. As it is told, the story is presented as a test to Abraham (Gen. 22:1-2). The question was whether he was as committed to his God as the people of surrounding nations were committed to their gods.

In order to fully comprehend the depth of this story, we must notice several significant items. First, Abraham had understood God's promise of a multitude of descendants as coming through Isaac (Gen. 21:12*b*). If Isaac were killed, how could this be? Second, Sarah is not mentioned in the story. She was clearly left behind, and apparently Abraham had not told her what he was about. She was surely aware of the practice and must have been beside herself with despair when the servants had told her what had happened. Third, Isaac was also quite aware of the practices. His question concerning the whereabouts of the sacrificial victim probably reflects his awareness that he was the likely choice (Gen. 22:7). Fourth, two of Abraham's statements present his utmost faith, which was greater here than it was earlier.

Abraham's statement to the servants, "I and the lad will go yonder and worship, and we will come again to you" (Gen. 22:5*b*, author's translation), clearly reflects an assurance on Abraham's part that somehow God was going to work out Abraham's dilemma. Furthermore, his answer to Isaac's question, "God will provide himself the lamb for a burnt offering" (Gen. 22:8), also expressed the same kind of total faith.

The fact that God did provide a substitute for Isaac by means of a ram caught in a nearby thicket was the way by which God kept His promise to Abraham. But the test of faith is trusting God when you do not know how He is going to work out the situation. This was what Abraham did. (We shall return to this episode later when we discuss its impact upon Isaac.)

The last episode of Abraham's life which we shall note was his provision of a wife for Isaac. Following the death of his own wife, Sarah, Abraham sent his servant to the region of Haran where the rest of his family had settled (Gen. 24:10). Abraham had two major concerns. First, he did not want Isaac to marry a Canaanite. Second, he did not want Isaac himself to go back. Both of these desires apparently stemmed from Abraham's own commitment to God. The Canaanites worshiped the Baals of the land. Abraham did not want Isaac involved with that. Furthermore, Abraham had been promised the land. He did not want Isaac to leave it. The servant returned from the journey with Rebekah as a wife for Isaac.

Abraham's careful provision for a wife for Isaac shows more than a father's normal concern for a good wife for his son. Rather, it reflects his dedication to God. He was seeking to provide as much assurance as possible that Isaac would follow in the faith of his father. No other significant events are recorded from Abraham's life except his death (Gen. 25:7-8). As far as the Genesis writer was concerned, the torch of faith had been passed to Isaac. Abraham could do no more.

Isaac

Some people who might otherwise be known as great have the misfortune to appear insignificant because of the greatness of those round about them. Such is the case with Isaac. Father of a great son and son of an even greater father, Isaac is frequently passed over in the patriarchal stories. Admittedly, we are not given the details about him that we are of his father and son, but what we are told about him allows us to see that the people of Israel remembered him as a man of great spirituality.

The very nature of his birth, a story which he certainly heard over and over again, should have made him believe that he was a child of destiny (Gen. 15:4-5; 17:17-19; 18:9-15; 21:1-3). This kind of childhood nurture makes an indelible impact upon one's life. Furthermore, the obvious devotion of his father to God also would have added to Isaac's spiritual growth.

The greatest impact, however, must surely have come from Isaac's near sacrifice. Being quite aware of the real possibility that he was about to be slain for God, he faithfully and obediently followed his father up the mount of Moriah. (This is identified as the Temple mount in Jerusalem by 2 Chronicles 3:1). Furthermore, once they arrived at the place, he was obediently submissive as his father bound him before placing him upon the altar (Gen. 22:9*b*). An old man could never have bound a vigorous young lad without his willing submission. Isaac was at least old enough and strong enough to carry the load of wood up the mountain. It is highly likely that Isaac's submission was not so much mere obedience to his father as it was surrender to the will of God. He was willing to be a sacrifice to God if that was what God demanded.

All of this certainly would have impacted upon Isaac's mind and heart in a major way. But the fact that, at the last moment, he was spared would have made an even greater mark upon his relation to God (Gen. 22:13). Isaac could never have forgotten that as long as he lived, his life was a real gift from God. Out of these experiences, Isaac developed a nature of deep spirituality. When compared with either Abraham or Jacob, Isaac appears to have been quiet and introspective, a man whose thoughts turned to God. He is later described as going "out to meditate in the field in the evening" (Gen. 24:63). Admittedly, the Hebrew word meaning *to meditate* occurs no where else in the Old Testament, but the Septuagint understood it to have this meaning, and it fits well into the context.

The human dimensions of Isaac began to show up in the narrative of his marriage to Rebekah. As was typical in the ancient Near East, the marriage had been arranged by his father and Rebekah's father, Bethuel (Gen. 24:1-9, 15,50-51). It is confirming of this kind of relationship that we are told that Rebekah became Isaac's wife first and that his love for her developed later (Gen. 24:67a).

We have been told of the conflict in Isaac's youth which surrounded him and his half brother Ishmael (Gen. 21:8-14). This apparently left no mark on Isaac's relation with Ishmael, for the two of them peacefully buried Abraham at his death (Gen. 25:9). However, the thing which Isaac did not learn from childhood experiences was the tragedy which can come to a family when partially is shown to children. When Jacob and Esau grew up, Isaac was partial to Esau while Rebekah was partial to Jacob (Gen. 25:28). It is highly likely that Isaac was trying to compensate for his retiring personality in the boisterous life of Esau. Much of the future trouble between Esau and Jacob can be traced directly to the parental partiality.

Isaac's retiring nature was certainly further accentuated as his advancing age brought blindness (Gen. 27:1). His planned blessing of his firstborn son, Esau, was disrupted by the scheming of Rebekah and Jacob (Gen. 27:3-17). This is also evidence of the deteriorating nature of Isaac's marriage. The deterioration may have begun when Isaac tried Abraham's trick of passing his wife off as his sister in order to save his own skin (Gen. 26:1-9). Be that as it may, the humanity of the biblical heroes is again clearly portrayed.

The problem of the stolen blessing is made more clear by an understanding of the nature of the spoken word in the ancient Near East. To us, it would appear that a blessing stolen in the manner by which Jacob stole Esau's would be wholly invalid. However, in that world, a word once spoken took on a concrete actuality. They took the spoken word much more seriously than we do. In an old Arabic story, for example, a father threw his son to the ground and covered him with his own body in order to protect him from an enemy's curses. To the Old Testament world, words once spoken became effective and real and could not be recalled.

Rebekah feared for Jacob's life after he had stolen Esau's blessing (Gen. 27:42-44). In order to deliver Jacob from Esau's wrath, she pleaded with Isaac to send Jacob back to her home for the stated purpose of getting a wife. In this, Isaac acquiesced, sending Jacob away (Gen. 27:46 to 28:5). Rebekah had plotted for Jacob's benefit. Perhaps it was only a just punishment that she apparently never saw him again, dying before his return. Isaac, on the other hand, lived to see his alienated sons reunited on the basis of Esau's forgiveness (Gen. 33:4,10). When he died, they were able to bury him peacefully (Gen. 35:28-29).

Quiet, retiring Isaac died as he had lived, in quietness and in confidence. His faith in the God of Abraham had sustained him as a youth. It upheld him to his grave.

Jacob/Israel

Of all the pre-Mosaic patriarchs, Jacob is usually the one who is most familiar to contemporary people. He is certainly the one who comes across as the most human. Jacob is also known by two names in the biblical traditions just as his grandfather Abraham was. But the name change in Jacob's life was far more significant. Furthermore, both names continued to be used both in the Psalms and in the preaching of the prophets. Therefore, rather than use just one of the names, as I did with Abraham, I will use both names, using each in those places where the Old Testament does.

The name *Jacob* appears to have originally meant "Supplanter." The name was originally given him when in the birth process, he seized his brother's heel, symbolically trying to "supplant" him as the firstborn (Gen. 25:26).

The name was quite descriptive of Jacob's character, for he was the confidence man *par excellence*. He was always out to get something for nothing, trying to supplant persons in their own heritage. Later in his life, when he was seeking for deliverance from a crisis from which he could not extricate himself, he struggled with God and begged for a blessing. The blessing came in the form of a changed name and nature. His new name, *Israel,* meant "He who strives with God" or "God strives" (Gen. 32:26-28). Although he was still human, from this time onward, there was a new dimension of spirituality in Jacob's life. The details of Jacob's life clearly reflect both dimensions of his nature, his humanity and his spirituality.

As a young man, Jacob was a retiring person with none of the adventuresome nature of his brother Esau (Gen. 25:27). As we have already noted, Jacob was the favorite of their mother, Rebekah, while Esau was the favorite of their father, Isaac (Gen. 25:28). In the process of their growth and development, Jacob took advantage of Esau's physical appetite to trade him out of his birthright for a mere dish of vegetable stew (Gen. 25:29-34). Although there is no excuse for the shabby way in which he treated Esau, Jacob's desire for the birthright reflected the value which he placed upon it. The birthright apparently carried not only monetary benefit and tribal authority but also the spiritual leadership of the family. Admittedly, at this stage in his life, Jacob would not have been much of a spiritual leader. At the same time, he at least showed an appreciation for things with an intangible value. Esau apparently valued little but his own satisfaction. Neither brother is particularly attractive at this stage of their lives.

Unfortunately, Jacob's life story went from bad to worse. At the time when Isaac was preparing to give the patriarchal blessing to Esau, Rebekah plotted with Jacob that he might get the blessing (Gen. 27:5-29). If it weren't so tragic, the story could be quite humorous. Preying upon Isaac's blindness, Jacob dressed himself in Esau's clothes and wrapped his arms in the skins of the kids which were being barbecued. Blind Isaac recognized the voice of Jacob, but the feel and the smell was that of Esau

(Gen. 27:22,27). It is no compliment to be identified with the smell of a goat!

Jacob compounded his crime by giving God the credit for his quick success (Gen. 27:20). The immediate result of Jacob's sins was that of the parental blessing which included prosperity, blessing, and authority over his family (Gen. 27:27b-29). Even though Jacob had gotten the blessing through deception, lying, and attributing the success of his scheming to God, the blessing was his. Under the beliefs of the day, a spoken word could not be recalled. Once pronounced, it became concrete and effective. Jacob at least valued the patriarchal blessing, but he was guilty of trying to get the good thing the wrong way. Here again, the Bible makes no attempt to hide the greed and sin of its heroes. At this point, Jacob appeared to be on top of everything, but the story was not over yet.

Discovering that he had once again been tricked by Jacob, Esau's anger was aroused. Yet, so great was his love for his father that he would not injure his father by striking out at his brother (Gen. 27:41). He bided his time, plotting to kill Jacob after Isaac's death. However, Rebekah was aware of the plan and arranged once again to deceive Isaac, getting him to send Jacob away from home on a false pretense (Gen. 27:46 to 28:5). Thus, at his mother's insistence and with his father's permission, Jacob left home to visit his Uncle Laban in Haran (Gen. 27:43). Jacob, who had been very much the homebody, was suddenly thrust out on his own, still trying to find within himself sufficient resources to preserve and advance his life.

With the skill of a gifted storyteller, the Genesis writer told of Jacob's flight toward Haran. In exhaustion, Jacob paused to rest once he felt that he was far enough from home to be safe from Esau. There he dreamed that he and God communicated with one another (Gen. 28:12-15). The angels of his dream ascending the ladder almost certainly represent his prayers going up to God, since angels were understood as divine messengers. A victim of his own fear and exhaustion, he apparently turned to God for help. Many of us can identify with that kind of plea for help. The most fascinating dimension of the story is that Jacob was assured that God's promises to Abraham and Isaac were going to be fulfilled to him. From a human standpoint, we must ask, "How can God use a man like Jacob?" Perhaps it is worth noting that the biblical message throughout is that God can use the worst people. Some of the best examples of the power of His love are seen in His use of the chiefest of sinners.

When Jacob awoke from his dreams, he realized that he had been given a profound spiritual experience (Gen. 28:17). He vowed to establish a shrine to God if he returned safely home (Gen. 28:20-22). Certainly the vow was self-serving. At the same time, it showed the awakening of something deep within. At that point, Jacob's relation to God was only a promise of what it was yet to be. So he went on his way to Haran.

With extreme skill, the narrator of Genesis told the story of Jacob's arrival in Haran and his love-at-first-sight meeting with Rachel. Having arrived in Haran, Jacob stumbled across the well where Laban's daughter Rachel watered her sheep. As soon as Jacob saw her, he was smitten. He did his best to send away the other shepherds who had gathered at the well so he would have Rachel all to himself (Gen. 29:7). As Rachel drew nearer, he saw her beauty and her wealth in sheep, and he immediately decided to try to impress her (Gen. 29:10). The stone upon the well had been too big for the other shepherds to roll away until they all had gathered. But as soon as Rachel drew near, Jacob rolled it away all by himself. He was a typical lovesick young man trying to impress a girl with his prowess.

Jacob was welcomed into the house of his mother's brother and settled down for a visit. Since he had no resources of his own in order to pay Laban the bride price for Rachel, he offered to work seven years for her (Gen. 29:18). This was perhaps the first really generous gesture which it is recorded that he performed. We are told that the seven years "seemed to him but a few days for the love he had for her" (Gen. 29:20).

Jacob was so much in love that it apparently never

entered his mind that others could be as deceitful as he had been. In his Uncle Laban, Jacob had met a man who was just as tricky as he was. When the time came for Jacob's wedding to Rachel, Laban apparently got Jacob so drunk that he was able to substitute brides on him. On the morning after the wedding when Jacob awoke, he discovered that he had married Leah instead (Gen. 29:22-25a)! It is obvious that this subterfuge had to have been done with Rachel's permission. It just could not have happened otherwise without a major brawl. Laban sought to appease indignant Jacob with a plea that younger girls couldn't marry before their older sisters, but if that were the case, it should have been stated earlier. It is more likely that because Leah had "plain eyes" (Gen. 29:17a, author's trans.) Laban had been afraid that he was going to be stuck with an unmarried daughter. Jacob completed his honeymoon week with Leah and then was allowed to marry Rachel. This time he got his wife before he performed the seven years of labor for her (Gen. 29:27-30). He was not about to risk being outdone by Laban again. It is worth noting that one human problem with polygamy immediately came to the fore in that Jacob "loved Rachel more than Leah" (Gen. 29:30).

During the passing years, Jacob became the father of several children (Gen. 29:31 to 30:24). The practices described in childbearing are well attested in other ancient Near Eastern documents.

When Jacob had completed his service for his two wives, he then entered into an agreement with Laban to continue serving him for the payment of any sheep or goats which were not solid white. Having spent at least fourteen years caring for Laban's flocks, Jacob was well aware that they were not pure bred. With a great deal of outward deception, Jacob slowly but surely began to take over more and more of Laban's flocks as they produced spotted offspring (Gen. 30:31-43).

As Jacob's wealth increased and Laban's decreased, the hostility of Laban and his sons began to be directed toward Jacob (Gen. 31:1-2). It is interesting that at this point Jacob became aware that God was calling him home (Gen.

31:3). Again, it appears that Jacob's fear made him sensitive to the call of God. That is an all too human reaction.

At a time when Laban was busy elsewhere, Jacob departed with his flocks and his family (Gen. 31:17-21). Rachel showed that she was the same kind of person as her husband and her father by stealing the household gods of Laban. As noted earlier, the possession of the household gods apparently carried title to the family property and a claim to the headship of the family. Thus, by stealing these, Rachel was laying claim to these things for her husband.

When Laban discovered that Jacob and his family were gone, along with the household gods, he set out in hot pursuit (Gen. 31:22-23). Due to Rachel's further trickery, Laban was unable to find his gods and returned home, allowing Jacob to depart in peace (Gen. 31:55).

But this left Jacob with a problem. He could not go back to Haran, for he was hated there. Yet he feared to go forward to his homeland, for he knew that Esau was there and hated him. In the midst of a crisis of his own making, the result of his own sin and treachery, he could see no way out. He tried to arrange his own situation by sending his possessions on before him, apparently as a bribe to Esau. He also sent his family on before him. Jacob was hiding behind his wives and children (Gen. 32:13-23). This left him alone with his conscience—and God.

The spiritual experience which Jacob had that night is couched in very prosaic terms. It would come across as nothing more than a wrestling match if it were not for the way in which it ended. Jacob's own description of the event leaves no doubt but that he was agonizing with God as he declares, "I have seen God face to face, and yet my life is preserved" (Gen. 32:30). Unable to go back, fearful of going forward, in desperation Jacob grappled with himself and God, seeking a blessing (Gen. 32:26). The blessing he received was a change of name and nature. No longer was he to be known as Jacob, a supplanter. From henceforth he was to be Israel, one who strives with God (Gen. 32:28). As we shall see, a new dimension was added to Jacob's life at this point. God was no longer merely an accessory to his life. Although Jacob's human nature was still with him, he also had, from this point on, a basic desire to serve God. Such was the ancient description of a religious conversion, set in the prosaic terms of historical events.

As the dawn came, we discover that Jacob's plight had not changed. His situation was still the same; it was just Israel who was new. God does not rewrite history. The new man Israel still had to face the same old danger from Esau. Here was a brother whom he had wronged, who hated him, and who had threatened to kill him. Now Esau was coming to meet him with "four hundred men" (Gen. 33:1). Four hundred men does not sound like a welcoming committee; it sounds like an army bent on destruction.

Suddenly we are shown the first difference in the man Israel. Whereas earlier Jacob had placed others between himself and danger, now he courageously stepped out in front (Gen. 33:3). Whereas before he had been generally arrogant and self-sufficient, now he approached Esau in humility, "bowing himself to the ground." In pride, he had stolen from Esau. In submission and surrender, he returned. He was truly a new man.

However, in the intervening years, something had happened to Esau as well. For "Esau ran to meet him, and embraced him, and fell on his neck and kissed him, and they wept" (Gen. 33:4). Instead of meeting his brother in anger, Esau welcomed Israel with acceptance and forgiveness. (How different from the older brother in Jesus' parable of the prodigal, see Luke 15:25-32.) Israel's new nature continued to reveal itself as he offered as presents to Esau that which he had intended to offer as a bribe. Jacob had never been generous, except in working for Rachel. However, Israel now showed a generous spirit. Furthermore, he who had once viewed Esau with contempt now greeted him with a generous compliment, saying, "to see your face is like seeing the face of God, with such favor have you received me" (Gen. 33:10). This becomes especially meaningful when we remember that Jacob/Israel had found acceptance and blessing from God that very morning. Esau was the rough, rugged outdoorsman who smelled like a goat. The only thing about him which could have reminded Israel of God was that he had seen a look of forgiveness and acceptance on the face of Esau. That reminds people of God!

Israel's generosity was not one of form only. He continued to urge Esau to accept the gifts until finally he did so (Gen. 33:11). A cynic might have questioned Israel's motives at the beginning. But his continued insistence that his gifts be accepted are the evidence of a new dimension to his nature. That apparently came from his experience with God.

Jacob had left Haran in fear that he could not really go home. But as Israel, he discovered that home was precisely where he was welcomed. As soon as he was able to obtain a piece of land on which to live, he erected an altar to El-Elohe-Israel, to "God, the God of Israel" (Gen. 33:20). No longer was God merely the God of his fathers, He had become the God of Israel.

Sometime after Israel and his family had gotten firmly settled in the land, he went to Bethel, the place of his initial experience with God when he had fled from Esau's wrath. Before approaching God, Israel's family and servants went through a purification, getting rid of all foreign gods and of their symbols (Gen. 35:1-4).

Bethel apparently was already an ancient shrine in the land of Canaan. But Israel transformed it into a shrine which he named El-bethel or "God of Bethel" or "God of the house of God" (Gen. 35:7). There, in a worship experience, Jacob's transformation to Israel was reasserted. (Gen. 35:10).

It is easy to assume that when people serve God they should have lives of ease and blessing and that none of the tragedies of life should befall them. Nothing is more foreign to the biblical message. Israel's experience was no exception. Immediately after the high point of his worship experience at Bethel, his beloved wife Rachel died in childbirth (Gen. 35:16-19). The son born to her was Benjamin. The fact that he was born at the time of Rachel's death is probably the basis for the extreme protectiveness which Israel later showed for him.

Not long after that Isaac, Israel's father, died (Gen. 35:28-29). Isaac had disappeared from the story until this point. It is worthy of note that Esau and Jacob were still getting along well enough to collaborate in Isaac's burial. The earlier vow of Esau to kill Jacob had long been forgotten.

As Jacob's old age drew on, he passed more and more into the background of the Genesis narrative. We see in the episode with Joseph and his brothers that Jacob had not become a plaster saint in his conversion. He learned nothing from his own childhood experiences of the dangers to a family when parents are partial to a particular child. Jacob was partial to Joseph, the firstborn of his beloved Rachel (Gen. 37:3). Not only was he partial but Jacob also used Joseph as a spy and talebearer on his brothers (Gen. 37:2,14). Such actions on Jacob's part could do nothing but engender hostility toward Joseph on the part of the brothers. We shall return to the Joseph stories shortly, but the end result of the brothers' growing hostility was that they sold their brother into slavery and told their father that he had been killed by a wild animal (Gen. 37:27,32-36). Jacob's grief was inconsolable. In spite of the fact that his own partiality had brought about the situation which created his grief, we cannot help but be moved at the tragic spectacle of Jacob's grief. Bereft of his beloved Rachel, his beloved Joseph, and his father Isaac, he was a sad figure.

Little more is heard of Jacob until the famous famine which had elevated Joseph to prominence in Egypt (Gen. 41:53-57). At that point, Jacob, still exercising the patriarchal leadership, sent his sons to Egypt to buy grain (Gen. 42:1-2). We shall return to the details of these events when we follow the Joseph narratives, but two events stand out as far as Jacob is concerned. The first of these is the pathos reflected in old Jacob's words as he wrestled with the necessity of sending Benjamin with the brothers when they made their second trip to Egypt after grain (Gen. 43:1-14). Here is the pathetic picture of Jacob giving up the last thing he apparently treasured on earth, Rachel's second son. Although we can surely understand the heartbreak of Jacob, we can also see the problems created by his obvious partiality to the sons of Rachel.

The second event of this series of stories which is important for our survey of Jacob's life is more joyful. This is when the brothers brought word to their failing father that Joseph was still alive and had invited them to come to Egypt to live (Gen. 45:26 to 46:7). The journey was made with joy and excitement, as well as with the blessing of God. Israel had his family reunited in Egypt. Perhaps for the first time since Rachel's death, there was a note of joy in Jacob's life. However, in looking back over his life, Jacob could not see much joy. He described those years to the pharaoh of Egypt, saying, "few and evil have been the days of the years of my life" (Gen. 47:9).

As was typical in the ancient Near East, when Jacob knew that the time of his death was approaching, he called his sons together to bestow upon them the patriarchal blessing (Gen. 49:1-27). The form of the blessing appears to be something which had been treasured and recited as a traditional statement of the tribal hopes, dreams, and relationships. We must remember that words, once spoken, had a concreteness to the Hebrew mind. Their very statement and repetition would have been seen by the Hebrews as being a guarantee that they were going to be fulfilled.

Following this patriarchal blessing, Jacob died (Gen. 49:28-33). Just before his death, Jacob expressed a desire to be buried in the old family burying plot at Machpelah. "There they buried Abraham and Sarah his wife; there they buried Isaac and Rebekah his wife; and there I buried Leah" (Gen. 49:31). The fascinating dimension to this request is that his final wish was to be buried beside Leah. She had obviously loved him over the years, being willing to serve him even in the face of his love for Rachel. In the end, her faithful love won out. She was not the beauty that Rachel was, but "she wore well."

Upon Jacob's death, Joseph asked for and received permission from Pharaoh to go up to Canaan in order to fulfill his father's request (Gen. 50:4-6). Jacob had died in peace and was buried where he wished. At his death, he was a different man from what he had been in his youth and young manhood. He had experienced the blessing of God.

Joseph

A pampered, spoiled brat is probably what Joseph's brothers would have called Joseph. That description would have been partially true. There is no question but that he was the apple of his father's eye and was surely spoiled by the lavish gifts of his father (Gen. 37:3-4). To be so singled out for Jacob's love surely aroused the hostility of his brothers, and that was to bear bitter fruit.

All of the blame for the brother's hostility toward Joseph cannot be laid at Jacob's feet alone, however, for Joseph himself added fuel to the fires of the hatred. Joseph had dreams of greatness (Gen. 37:5-11). It might be well asked, What young person does not have dreams of greatness? The question is legitimate, but Joseph apparently not only believed his dreams but also arrogantly described them in all their detail to his already hostile brothers. Such was his attitude that when his dreams of power also included authority over his father, even Jacob was forced to rebuke his favorite son (Gen. 37:10).

As the story is told, it is of little significance at this point that Joseph's dreams were going to come true. He did rise to power and to an authority over his family, including his father. That was not really the problem. The real problem rested in the fact that Joseph was apparently trying to lord it over his brothers before he had either the power or the authority. Jacob's love and Joseph's dreams stirred the monster of jealousy. That was to have tragic consequences for all concerned. On the other hand, in spite of rebuking Joseph, Jacob continued to ponder the dream, seeking to understand what was happening to his son (Gen. 37:11).

Unfortunately, Jacob himself continued to antagonize his other sons by using Joseph as a spy and a talebearer (Gen. 37:14*a*; see 37:2*b*). The problem was further augmented by the fact that Joseph was now being spared from the labor of shepherding the sheep. When Joseph went to seek his brothers, he discovered that they had moved the flocks from where they were supposed to be (Gen. 37:15-17). It may be that they had moved simply because the pasturage had given out. As the story is told, however, they may also have gone elsewhere just to avoid the tattling of Joseph. But he found them anyway, and that was the straw which broke the camel's back. The brothers plotted to kill him (Gen. 37:18).

Without question, the narrative is a bit confusing at this point. Either Reuben or Judah or both set out to spare Joseph (Gen. 37:22,26-27). Either the brothers sold Joseph to the Ishmaelites or Midianites found Joseph in the pit and sold him to the Ishmaelites (Gen. 37:27-28). Furthermore, Reuben was distressed to find Joseph gone, as if he had not known of any of this (Gen. 37:29). Finally, either the Ishmaelites or the Midianites took Joseph to Egypt (Gen. 37:28*b*,36). However, the central theme of the narrative is quite clear, regardless of how the details are worked out. Joseph was seized by his brothers and was carried into Egypt to be sold as a slave. The brothers conspired to deceive Jacob, leading him to believe that Joseph had been killed by a wild beast (Gen. 37:30-35). An intriguing dimension of human interest is that the brothers did not refer to Joseph as "our brother" but as "your son" (Gen. 37:32).

A new dimension of Joseph's character was revealed when he found himself a slave in Egypt. He showed himself to be a hardworking, loyal servant. He did not bemoan his fate. Neither did he lose his dreams of greatness but seems to have decided to be great in whatever life situation he found himself. His faithfulness and hard work were rewarded by rapid advancement in the staff of his master until he was finally made chief steward (Gen. 39:1-6*a*). So diligent and effective a servant was Joseph that his owner was able to turn over all of his business concerns to the young Hebrew.

At this point, tragedy struck. Joseph had grown from his teens into a "handsome and good-looking" young man (Gen. 39:6). The wife of Joseph's master became infatuated with him and sought to seduce him. However,

Joseph's good sense and loyalty kept him from falling into this pit (Gen. 39:7-10). He had obviously learned the value of the word *no*. However, his refusal apparently made him more attractive, so the Egyptian's wife persisted. Finally she sought to force him, but he fled from her, leaving his outer cloak in her hand. At this final rebuff, the woman turned on him, accusing him of having tried to rape her (Gen. 39:11-18). As a result of this, Joseph was sent to prison. It would appear that all of his loyalty and faithfulness had gotten him nowhere but worse off.

The strange thing about this is that, given what we know of ancient law, we would have expected Joseph to have been executed not just imprisoned. Slaves had no rights in ancient society. This kind of insult to an owner's wife should have resulted in the slave's death. Not only was he not killed, Joseph was immediately put in charge of the prisoners and the prison (Gen. 39:22-23). This is even more strange.

We note, however, that the officer in charge of the prison was "the captain of the guard" (Gen. 40:3). Furthermore, Joseph's original master, Potiphar, was also "the captain of the guard" (Gen. 39:1). Joseph was not executed by Potiphar; he was given a new responsibility by the same man. It would appear that Potiphar had not believed his wife. Rather than suffer the public embarassment of admitting his wife's flaws, he had sent Joseph to prison. But at the same time, trusting Joseph, he made him overseer of the prison. Joseph on the other hand could have given up, having been moved from slave to prisoner. But he continued to try to be great in whatever place life gave him.

In prison, Joseph was faced by two notable men of Pharaoh's court, the chief butler and the chief baker. While there they each had a dream which Joseph interpreted for them, promising the chief butler release and a restoration to favor (Gen. 40:5-13,16-19). Joseph pleaded with the butler to present his case before Pharaoh (Gen. 40:14-15). In an all too human dimension, when the butler was restored to Pharaoh's favor, he immediately forgot Joseph's friendship and request (Gen. 39:20-23).

Two years elapsed before the situation was corrected. At that time Pharaoh had a dream which he wished to have interpreted, but his own attendants were unable to help him (Gen. 41:1-8). The chief butler then remembered Joseph and told his story to Pharaoh, who called for Joseph to be brought to him. It is worth noting that Joseph's attitude toward dreams was that of a servant of God. He did not claim any power in himself for their interpretation (Gen. 40:8; 41:16). In interpreting the dream of the seven years of plenty followed by the seven years of famine, Joseph had done what Pharaoh's own attendants had not been able to do. When he further suggested how to deal with the problem, Joseph said, "Let Pharaoh select a man discreet and wise, and set him over the land of Egypt" (Gen. 41:33). This was a rather obvious recommendation of himself. Pharaoh immediately accepted the suggestion of Joseph, elevating him to the position of chief steward or prime minister of Egypt (Gen. 41:37-45). At the age of thirty, Joseph had attained the greatness of which he had dreamed (Gen. 41:46).

Under Joseph's administration, grain was gathered from the people of Egypt during the years of plenty, being stored for the famine years to come. When the famine arrived, Joseph began to sell the stored grain to the Egyptians (Gen. 41:56). When the people ran out of money, the famine was still with them; so they began to sell their cattle and land to Pharaoh for grain. Eventually, the people wound up selling themselves as slaves to Pharaoh, so that they would not starve (Gen. 47:15-21). Before the crisis, Egypt had been filled by a multitude of free landholders. After the crisis, Egypt belonged to the pharaoh, and the people were little more than serfs upon his land. (We shall return to this idea in the next chapter.)

During the years of famine, people began to come to Egypt from surrounding regions in order to buy grain (Gen. 41:57). Among these were the brothers of Joseph, coming from Canaan (Gen. 42:1-5). When they arrived at the grain market, they were recognized by Joseph, but he was not recognized by them. This is quite understandable, considering that he was merely a teenager when they sent him away.

The whole episode between Joseph and his brothers is one of deep emotion. Accusing them of being spies, Joseph found out from them the present state of the family and that Jacob was still living. Pretending not to believe them, he demanded that they return with their youngest brother, Benjamin. In order to bring about this end, he had Simeon arrested, sending them home with the money for their grain having been surreptitiously returned to them. The brother's fear when they discovered this was unbounded (Gen. 42:6-28).

Jacob, as might have been expected, refused to allow Benjamin to make the journey to Egypt (Gen. 42:38). But the famine persisted, and finally there was no other way of survival but to return to Egypt. In order to try to alleviate Jacob's fears for Benjamin, Judah offered himself as surety for the young lad (Gen. 43:8-9).

When the brothers returned to Egypt, they were brought to Joseph. They showed their honor and honesty by trying to return the money for their first purchases to Joseph (Gen. 43:20-22). Again, the pathos of the situation is vividly described, as Joseph had to seek a place to weep privately (Gen. 43:30). As the brothers prepared to return to Canaan, Joseph put them to the test by hiding his personal silver cup among the possessions of Benjamin. When the cup was found there, they all came back before Joseph (Gen. 44:4-13). They had matured over the years, for they were obviously no longer jealous of their father's special love. Rather, they were compassionate for their father's concerns and for their youngest brother. One of the most moving and beautiful passages in all the world's literature is Judah's plea for the release of Benjamin, offering himself as a slave in Benjamin's place (Gen. 44:18-34).

At this point, Joseph knew that they were different men from the ones who had sent him into slavery. For that matter, he was different as well. He revealed his identity to them and offered them forgiveness (Gen. 45:3-8). He also showed a deep commitment to God and His divine purposes, for he said, "God sent me before you to preserve life" (Gen. 45:5).

Joseph then urged his brothers to go home and bring their father and all their families to Egypt, for the famine would continue for five more years (Gen. 45:9-11). It goes without saying that the reunion of the family was joyous. When they arrived in Egypt, they were made welcome by Pharaoh and were allowed to settle in the lush grassland of Goshen (Gen. 47:1-12). Little more is known of Joseph's relations with his family. Just before his father's death, Joseph was promised that God would one day bring the family of Israel back to Canaan (Gen. 48:21). After Jacob's burial, the brothers feared that Joseph might then seek revenge upon them (Gen. 50:15-17). However, Joseph showed that he was a truly great person by reassuring them of his forgiveness and his care for them (Gen. 50:19-21). He maintained them and their families until his death. His last request was that whenever they should return to Canaan, they would carry his body back to the land of promise (Gen. 50:24-26).

Joseph died, and the passage of time took away all of that generation (Ex. 1:6). The famine ended, but the descendants of Jacob remained in Egypt.

The Significance of the Period

The prime concern of the biblical writers never seems to have been the mere recording of history. Rather, what they appear to have recorded was significant history. For them, that meant not what people were doing so much as what God was doing with people. What, then, appears to be the significance of the history of the patriarchs?

As we review the narratives, perhaps the first thing which strikes us is that the patriarchs were people. They were human, with all of the intermingled strengths and weaknesses which we have learned to expect in humanity. The patriarchs and their families were not plaster saints. They had their moments of greatness and their moments of weakness. They could be generous and jealous. They were also lustful and loving. In short, they were just as human as we have learned to expect all people to be. This is quite important. For it shows that the biblical writers had no illusions about their ancestors or themselves. You do not have to be unusual to be a part of God's plan.

A second thing which strikes us in these ancient stories is that the patriarchs were people of their times. By and large, their customs, habits, practices, and understandings were essentially those of the other people who were living at the same time. We have seen again and again how their social customs paralleled those of the surrounding cultures. They were not culturally different from the people among whom they lived and around whom they moved. This, also, is of great significance. The people whom God uses are not necessarily different from those around them. This means that God can use you and me.

Admittedly, the patriarchs were human and were people of their times, but there was a difference. They were used by God, according to the biblical authors. This brings us to the third point of significance, for it says something to us about the sovereignty of God. He can choose to use whomsoever He pleases. He could have used another family from another place rather than Abraham from Ur. But in His sovereignty, He chose to use that family. On the other hand, there is every indication that Abraham (and the others) allowed themselves to be used. Thus there is always the note of surrender and submission. Even when this may at times be self-serving, as in the early days of Jacob, it at least involves some form of belief and submission. Further, the very fact that God could use a man like Jacob allows us some hope that He can also use us. Even our weaknesses can be transformed for God's purposes.

Finally, the patriarchal narratives are significant because they explain to us several things of importance for the subsequent history of Israel. They explain why Israel was in Egypt. They also set the stage for God's greatest act of redemption in the Old Testament, the Exodus from Egypt. Furthermore, from these we begin to gain an understanding of the heritage to which both ancient and modern Hebrews look. The very longing for the land of

Israel today has its roots in the Israelis' understanding of God's promises to Abraham, Isaac, and Jacob. Their racial pride has its basis in these stories as well. Much of the New Testament is relatively meaningless without some knowledge and understanding of these events.

Through the patriarchal narratives, we see how the stage was set for the next great step in God's plan of redemption. Using human beings, God had prepared a people to effect his purpose.

3
Israel's Birth: The Exodus and Wilderness Wanderings

Historically and theologically, the experience of the Exodus from Egypt was the most significant event in the entire Old Testament. From a theological standpoint, the experience of the Exodus was the focal point of all of Israel's subsequent faith. From that experience, the Hebrews believed that God had chosen them to be His special people. Unfortunately, they frequently forgot that they had been chosen to be His agents of redemption, not merely the recipients of His blessing. That forgetfulness, however, does not change the centrality of the Exodus event for their faith. In a very real sense, the Exodus of the Old Testament was for Israel what the Calvary of the New Testament is for Christians.

More important from the historian's standpoint, Israel's Exodus from Egypt was the primary historical event in their heritage. It was through the Exodus experience and its meaning that a loosely knit group of enslaved families were welded into a united people which was to become a great nation. Almost every significant feature of Israel's sense of national identity had its roots in the experience of the Exodus. If we are to understand Israel's subsequent development, we must understand the events of the Exodus. The historian can deal with Israel's history without really focusing upon the patriarchs. There is no way, however, to deal adequately with Israel's historical identity and ignore the Exodus. It would be like trying to understand the United States while ignoring the American Revolution.

In dealing with the period of the sojourn and the Exodus, we need a clear understanding of the period with which we are dealing. The sojourn began with the descent of Jacob and his family into Egypt as a result of the famine during the administration of Joseph. From that point until the time the Hebrews left Egypt is the period of the sojourn. In the Exodus period itself, I am including those events which essentially involved the career of Moses. This covers the immediate events leading up to the Exodus, the actual departure from Egypt, the journey to Sinai, the covenant experience at Sinai, the wilderness wanderings up to the encampment on the plains of Moab, and the subsequent death of Moses.

Sources for the Study

The basic sources for studying the history of the period are Exodus, Numbers, and Deuteronomy. (Leviticus is left out for it is primarily legal material. Furthermore, parts of the other three books could be omitted for similar reasons.) In addition to these major biblical sources, numerous minor biblical references reflect the traditions in Israel regarding this period. These occur in the sermons of the prophets and in occasional psalms. Among these are two psalms which give a rather extensive summary (Pss. 78; 105).

Outside the Bible, there are significant historical records from Egypt which give us the background of the Egyptian Empire of this era. The pharaohs' territorial domination extended from Egypt all the way through Canaan during almost the entire period. This means that we have fairly adequate (for this period) historical records for the entire geographical region in which the Hebrews were involved throughout this period.

Furthermore, the Egyptians were significantly involved in the erection and decoration of monuments. Many of these monuments add background knowledge of the period to our store of information. For example, the first extrabiblical reference to Israel is found on the Merneptah stela which comes from the late thirteenth century BC.

On the opposite extreme, we have also gained some significant information of the era from graffiti. There are such inscriptions on the walls of Egyptian copper mines in the Sinai Peninsula. These were apparently written by Semitic slaves in the early fifteenth century BC. (It is worth noting that the Hebrews were Semites. It is fascinating to ponder whether this graffiti came from them.)

In addition to these Egyptian records, there are the so-called Amarna letters from the fourteenth century BC. These generally are official correspondence from Egyptian vassals in Canaan and Phoenicia written to the court of Egypt. However, some of them came from as far north as Mitanni and from as far east as Babylon. They give us a rather vivid picture of the chaotic condition in Canaan during the era.

Adding further to our knowledge of the era are the treaties of the Hittites, along with legal codes and religious documents from several nations of the region. These all add depth to our knowledge of world events during the period, as well as to our understanding of legal and religious concerns. Further, these help us identify similarities and differences between the Hebrew traditions from the period and those of the surrounding nations.

Beyond the actual written materials, there is, as usual, the evidence added to our study from the archaeological excavations and the surface explorations of the region. To these must also be added the geographical and climatic features of the region. Only as we understand this information can we come to grips with many of the details of the biblical narratives. The understanding of the former also adds depth to our grasp of the common cultures of the day. Daily life of people has a significant bearing on the history of any era. As we draw all of this material together, we are able to depict fairly well the world in which Israel was born and grew.

Major Problems for Consideration

From the historian's standpoint, there are several significant problems regarding Israel's sojourn in Egypt, the Exodus, and the wanderings between Egypt and the entrance into Canaan. We must direct our attention to these

ISRAEL'S BIRTH

problems before we seek to reconstruct the history of the era. In a very real sense, several of these problems impinge upon one another and upon related problems in earlier and later eras. In addition to the historical problems, some theological problems are of major importance for the theologian which the historian cannot ignore. In a survey such as this, we cannot probe any of these in depth, but we must at least give some consideration to them.

The Silence of Egyptian Records

The question is frequently raised, particularly among beginning students of Old Testament history, Is there any record of Israel in Egypt or of the Exodus events in the ancient Egyptian records themselves? The answer to this question at this time is a categorical no. Unfortunately, there is a universal silence in the Egyptian records of any involvement with Israel insofar as these events are concerned.

In spite of our opinions to the contrary, no matter how important the events of the Exodus were to Israel, nor how important they may be to Christians, they simply were not important to Egypt. The departure of a group of slaves was not the sort of thing which was recorded in the Egyptian annals. Further, the destruction of an Egyptian army at the sea was not the sort of thing which was recorded in official court records either. They did not normally record defeats.

As to the question of why Joseph is not mentioned, we face different problems. It is possible that Joseph was not as important in the eyes of the Egyptians as he might have seemed to his own people. It is also quite likely that he achieved his importance during the time of the Hyksos rule in Egypt. The Hyksos were a Semitic dynasty who ruled over Egypt from around 1750 BC to about 1550 BC. As Semites, they were foreigners who were hated for that very reason. However, since Joseph himself was a Semite, it is quite easy to understand his elevation to power under such rulers.

When the Hyksos were finally expelled from Egypt,

the new, native Egyptian rulers did their best to eliminate as much evidence of the Hyksos presence as possible. Thus, if Joseph had served under the Hyksos, his name might have become lost in this purge of records and monuments. It is also possible that Joseph might have been known in Egypt under an Egyptian name rather than under his Hebrew name.

However, there is one bit of evidence from ancient Egypt which might reflect the presence of Israel in Egypt. The Genesis narratives tell us that during the famine in Egypt, Joseph sold grain to the Egyptians until they ran out of money. Finally the people had to sell their cattle, their property, and at last themselves to Pharaoh (Gen. 47:14-21). While there is no record of this in the Egyptian annals, there are two striking facts which must be considered. Prior to the rule of the Hyksos, Egypt was filled with many small landholders and the people were essentially free (at least by ancient standards). After the period of the Hyksos, the pharaoh owned all the land and the people were essentially serfs of the Egyptian king. Although this does not prove the presence of Joseph or his administration, it certainly fits.

The Date of the Exodus

Probably the most significant historical problem related to the Exodus is when it occurred. Are we able to date this event? In order to try to answer this question, we must begin by getting the chronological data before us.

The author of Kings tied in the building of the Temple with the Exodus. "In the four hundred and eightieth year after the people of Israel came out of the land of Egypt, in the fourth year of Solomon's reign over Israel, . . . he began to build the house of the Lord" (1 Kings 6:1). The building of the Temple is usually considered to have begun between 960 and 966 BC. This would place the Exodus 480 years earlier, about 1440 to 1446 BC. However, this information is confused when we consider that the Septuagint dates the Exodus as 440 years earlier than the Temple.

In addition, this tradition must be confronted with the archaeological evidence from the period. Surface exploration of the regions of Edom and Moab indicate that there were no significant settlements at all in these regions until about 1300 BC. Thus Moses and the Israelites would not have had to ask permission to go through these lands in the earlier period. They could have marched on through unopposed. The only opposition to their advance which they would have faced would have to have come after 1300 BC. (See Num. 20:14-21; 21:4,13,21-23). Furthermore, there is no significant archaeological evidence of any major influx of people into Canaan around 1400 BC. (If the Exodus were about 1440, the conquest would have been about 1400, since the wilderness period took forty years.) The Amarna letters reflect problems in Canaan with insurgents or rebels called the Habiru' about 1400, but there is no evidence from excavations of major military destructions at that time. (The earlier claim that Jericho fell about this time has been shown by subsequent investigation to have been in error. Due to weathering and robbing of stone from the mound, there are no remains from Jericho which date to this period.) However, there is a significant amount of destruction evidence from numerous sites in Palestine which can be dated to around 1230 to 1210 BC. In each of these instances, the new culture was more primitive than the one replacing it. Furthermore, a victory stela of Pharaoh Merneptah indicates that a group of people called Israel were in Palestine about 1220 BC. They are not called a nation or a kingdom but are identified as only a loosely organized group of people. This is precisely what would be expected if they had only recently entered the land. If, on the other hand, they had been in the land for at least 150 years, we would have expected a different designation.

It appears that there are at least four ways to deal with the problem. We can ignore it, which is what most people do. But ignoring a problem does not solve it. We can also assume that either the biblical or the archaeological evidence is wrong. This has been done by numerous people who have decided one way or the other, usually based upon a theological bias. It is possible, however, that the problem lies not so much with the data as with our understanding of it. For example, 480 years sounds remarkably like twelve times forty. It is common both in the Bible and out of it to use forty as a round number indicating a long period of time. It is also demonstrable that forty is sometimes used as a synonym for a generation. Could it be that the biblical author received a tradition that the Temple was erected twelve generations after the Exodus and simply supplied the numbers on his own? If a generation is assumed to be more like twenty-five to twenty-seven years, then twelve generations would be about three hundred years. This would then place the Exodus about 1260 to 1280 BC (three hundred years earlier than Solomon's Temple) and the entrance into Canaan about forty years later. This would fit the archaeological data much better.

A fourth solution is also worthy of consideration. There are many indications, as we shall see in the next chapter, that when Joshua led Israel into Canaan he found a significant number of related people who were already there. It is possible—in fact, it is highly probable—that there was more than one departure from Egypt. It could be that the archaeological data reflect the Exodus and conquest under Moses and Joshua, while the Temple was dated by the departure of a different group which infiltrated the land in a more peaceful manner.

It appears almost certain that the Exodus under Moses must have occurred around 1280 to 1260 BC in the Nineteenth Dynasty of Egypt. There may have been and probably were other departures as well. (We know that the Bible only tells those details which are significant for the main story. For example, Moses had an older brother and sister, but we would never know it if all we read were Ex. 2:1-2. The birth of Miriam and Aaron are totally ignored.)

The entrance into Egypt offers a different set of problems. The author of Exodus simply said: "The time that the people of Israel dwelt in Egypt was four hundred and thirty years" (Ex. 12:40). We become confused however, when we read in Genesis: "They will be oppressed for four hundred years; . . . And they shall come back here in the fourth generation" (15:13-16). Information from Paul further confuses our data. Paul said that the law came 430 years after the promises to Abraham. This would make the sojourn in Egypt and the patriarchal period together cover 430 years. In addition, Exodus 6:13-26 would cause the period of Jacob through Aaron's son Eleazar to cover seven generations. It is possible to interpret this as saying that four generations was the length of the period of the sojourn. Our understanding of this data may also be confused due to different departures from Egypt. However, the 430 years is not the kind of number which ever appears to have had any kind of symbolic significance for Israel. Thus I conclude that if the Exodus occurred around 1280 to 1260 BC, then the entrance into Egypt must have occurred around 1710 to 1690 BC. If this is the end of the patriarchal period, it would place the dates of the patriarchs precisely where they best seem to fit into the ancient Near Eastern culture. This would be a further confirmation of the probability of the accuracy of our conclusion.

The Numbers Involved in the Exodus

Another major problem for the historian who is seeking to understand the Exodus events relates to the number of people involved in the process. When the Hebrews prepared to depart from Sinai, a census was taken of the tribes (Num. 1:17-46). The purpose of the census was to establish the number of fighting men which Israel had available. The census revealed that there was a total of 603,550 fighting men among the Israelites.

These figures have appeared to be excessively large for a number of reasons. With that many fighting men, the total population would probably have numbered about two million people. Some scholars have suggested that that many people and their flocks would have been impossible to feed in the wilderness. Granted that God could have supplied such a multitude, did He? Other objections are much more significant. Such a group of people, marching fifty abreast, would have formed a column of more than twenty-two miles. Yet this army was controlled by only two trumpets (Num. 10:2)!

Furthermore, while still in Egypt, all of the children born to the Hebrew women were delivered by only two midwives (Ex. 1:15). In addition, Moses warned Israel that they would confront armies greater than they were (Deu. 7:17-24). Not one of the peoples whom Israel confronted came anywhere close to having an army this size. Beyond this, all of the effort to free Israel from Egypt would have been nonsensical. A people led by an army of 603,550 men could have left Egypt anytime they pleased and should have felt no threat at the approach of an Egyptian army at the sea. Finally, given what is known of ancient birth and death rates, the probability of the 70 people who entered Egypt with Jacob multiplying to more than 2 million people in this period is quite unlikely.

Some have sought to remove the difficulty by suggesting that a later census list of David had gotten mixed up with the list from Moses' time. But this just substitutes one problem for another. There is a better solution, it appears to me.

The Hebrew word for thousand is *'eleph*. But *'eleph* can also mean family, clan, tribe, or fighting unit (such as a squad or a platoon). Suppose that here it were to have that latter meaning. How would this affect our understanding? The census list would then appear as the following table indicates.

Census List

Tribe	Number	Proposed Translation
Reuben	46,500 men	46 units, 500 men
Simeon	59,300 men	59 units, 300 men
Gad	45,650 men	45 units, 650 men
Judah	74,600 men	74 units, 600 men
Issachar	54,400 men	54 units, 400 men
Zebulun	57,400 men	57 units, 400 men
Ephraim	40,500 men	40 units, 500 men
Manasseh	32,200 men	32 units, 200 men
Benjamin	35,400 men	35 units, 400 men
Dan	62,700 men	62 units, 700 men

Asher	41,500 men	41 units, 400 men
Naphtali	53,400 men	53 units, 400 men

This would give a total of 5,550 men and a complete population of about 20,000 people. This hypothesis meets most objections. Though it does not eliminate all problems, it does appear to be the best solution which has been offered in the light of our present knowledge.

The Location of Sinai

One of the problems in trying to reconstruct ancient history is that of locating ancient places. A city like Jerusalem which has been in continuous existence for all the intervening years offers no difficulty. But the location of Sinai and of the route used by Israel to get there is a different matter. Of all the places listed in the route of the Exodus, there are very few which can be located with certainty. Due to this difficulty, there have been at least three major suggestions made as to the location of Sinai. It has been suggested that Sinai was located in the north of the Sinai peninsula, somewhere near Kadesh. It is normally suggested that the traditional location of the Jebel Musa (Mount of Moses) where the Monastery of Saint Catherine is situated is the correct location. But it has also been maintained that a third location in the region of Midian, on the eastern side of the Gulf of Aqaba is the correct location.

If the location is near Kadesh, then the crossing of the sea and the wilderness journey would have been in the northern part of the Sinai Peninsula. If the location is the traditional one near the south-central part of the peninsula, then the crossing of the sea and the journey would have been more to the south. If the location in Midian is correct, then the crossing and the journey would still have been in the south, but the journey would have been considerably longer.

The name of the sea which Israel crossed offers no real help. The Hebrew literally means the "Sea of Reeds." It was probably not the Red Sea, for no reeds grow there. There are numerous other bodies of water which would have met the requirements, but we do not at present know of any which was called by this title. The quails which were supplied to Israel would make the northern route appear more likely, for even today when the quails migrate across the Mediterranean they alight in great droves at the northern edge of the Sinai Peninsula. Some geographers also suggest that Sinai appears to be near Kadesh. However, it appears probable that if Sinai had been that close to the southern territory of Judah, it would have become a major national shrine with regular pilgrimages there. Only Elijah made such a pilgrimage, and that appears to have been quite a journey (1 Kings 19:3-8).

The location in Midian has been suggested because so many of the details of the story appear to be volcanic in nature. The fire on the top of the mountain and the pillar of smoke by day and of fire by night could have been descriptive of volcanic eruptions. Further, the ease with which Moses' father-in-law, the priest of Midian, communicated with Moses also commends this suggestion. But the region of Midian was not so much a nation over which people ruled as it was a territory through which they wandered. There is abundant evidence that Midianites were frequently found far out in the Sinai Peninsula. Further, the clouds and flashing fire on the top of Sinai far better fit a storm than a volcano, if a natural phenomena has to be identified for it. Therefore, although there is no certainty as to the location of Sinai, it appears that the best suggestion is still that of the traditional location in the heart of the southern part of the peninsula.

The Nature of the Covenant at Sinai

From a theological standpoint, there are few events in Israel's history which were as significant as the giving of the covenant at Sinai. Whether or not it is the central feature of Israel's faith, as some have suggested, there is no question but that it was of major significance. From the historian's position, however, we are more concerned with the nature of the covenant than with its theological import.

In the ancient Near East, there were two basic types of covenants. There were the parity treaties (covenants) and the suzerainty treaties. The parity covenant, as the name implies, was made between two individuals or nations of approximate equal stature. Such covenants might be negotiated by the parties, until both were pleased with its final form. These might cover international agreements or personal agreements, such as property transactions and marriage arrangements. For a long time, it was thought that this was the only kind of covenant found in the ancient Near East. It was certainly quite common in the Old Testament (see Gen. 21:32; 26:28; 1 Sam. 11:1; 23:18; 1 Kings 20:34).

Beginning in the period after World War II, however, it was discovered that there was a different kind of treaty which began to be common in the second millennium BC. This has come to be known as the suzerainty treaty. A suzerain was a great king, a ruler of an empire. When he made a covenant with one of his vassals, the covenant was not negotiable but was simply handed down. The vassal could either accept it or reject it, but he could not alter it. Further, the suzerain was frequently called by the title "king of kings and lord of lords," indicating his authority over other rulers in the area. These covenants had seven basic features. Not every suzerainty covenant had all of these features; nor were they always in the same order. However, the following is the more usual order.

Such a treaty usually began with the identification of the great king as the one who gave the treaty. It might be phrased as: "I am ABC, the great king, king of kings and lord of lords." This immediately brings to memory the beginning of the Sinai covenant statement: "I am the Lord your God" (Ex. 20:2).

The next feature of the typical suzerainty treaty was a statement of the historical relations between the suzerain and his vassal. It usually placed a special emphasis upon the benevolent acts of the suzerain on behalf of the vassal. This, too, parallels the Sinai document, "who brought you out of the land of Egypt, out of the house of bondage" (Ex. 20:2).

The third item in the suzerainty treaty was a prohibition against the vassal entering into any other foreign alliances. There were to be no other commitments than with the suzerain. This is a striking parallel to the Sinai statement: "You shall have no other gods before me" (Ex. 20:3).

Following this, there was usually a statement of the basic obligations of the vassal and of the stipulations controlling his behavior. Here again, our attention is called to the Mosaic covenant.

> You shall not make for yourself a graven image, . . .
> You shall not take the name of the Lord your God in vain; . . .
> Remember the sabbath day, to keep it holy. . . .
> Honor your father and your mother, . . .
> You shall not kill.
> You shall not commit adultery.
> You shall not steal.
> You shall not bear false witness . . .
> You shall not covet (Ex. 20:4-17).

These were set forth as Israel's duties to God. They were owed to Him because of what He had done for them.

The fifth feature of this kind of treaty was usually a statement of where the covenant document was to be kept and when it was to be read. It was normally kept in the chief sanctuary of the vassal and was taken out and read publicly on frequent occasions. Israel was commanded to keep the two tablets of the covenant in the ark that was to be placed in the holy of holies (Ex. 25:21; 1 Kings 8:6-9). In addition, there were frequent occasions when the basic covenant document appears to have been reread (Ex. 34; Deut. 5; Josh. 24).

A sixth part of the suzerainty treaty involved the naming of the witnesses to the treaty. These were usually the gods of the suzerain and of his vassal. This was then usually followed by a call to the heavens and the earth to serve as witnesses. As might be expected, such witnesses are absent in the Sinai covenant. However, Joshua called the people themselves to be witnesses, and the prophets regularly called upon the heavens and the earth to testify against Israel for covenant breaking (Josh. 24:22; Isa. 1:2-3; Mic. 6:1-2).

The final portion of the suzerainty treaty was a list of blessings which would come to the vassal for obedience and of curses which would befall him for disobedience. Although these are not a part of the basic Sinai covenant document, there are frequent lists of such in covenant contexts in the Old Testament (Ex. 23:20-33; Lev. 26; Deut. 27—28).

It appears to me that there is an overwhelming amount of evidence that the covenant statement of Exodus 20:1-17 was framed in the normal form of an ancient suzerainty treaty. It would certainly have been possible, for such forms were common in international affairs of the precise period with which we are concerned. Furthermore, the purpose of such a framework is quite obvious. It was a blunt statement to Israel and to all who might hear of it that God was Israel's king. Moses would certainly have been familiar with such forms, for he had been raised in the palace of the king of Egypt himself where such documents would have been a part of normal daily affairs.

The Background of the Period

During the period of the Exodus and the wilderness wanderings, Egypt was the only major power of significance in the geographical regions in which we are interested. As we have noted, the land of Egypt was ruled by Semitic rulers known as Hyksos from about 1700 to about 1550 BC. Around 1550, the New Kingdom or the Empire of Egypt was established by the expulsion of the Hyksos and the founding of the Eighteenth Dynasty under Amosis. For our purposes, the two major items of significance which can be dated to this dynasty are the Amarna letters from Palestine and the Akhenaten heresy. (We shall consider each of these later in this section.)

The Eighteenth Dynasty was one of great military genius and extreme energy. The territories which Egypt controlled were expanded, while the regions over which they exerted significant influence reached far to the north of Palestine. Part of the great success of Egypt was due to the invention of a light, horse-drawn chariot and of the composite bow. The speed and mobility of the Egyptian army revolutionized the warfare of the period.

This dynasty was replaced about 1300 BC by the Nineteenth Dynasty founded by Sethos (sometimes known as Seti). He began great building programs which were further carried on by Ramses II who became pharaoh about 1290 BC and ruled until the last third of the century. After a reign of more than sixty years, he was succeeded by his son Merneptah, who was already quite old. Under his inept rule, most of Egypt's control of and influence in Palestine came to an end. If our dating of the Exodus is correct, it was under the reign of Ramses II that the Hebrews fled the land of Egypt and during the days of Egyptian weakness near the end of the century that they entered into the land of Canaan. Within this overall historical background, there are five specific features to which we must give serious consideration.

The Hyksos

We have already noted the possible significance of the Hyksos rulers insofar as they might have afforded the historical opportunity for Joseph's rise to power. Furthermore, these Semitic rulers of Egypt ruled over the land at a time when the land of Egypt came to be the property of Pharaoh and the Egyptians came to be his serfs.

These people were hated with an unbounded passion by the native Egyptians, even as most foreign rulers are hated by those who are their subjects. When the Hyksos were finally expelled from Egypt (about 1550 BC), the rulers of the New Kingdom sought to remove every vestige of the Hyksos' presence in the land. This may also offer us a reason for the absence of any mention of Joseph or the Hebrew tribes in the Egyptian records.

It must be clearly understood that there is no direct Egyptian evidence for the presence of the Hebrews in Egypt. But what we do know of the Hyksos period certainly gives us an appropriate background for understanding the beginning of the Hebrews' sojourn in the

ISRAEL'S BIRTH

land. It may also offer an explanation for the later hatred and fear of the Hebrews by the Egyptians, which the Book of Exodus reflects (Ex. 1:9-12).

The Amarna Letters

Archaeologists found a collection of letters in Egypt near Tell el'Amarna that apparently came from the royal archives of the late Eighteenth Dynasty. Among the almost 400 clay tablets, there were about 150 letters written by Canaanite vassal-kings to the Egyptian pharaoh. These date from the period between 1400 and 1350 BC.

The Canaanite kings of that period were pleading for help in dealing with a problem created by invading Habiru'. In the preceding chapter, we raised the question as to whether these people could be identified with the Hebrews of the Old Testament. Although the similarity of the name makes the idea quite attractive, there are several reasons for rejecting it. The time does not fit with much of the evidence of the timing of the invasion of Canaan by Israel. Furthermore, the Habiru' are clearly not a racial group but a mixed group of peasants who were trying to overthrow their lords. However, if we believe that the biblical evidence might reflect more than one group of Hebrews coming into the land, it is possible that there were some Hebrews among the Habiru' who were giving the Canaanites troubles.

For our purposes, the major value of the Amarna letters is that they give us a picture of Canaanite life shortly before the Israelite invasion. Canaan was not made up of one major power. Instead, it was composed of numerous small city-states, each ruling over a very limited territory which surrounded the city. All of these were primarily dependent upon Egyptian arms and resources for maintaining their own existence. Thus, when Egypt was weak, these city-states became relatively helpless. This was the situation seen by the Hebrew spies who first entered the land from Kadesh-barnea in the south (Num. 13:17-33).

The Akhenaten Heresy

Another item of interest for understanding this period comes from the reign of Pharaoh Amenhotep IV. Throughout most of its history, the Egyptians worshiped many gods, with the chief on being Amun. Amenhotep IV became convinced that there was only one god, the sun disc known as Aten. In honor of his new god, he changed his name to the "Splendor of Aten" (Akhenaten). He tried to stamp out the worship of other gods and established a new city, Akhetaten, as his capital. To the Egyptian people and to the powerful Egyptian priests, this was wholly heretical. The new religion was quickly abandoned after the death of the pharaoh in 1347 BC.

However, some historians have suggested that the monotheism of Israel had its roots in the religion of Egypt under Akhenaten. First, there is little real relationship between the religion of Aten and the faith of Israel. On the other hand, the religious unrest and thought which this Egyptian innovation produced certainly would have provided a fertile ground for Moses and his people to be searching for the nature of God. To say that there is a direct connection between the two would be wholly false. However, to say that there is no connection would probably be just as false. The religious controversies of the Egyptians would surely have caused a religious people like Israel to ponder the nature of their faith.

Building Programs

The pharaohs of the early Nineteenth Dynasty were involved in a number of major building programs. We are told in the Bible that the Hebrews were forced to labor in the building of Pithom and Raamses (Ex. 1:11). It is almost certain that these two cities have now been located. Although the building of one of these sites was begun by Sethos, both of them had major building projects erected by Ramses II. In carrying our these building projects, there is abundant evidence that large numbers of slaves were used. It is quite likely that these sites in northern Egypt contain the ruins of buildings erected by these ancient Hebrew slaves. A very vivid relief from a slightly earlier period shows slaves being supervised by taskmasters in making bricks and constructing buildings.

Law in the Ancient World

Although the problem of ancient law is far too complex to go into in detail here, numerous law codes from the ancient Near East have survived to this day. We discover from these that the world of Moses' day was a world which was governed by law. There were civil, criminal, and religious laws. Many of these ancient laws are remarkably similar to the laws of the ancient Hebrew codes. This is only to be expected. Effective laws are good, no matter what the race or nationality. Further, law codes in ancient times, even as in modern times, were constantly undergoing change and development.

In comparing the laws of Israel with those of the peoples surrounding them, two features stand out. First, it is quite obvious that the notion of law was not an invention of either Moses or Israel. Laws had been around for centuries. Moses and Israel were obviously quite familiar with the laws of the peoples who were around them. On the other hand, the laws of Israel make some significant advances over some of the codes of the nations around them. Compared with Christian standards, the Hebrew laws governing slavery, for example, seem unbelievably harsh (Ex. 21:1-11). On the other hand, when placed against their ancient cultural background, they are a step forward, for those laws teach that slaves have rights too. Prior to this, slaves were nothing more than property. But the law granted legal rights to slaves. It was a giant step for its day.

The History of the Period

In the light of the background of the Exodus period, we are now ready to examine the actual history of the Exodus era. Admittedly, there are numerous unsolved problems with understanding the sources, the chronological data, and the geographical data. But this does not invalidate the basic conclusions concerning the period.

The Sojourn in Egypt

Joseph and his family apparently migrated to Egypt about 1700 BC, in the time when the foreign Hyksos dynasty was consolidating its power. The biblical material passes very quickly over most of the years of Israel's sojourn in Egypt, saying simply: "Then Joseph died, and all his brothers, and all that generation. But the descendants of Israel were fruitful and increased greatly; they multiplied and grew exceedingly strong; so that the land was filled with them" (Ex. 1:6-7). The events of almost four hundred years of living are summed up in these two verses.

From Israel's standpoint, the living was easy. Goshen, the region of their settlement, was a lush grassland with abundant water, an ideal place for shepherds to prosper (Gen. 47:6). And prosper they did. That, perhaps, was a part of their problem. The living was so easy that they who had come to escape a famine stayed to enjoy a feast.

In the ancient world, as so often in the modern, people clearly believed that prosperity was a sign of God's favor and blessing. (Large portions of the Bible attack that very belief, but many people still hold to it.) From Israel's standpoint, their prosperity in Goshen was apparently interpreted as indicating God's pleasure with them. They were wrong. They had been called to Canaan, not to Goshen.

In the intervening years, numerous world-shaking events occurred, but Israel was apparently not involved. With the expulsion of the Hyksos, the native Eighteenth Dynasty began its steps toward empire about 1550 BC. Apparently none of the Hebrews had been involved in any positions of authority since the time of Joseph, so they were not thrust out with the Hyksos. It is even possible that the new rulers were aware that the new wealth of Pharaoh was the result of Joseph's labors and, in honor of that, continued to allow the Hebrews to live in peace.

But a somber note makes its way into the narrative with the announcement that "there arose a new king over

Egypt, who did not know Joseph" (Ex. 1:8). With the "new king," there began a systematic attempt to oppress the people of Israel. The question arises as to the identity of the king. In seeking to make a decision, we must be aware that the word translated *know* implies intimate personal knowledge, not merely something which one has been taught. Based upon this, some have suggested that this "new king" was Ahmose (about 1555-1527), the founder of the Eighteenth Dynasty. Certainly, he had not personally experienced Joseph, but he just as certainly reaped the benefits of Joseph's administrative policies. If this is a proper identification, then the harsh oppression of Israel would have lasted from about 1550 to the time of the Exodus, about 1280 BC. The basic problem with this identification is that Ahmose was not involved, as far as we know, in major building programs.

On the other hand, if the "new king" were the founder of the Nineteenth Dynasty, Seti (about 1305-1290 BC), he would better fit the picture. Not only would he not have heard of Joseph, he would not even have known that Joseph's administration had brought wealth to the Egyptian kingship. He truly "did not know Joseph." Furthermore, he was also involved in major building programs in precisely the regions where the Hebrews are said to have labored, Pithom and Raamses (Ex. 1:11). Israel had prospered in Egypt, but they were beginning to pay a high price for their prosperity.

The Oppression of Israel

It is quite obvious as we deal with the narrative of the Exodus event that Pharaoh's fear of Israel was not nearly as overwhelming as some translations make it appear. His fear was based upon Israel's potential danger, rather than any real threat (see Ex. 1:9-10). If his fear had been so overwhelming, he would have trembled before Moses' later demands that Israel be released from their bondage. The subsequent narrative makes it quite clear that Israel would not have gotten out of their slavery at that time if it had not been for their deliverance by the mighty acts of God.

In seeking to remove the potential danger of the Hebrews, the pharaoh began a program of forced labor directed against Israel. If we are correct in dating this to the reign of Seti, he began his major building programs by enslaving numerous other peoples as well. The purpose of his enslavement of Israel was apparently threefold. First, he was seeking to remove the danger of revolt by keeping the people busy and exhausted. Second, he was trying to accomplish major building activities, and this could not have been done without slave labor. We have numerous records of the fact that such building projects were carried out by the appointment of Egyptian overseers to direct the efforts of conscripted laborers. Third, the pharaoh apparently thought that by exhausting the Hebrews with their forced labors, he could effectively reduce their birth rate.

While the oppression may have accomplished the first two objectives with his practices, the third was a total failure. The birth rate kept on climbing (Ex. 1:12). More than one conqueror has discovered a rising birth rate among oppressed people. When all else is gone, such peoples find their consolations at home.

As the pharaoh's policies obviously failed in reducing the Hebrews' birth rate, he was forced to a new approach of the systematic killing all of the boy babies born to the Hebrews (Ex. 1:15-16). The pharaoh's decision almost appears to have been based upon panic. The continual increase of the Hebrews in spite of the oppression had produced a feeling of superstitious dread in the hearts of Pharaoh and the Egyptians (Ex. 1:12). Tyrants cannot afford any kind of failure or they lose their power over all their servants. For the tyrant, failure is always a sign of weakness and weakness is the prelude to downfall.

Pharaoh's first attempt to incapacitate Israel by having the Hebrew midwives kill all the boy babies was equally as great a failure as the attempt to weaken the Hebrews through forced labor. Thus he was forced to devise another plan. He turned to his own soldiers with orders to kill all the boy babies. This was a much more gruesome and sadistic plan than anything yet devised. The Hebrew literally says, "Every son that is born to the Hebrews you shall cast in the direction of the Nile" (Ex. 1:22). Throwing the children into the Nile would have drowned them, and death would have been relatively quick. This plan was one of death by exposure, which was long and drawn out. It would certainly have been much more heartbreaking for the people of Israel.

We are not told how long this process of attempted extermination was carried on. Apparently, it was not carried on too long. Aaron, Moses' brother, was three years older than Moses; so the plan had not been enforced longer than three years before Moses' birth (see Ex. 7:7). Furthermore, when Israel was finally released from Egypt, there does not appear to be any significant gap in the spread of the population. If the plan had been enforced for a period of ten, twenty, or more years, there would have been a significant range of age where there were no fighting men. This just does not appear to be the case. Apparently, this was a procedure developed under panic and eliminated after a short time, following more serious thought. It may have been stopped when Seti died and his son Ramses succeeded him upon Egypt's throne, but more likely this procedure did not last that long.

The Early Days of Moses

Most Christians are fairly familiar with the story of Moses' birth and his protection by his mother. One feature of the biblical narrative is of basic significance for understanding a major aspect of Old Testament historiography. The record would make it sound as if Moses was the first child of Amram and Jochebed (Ex. 2:1-2). However, later in the birth narrative, we are introduced to his older sister, Miriam (Ex. 2:4; Num. 26:59). We have already noted that Aaron was three years older than his brother, Moses (Ex. 7:7). This is a clear illustration of the point that the biblical authors followed the mainline of their story while ignoring other events which had happened. This was frequently done even when omitting such details might give a superficially false view of the history. Their primary concern was to communicate a message about the activity of God, not to record history as such.

When the infant Moses was too old to be hidden any longer, Moses' mother carefully placed him precisely where Pharaoh's daughter bathed (Ex. 2:3-5). She was presuming upon the compassion of one woman for another's child. The plan worked, and the baby was allowed to live under the protection of Pharaoh's daughter. It was one thing for the young woman to be aware of the systematic extermination of the boy babies of the Hebrews. But the sight of one helpless child moved her with compassion.

The end result was that Moses' mother was allowed to care for her child as long as he needed to nurse. When he was weaned, he was turned over to Pharaoh's daughter to be raised at court (Ex. 2:10). In a real sense, this gave Moses the best of both worlds. The time of weaning was normally between the ages of three and four. For those very formative years, he was raised in his own home. While we do not know what he learned there, we do know that a child can learn a great deal during that period of life. He certainly learned that he was a Jew, for he later recognized the Hebrew slaves as his own people (Ex. 2:11). He also would probably have had instilled in him something of his heritage. Probably, he would have further heard his mother tell of his special deliverance, suggesting that God must have some great purpose for him.

In the court of Pharaoh, on the other hand, Moses would have learned the kinds of things that a male member of the royal household would have been expected to know. This would have included the law codes, the forms of international treaties, and how to organize and lead an army. All of these things were skills which he was later called upon to demonstrate as he lead Israel through the wilderness. The name which he was given is explained as meaning "to be drawn out" in the Hebrew. But in the Egyptian, it simply meant "son." It shows up regularly in Egyptian names, such as Ahmose and Thutmose.

In young manhood, Moses became aware of the helpless plight of his people. Deeply concerned, he took matters into his own hands, murdering an Egyptian who was oppressing a Hebrew (Ex. 2:11-12). Obviously, Moses thought his crime could pass unnoticed. He was wrong.

Moses' action revealed not only his humanity but also a burning passion for justice and a quickness of decision and action. However, when he became aware that his crime was known, he fled from Egypt in terror (Ex. 2:14-15). Moses had apparently failed to consider that to the Hebrews he looked like an Egyptian. Therefore, the Hebrew who had been delivered by Moses' act of violence would certainly talk about it.

Moses fled to Midian where, in a very human story, we find him showing off before an attractive Midianite girl. He later married her and settled down there, working for his father-in-law, a priest of Midian. The Midianites were considered to be descendants of Abraham (Gen. 25:2). This may explain why Moses fled there in the first place. He may have been trying to find a home among related people. He did not dare go toward Canaan, for that was still under Egyptian control.

It is quite likely that Moses' father-in-law was a worshiper of the God of Abraham. If so, Moses would have found in Midian a faith similar to that which he had learned at his mother's knee.

It would appear that, even though Moses had settled down in Midian to stay, Moses' heart turned back to his people occasionally. The very fact that his first son was named Gershom would tend to support this. The name means "stranger" or "sojourner." It was selected because Moses felt that he was "a sojourner in a foreign land" (Ex. 2:22). He had settled in Midian, but his heart was still with his people and their sufferings. The tragedy for him was that he could not return to help, for he was a wanted man in Egypt. Moses' own rash act had prevented him from being able to help his people.

During Moses' stay in Midian, Pharaoh died (Ex. 2:23). However, Moses did not know that. As far as he knew, he was still a fugitive criminal with a price on his head.

It is at this point that we begin to tread on holy ground, for we are next told of Moses' experience with God in the wilderness (Ex. 3:1 to 4:17). Moses led his flock to the "mountain of God" (Ex. 3:1; it is known both by the names of Sinai and Horeb). We do not know if it began to be called the "mountain of God" after this experience or if it had been pointed out as such to Moses by his father-in-law. Moses became convinced that God was about to deliver Israel from Egypt and that he had been chosen as the human instrument of that deliverance. Try as he might to avoid responding affirmatively, however, Moses felt utterly overwhelmed.

Three dimensions of Moses' call experience are quite important. First, it was here that to Moses was revealed the meaning of God's name, Yahweh. Given the Old Testament understanding of names, this was also a revelation of God's very nature (Ex. 3:14). This was the very sacred personal name for the God of Israel. Second, the confirming sign to Moses that God had called him would be the ultimate success of his mission. He would lead Israel back to Sinai (Ex. 3:12). It is obvious that this would leave a great deal to be desired in the way of assurance. But that is the nature of faith.

The third feature of significance is that Moses finally responded to God's call to return to Egypt without knowing that he was no longer a wanted man. When he submitted, he still believed that returning to Egypt might cost him his life. Only after he had accepted the task did Moses discover that his greatest fear had already been removed by God (Ex. 4:19). Seti had died, and Ramses had become Pharaoh. At this point, Aaron came out seeking Moses; and the two of them returned to Egypt to start the struggle for freedom (Ex. 4:27).

The Deliverance from Egypt

From a theological standpoint, the deliverance of Israel from Egypt was viewed primarily as a contest between the God of Israel and the gods of Egypt. From a historical standpoint, it was more of a confrontation between a hardheaded king and a strong-willed slave.

As might have been expected, when Moses and Aaron told the leaders of the Hebrew slaves that there was a plan afoot to deliver them from Egypt, there was an overwhelming sense of joy (Ex. 4:29-31). Equally as expected was the clear-cut refusal of the pharaoh to pay any attention to Moses' demand for the release of his people (Ex. 5:2). In fact, the king of Egypt assumed that the only reason that the Hebrews had made such a request was that they had time on their hands (Ex. 5:8). Thus, the response to Moses' demand was that more labor was required from the Hebrews (Ex. 5:6-7,9).

We must clearly understand that Pharaoh was not ordering his slaves to make bricks without straw. Such bricks would have been totally worthless. He was commanding that the Hebrews must henceforth gather their own straw while at the same time producing the same amount of bricks daily. This was essentially requiring an extra shift of work from each slave (Ex. 5:10-11). When the Hebrews became aware of the increased labor required of them and the punishment when it was not delivered, they turned with hostility upon Moses (Ex. 5:21).

With this impass, the stage had been set for the so-called plagues of Egypt. Actually, the Old Testament calls them "signs and wonders" (Ex. 7:3). In seeking to understand these events which brought about Israel's deliverance, we must come to grips with the Old Testament's understanding of what we call a miracle. There are three basic characteristics which were always present. (1) There is an actual event. Something happened. (2) There is also always a sense of timeliness and location. It happened at the right place and time. (3) Finally, there was a faith interpretation. There was someone present who said that God had done it.

Of all the plagues, only the last one—the death of the firstborn—has the markings of a wholly supernatural event. Each of the others reflects something which Egyptian records indicate may have happened occasionally in Egypt. For example, the Nile infrequently turned a bright red, either with red clay from its Ethiopian headwaters or with a massive growth of red plankton. Such can be described as the water being turned to blood, if "blood" is seen as a figure of speech. Thus this may have been supernatural or just abnormal. But from the Old Testament standpoint, even if this is what happened, the miracle is still there because it happened when and where Moses said it would; and Moses, with the eyes of faith, pointed out that God had done it (Ex. 7:17). In seeking to understand what really happened, we must note that the Old Testament itself says that the Egyptian magicians duplicated the feat (Ex. 7:22). I, for one, do not wish to ascribe to Egyptian magicians any supernatural powers!

It is of importance to note that each of these events was aimed at the basic religious faith of Egypt. The three chief gods of the Egyptians were the Nile, the sun, and the pharaoh. Each of these was shown to be powerless before the God of Israel. There were gods in the Egyptian pantheon who were responsible for protecting the land from frogs, from locusts, from other flying insects, and from damaging storms. Further, the health of cattle and people was the concern of some of their gods. The events were selected as being clear demonstration of the superiority of Israel's God over the gods of Egypt. The end result of this sequence of events was freedom. The pharaoh of Egypt thrust Moses and the Hebrews from the land (Ex. 12:31-33).

The historian must seek to identify the time frame of the plagues, if that is possible. Several hints are given to us. The final plague is clearly identified as occurring "in the month of Abib" (Ex. 13:4). Further, the institution of the Passover was on "the fourteenth day of this month" (Ex. 12:6). Abib overlaps our March and April. Therefore the middle of Abib would be the end of March or the first of April.

The plague of hail is also clearly established, for we are told concerning it that "the flax and the barley were ruined, for the barley was in the ear and the flax was in bud. But the wheat and the spelt were not ruined, for they are late in coming up" (Ex. 9:31-32). Thus the hail storm would have to have occurred in mid-January, for that is when this bit of agricultural detail was true in Egypt. The plague of locusts would have been from four to eight weeks later, giving time for the wheat and spelt to sprout and attract the locusts. The plague of locusts then would have been between mid-February and mid-March. It clearly had to be far enough before the final plague to allow for the darkening of the sun to occur between them.

The only other plague which may give us some indication of time are the first two, the turning of water into blood and the plague of frogs. If the first of these is to be connected with the annual flood of the Nile when its normal life-giving qualities were turned into death-dealing ones, a most appropriate time, this would have been at the time when the snows melted in Ethiopia. This normally occurs sometime between June and October. The earlier it is, the more likely it is for massive amounts of red clay silt to be in the water. If this latter item gives us any help at all, it would date the first plague about June. Further, if Egypt ever had a problem with frogs, it always occurred right after the annual flood of the Nile when the frogs were driven from their homes in the marshes along the river. Thus this plague is also to be dated in connection with the annual flood.

The very minimum time in which the plagues could have occurred is from early June of one year to mid-April of the next, a period of about ten to ten-and-one-half months. Of course, they could have been spread out over a longer period, but their impact would have lessened if this had been true. The period might have been a bit shorter if the annual flood were late.

In celebration of their deliverance from Egypt, the Hebrews held the feast of unleavened bread and the Passover (Ex. 12:1-28). These two festivals share some similarities with spring festivals celebrated by pastoral and agricultural peoples throughout the ancient Near East. It is possible that Israel took old festivals and poured new meaning into them, just as Christians have done with their Christmas and Easter celebrations. The Hebrews may also originally have had separate festivals which were tied together by their nearness to each other and by the historical meaning given to them.

After Israel had departed from Egypt, Pharaoh changed

his mind. Their departure had done away with a major source of cheap labor. When Pharaoh became aware of Israel's apparently aimless wandering while still near to Egypt, he decided this provided him with an opportunity to rectify his mistake in giving them freedom (Ex. 13:20; 14:2,6-7). The swift pursuit of the Egyptian chariotry caught the Hebrews in the difficult situation of having their backs to the sea. As we haved already noted, the location of the sea is unknown, but it was clearly an insurmountable barrier.

Israel's deliverance from the Egyptians was made possible by another one of the wonders of time and place. All night long "a strong east wind" drove back the waters (Ex. 14:21). The Hebrews were able to cross the body of water on foot; but when the Egyptians tried to pursue them, their chariot wheels became bogged down in the mud, the wind stopped, and the waters returned in a devastating flood (Ex. 14:25,28). But Israel was out of Egypt. The trial of slavery was behind. The trial of freedom was about to begin.

The Journey from Egypt to Sinai

As I have already indicated, the route by which Moses led Israel through the wilderness is quite uncertain. There is no way, given the present state of our knowledge, by which we can identify it. However, there are three features of significance which are related to that journey with which we need to deal.

First, there was the problem of water. The wilderness region through which the Hebrews wandered was obviously a desert. This, however, still gives us no help in establishing the route. Three days after the Hebrews' departure from the sea they did come upon an oasis, but the water was too bitter for human consumption. A three days' journey with a group made up of women and children, along with flocks and herds, is quite limited. They could hardly have covered more than forty-five miles in that period. That effort and the length of time involved would have been sufficient to put them in rather desperate straits in regard to thirst.

We are told that "the Lord showed him [Moses] a tree" which would make the bitter water palatable (Ex. 15:25). From the historian's standpoint, it is possible that Moses had learned of a variety of tree with such qualities during his long years of shepherding his father-in-law's sheep in the desert. Modern Arabs say that there is such a tree. In such a desperate situation, a man of faith would have given God the credit for leading him to such a tree. It is just as possible, from the standpoint of faith, that the event was wholly miraculous. Either way, the people of Israel had received their first lesson of God's providence. That is the point.

The second major crisis in the journey of Israel occurred about two months later (Ex. 16:1). Apparently they had then run out of food or at least were on reduced rations. This time, by God's providence, they were provided "bread from heaven" and quails (Ex. 16:4,12-14). Again, the miracle may not have been supernatural but may have been one of time and place. Quails, in the late spring and early summer migrate across the Mediterranean. When they reach the Sinai Peninsula, they are so exhausted that after landing they can be easily captured. It has also been suggested that the manna was a sweet secretion from desert trees. When it drops upon the ground, it turns white. This also normally occurs in late spring or early summer. If this is what happened, the timing of the events would have been in early June. This date fits in quite nicely with the biblical schedule. Again, the basic meaning of the events would have been to show to the Hebrews that God was providential in His care.

The third major crisis which confronted Moses and the Hebrews was the attack by the Amalekites (Ex. 17:8-13). The reason for the attack is not stated. It can only be presupposed that the Amalekites were either protecting territorial rights or were facing the harsh reality of two groups of people trying to sustain both themselves and their flocks on quite limited resources. From a historical standpoint, perhaps the most significant event here was the introduction of Joshua as the military leader of the Hebrews. From a faith standpoint, the Hebrews saw their deliverance as the miraculous intervention of God on their behalf.

Apparently, in the journey to Sinai, the Hebrews had drawn close enough to the region of Midian that Jethro (Moses' father-in-law) heard of their presence and came to meet them. Jethro brought Zipporah whom Moses "had sent . . . away" (Ex. 18:2). It is possible that Moses had sent his family away for their protection during the dangerous days leading up to the Exodus. However, the word used here is the normal Hebrew expression for divorce, so there may have been family difficulties. This may explain why Moses apparently greeted his father-in-law with more welcome than he did his wife (Ex. 18:7). Be that as it may be, Jethro did help Moses get himself better organized to furnish administration and leadership to his people (Ex. 18:17-24). This was the last significant development before the people of Israel actually drew near to the mount of God.

Israel Before the Mount

History writing can be a simple recital of events. It can be a very ardent attempt to understand the meaning of events. But it can also be an attempt to get inside the mind of the people who lived those ancient events. As Moses and his people drew near to Sinai, it is easy to understand something of the emotions which they must have felt. For the Hebrews, it was the goal toward which they had been striving ever since Moses had first begun to try to win them their freedom. All of the doubts, all of the fears, all of the difficulties would have faded into insignificance as they saw the mountain of God rising up out of the plain. But Moses, in drawing near to the mount, must have felt something of the awe and fearful wonder of knowing that God had been with him all of the way. The original sign he had been given that God had called him was that he would bring Israel back to the mount (Ex. 3:12). In his approach to the mount, he would have found the assurance of his call. His faith had found confirmation.

The time of Israel's arrival at Sinai is given as "the third new moon after the people of Israel had gone forth out of the land of Egypt" (Ex. 19:1). They had departed on the fifteenth day after a new moon, so the first new moon would have been about fourteen days later. Thus the "third new moon" would have been about two and a half months after the Exodus event. There is nothing about these numbers which would appear to be questionable. These numbers are not at all like those which appear to have either a symbolic function or to be some sort of schematic structure.

Obviously, the entire episode at Sinai is one of deep faith. This is just not the kind of thing which the historian can investigate. Only the eyes of faith can evaluate the covenant experience of Israel.

We have seen how the form of the covenant appears to fit into the cultural background of the period. The form was one with which the people of Israel probably and Moses certainly would have been familiar. There is nothing improbable in the form.

But the concept of the covenant has been under attack by some theologians and historians in at least two different periods of Old Testament studies. It appears to me that there is absolutely no basis for such attacks. Other than being a matter of faith, there are two very concrete reasons for this judgment. Both of these are found in the narrative of the sealing of the covenant in Exodus 24:1-18.

It is quite significant to note that, at the sealing of the covenant, the burnt offerings and sacrifices were offered by "young men of the people of Israel" (Ex. 24:5). If, as some have suggested, this whole covenant was the creation of priests after the Exile, they most certainly would not have ever described the event this way. Every document which the priests produced clearly portray that sacrifices were only offered by priests and Levites. They certainly would not have left themselves out of what was to them the central event in all of Israel's pilgrimage of faith. We do know that prior to the time of the Exodus event, throughout the entire patriarchal period, sacrifices were offered by people who were designated to do them by the leader. The event as desired here clearly places the stamp of antiquity and authenticity upon it.

It is equally as significant that, when the covenant was sealed, "Moses and Aaron, Nadab, and Abihu, and seventy of the elders of Israel went up, and they saw the God of Israel" (Ex. 24:9-10). Admittedly, this appears to be a sacred figure of speech, describing an indescribable event. At the same time, no priestly author of the Exile would ever have created such a statement, for they clearly believed that any such experience with God would have resulted in immediate death. To them, men just did not look on God and survive. In this part of the event, although Moses is clearly the leader, he is seen as the first among other leaders. In the postexilic period, Moses was seemingly viewed as a figure who towered so far above others that there was just no comparison. If this narrative were a postexilic creation, they surely would not have told the story so as to allow others to have this kind of experience.

Further than this, however, the historian just simply cannot go. The covenant experience at Sinai became to Israel one of the major concepts of faith, if not the very center of it. Whatever happened there, Israel was never the same after it. Many of the people and their leaders later rebelled against the teachings of faith and turned their backs upon the worship of God. At such times, the prophets called them back to that covenant commitment. They never seem to have questioned the authenticity of that part of the prophetic message.

Other peoples in the ancient Near East also had stories of their origins. But such stories always looked back to a golden age when they were the darlings of the gods. Israel told a story which no one would have invented. They told how they had been helpless slaves until God had chosen and delivered them.

The details of this period are quite hazy. After the initial sealing of the covenant, Moses disappeared upon the mountain. People have difficulty serving God whom they cannot see. For Israel, it became an impossibility when the leader whom they could see also disappeared.

In the modern world, religious people have little trouble believing in an invisible God. In fact, most people would have trouble believing in a visible one. In the ancient world, it was not so. In fact, the very idea of an invisible God was something wholly new to Israel. The world of Egypt from which they had come and the world of Canaan to which they were going were filled with representations of the gods. The newness of this concept was frightening to the people when the presence of Moses was taken from them. Not even his brother, Aaron, could hold onto that faith.

In anxiety and fear, the people turned away from Moses and God and commissioned Aaron to make gods for them (Ex. 32:1). To the people of Israel, a covenant was one thing but an invisible God was another. They wanted a god they could see.

Aaron made a molten calf and commanded that a day of worship and celebration be set aside (Ex. 32:3-5). Given what we know of such idols in the ancient Near East, the calf was almost certainly made out of wood and overlaid with gold. The question arises as to why the figure of a calf was made in the first place. Why not a sun disc or some kind of human-animal figure? Two suggestions have been made. The first is that Israel was adopting the worship of Egypt's Apis bull. This is not likely since nowhere is Israel's idol called a bull; it is always a calf. Further, the worship of the Apis bull was not of major significance in Egypt. If Israel had been adopting an Egyptian god, there were others far more prominent which they might have chosen.

On the other hand, Israel was on its way to Canaan. They most likely were already possessed of some knowledge of what they would face once they arrived there. Archaeologists have discovered some representations of the Baal of Canaan riding on the back of a calf. It could have been that Aaron was trying to appease the people and remain loyal to God by making a calf and assuming that the invisible God was riding on the back of that calf. Then the people would have some form to see, yet Aaron might think that he was off the hook.

Regardless of the reason for making the calf, Moses was incensed when he returned to the camp. Such rebellion on the part of his people broke the heart of Moses. In this episode, Moses revealed himself as a man of great compassion. Even though he dealt swiftly and severely with those who had rebelled, yet he still remained one of them (Ex. 32:25-34). He did not and would not turn his back upon them. The leadership skills of Moses are never more visible than they were in the episode following the rebellion of his people. Admittedly, the entire sequence of events is on a far lower plain than that of the New Testament. But Moses lived at least twelve hundred years before the New Testament. Tragically, there are many episodes in Christian history where leaders have not stood as tall as Moses did in dealing with Israel's rebellion at Sinai.

The Rebellion at Kadesh

Following the experience with the golden calf, Moses and the people settled down in the vicinity of Sinai for an extended period. They were still there for the celebration of the Passover festival two years later (Num. 9:1-3). A little more than a month following that Passover, the people of Israel finally departed from the region, going toward Kadesh which is also known as Kadesh-barnea (Num. 10:11-12; 13:25; Deut. 1:2).

During the time that the people of Israel stayed at Sinai, at least two things were going on. First, they were obviously getting used to their freedom, and they were getting themselves organized to face what lay before them. A part of this is probably reflected in the census of the men of fighting age which Moses took (Num. 1:2-3). The second thing which went on during the time at Sinai is reflected in the law codes of Israel. Israel's worship was being organized and regulated. In the ancient Near East, the worship of a people was so involved with their national identity as to be inseparable. There was no way to consider one without the other. Slaves had been ruled by foreign masters. Now that they were no longer ruled by masters, a considerable period of time was needed to prepare to exist without masters, either in matters of government or religion.

We know nothing of the journey from Sinai to Kadesh, except that it was said to have been an "eleven days' journey" (Deut. 1:2). This is obviously rather indefinite. Kadesh itself is located in the region of the Negeb, south of the central hill country of Canaan. In a sense, it was the southern gateway into the land.

When they arrived at Kadesh, in a move of careful military strategy, Moses selected twelve men and sent them northward into Canaan as spies (Num. 13:17-20). They were instructed to look for the precise kinds of information any military leader would need to know before making an attack. Upon returning, the spies brought a mixed report. There was unanimous agreement as to the attractiveness of the land, but there was significant disagreement as to whether a military attack was a feasible enterprise (Num. 13:27-33; 14:6-9).

The people of Israel, as might have been expected, were overwhelmed by the difficulties presented in the majority report. Their immediate desire was to reject Moses as their leader, since he had brought them to that place, to select a new leader, and to return to Egypt (Num. 14:4; Deut. 1:26). It is obvious in this episode that Israel was operating on some form of democratic principle and had no idea of following Moses simply because he was the authoritative leader. It is also obvious that their past successes had given them no confidence in future achievements.

The reaction of the people in rejecting the proposed advance into Canaan under the leadership of Moses also had a religious dimension. When Moses pronounced God's judgment upon the people for this, they were overwhelmed. This is a fascinating response. So much was their religion a part of national life and so fresh in their memories were the faith statements of Moses that, when he announced a judgment, their self-confidence was devastated (Num. 14:39). They had been willing to reject him as leader but could not separate that from their fear of him as the representative of God.

In a clear demonstration of the power of public opinion and mob reaction, the people swung violently from one purpose to another. They who had so recently been eager to depart from Canaan and return to Egypt were suddenly just as eager to make an attack upon Canaan (Num. 14:40; Deut. 1:41). But during the time of rebellion toward Moses (and God), they had lost the benefit of surprise. Moses was wise enough to realize this, but the people were not. We must remember that he had probably received military training in the palace of Pharaoh, but they had no military training. With the precipitousness of slaves, they were eager to act without thought or plan. And act they did. In an ill-planned attack, the people made an abortive advance northward from Kadesh. They were thoroughly defeated (Num. 14:44-45). The Hebrews were not just defeated; the Canaanites totally routed them, driving them back from whence they had come. They returned to Kadesh a thoroughly humiliated and chastened group (Deut. 1:45).

From the standpoint of Moses, the people had rebelled twice at Kadesh. They had rebelled in refusing to attack at the first. Then they had also rebelled in attacking when the opportunity had passed (Deut. 1:26,43). Such rebellion was understood not merely as a rejection of Moses' leadership but also of God. To an outside observer, it would have appeared that the dreams which Israel had brought with them when they came out of Egypt had been merely delusions of grandeur. Moses, however, assured the people that one day they would achieve that victory. In the meantime, they remained in the vicinity of Kadesh.

From Kadesh to the Plains of Moab

The historical details of the time the people of Israel spent in the wilderness are wholly impossible to recover. For at least a generation, they roamed in the vicinity of Kadesh. This must have been a time of great frustration. They did not dare to return to Egypt, and they had not been able to enter Canaan. They were, in truth, a people without a country.

Finally, Moses announced that the time was right for them to make a renewed approach to Canaan. However, instead of trying to enter the land from the south, he determined to lead Israel to the east of the Dead Sea, up the King's Highway on the Transjordan Plateau, then across the Jordan in a surprise attack from the east. Unfortunately, the lands of Edom, Moab, and Ammon stood in his way, along with several minor city states.

The first obstacle was Edom (Num. 20:14-21). Moses sought a peaceful passage through Edom, which was denied to him by the Edomites. Rather than risk a military confrontation, Moses led the people around the south and east of Edomite territory. Unnecessary military action would certainly have weakened Israel's army for the later campaign against Canaan. It might also have demoralized them.

Furthermore, rather than even risk a confrontation, Moses bypassed the Moabites (Deut. 2:9). However, Moses determined to make his approach to Canaan through the less strongly defended region between the territory of Moab and Ammon. In that region, they faced the opposition of two minor kings, Sihon and Og (Num. 21:21-24,33-35). Both of these kings were apparently fairly easily subdued.

In a fascinating little interlude, the biblical narrator recorded the story of the attempt made by Balak, king of Moab, who sought to defeat Israel by divination. Balak sent for a diviner or seer by the name of Balaam, a native of upper Mesopotamia (Num. 22:4-5). The region was regarded throughout the Old Testament era as a center of divination. Two features of the story stand out. First, Balaam is presented as a foreigner who was subservient to the God of Israel. Here was an oblique claim to the sovereignty of the God of Israel over all peoples. The second significant feature lies in the fact that Balaam's blessings upon Israel, once spoken, were assumed to be certain and sure. This is just one more indication of the seriousness with which ancient peoples took the spoken word.

It is interesting to note that the Moabites did not

militarily attack the Hebrews but sought to defeat them through divinatory practices. This would be an incomprehensible practice to us, but in that time was a natural attempt to utilize supernatural powers to augment physical ones. In this, the Moabites clearly failed.

Along the journey from Kadesh, some of the same kinds of problems had showed up which Israel had faced when they had first left Egypt. There was the continual problem of supplies of food and water. This is not surprising, given the nature of the region through which they were moving.

When Israel finally arrived in the plains of Moab, they were confronted with a problem of a different kind. In the regions of Shittim and Beth-Peor, they became involved with the Canaanite fertility cult (Num. 25:1-3; Deut. 3:29). The Canaanites worshiped Baal who was supposed to insure the fertility of the land, the flocks, and the people. The worship was highly sexual in nature. Thus, when the biblical author states that they "began to play the harlot with the daughters of Moab," it is a description not only of their sexual sin but of their apostasy as well (Num. 25:1).

When the people of Israel arrived in the plains of Moab, Moses allowed some of them to claim land there and to settle in the territory which they had already captured (Num. 32:1-5,33). However, he did exact a promise that they would continue to assist their brothers in the conquest of the land of Canaan (Num. 32:6-7,16-18).

The time in the plains of Moab was apparently one of consolidation and reorganization. It was also the time of Moses' death (Deut. 34:5). Joshua had already been designated as Moses' successor and upon Moses' death began to assume the leadership of the forces of Israel (Num. 27:18; Josh. 1:1-2). About thirty-eight years after the abortive attempt to take Canaan from the south, the people of Israel were ready to try again (Deut. 31:1-6). This time, they would approach from the east.

The Significance of the Period

As I have pointed out before and as you have clearly noted in the biblical material related to Israel's deliverance from Egyptian bondage, these narratives are not at all like the history which a modern historian would write. Rather, the biblical authors recorded history because of its significance for their faith. Therefore, we really have not fully understood these narratives until we have at least given consideration to what the Old Testament writers perceived as the significance of these events. It appears to me that this can be summarized in four basic categories.

The Concept of God

From the standpoint of Israel's faith, the basic focus of the Exodus experience came to bear on their understanding of the nature of God. In all of Israel's subsequent history and in the whole of their religion, their concept of God was essentially little more than the lengthened shadow of the understanding of God which they gained through these formative days of faith and national existence.

First of all, the Hebrews felt that God had come to them in an act of sovereign choice. When they were helpless slaves to the power of Egypt, God chose to love and deliver them (Deut. 4:37; 7:7). They were firmly convinced that all which He did for them was the result of that loving choice. Although in Israel's subsequent history there were many times when they believed that God loved them because they were something special, that is in no way reflected in the Exodus narratives. There they clearly knew that they were slaves who had no basis by which to claim or to have deserved that loving choice. They were convinced that every act from the coming of Moses, through the plagues in Egypt, to the sealing of the covenant on Sinai was the result of God's free choice.

But this brings us to the second aspect of Israel's understanding of God through the Exodus events. Because He chose them, He delivered them. They never perceived of

God as far removed from their condition and their plight. When there was nothing which they could do for themselves, God had acted to deliver them. This deliverance by God served as the basis of both the Old Testament and the New Testament concept of salvation. When they were slaves in Egypt, God intervened to bring them forth from the land through a series of miraculous events. When they appeared to be helplessly pinned against the sea, God acted to deliver them once and for all from Pharaoh's power. When they were starving and famishing in the wilderness, God acted to give them food and drink. When they were confronted by enemies, God acted to bring victory to them. When they knew not which way to go in the wilderness, God furnished guidance so that they would not be swallowed up by the desert. This constant sense of His powerful acts of deliverance served as their basis for their next perception of God.

Because they had seen God regularly at work to deliver them from real historical crises, they perceived that God was the sovereign Ruler of the world. Moses and Israel were promised that through the events of the Exodus they should "know" God (Ex. 6:7). Furthermore, Israel also believed that both Pharaoh and his people would "know" that the Lord was God through the catastrophic events of the so-called plagues (Ex. 7:5,16). It is imperative to note that the Hebrew word meaning to know always implies something learned or perceived through intimate personal experience. Thus Israel believed that all involved in those events had experienced the sovereign power of God. They also perceived this in God's acts in the wilderness in controlling natural and supernatural events. And they also perceived this in the fact that a foreigner, such as Balaam, was submissive to their God.

To Israel, these were the primary meanings of those great events. God was choosing. God was active in delivering those whom He chose. And God was sovereign over all men and nations, as well as over all natural and supernatural events.

The Concept of Rebellion and Forgiveness

What Israel perceived of God in the Exodus events does not exhaust all of the theological insights which they gained through this part of their history. From Israel's own standpoint, the events of the Exodus do not portray a pretty sight. It surely took all of the honesty which they could muster to report the whole series of acts of rebellion and faithlessness which we find in these narratives.

Perhaps one of the most striking features of these stories is the frankness by which the Hebrew writers recorded and described Israel's utter inconstancy. Just about every time the going got difficult, Israel turned away from God in disbelief or in utter rebellion. There was little evidence of loyalty or faithfulness shown on their part. At the very best, it is a relatively ugly story which they told about themselves.

But the ugliness of Israel's experience makes the wonder of their perception of God's response even more remarkable. For they perceived that God was a God who forgave. This does not ever appear to have been understood by Israel as an indication that God did not care but that He cared very much. Their rebellion was always viewed as serious and as something which had to be punished. But it was also perceived that beyond God's punishment was mercy. The forgiveness of God always came from the overflow of His love, never because they deserved His love.

The Concept of the Chosen People

If we are not familiar with the Exodus experience and Israel's understanding of it, one feature of Israel's subsequent faith would become either incomprehensible or evidence of utter arrogance. Throughout Israel's history, the people perceived themselves as God's Chosen People. This has frequently been understood as the fruit of an inordinate pride and haughty presumption. But Israel's experience as freed slaves and as forgiven rebels served as the foundation for that belief. Their history was viewed as demonstrable evidence of the truth of that belief. They were the Chosen People because they had experienced being chosen. For them, it was just that simple. Some of this may even explain the belief of the modern Hebrew that the land of Israel belongs to them regardless of any other consideration. As Chosen People, they have always had and still have that utter sense of destiny.

The Basis of Hebrew Prophetism

Seemingly of much less theological significance, but actually one of the more important items of significance which Israel gleaned from the events of the Exodus, is that here we find the basis for the future development of the Hebrew prophetic movement. Moses was always viewed as the epitome of Hebrew prophets. This is pointedly stated in the words: "There has not arisen a prophet since in Israel like Moses, whom the Lord knew face to face" (Deut. 34:10). Such an impact did Moses make upon Israel's concept of the prophet that they even recorded the future details of other prophet's calls in the same basic outline as that of Moses (see Ex. 3:1 to 4:17; Isa. 6:1-12; Jer. 1:4-10; Ezek. 1:4 to 3:15).

Equally as important for Israel's future understanding of the role of a prophet was the relationship established between Moses, Aaron, and Pharaoh. "See, I make you as God to Pharaoh; and Aaron your brother shall be your prophet. You shall speak all that I command you; and Aaron your brother shall tell Pharaoh" (Ex. 7:1-2). Here was the basis for viewing the prophet as the messenger of God to God's target audience. Further, Moses' own life also served as the basis for Israel's future understanding of prophetism. He identified himself with his people and spoke to God on their behalf. All of these things in Moses' life bore fruit in prophetism as it developed in Israel. Other nations had prophets to whom they could go for a message from their gods. Such were received after the appropriate methods of divination. Other nations also had prophets attached to the royal court, who would give a king a "message from god" whenever he needed advice. Israel alone developed the idea that God could and did speak directly to a person who would then carry that message to the audience God had chosen, whether they wished it or not.

These things made the events of the Exodus most meaningful to Israel. In fact, were it not for these meanings which they perceived in the Exodus, it is doubtful that we would ever have heard of it. If they had not heard God speak through these events, these events would have passed unrecorded on the pages of history. It was because they heard God speak that they were moved to record what He had done.

4
Israel's Land: The Conquest and Settlement

As the Exodus from Egypt gave Israel a faith and sense of self-identity, so the conquest gave them a land. From the time of Abraham, Israel had looked forward to the land of promise. Throughout the whole Exodus experience, the hope of that land was a major motivating force which kept the people going. But entering and possessing the land was not as easy as they had anticipated.

This period, like that of the Exodus, was also quite formative for Israel's faith. As the Exodus left the Hebrews with a firm conviction of God's redemptive choice, just so the experiences of conquest and settlement left them with an equally firm sense of the land as God's gift. Their ties to the land never wavered throughout the Old Testament era. Indeed, those same ties call forth the exuberant zeal of their modern brothers for the land of Israel. No matter how they had to struggle to enter or maintain their existence in the land, it was to them first and foremost the gift of God.

Sources for the Study

In seeking to understand this highly complex period of Israelite history, we must first identify the basic sources from which we gather our information. As is true throughout the entire Old Testament era, the basic source is, of course, the Bible.

Among the biblical sources, the primary ones are the Books of Joshua and Judges. Even though in the Old Testament canon, these books are separated from Deuteronomy as being the beginning of the section known as the Former Prophets, they carry on the story line from the period of the Exodus. These two sources, however, must be supplemented with a number of other less significant, but important, biblical materials.

We must also include here the information about the settlements in the Transjordan region by two and a half tribes of the people which is recorded in Numbers. Furthermore, we must consider the various tribal lists in the Pentateuch (Genesis through Deuteronomy). The first part of 1 Samuel must also be included, for Samuel represents the last of the Israelite judges. To these sources, we can also add scattered references throughout the Old Testament which appear to have some bearing upon our understanding of this period.

In addition to the biblical material, however, there is a tremendous amount of archaeological, historical, and geographical material which must be considered. There are few, if any, periods of Hebrew history where a thorough familiarity with the geography of the area is as important as it is here. To fully understand, or even to begin to partially understand this period, the student must be reasonably familiar with the basic geographical features of the land of Palestine. The locations of hills and valleys, of lowlands and plains, and of mountains and rivers is quite significant in seeking to grasp not only what but also why many events took place as they did. In addition to the natural features, the student of history must also be aware of the locations of cities and towns, and of the general border regions between the various political divisions.

There are also a number of ancient monuments which shed light upon our perception of the events of these days. There is a long list of Canaanite cities on the wall of Thutmose III's temple at Karnak in Egypt. This comes from the period about 1184 to 1153 BC. We have already referred to the Merneptah stela which lists the Israelites among peoples with whom he did battle in Canaan, dated about 1220 BC. In addition, there are other less significant monuments and stela from which we can draw some important contemporary information relating to the period.

To these monumental sources, we must also add other

ancient literary sources. There are the Amarna letters to which we have referred earlier. Among these are letters from the rulers of some of the Canaanite city-states to their Egyptian overlords. Even though they date from about 150 years earlier than this period, they do give us some insights into the political organization of Canaan. To these must be added some texts from Taanach (in the Valley of Megiddo) which date from the same period. Their value also rests in allowing us to gather further insight into the political situation just prior to Israel's entrance into the land.

Far and above the largest amount of external information which deals with this period comes from archaeological excavations and surface explorations. Numerous cities have been excavated whose history clearly included this era. Even though not all of them have been positively identified with biblical sites, many of them show a violent overthrow in the period from 1230 to 1210 BC. In most instances, this overthrow was followed by a subsequent resettlement made by a people with a culture which was considerably more primitive than that of the peoples who had been defeated. Some of these sites, however, were not resettled immediately. Further, other sites which have been identified with biblical sites in our narratives do not even seem to have been inhabited at this time. Among these are Ai and Jericho. Our understanding of the history must deal with these facts.

Furthermore, surface explorations of Palestine show a number of previously unsettled sites which were settled with small towns during the period from about 1220 to 1150 BC. The culture seen in these settlements is quite similar to the new culture which showed up in the cities which had been overthrown.

In addition to this evidence, we must also bring to bear upon our study such evidence as can be gleaned from archaeology, as it reveals to us an understanding of the conditions which existed in the regions around the territory which Israel is said to have occupied. This particularly applies to the areas invaded by the Sea Peoples to the west and southwest as well as to the northeast. One of

Israel's greatest problems immediately after their settlement came from their conflict with and domination by the Philistines. These were a part of the Sea Peoples. Furthermore, in the south and in the Transjordan, there were the settled states of Edom, Moab, and Ammon, each of which played some part in Israel's entrance into the land. Beyond these were the more nomadic peoples who were Israel's enemies, such as the Amalekites and Midianites. These clearly had an influence upon Israel's subsequent settlement and security.

Israel did not enter into Canaan in a vacuum. That region was already inhabited, and everything we can learn about it will help us to grasp what really did happen in this period.

Contemporary books which deal with this period are numerous. There is probably no period in Israel's history which has brought forth as many books with as many different approaches to unraveling this tangled skein of events. Any attempt to study this period in more depth will require the student to become familiar with several different approaches. Limiting yourself to just one or two books here will give a distorted view of both the complexity of the problems and the difficulty of their solution.

Major Problems for Consideration

Before we can begin to reconstruct the history of the period of the conquest and settlement, there are some basic problems to be considered. In fact, unless these problems can be solved by the historian, it will be impossible to give anything but a very rough summary of this period.

The Geography of Palestine

In order to deal properly with the major geographical details of the period of Joshua and the judges, we must begin with a basic summary of the major geographical features of Palestine. The land of Canaan served as the land bridge between the Mesopotamian Valley and the Nile Valley. Every army, every caravan, and most pilgrims which moved between these regions had to pass through Canaan. This made the little land far more significant than its actual land area might otherwise have suggested.

Palestine itself is divided into four major north-south regions. We shall consider these, beginning at the Mediterranean and moving eastward. First, there is the coastal plain. This is wider in the south and becomes decreasingly smaller as we move northward until it ceases to exist at Mount Carmel. North of Carmel, the plain begins again and continues further north in a very narrow strip along the Mediterranean. The plain was fertile and very desirable. During this period, the southern part of it was settled by the Philistines and the region north of Carmel was settled by the Phoenicians.

Next comes the major segment, the mountainous region known as the central highlands. These rugged mountains form a backbone which extends the entire length of the land. Just north of Mount Carmel, however, a narrow valley extends inland from the Mediterranean, reaching almost to the Jordan Valley. This finger effectively divides the central part of the highlands from the northern part. The valley is variously known as the Valley of Megiddo or the Plain of Esdraelon.

The third major north-south division is the great Jordan rift. It begins north of the Sea of Galilee, continues down the Jordan Valley to the Dead Sea. There its elevation rises slightly, but continues on southward all the way to the Gulf of Aqaba. The Sea of Galilee, the Jordan River, and the Dead Sea are all below sea level. The Dead Sea is the lowest surface on earth, being about 1275 feet below sea level. The Dead Sea has no outlet and over the centuries has become highly salty. No form of life survives there.

Across the Jordan Valley, the land rises sharply to the Transjordan Plateau, which is the fourth major north-south division. The plateau quickly fades away into the great Arabian Desert, a region which is totally inhospitable.

In addition to these four major divisions, there are two

others of which we need to be aware. In the south of the land, essentially parallel to the Dead Sea, there is a wedge-shaped region of foothills which separates the central highlands from the coastal plain. This is known as the Shephelah. To the deep south, the entire land fades away into a desert wilderness. This region is rough and rocky, and is known as the Negeb (RSV), today known as the Negev.

The major significance of these geographical features for the period of the conquest and settlement has to do with the settlements and the people which were there. First of all, the plains and valleys were the most attractive for settlements. They were fertile and had adequate water supplies. The hills and mountains were unable to maintain any significant settlements except where there were major springs. When there was a significant water supply on a mountain, it could support a city which then became almost impregnable given the state of conducting warfare in the ancient Near East. This probably explains why the ancient city of the Jebusites, Jerusalem, was able to withstand any attack until the time of David. Generally, cities were built on hills or valley sides where there was an abundant supply of water. This may explain why Joshua chose to attack the cities which he did.

Up to this era, the central highlands had never been able to maintain any significant population. This probably explains why the patriarchs had been able to move through that region so freely. It could maintain wanderers and their flocks but no significant cities or major settlements.

Two historical features when coupled with the geography made it possible for the Hebrews to settle into the central highlands during the time of their entrance into the land. The first of these was the fact that the Egyptians had just about two centuries earlier invented the light chariot. For organized armies, it had become the major weapon of attack. By this period of history, it had begun to be adopted by most military powers of the era. But the chariot had a major drawback. It could not operate in mountains. It could only be used effectively in valleys and on rolling hills. By devoting military strategy to the primary development of one weapon, the armies lost their mobility in mountainous terrain. This clearly served to Israel's advantage. Although they had constant problems in any attempt to seize plains, they were able to seize mountainous regions fairly effectively.

However, seizing something and settling it are two different things. At about the time when Israel was invading Canaan, slaked lime had been invented. This major advance made it possible to line limestone pits and make them waterproof. It was this which in turn made it possible for people to dig cisterns in the mountains, to collect the rainwater in the rainy season, and to have a water supply for the entire year. This historical development coupled with the geography made it possible for Israel to do what no people had ever been able to, occupy and settle the central highlands. From a historical standpoint, it was this which made the land of promise become the land of Israel.

The Nature of the Conquest

A hasty, superficial reading of the biblical narratives dealing with the Israelite conquest of Canaan raises no significant problem. But a more thoughtful reading of the material raises several questions. First, how do we deal with the statement that "Joshua took the whole land" in the light of the fact that he was later told that "there remains yet very much land to be possessed" (Josh. 11:23; 13:1)? This is further compounded by the statement that "the Lord gave to Israel all the land which he swore to give to their fathers; and having taken possession of it, they settled there" (Josh. 21:43). This is made yet more confusing by an additional statement that several nations had been left in the land of Canaan by Joshua (Judg. 2:21 to 3:5). Did or did not Joshua take the whole land?

If that did not create enough of a problem for the historian and interpreter, there is another perplexity. After the Israelites had finally defeated the men of Ai, thus gaining a lodgment in the middle of the central hill country, Joshua was able to turn northward and march about twenty-five miles to Mount Ebal and Mount Gerizim and have a major covenant ceremony there with absolutely no opposition (Josh. 8:30-35). Yet the major city of Shechem lies in the valley between these two mountains. In fact, there is another covenant ceremony recorded at Shechem (Josh. 24:1-28). Yet there is no record at all that any battle was ever waged in its vicinity.

Furthermore, as we notice the cities which Joshua is said to have captured after his initial thrust into the land, the only ones which are named are six cities in the southern hill country and Hazor far to the north of the land (Josh. 10:28,29,31,34,35,38; 11:10). This left several cities of the south unassaulted and the entire central and northern part of the land in peace. Joshua is said to have fought pitched battles with numerous kings, but he is not said to have captured any more cities (Josh. 10:1-27; 11:1-9; 12:1-24). In spite of the fact that Joshua's troops are not said to have captured more territory, they could move fairly freely throughout the central hill country.

All of these factors add further confusion to our understanding of the nature of the conquest. Generally, the problems are ignored. But the historian is not allowed that luxury. We must try to find some sort of order.

There have been several solutions suggested which we must consider. One suggestion is that, since we have noted how many elements are left out of the biblical narrative simply because they just don't add significance to the basic story, this has happened here. This is possible. But it appears to me to be unlikely that, since Shechem and the covenant renewal ceremony figure so significantly in the narrative, the biblical narrator would have left out the detail of how that city was captured.

It has also been suggested that no one but people who have no faith commitment to the God of the Bible would ever ask such questions. But the Bible makes so much of discipleship, (being a disciplined student) it appears to me to be the height of folly for the disciple to fail his Master by not giving serious study to the Bible. The Christian has nothing to fear from truth. But we do have the responsibility of seeking to know the truth. Closely related to this suggestion is the idea that, since we obviously know so little about the period, we should not ask such questions. There may be some truth to that. On the other hand, we know so much about the period that these questions leap out at us.

It appears to me that the best solution is one at which I have already hinted in dealing with the problem of the date of the Exodus event in the preceding chapter. There I noted that there is a growing belief among Old Testament historians that there was more than one group of people who had come out of Egypt. This might explain the fact that we apparently have at least two traditions as to the date of the Exodus. It might further explain the fact that Joshua and his troops did not have to fight for Shechem. Perhaps it was already in the hands of people related to Israel. This might also have been true in several of the mountainous regions in the northern part of the land. There are other indications scattered throughout this biblical material which make this appear to be an even more attractive theory. However, such a detailed study of this particular material is beyond the purpose of this book. Let me make perfectly clear that what I am suggesting is not a fact but merely a human theory to try to explain the facts as we now perceive them.

This theory of at least two (and perhaps more) incursions into the land of Canaan offers a solution to the second and third problems noted at the beginning of this section. The biblical narrative would then be following the story of the incursions under Joshua, but this does not mean that others did not happen, just as Moses' birth narrative did not mean that Miriam and Aaron were not born prior to Moses (Ex. 2:1,4; 7:7).

We still have not dealt with the problem of whether the land of Canaan was wholly in Israelite hands when Joshua had completed his mission. Part of this may be solved by the foregoing theory, that perhaps some land was already in Hebrew hands which Joshua did not actually have to capture. This still leaves us with the fact that "much land" still remained to be taken (Josh. 13:1). How are we to understand this? An examination of a good Old

Testament map helps here. It becomes obvious that what Joshua had done when he came to the end of his attack was to encircle the land. His initial attack split it through the middle. He then surrounded the southern section on all sides but the east, which is bordered by the Dead Sea, and then he cut off the only major approach to the land from the north. Thus he had effectively interdicted the land. No outside help was available to the people on the interior of the land as long as the Israelites could maintain those positions.

In essence then, it could be said from a military standpoint that the land had been taken. Yet, at the same time, there did remain much land on the interior which had not been captured. This problem then appears to be more one of semantics than of real difficulty. The ancient biblical authors were not nincompoops. They could read just as well as we can. If the apparent problem here had offered a problem to them, it could have been dealt with. The fact that it was not indicates that they did not see a problem.

What we are left with is a slightly different picture of the conquest than we are used to facing. It appears that Joshua's attack on Canaan was merely the last in a series of incursions which had begun long before. The biblical narrative follows the mainline but that does not mean that something else had not happened in the meantime.

The Chronology of the Conquest

Closely related to any attempt to reconstruct the chronology of the conquest is the problem of the chronology of the exodus. One obviously affects the other. I would suggest that you review that section in the preceding chapter. At that time, I concluded that the probable date for the beginning of the conquest under Joshua was about 1230 BC. The evidence for the date of the conquest appears to further corroborate this conclusion.

At the time of this writing, neither Jericho nor Ai offers any archaeological data indicating a major overthrow about 1230 BC, or at any other time within reason. The top of the mound of Jericho has been weathered and plundered over the centuries so that there is just no surviving evidence of any kind. Furthermore, Ai does not seem to have been inhabited at the time under investigation. Its very name may verify that, for in the Hebrew Ai means "ruin." However, nearby Bethel slightly to the west of Ai did have a massive overthrow about 1230 BC, with the total destruction of everything in the city which would burn. Since Bethel is not mentioned in the biblical narrative, it is possible that the mound of ruins called Ai was simply a military outpost for Bethel. When it was captured, the city which it guarded was put to the torch.

Gibeon, whose inhabitants are said to have made peace with Joshua through subterfuge, shows absolutely a steady pattern of occupation with no signs of an overthrow (see Josh. 9:3,15). This is precisely what we would have expected.

The site which has been identified as Makkedah has not yet been excavated. Further, the site of ancient Libnah has been identified as the modern Tell es-Safi. Since it is still being occupied, no significant excavations have been made. On the other hand, Lachish has been excavated, and it did suffer a major destruction about 1230 BC.

Eglon has been tentatively identified as Tell 'Atun, although some scholars would now dispute this. It was clearly a fortress city and apparently underwent a fairly massive destruction in the late 1200s. This has been determined by sinking several pits, with an appropriate ash layer being turned up in each. Hebron also appears to have fallen at about the same time, although it was not immediately resettled. Debir, about seven miles north of Hebron, was also overthrown at the same time, but it was immediately resettled. This might possibly indicate that, while Hebron had been overthrown, the Hebrews did not wish to extend their lines quite so far to the south.

The final city listed in the Old Testament as having been destroyed by Joshua is Hazor. Judging from the size of its ruins, it was probably one of the largest cities in ancient Canaan, having perhaps forty thousand inhabitants. It also shows evidence of a massive overthrow near the end of the thirteenth century BC.

In addition to these evidences, two other things stand out. There were other cities which are not mentioned in the Bible which do seem to show evidence of a violent overthrow in the last quarter of the thirteenth century BC. When any of these cities were resettled, the new inhabitants had a more primitive culture than the one which they had overthrown. Related to this, throughout this same period, there were numerous small settlements which were inhabited for the first time in the central hill country where no previous settlement had been before. The remains of their material culture appear to be quite similar to that new culture found in the cities which had been destroyed.

Thus, while the picture can by no means be said to be absolutely clear-cut, there is a massive amount of evidence that the land of Canaan did experience a rather violent overthrow about the last quarter of the thirteenth century BC. It was subsequently resettled by a more primitive people.

This must be added to the evidence of the Merneptah stela. Pharaoh Merneptah recorded his invasion of Canaan about 1220 BC. He listed those nations and peoples with whom he fought or with whom he came in contact. Among these appears the name of Israel. In Egyptian hieroglyphics, what is known as a determinative was used to indicate the nature of any particular word picture. Thus a word could be used with one determinative to indicate the name of a town, with a different determinative to indicate the name of a person, with a different determinative to indicate the name of a nation, and so on. The name of Israel on Merneptah's monument was used with the determinative of a people, not with one which represented a nation or a kingdom. Thus, his monument would indicate that, at that period of history, Israel was in the land but still was not fully settled, and in no way were they to be considered as having national status. This also fits the prevailing evidence. It would appear then that we are on fairly safe ground to conclude that the invasion of Canaan under Joshua began about 1230 BC.

The Nature of the Oppressions

The period of the judges gives us a number of problems in dealing with Hebrew history. In reading the Book of Judges, we get a first impression that what we are dealing with is one long narrative made up of a series of events which followed one after the other in sequence. But a more careful study of the various oppressions causes us to raise some serious questions about this.

First, there are problems with the chronology. If we add up all the years of the various periods of oppression and deliverance, we have far too many to fill the time between the invasion under Joshua and the rise of the kingship under Saul. Now the date of the rise of the Hebrew monarchy is fairly well established as being about 1020 BC. At the most, it can only vary from that date by a few years. It certainly cannot vary enough to solve the problem of the length of the period of the judges. On the other hand, to push the date of the Exodus far enough back to fit in all these years flies in the face of all the evidence which has caused us to decide that the Exodus and conquest probably occurred in the thirteenth century BC. There are two other possibilities in interpreting the data of the Book of Judges which may alleviate the problem. The idea that there may have been some Hebrews already in the land of Canaan when those under Joshua invaded the land may offer an explanation for the rather extended length of the period when all of the years are added up. It may have been, in other words, that the Hebrews in the land were already facing some oppressions prior to the invasion of Joshua. That is certainly possible, but it creates other problems, for the judges all appear to have arisen after Joshua's invasion.

However, a closer reading of the book suggests another possibility as a way to deal with our problem. In a thorough examination of each of the oppressions, we discover that in most instances only one or two tribes appear to have been involved. Even in the case of the period of Deborah, only ten tribes are mentioned, and two of those, Machir and Gilead, may only have been clans from a tribe instead of the entire tribe (Judg. 5:14-18). Consider the following table.

Judge	Oppressed Tribes Tribe(s) Involved	Reference
Othniel	?? (Caleb of Judah?)	3:7-11
Ehud	Benjamin, Ephraim	3:12-30
Shamgar	??	3:31
Deborah	Ephraim, Benjamin, Machir Zebulun, Issachar, Reuben, Gilead, Dan, Asher, Naphtali	4:1 to 5:31
Gideon	Manasseh, Asher, Zebulun, Naphtali, Ephraim	6:1 to 8:35
Tola	Issachar, Ephraim	10:1-2
Jair	Gilead (?)	10:3-5
Jephthah	Judah, Benjamin, Ephraim	10:6 to 12:7
Ibzan	?? (Judah?)	12:8-10
Elon	Zebulun (?)	12:11-12
Abdon	Ephraim (?)	12:13-15
Samson	Dan, Judah	13:1 to 16:31

A quick look at the table and a more thorough examination of the passages involved begins to leave us with the impression that most, if not all, of the oppressions were rather limited in scope. It would appear probable that none of them involved the entire nation.

This idea of limited oppressions with a specific tribal or geographical focus might also be suggested by the use of a good map while reading Judges. For example, the Philistines might be expected to create problems near their own territory, the southwest of Canaan. The Canaanites might be expected all over the land but probably more to the north and central where there were no major territorial conquests under Joshua. The Midianites might be expected to give trouble from either the south or the east as they made their raids upon the land from the desert. The Ammonites and the Moabites would be expected to give problems near their lands across the Jordan. Thus, for them we would look to the east, both in the central and southern regions of Palestine.

It would appear to be quite likely that some tribes

might have been having problems with one enemy at the same time that other tribes were having problems with another enemy. A bit of thought may make this even more probable, for events which are going on at the same time cannot be written about in the same place. One has to follow the other. This proposal, which the narrative itself suggests, offers a solution to the extended period which a first reading of the chronological data suggests. (I shall return to the chronological problem in the following section.)

The other feature of the oppressions which we must consider is the way in which they were viewed by the Hebrews. In every instance, the oppressing enemy was seen by the Hebrews as being God's punishment upon them for sinful rebellion. In this material, the ancient inspired writers began to view God as using human instruments as agents of temporal judgment. Thus they understood such oppressions not as the result of their ill fortune but as the result of their folly. This belief was to have a significant influence upon Israel's subsequent understanding of history and of God's sovereignty. They clearly believed that God could and did use men and nations without their own knowledge as agents of His will.

But just as the oppressors were seen by Israel as agents of God's judgment, the judge was seen as the agent of God's grace. God's judgment was understood as being brought to an end by His love and mercy. We shall come back to this idea later.

The Chronology of the Oppressions

As noted in the preceding section, when we add all of the various chronological data for the various oppressions and the judges together, the total is far too long to fit into the period of history into which they must be fitted. In fact, all of the years added together give a total of 410 years. If we add to this the time of Samuel, the total is about 440 years. Yet the period of the judges must be fitted into the gap from approximately 1220 BC to about 1020 BC (from the conquest to the reign of Saul). I have already suggested that the best solution to the problem is the one which becomes obvious in a detailed reading of the material. The oppressions generally appear to have been localized and thus there was most likely significant overlapping. This will eliminate the major problem which confronted us.

However, there is another problem which we must at least consider. This is the large number of references which appear to be some multiple of forty.

Period	Years	Reference
Peace after Othniel	40	3:11
Peace after Ehud	80	3:30
Oppression by Jabin	20	4:3
Peace after Deborah	40	5:31
Peace after Gideon	40	8:28
Oppression by Philistines	40	13:1
Samson's judgeship	20	15:20 (16:31)

We noted earlier that *forty* appears to be used throughout the Bible as indicative of a long, indefinite period. It is also sometimes used in connection with years as apparently indicating a generation. The surprising number of occasions in Judges where a multiple or a fraction (½) of forty is used appears far too frequently to be a coincidence. It is possible, perhaps even probable, that the author was using these in reference to a generation, two generations, or half a generation. This proposal may further help us make sense out of the chronological data which we are given concerning the period of the judges.

If we do not adopt some such proposals as these which have been suggested, then we must assume that a significant part of the activities of the judges was carried out before the Hebrews entered into the land under Joshua. This is possible provided that many, if not most, of the Hebrews entered the land earlier. While it does appear that some entered earlier, I do not believe that the majority of them did so.

The Nature of a Judge

One of the more frustrating problems in understanding the events of the period of Israel's settlement in Canaan is that of the nature of a judge. The very title is misleading.

To begin trying to understand what a judge was we need to eliminate what a judge was not. A judge was not normally one who rendered judgments upon cases or complaints brought before him. In fact, such a function is only seldom attributed to any of the people whom we call judges in this period. Furthermore, in general, the persons whom we call judges in this era are not so identified in the Book of Judges. They are usually described by a verb as having "judged" but seldom are given the title of judge.

The basic function of these people seems to have been that of savior or deliverer. They apparently furnished some sort of military leadership to their people in order to overthrow their oppressors. Furthermore, they were in their positions of leadership because of the obvious native gifts which they possessed and because God had raised them up. In that sense, we might even call them charismatic leaders. In addition, when the basic need was over, they seem to have faded into the background.

The judges came from differing backgrounds. Deborah was a prophetess (Judg. 4:4). Gideon was a farmer (Judg. 6:11). Jephthah was a soldier (Judg. 11:1). Samuel was both a priest and a prophet (1 Sam. 3:1-3,20). But they were all raised up by God to deliver the people from an oppressing enemy. They were instruments of God's deliverance.

However, admitting that our term *judge* is probably not the best one to apply to these people if we are trying to describe their function, we shall stick with it because it has become too much a part of our vocabulary. At the same time, we need to recognize that the function of the Hebrew judges was far different from modern judges. In general, they were not even spiritual leaders but were people who allowed God to use their strengths and weaknesses in accomplishing His purposes for the people of Israel.

The Background of the Period

Before we can really understand the period of the conquest and the settlement of Canaan by the Hebrews, we must consider the historical background of the era. The culture and the political activities of the peoples in and around Canaan played a significant role in setting the stage for Israel's history. Some of the biblical events beginning with the time of Joshua and continuing through that of Samuel make no sense at all apart from a knowledge of this background. Other events make much better sense when we place them against this background.

The Major Powers

Shortly before the time when Joshua's armies invaded Canaan, the international situation of the ancient Near East went through a major transformation. At the beginning of the thirteenth century BC, there were two major powers on the scene alongside of one minor power which was growing in importance. We are already aware of the strength of Egypt, whose empire extended far to the north of Palestine on beyond the northern reaches of Syria. Further north, there was the great Hittite empire of Mitanni, basically ruling over the region we know as Asia Minor. Alongside of these two major powers, the Assyrians were beginning their first rise to power in the upper part of the Mesopotamian Valley.

The Egyptian control of Canaan began to wane under the kingship of Akhenaten. His concern with religion and internal affairs caused him to neglect his foreign possessions. This was certainly to the benefit of the Hittites, who wished to extend their control southward. But it began to create problems for his Canaanite city-states because they were again confronted by revolt and invasion, as well as by attacks upon one another among themselves, as each sought to gain supremacy over the other.

With the beginning of the Nineteenth Dynasty in Egypt (about 1306 BC), Sethi sought to regain control of his Asiatic provinces. Since these bordered on the Hittite territories, war between Egypt and Mitanni became inevitable. With the accession of Ramses II (about 1290 to 1228 BC), the long-threatened war became a reality. The two nations brought into the field major armies made up of native troops as well as foreign mercenaries. About 1285 BC, Ramses led his troops northward into Hittite territory where they were ambushed at Kadesh on the Orontes River. (This is not to be confused with Kadesh-barnea, to the south of Canaan.) Although both nations claimed a victory, it was apparently an indecisive, decimating battle for both armies. Egypt's armies returned home and were never again a threat to the Hittites. At the same time, the Hittites were too decimated to pursue Egypt and made no serious threat toward seizing control of Egypt's northern possessions. About ten years later, the two nations entered into a treaty which effectively settled the conflict.

This allowed Ramses to turn his attention fully toward his internal building programs. This resulted in the Egyptians' neglect of their Canaanite territories. In turn, this further intensified problems for the Canaanite city-states. With the death of Ramses and the accession of his son Merneptah, there were two events of significance. The pharaoh made an invasion of Canaan to try to strengthen his hold on those regions, but this was apparently rather unsuccessful, his stela to the contrary notwithstanding. Egyptian influence in Canaan was clearly waning and well on the way toward its end. This was further augmented by the attack of the Sea People on Egypt. It was only by the barest margin that these invaders were repulsed. A part of these Sea People were the Philistines, and another part were the Phoenicians. When these finally settled on the coast of Palestine, Egypt was unable to do anything about it. Egypt's control of Palestine was gone.

In the north, Mitanni was facing similar problems. The rise of Assyria became a new threat to the Hittites. Their attention was wholly directed to trying to defend themselves from Assyria's territorial expansion, which began around 1240 BC. Shortly thereafter, the Sea People also began to land on the coastal regions which the Hittites controlled. With the major onslaught of Assyria and the minor conquests of the Sea People, the end came rapidly for Mitanni. By the early twelfth century, Mitanni had ceased to exist.

Upon the end of the Hittite Empire and with the onset of a period of great weakness in Egypt, there was only one major power in the Fertile Crescent which could have exerted influence over Canaan. That was Assyria. But the Assyrians turned their attention southward in the Mesopotamian Valley, directing it toward the threat of Babylon. At the same time, they made minor attacks westward into the decaying remnant of the Hittite Empire. Assyria does not appear even to have made a threatening move in the direction of Canaan at this time.

The fascinating result of this century of international conflict was that each of the major powers on the scene at its beginning had very quickly either been destroyed or seriously weakened. At precisely the time that Israel was trying to wrest control of Canaan, there was a major power vacuum in that region. The invading army of slaves from Egypt had no international threat to face. For Israel, the international situation had truly left them with a fullness of times.

The Canaanites

Since there was no international threat with which Israel immediately had to deal upon their entrance into Canaan, we must consider what they faced in Canaan itself. Who were the Canaanites? What was their culture like?

Most of our information about the Canaanites comes from external sources, for they have left us little record of their own activities. It appears that "Canaanite" is neither a racial nor, strictly speaking, a cultural designation. Both the biblical and the extrabiblical sources give us the distinct impression that the people of Canaan were made up of many different peoples. The Book of Joshua describes the inhabitants of Canaan as "the Amorites, the Perizzites, the Canaanites, the Hittites, the Girgashites, the Hivites, and the Jebusites" (Josh. 24:11). The people who had originally settled in Canaan were apparently fragments of several nations and peoples, some of whom fled there as refugees, others of whom came as conquerors, while others apparently came as migrants. The name *Canaanite,* therefore, apparently only applied to those who lived in Canaan.

Politically, the land of Canaan was basically made up of numerous city-states. Each of these was ruled by a monarch and controlled as much of the territory surrounding itself as it could. This was generally not very much. The major city-states were identified in the Amarna letters as Shechem, Gezer, Hazor, Megiddo, Jerusalem, and Lachish. At least the first two of these were seeking to gain control over larger amounts of territory. These city-states had essentially been under Egyptian suzerainty for a very long period of time. However, beginning in the fourteenth century BC, they had been faced with uprisings from within and attacks from without. By the time of the Israelite invasion, they had generally grown rather weak. This may have been due both to their internal social collapse as well as due to their conflicts with one another. Again, such a political situation left them fairly ready for an external overthrow.

Culturally, the Canaanites had developed into fairly successful merchants. This was so true that, throughout the rest of the Old Testament period, the very name *Canaanite* had become synonymous for merchant. This was probably due to the fact that Canaan was the land bridge between Egypt and Africa on the one hand and Mesopotamia and Asia Minor on the other. All the goods which were traded between those regions had to pass through Canaan. The Canaanites apparently became known as brokers of international merchandise. In addition, they also imported goods from Crete, Cyprus, and the whole Aegean region. Such successful trade, however, had apparently given rise to a wealthy merchant class and a rather impoverished lower class. This in turn had given birth to a social unrest which may have played a part in the collapse of Canaan before the incoming Hebrews.

We know more about the religion of Canaan than about any other aspect of Canaanite life. The ancient materials found at Ugarit have brought new meaning to many of the biblical references relating to the practices of Canaanite worship. Their religion was essentially a fertility cult with the avowed purpose of ensuring the fertility of the land, the flocks and herds, and the people. This was to ensure abundant crops, increasing flocks, and a growing population to maintain its hold on the land. Each hill or "high place" in Canaan was thought to have its own baal or lord who ruled the surrounding region up to the next "high place." On the high places were sacred groves and both priests and priestesses. These priests and priestesses were little more than sacred prostitutes. Among other things, the worship at those high places involved having sexual intercourse at the shrine. Such worship appealed to the basest part of human nature and was a constant problem to the people of Israel after they settled in the land.

These were the people whom Israel had to face first when they came into the land of Canaan. The later assimilation of many of these people and their practices into Israelite life and worship again and again brought forth the scathing attack of the prophets.

The Philistines

Most Christians know of the Philistines primarily from the biblical stories of Samson and of David and Goliath. That is an unfortunate limitation, for they were a significant people both in the ancient world and through the pages of the Old Testament. They were important enough that they gave their name to the whole land, for Palestine is derived from "Philistine."

In spite of the importance of the Philistines in the ancient world, however, a great many things about these people still remain unknown to us. Their settlements on the coastal plain may have begun as early as the late thirteenth century BC. Certainly, they began arriving in earnest by the early twelfth century, at least by 1175 BC.

The Philistines were apparently made up of several

different tribal groups of the Sea People. In the period from the late 1200s to the early 1100s, these people were attacking almost the entire eastern end of the Mediterranean. They apparently came from the regions of Crete and the Aegean. Some of their ancestors appear to have initiated attacks on the eastern Mediterranean about a century earlier, but at that time there was no apparent attempt at settlement. However, by the time in question, they were coming with an intent to stay.

These Sea People came very close to defeating the Egyptians during this period of expansion and settlement. Only by the barest margins were they beaten off without at least conquering the coastal regions of Egypt. For a long time, historians thought that the Sea People's ultimate settlement in Palestine came about after they were driven away from Egypt. More recent interpretation of the evidence suggests a different picture. While some of the people who were eventually known as Philistines came to the coastal plain of Canaan apparently without ever having been involved in attacks on Egypt, others of them came directly from their Egyptian attacks. However, it now appears that these did not come because they had been driven away from Egypt but because Egypt had employed them as mercenaries. It appears that Ramses III (about 1185-1150 BC) was impressed with their warrior abilities and employed them to create problems for the territories of Canaan which Egypt had once controlled. Thus the Philistine settlements were at least partially intended to benefit the Egyptians by oppressing their former vassals. The people who settled the region we know as Philistia were also closely related to these who settled the northern coastal plain. These have become known to us as the Phoenicians.

The Philistine invasions seized the coastal plains. It was a highly fertile region, well situated for the production of grain which was the major Philistine agricultural product. Philistine settlements centralized in five cities: Ekron, Ashdod, Ashkelon, Eglon, and Gaza. Each of these city-states controlled the territories which bordered upon it. Each was ruled by a lord, or "tyrant." These five city-states formed the Philistine confederation. It appears that no one city and no one ruler ever gained supremacy. Apparently they did not even try to do so. This rule by confederation or by committee seems to have functioned unbelievably well.

The Philistine presence on the coastal plain was a source of major problems for the Hebrews throughout their history. The Philistines were clearly militarily superior to the Hebrews from the days of their arrival at least until the time of David. The reason for this shows up both in archaeological excavations and in the biblical narratives. We are told that

> there was no smith to be found throughout all the land of Israel; for the Philistines said, "Lest the Hebrews make themselves swords or spears"; but every one of the Israelites went down to the Philistines to sharpen his plowshare, his mattock, his axe, or his sickle; . . . So on the day of the battle there was neither sword nor spear found in the hand of any of the people with Saul and Jonathan; but Saul and Jonathan his son had them (1 Sam. 13:19-22).

Archaeological excavations demonstrate that the Philistines had learned the process of manufacturing iron long before anyone else in the region did. It was this scientific advance which allowed them to win the arms race and to gain supremacy for a while. It is quite obvious what an advance iron swords were over those made of copper or bronze. When Israel finally gained this knowledge, they were able to fight on a more equal footing. It was then that the Philistine supremacy came to an end.

The Philistines' religion seems either to have been adopted or significantly modified after their arrival in Canaan. The three names of their gods which we know are all Semitic, with their origins resting in Canaan. Dagon was worshiped at Gaza and Ashdod; Baal-zebub was worshiped at Ekron; and Ashtaroth was worshiped somewhere in the region of Philistia (Judg. 16:21-23; 1 Sam. 5:1-2; 31:9-10; 2 Kings 1:2).

Further, the Philistines never seem to have abandoned their heritage as Sea People. In spite of very poor harbor facilities along the coastal plain, they do appear to have engaged in sea trade throughout their history. They were an aggressive people of high achievement. Their presence certainly influenced Hebrew history at many points.

The Transjordan Peoples: Edom, Ammon, and Moab

In the Transjordan region, there were three nations which were to be constant sources of difficulties for the people of Israel. In the far south was Edom; to the north of them was Moab; and to the north and east of the territory of Reuben was Ammon. These people were all understood to have been related to the Hebrews (Gen. 19:37-38; 25:29-30; 36:1,8,19).

All three of these nations appear to have come into national existence in the early part of the thirteenth century BC, although Ammon was slightly later than Edom and Moab. (We have already noted the impact that this fact makes upon our attempt to arrive at a date for the Exodus from Egypt.) Unlike the Canaanites who had city-states and the Philistines who had a confederation, these three nations were all monarchies, ruled over by kings.

By reputation, the Ammonites and the Moabites were essentially engaged in sheep herding while the Edomites were better known as traders and merchants. Edom was also reputed to be a center of ancient Near Eastern wisdom. All three nations were at least resistant to, and were probably opposed to, the settlement of Israel in the land of Canaan. Although we cannot really identify the reasons for this, it was probably due to the fact of sibling competitiveness and of the desire to occupy the same territory. These Transjordan people were apparently threatened by Israel's presence, being fearful of being driven away from their own territories. They were also apparently envious of the fact that Israel's territory was more fruitful than what they occupied. Part of the hostility might also go back to the fact that Israel had been opposed in their migration toward Canaan by Edom and Moab.

The constant enmity between these peoples and Israel, which existed throughout Israel's history, had its basis in the time of the conquest and settlement. It appears that every time the people of Israel were brought under pressure by other enemies, one or more of these Transjordan nations took advantage of it by raiding Hebrew towns. We know very little of the culture of these peoples. There were few cities in these regions, and the peoples were much more nomadic than the Hebrews.

The Transjordan peoples' territory was less precisely defined than Israel's due to the existence of the Arabian desert on their eastern borders. Also, other than knowing that the chief god of Moab was Chemosh, we know almost nothing of their religion.

Because of the constant enmity between these nations and Israel, a steady pressure was exerted by them upon Israel's land from the south and east. This pressure helps us understand some of Israel's problems during the time of settlement.

The Midianites and Amalekites

The only other people whose existence had a major impact upon the history of the Hebrew people in this period was the Midianites. They played a part in Israel's earlier history as the place where Moses found refuge when he fled from Egypt (Ex. 2:15). Midian does not seem to have really had an existence as a nation. Rather, the Midianites were apparently nomadic peoples who wandered fairly freely throughout the Sinai Peninsula and the Arabian desert.

At about the time the Hebrews were settling into the land of Canaan, the Midianites made a significant advance in their cultural development which changed their whole future and the relationship which they were to have with Israel during the period of the judges. This development was the domestication of the camel. This one thing made possible a number of changes in the culture of anyone who lived in or on the edges of a desert region. Camels are able to survive for long periods of time without water. Therefore those who use them can venture far deeper into the desert than those who are dependent upon other animals. Furthermore, camels are quite swift and possess amazing stamina. Camels can travel seventy-five miles a day for several days in a row.

The Midianites were apparently the first people with whom Israel came in contact who used camels in significant numbers (Judg. 6:5). These beasts made it possible for the Midianites to make swift raids from out of the desert. They could in one day's time reach almost any point in Hebrew territory from the desert. Furthermore, to those unfamiliar with these great beasts, their very appearance in such large numbers would have been quite frightening. Camels also allowed the Midianites to transport significantly larger amounts of plunder than any other beast of burden could have done. Finally, after such raids into the land, the Midianites could race back out into the desert at a pace which the Hebrews could not hope to match. They could also go deeper into the desert than Israel could hope to follow.

Such speed and mobility made it quite possible for the Midianites to develop the raiding techniques which are so clearly described in the biblical material (Judg. 6:1-6). The Midianites apparently made no attempt to conquer territory. Rather, it was their intent to plunder the land, seizing wealth and produce and keeping Israel weak, so that the Hebrews could not effectively resist or defend themselves. The speed of the Midianites' raids made effective defense quite difficult.

The Midianites are said to have been accompanied by the Amalekites (Judg. 6:3). They were apparently another desert tribe. At times they may have served as mercenaries for the Moabites (Judg. 3:13) and may have aided the Midianites in the same manner. However, they seem almost to have been partners of the Midianites, rather than their employees. They, too, were to become a rather constant source of problems for Israel.

Since both the Midianites and the Amalekites were more or less desert nomads, they have left almost no identifiable material remains. What little we know of them comes from ancient references rather than from archaeological investigation.

The History of the Period

It was one thing for a group of slaves to find deliverance from their slavery. It was quite another for those former slaves to become sufficiently well enough organized to overthrow a long-established culture. And it was still another for those insurrectionists who had defeated the inhabitants of a land to so consolidate their conquests that they were able to defend it against all comers. But these are precisely the things which the Israelites did in Canaan. They overthrew the inhabitants sufficiently to gain control of the land, and they did it well enough to maintain and expand their hold upon it. This process was begun under the leadership of Joshua.

The Work of Joshua

Little is known of Joshua prior to the time he led the people of Israel in the conquest of Canaan. But that little is so instructive. He is first introduced as the leader of the Hebrew soldiers when they went into battle during the Exodus from Egypt (Ex. 17:9,13). We also see him as the companion of Moses on the mountain when the Hebrews led by Aaron rebelled with the golden calf (Ex. 32:15-18). Joshua's warlike nature was further revealed at this time when he immediately interpreted the noise of Israel's idolatrous celebration as being that of war.

Joshua also had some kind of responsibility over the tent of meeting in Israel (Ex. 33:11). This may imply some kind of spiritual responsibility but more likely only indicated that he was placed on guard to protect the tent. This fits in well with Joshua's obviously military responsibilities.

When Israel first approached Canaan, Joshua was one of the twelve leaders selected by Moses to serve as spies in the land (Num. 13:8,16). At great risk to his own life, he brought back a minority report, insisting that Israel should trust the Lord and proceed with the task of conquest (Num. 14:6-10).

As the final days of Moses' leadership came on, Joshua was publicly set apart as Moses' successor (Num. 27:18-

23). This was a clear indication of the fact that he was to be not only Israel's military leader but their spiritual leader as well. Ancient society made no distinction between sacred and secular responsibility.

Joshua was the son of a man named Nun who is otherwise unknown in the Old Testament (Ex. 33:11; Num. 13:8,16; 27:18; Deut. 34:9; Josh. 1:1; 1 Chron. 7:20,27). However, this ancestry clearly identifies Joshua as an Ephraimite. If, as it appears, some of the northern and central tribes were already in the land when Joshua arrived in Canaan, this relationship with them would surely have made their acceptance of his leadership easier.

The Initial Campaign. In spite of his obvious abilities, Joshua was apparently quite intimidated by the awesome responsibility which fell upon him following the death of Moses. So great was his fear that he had to be encouraged on at least four occasions when he assumed the leadership of Israel (Josh. 1:6,7,9,18).

In planning his initial campaign to get a lodgment in the land of Palestine, Joshua took two separate actions. First, he got his armies organized and prepared for battle (Josh. 1:10-11). But he also determined what his first target would be and sent spies into the land to gather such information as a military commander might need (Josh. 2:1). Joshua was well aware that, from a human standpoint, the success or failure of a military campaign depended upon the adequacy and accuracy of information.

In the visit of the spies to Jericho, an event occurred which was to have an impact upon the whole of Israel's subsequent history, as well as that of the New Testament. The spies were almost discovered by the ruler of Jericho and were hidden by a prostitute named Rahab (Josh. 2:2-7,15-16). Upon her subsequent entry into the Israelite community, she became an ancestor of David and of great David's greater son, Jesus (Matt. 1:5-16).

Upon receiving the report of the spies, Joshua led his people across the Jordan River. There they encamped at Gilgal (Josh. 4:19). The name means "circle." It was apparently a place where there was a prehistoric stone circle and which had long served as a sacred shrine. To that stone circle, the Hebrews apparently added other stones which were to serve as a memorial to future generations of Israel's successful entry into Canaan.

The reason for crossing the Jordan at the plain of Jericho was clearly based upon strategic factors. The only significant crossing place of the Jordan was on the east-west highway which came from the Transjordan region at Jericho. In order to sucessfully control entrance into Canaan from the east, it was imperative to control the highway and the city of Jericho. On the other hand, there was no way by which an army could bring a large number of troops into the central part of land without using that highway and gaining control of Jericho.

Having once gained entrance into Canaan, Joshua's first military move of necessity had to be against Jericho. It is impossible from a historian's standpoint to describe what happened in Jericho. As we have already noted, there are no remains of Jericho which can be ascribed to the destruction under Joshua. Over the centuries the top of the ancient mound has been plundered for stone and has weathered. We just have no other information than the biblical narrative of Israel's miraculous victory (Josh. 6:12-21).

One of the more difficult things for modern readers to comprehend is the absolute destruction of the city. This appears to be so different from the New Testament ethic. Of course, it is! If these ancient peoples had lived by the standards of Jesus, then we would not have needed the message of Jesus. On the other hand, we must try to grasp the ancient practice of *cherem*. This term was applied to the total destruction of a city which was devoted to or dedicated to the god of the conqueror. The intent was that a conquering army should not enrich itself by conquest. Everything in that city was considered to be property of the conqueror's god and had to be offered to him. The background behind this was that a major part of the pay of a soldier normally came from the booty which was captured. The practice of *cherem* was established to eliminate the accusation that an army was fighting only for profit.

Following the victory at Jericho, Joshua and his troops moved on into the central hill country toward Bethel and Ai. A victory here would not only have left Joshua in control of the central part of the land but also would have interdicted the major north-south highway through the region. That would have effectively separated the northern part of the country from the southern. Strategically, it was a magnificient plan.

There is a problem concerning this point of attack. The biblical material mentions an attack on Ai but does not mention Bethel. Archaeologically, there is no evidence of any settlement at Ai from this time and on backward for about six centuries. However, there was a major overthrow at Bethel at about this time. Both Bethel and Ai were settled about 1230 BC with a common but primitive culture.

The Hebrew word for Ai means the "ruin." It has been suggested that the Hebrews attacked and defeated Bethel, but that over the years, the story of this attack was transferred from Bethel to this obviously ruined city. It is more likely that Ai served as the military outpost of Bethel, the soldiers establishing themselves among those ancient ruins. The end result of the defeat of Ai was the defeat of Bethel. From a military standpoint, however, it was the defeat of the garrison at Ai that was important. With our present state of knowledge, no final conclusion as to precisely what happened to both of these places is possible.

Having had an easy victory at Jericho, Joshua assumed that a small place like Ai would offer no real resistance. Unfortunately, his confidence was misplaced, and the initial attack was repulsed (Josh. 7:3-5). The whole description here would make Ai appear relatively insignificant and support the idea that it was primarily a military garrison, not a city. The reason for Israel's defeat was given as due to the fact that they had not been faithful with the *cherem*. A soldier by the name of Achan had enriched himself at Jericho. The entire narrative reflects the absolute seriousness with which Israel took the practice of *cherem* (Josh. 7:20-25).

The second attack was more carefully planned. The strategy of pretending to flee, thus drawing the defenders out from their fortifications until they could be destroyed, has been used again and again by military commanders (Josh. 8:3-8). The fact that we are told that the people of Ai and Bethel fell for this ruse further supports the idea of Ai being Bethel's outpost (Josh. 8:17).

With the defeat of Bethel-Ai, Joshua was in firm control of the central part of the land. The territory he had conquered reached into the very heart of Canaan, like a wedge. The Hebrews were in a firm position to establish a base from which to extend their attack. They were no longer in danger of being driven back from the land.

The Covenant at Shechem. Following the capture of Bethel-Ai, Joshua and the people of Israel apparently paused to consolidate their gains and to regroup before the next part of the campaign. In that interlude there was a very surprising event. We are told that "Joshua built an altar in Mount Ebal to the Lord, the God of Israel" (Josh. 8:30).

Mount Ebal is about twenty-five miles north of Bethel on the only highway which runs north-south through the central hill country. It is directly opposite Mount Gerizim with the city of Shechem being in the valley between them. At that place Joshua had a covenant renewal ceremony (Josh. 8:32-35). This whole episode raises three very important questions.

First, how was it possible for Joshua and the people of Israel to march twenty-five miles through hostile territory without a hint of battle or of any opposition? This is a serious problem and must be seriously dealt with.

Second, how could Joshua station the people on the slopes of Mount Ebal and Mount Gerizim with many of them filling the valley between the two, precisely where Shechem was, without having conquered Shechem? Shechem was a major Canaanite city-state. It is inconceivable that such could have happened without a major battle. This problem further accentuates the issue raised by our first question.

The third question is less involved but is equally as important. Why was it necessary or important for Joshua to journey to Shechem for such a covenant ceremony at all? It would have made much more sense, with the northern regions being inhabited by enemies, for the people to have held the covenant renewal ceremony where they had won a victory, at Jericho or Bethel-Ai. This question merely points up the apparent military foolishness in making such a journey unnecessarily. Whatever else we may have seen in Joshua's leadership, he had done nothing foolishly. He was in every instance an able general and a competent national leader. What solution can we find to these issues?

It is certainly possible that there was a major campaign fought as Joshua advanced up the central highlands highway. It is also possible that he waged a major campaign for the capture of Shechem. It is clearly possible that these things happened and that the Bible just does not mention them. But it seems to me to be unlikely that such significant events occurred without there being any biblical or archaeological record of them.

Another suggestion to which I have alluded earlier may offer us some help in dealing with these questions. Is there any possibility that the inhabitants of Shechem and this part of the central hill country may have been related to those Israelites who had invaded the country under Joshua? I have already noted that this hypothesis would help solve some of the problems relating to the dating of the time Israel came out of Egypt. If the people who were in this region had settled there more than a century earlier, the land would not have had to be conquered by Joshua. At the same time, this would offer a rationale for going to Shechem for a covenant ceremony. If these people had not been at Sinai with those who had come out in the Exodus, they would not yet have been a part of the covenant community. In order to fully incorporate them into the invading people of Israel, they would have had to participate in a covenant ceremony.

If this hypothesis is correct, it would solve several of our problems and make sense out of a number of questions. It is by no means certain, but it does appear to me to be highly probable that Joshua found friends and relatives in this region. Therefore, before proceeding with military campaigns, he paused to rest and to unify the people of the Exodus with those who were already there from an earlier entrance into the land.

Before Joshua renewed his attack upon the Canaanite territories, he was visited by emissaries from Gibeon. This was apparently located about seven miles southwest of Ai. Those people were both fearful and deceptive. They wholly fooled Joshua and the Israelites into believing they had come from a great distance. They, too, made a covenant with Israel (Josh. 9:3-6,15). Here is a specific example of people being allowed to remain in the land through a covenant with Joshua. It is possible that this lends credence to our theory that the men of Shechem were also incorporated into Israel through the covenant ceremony at Mount Ebal and Mount Gerizim.

The Southern Campaign. Regardless of how Joshua had gotten control of the region between Ai and Shechem, he and his people had a major power base right in the heart of Canaan. He was literally sitting astride the saddle of the land. He had effectively isolated the south from the north and the main body of Canaan from the Transjordan region. He was literally practicing the strategy of divide and conquer.

At this point, five kings in the southern region of the land, led by the king of Jerusalem, made an attack upon Gibeon (Josh. 10:3-5). This was an attempt to recapture lost territory as well as to punish the Gibeonites for their treachery to the Canaanite cause. At this period in history, the normal relationship between the Canaanite city-states was one of gentle hostility and distrust. But the fact that Joshua had successfully occupied so much of Canaan, sometimes with no loss and no military campaign, had forced the kings to take Joshua's invasion seriously. The coalition among the kings was evidence that their fear of each other was less than their fear of Israel.

Joshua rushed to the aid of Gibeon from his base at Gilgal (Josh. 10:9). It is possible that this base was at the

Gilgal where Israel first encamped upon crossing the Jordan. But there was another Gilgal located halfway between Bethel and Shechem. This was more likely the place where Joshua had established a center of operations.

Joshua led his troops on an all-night forced march, arriving much sooner than the Canaanite coalition had expected and throwing them into a panic. At the same time, there was a massive hailstorm, which severely decimated the Canaanite armies (Josh. 10:9-11). The end result was the deliverance of Joshua's allies at Gibeon and the total defeat of the Canaanites. This included the death of the attacking kings.

Having moved his army back on the offensive, Joshua began to implement his southern strategy. He moved first to Makkedah, which he captured and totally destroyed (Josh. 10:28). From there he attacked Libnah, with the same results (Josh. 10:29-30). Makkedah has not been certainly identified, but two sites have been suggested on the north side of the Valley of Elah where it enters into the central hill country from the east. Libnah was a little west of Makkedah and on the southern side of the valley. Both were fortress towns, guarding access into the central highlands. This valley led directly into the highlands from the northern reaches of the Philistine Plain. (The Philistines may have been beginning to settle there at about this time.) Libnah also controlled the only north-south highway through the Shephelah, the southern foothills.

Joshua continued his southern campaign by attacking and destroying both Lachish and Eglon (Josh. 10:31-32, 34-35). These fortress cities guarded the entrance of the next two major southern valleys leading from the coastal plain into the central highlands.

Having cut off the entrance of the major valleys which led into the central highlands from the Philistine Plain, Joshua next drove eastward, right into the heart of the south central highlands. There he attacked Hebron (Josh. 10:36-37). Hebron sat directly astride the central highlands highway, about twenty miles south of Jerusalem. From there Joshua turned southwestward and attacked

Debir (Josh. 10:38-39). This was one of the strongest Canaanite fortresses of the period. Excavations indicate a massive overthrow near the end of the thirteenth century BC. By attacking it from the direction of Hebron, Joshua advanced upon it from the rear, an unexpected direction.

Every step of the southern campaign bears the stamp of a military genius. By the time this campaign was concluded, Joshua had effectively isolated the entire southern part of Canaan. He controlled the major highway entrances into the region from the east, from the north, from the west, and from the south. No significant aid could reach the city-states in that region from the outside, for Joshua controlled every significant highway and valley approach. The capture of the territory inside that encirclement, while not accomplished, was only a matter of time as long as Israel was able to control what it had seized.

The Northern Campaign. At this point in Israel's invasion of Canaan, several options were open to Joshua. Having surrounded the southern regions, he could have advanced into the southern part of the central hill country and tried to capture every city. This would have been both a very costly and a long campaign. He could have sat back and waited for those isolated regions to weaken, making no effort to take them until they were weaker. As far as the south was concerned, that was precisely what he did.

Having adopted this southern strategy, Joshua turned his attention toward the north. He apparently decided to utilize a similar approach to that which he had made in the south. He moved the army northward to attack Hazor. From a strategic standpoint, Hazor controlled the major highway entrance into Canaan from the north. A modern judgment, based upon the size of its ruins, would lead us to conclude that this was one of the largest cities in ancient Canaan, holding a population of some forty thousand people. Archaeologists report that Hazor was totally destroyed a bit later than the cities in the south. This was certainly the greatest feat of arms which the attacking Hebrews performed. The king of Hazor and his allies tried to ambush Joshua as he approached Hazor.

The northern coalition was defeated by the waters of Merom, and Hazor was destroyed shortly thereafter (Josh. 11:1-11).

Following the capture of Hazor, Joshua captured several other cities of the region, but they are unnamed. However, it is apparent that there was nothing like the southern campaign carried out in the north. This again raises the possibility that some of those northern peoples might already have been incorporated into Israel through the covenant at Shechem.

Be that as it may, with the capture of Hazor and the nearby regions, Joshua had isolated the northern hill country just as he had the south. No significant military aid could reach the interior of the land of Canaan as long as Joshua was able to hold the fortress cities which he had captured. The next step in the campaign, if there was to be another, had to be some kind of systematic attempt to reduce the interior of the land. Although it was isolated, Joshua's conquests were not safe as long as the Canaanite city-states in the interior were free and independent. Joshua next turned his attention to that problem.

The Division of the Land. In spite of the fact that the first part of the Book of Joshua draws to a close by stating, "So Joshua took the whole land," the second half begins with the assertion, "There remains yet very much land to be possessed" (Josh. 11:23; 13:1). As we have noted, for all practical purposes, the land had been surrounded and isolated. At the same time, a large number of city-states and their territories were still free and a threat. What was needed from this point onward was some form of organized guerilla warfare in order to gain control of the whole land.

The Book of Joshua describes this effort as being organized by the systematic assignment of various tribal territories. The whole arrangement of tribal allotments is set forth, beginning with those made by Joshua (Josh. 13:7 to 19:51). The entire process is quite complex. It is made so by the fact that there are some differences in tribal names. Also bearing upon the complexity of the problem is the possibility (probability?) that some of the Hebrews may already have been in the land before the arrival of Joshua. Making it even more difficult to unravel is the problem of identifying many of the ancient geographical references. To try to unravel this highly complicated problem is beyond the purpose of this survey of Old Testament history. (There are a number of books which deal with this particular issue.)

Two or three features of this process of land allotment are important for our consideration here. Shortly before World War II, it was suggested that the Hebrew tribal organization should be described as an amphictyony. This is a term which had been applied to the grouping of the city-states of ancient Greece into a common confederation with a central sanctuary and with a commitment to the common god(s) of the cities. While the idea clearly offered some insights into the centrality of faith to Israel's national commitments, the term *amphictyony* is no longer applied to Israel's tribal organization. There are just too many differences between the confederation of city-states in Greece and the tribal league of Israel.

It does appear that the people of Israel usually gathered themselves together around some particular sanctuary. They were certainly held together by a common covenant commitment to one God. However, in the early days of Israel's presence in Canaan, there do appear to have been several sanctuaries or shrines around which Israel gathered and at which they worshiped.

When Israel first entered the land with Joshua, Gilgal in the Jordan plain became a center of worship (Josh. 4:19-24). Following the battles for Jericho and Ai, there was a major gathering at Shechem for the purpose of worship. This also was the place to which all Israel gathered as Joshua neared the end of his life (Josh. 8:30-35; 24:1). Shortly after the first tribal gathering at Shechem, the tribes seem to have made Gilgal in the central highlands their base (Josh. 10:9,43). It is possible that this was not a center for worship but simply a base for military operations. However, it was back to this Gilgal that

Joshua went to divide the land into tribal allotments (Josh. 14:6). This whole process was clearly considered to be quite sacred, so it may strengthen the claim that Gilgal in the central highlands had become a worship center. It appears then, at this stage of Israel's settlement in the land, that there were several worship centers. It would also appear that it was not the shrine but the faith which held Israel together.

The Covenant Renewal. The final major act in the life and ministry of Joshua was the covenant renewal ceremony at Shechem (Josh. 24:1-28). This may have been nothing more than the last attempt of a dying leader to remind his people of their common commitment to the God who had led them. But it may also have been his attempt to bring others into the covenant community who had not been present at Sinai. If this were its purpose, then the emphasis upon the ordinances and statues takes on an added significance (Josh. 24:22-27). Even if everyone there were already worshipers of the God of Israel, they would not have known the demands of that faith set forth in the covenant. If, on the other hand, some of those present had their faith in pagan gods, then this would have been incorporating them into the fundamental commitment of Israel to God. The long recititation of what God had done for His people might have been more necessary for those who had not experienced it all than for those who had (Josh. 24:2-14). Either way, it was Joshua's last chance to affirm his personal faith before those who had followed him, saying, "As for me and my house, we will serve the Lord" (Josh. 24:15).

This final act of Joshua's ministry served as the seal upon all of his life. It clearly points up that in Israel there was no assumed separation between sacred and secular leadership. Joshua had been the military leader who had led the people forth to war. He had been the strategist who had masterminded the whole attack. But he was also the administrator who had organized the people for the later assimilation of the entire land. To both of these must be added the fact that he was Israel's spiritual leader as well. The conquest of the land would have been of no ultimate significance if the people had not also been united in their covenant commitment to God and to each other. It was a part of Joshua's genius that he had led the people in the accomplishment of all of these. Israel was now solidly in the land. The next issue was: Could they remain there? Perhaps even more fundamental, the people of Israel were now publicly commited to God. The real issue was whether they could maintain that commitment. The answer to the latter question was to seriously affect the answer to the former.

The Period of the Judges

With the death of Joshua, Israel entered a decidedly new era of history. The tribal confederation which Joshua had apparently established appears to have begun to come apart. It would seem that the tribes had been held together by the impact of a strong leader. When that leadership disappeared, each of the tribal groups appears to have become more concerned with its own interests than with the concerns of the entire land. While it is almost impossible to establish the chronology of many of the events of the period, the whole era seems to have lasted from about 1200 BC to about 1020 BC.

The Functions of a Judge. As we have already noted, the judges who functioned during this period did not at all act in the manner in which we normally assume a judge will act. They appear essentially to have been military leaders. Even when that was not the case, their major function was that of deliverer.

While this is quite true, most interpreters of this period and of this material generally separate the judges into the categories of major and minor judges. In general, the decision as to which way to classify a given judge depends upon the amount of material devoted to each within the Bible. While this appears to be an artificial separation, it may not be quite as artificial as it first seems. However, before we can make that assessment, we must separate them. Examine the following table.

The Judges

Passage	Major Judges	Minor Judges
Judges 3:7-11	Othniel	
Judges 3:15-30	Ehud	
Judges 3:31		Shamgar
Judges 4:4 to 5:31	Deborah	
Judges 6:11 to 8:32	Gideon	
Judges 10:1-2		Tola
Judges 10:3-5		Jair
Judges 11:1 to 12:7	Jephthah	
Judges 12:8-10		Ibzan
Judges 12:11-12		Elon
Judges 12:13-15		Abdon
Judges 13:2 to 16:31	Samson	
1 Samuel 2:27-34; 4:12-18	Eli	
1 Samuel 3:1 to 4:1a; 7:3 to 8:22	Samuel	

In considering the differences between the major and minor judges, let us first examine the minor judges. We are told almost nothing about these men except their heritage. This was always important in Israel. However, based on the size of the families given for Jair, Ibzan, and Abdon, they must have been men of some means. To have had as many children as are attributed to them would have demanded multiple wives. This clearly required significant economic resources. It has been suggested that the six minor judges actually functioned in the legal sense of judge. There is absolutely no basis for this suggestion. It is far more likely that they functioned as the major judges did. Clearly, with no more information than we are given about the minor judges, we cannot reconstruct the history of their judgeships with any accuracy.

Shamgar is said to have confronted the Philistines. This was probably at the time of their initial invasion of the coastal plain, shortly after 1200 BC. As regards the other minor judges, we are not even told from which enemies they delivered the people. Any conclusions as to their dates would be little more than educated guesses. We can do a bit better, however, as we seek to reconstruct the periods of activity of the major judges. This is possible because we have more detail concerning the oppressions which they faced.

The Major Oppressions. The Book of Judges, edited with a Deuteronomic outlook, presents the period of Israel's settlement in Canaan from a cyclical standpoint. Each cycle began with the apostasy of Israel as people turned away from God to the Baals of Canaan. "The people of Israel did what was evil in the sight of the Lord and served the Baals" (Judg. 2:11). This religious rebellion was then seen to be punished by the raising up of oppressors. "So the anger of the Lord was kindled against Israel, and he gave them over to plunderers, who plundered them" (Judg. 2:14).

Out of the midst of Israel's oppressions came the cries of the oppressed people. Those cries were neither described as pleas for mercy nor as cries of penitence. Rather, they were simply the groans of an oppressed and hurting people. But God is described as responding in pity to those groans, "for the Lord was moved to pity by their groaning because of those who afflicted and oppressed them" (Judg. 2:18). It was at those points in time that the Hebrews understood that "the Lord raised up judges, who saved them out of the power of those who plundered them" (Judg. 2:16). However, as soon as peace and prosperity returned, the people of Israel forsook God and turned back to the Baals (Judg. 2:17).

This continuing cycle of apostasy, oppression, and deliverance was repeated over and over again. Those ancient peoples recognized that prosperity frequently appears to bring a sense of security, self-sufficiency, pride, and sin. This has been amply illustrated in contemporary history.

Against the background of this understanding of spiritual cycles, we must attempt to reconstruct the history of the settlement of Israel into Canaan. I have already pointed out that it appears to be probable that each of the oppressions should be seen as involving a limited number of tribes and a limited region. It is not always possible to assign each oppression to a specific time, but I shall do the best that I can. Insofar as the minor judges and oppressions are concerned, we are given so little information as to make it virtually impossible to do any more than just guess at a possible chronological framework. Therefore, we shall confine our attention to the major judges and the oppressions with which they dealt.

Othniel and Cushan-rishathaim of Mesopotamia.—The identity of the Cushan-rishathaim is otherwise unknown, except for the reference in Judges (3:7-11). The name itself may even be a nickname, for it can be translated as "Cushan of the double wickedness," that is, he was twice as bad as anyone else around. Some historians have suggested that we have a scribal error here and that the oppressor came from Edom rather than from Mesopotamia. They make this suggestion due to the fact that Othniel obviously came from the southern hill country, being a nephew of Caleb. It is admitted that this would have been a typical kind of scribal error, for it merely requires that two similar letters have been interchanged. However, there is no evidence that this error occurred, for our oldest manuscripts still have the same text. Furthermore, there is evidence from Egyptian city lists that there was a region named Qusana in northern Mesopotamia, and ancient kings frequently bore names similar to the city from which they ruled.

It would appear, therefore, that shortly after Israel began to settle in Canaan, this Cushan must have led an army down the King's Highway on the edge of the Transjordan Plateau. Probably at about the same place where Joshua had earlier crossed the Jordan, Cushan marched down from the plateau, crossed the Jordan, and attacked the Hebrews in the central hill country. The period of conflict lasted for eight years until Othniel was able to drive Cushan out of the land. This eight-year oppression is probably to be dated about 1200 BC.

Ehud and the Moabites.—Prior to Israel's arrival in the Transjordan region under the leadership of Moses, the Moabites had lost their territory north of the Arnon River to an Amorite king by the name of Sihon (Num. 21:26). It was from Sihon that Israel took the land, ultimately allowing the people of Reuben to settle there (Num. 21:23-24; 32:33,37-38).

It appears that during the time of the Hebrew conquest the Moabites had recaptured part, if not all, of this territory. In addition, they had moved on across the Jordan and taken part of the Jordan plain around Gilgal. This would have been Benjaminite territory. Ehud, a left-handed deliverer, was able to assassinate Eglon the king of Moab because the king did not watch the Israelite's left hand (Judg. 3:21).

Ehud then gathered warriors from the nearby hill country of Ephraim and ambushed the fleeing Moabites as they sought to cross the Jordan (Judg. 3:27-28). This delivered the Israelite land west of the Jordan from Moabite control. Not a thing is mentioned about the Transjordan territory. It is possible that Moab maintained its hold on the Reubenite territory. This may even be the explanation for the virtual disappearance of the tribe of Reuben from subsequent Hebrew history.

This subjection of the Israelite territory in the plains of the Jordan is said to have lasted eighteen years. It is even possible that Cushan-rishathaim's deeper penetration into the central hill country from the west is to be connected to the Moabite invasion. They probably had formed a coalition. This would place the Moabite oppression as beginning about 1200 BC.

Deborah and the Canaanites.—The Canaanite oppression at the time of Deborah offers a number of problems and interesting sidelights. The most fascinating dimension of this period is the fact that Deborah is identified as both a prophetess and a judge (Judg. 4:4). This is especially unusual when we consider that this was in a time when women were little more than chattel. The very fact that she should have been functioning in two positions which the Hebrews considered to be God called is striking. The further fact that no particular attention is paid to this makes it even more so. Apparently, even at this early stage, the Hebrews had developed an awareness that God can and does call whomsoever He wishes.

This episode takes on even greater importance when it becomes obvious that Deborah was both braver and more faithful to God than her male counterpart, Barak. He was wholly unwilling to face the Canaanite enemies without the presence of Deborah (Judg. 4:8).

The nature of the Canaanite oppression offers some real problems to the historian. The primary enemy appears to be "Jabin king of Canaan, who reigned in Hazor"; but the battles were actually fought by "the commander of his army . . . Sisera, who dwelt in Harosheth-ha-goiim" (Judg. 4:2). We have already seen that there were many Canaanite kings, not just one. Each city-state had one. Perhaps it would be better to identify him as "a king of Canaan," or he may have simply been the only Canaanite king still left.

A more difficult problem is that Jabin is identified as reigning in Hazor. Joshua had already taken Hazor from Jabin, killing him (Josh. 11:1-13). It has been suggested that we have duplicate accounts of the same basic event. That hardly seems to be possible, for there are too many details of the two battles that do not at all match. It is also possible that the son of the Jabin Joshua killed had the same name as his father. That was a common practice in the ancient Near East. The more difficult problem is the fact that Hazor again appears to be in Canaanite hands following its destruction by Joshua. Occasionally, however, when a defeated king was driven from his capitol, he renamed whatever city where he established himself by the name of the former capitol. He also was still known as the king of the defeated territory. Either of these possibilities may offer an explanation for the difficulty.

Still another problem has to do with the home of Jabin's general, Sisera. Harosheth-ha-goiim can also be translated as Harosheth of the Gentiles. This coupled with the fact that he had nine hundred chariots of iron (Judg. 4:13) may indicate that he was a part of the Sea People who were settling all along the eastern Mediterranean. Sisera and his army were possibly mercenaries who had been employed by Jabin.

The prose account of the Israelite victory is followed by an ancient war song which commemorated it (Judg. 5:2-31). The geographical references indicate that the battle was fought in the Plain of Esdraelon, which reaches like a long finger into the heart of the northern highlands. The song reflects the fact that a great rainstorm caused the river Kishon in the valley to flood (Judg. 5:20-21). This would have totally incapacitated the Canaanite chariots, thus destroying Sisera's advantage of arms. Furthermore, this would also have incapacitated Sisera's army before the hordes of Israel. Sisera fled the battle scene, only to be betrayed and assassinated by another woman, "Jael, the wife of Heber the Kenite" (Judg. 5:24). This may be another indication of the inclusion of elements other than Hebrews among the people of Israel.

Many of the tribes were urged to participate in this battle (Judg. 5:14-18). The southern tribes of Simeon and Judah are not mentioned at all. Zebulun and Naphtali apparently bore the brunt of the battle (Judg. 5:18). It would appear from the roll call that this conflict was limited to the northern tribes and that even those participated in proportion to their nearness to the crisis.

The dating of this oppression is hinted at by the statement that:

> The kings came, they fought;
> then fought the kings of Canaan,
> at Taanach, by the waters of Megiddo (Judg. 5:19).

Archaeological excavations clearly demonstrate that Taanach was totally destroyed about 1125 BC. Since it was in existence as a fortress in the pass at Megiddo when this war was fought, we must date the war earlier. If this war was the time of its destruction, then this oppression of northwestern Palestine can be dated no later than from 1145 to 1125 BC. On the other hand, if the army of Sisera is in any way to be connected with the invasions of the Sea People, then this oppression can hardly be earlier than from about 1175 to 1155 BC. It appears to me to be more likely that the oppression ended with the destruction of Taanach in 1125 BC.

Gideon and the Midianites.—The next oppressor was the Midianites, apparently allied with some mercenaries from the Amalekites. This oppression was apparently not an invasion but a series of annual raids made for the purpose of seizing plunder (Judg. 6:1-6). The camel had just been domesticated, and this allowed the Midianites to move more rapidly than the Israelites, as well as to go further into the Arabian desert. The very appearance of such beasts would most likely have terrorized the Israelites.

The tribes related to this oppression make it appear that the territory involved was the central and northcentral regions of the country. This would make good sense when coupled with the fact that the Midianites were desert nomads and would have invaded from the Transjordan region.

Gideon, a member of the tribe of Manasseh, was selected to be the deliverer. From a human standpoint, he was a strange choice for such a leader. He appears to have been quite a coward, hiding in a wine pit to try to thresh out his wheat (Judg. 6:11). Such a job was normally done on a hilltop where the wind could separate the chaff from the grain. Gideon also tried to avoid leading his people by the double episode of the fleece, posing impossible conditions.

The strategy which was used to drive the Midianites from the land was one of terror. The sudden flashing of the lights and the sounding of the trumpets in the dark of the night struck fear to the hearts of the oppressors. Such flashing light was utterly unexpected. Further, a trumpet was normally blown to control each fighting unit. Three hundred trumpets would have convinced the Midianites that they were hopelessly outnumbered. The entire event made them flee from the land in terror.

There appears to be nothing in the story of Gideon to help us establish an approximate date for the oppression and deliverance. On the other hand, we may get some help by what follows. After Gideon's amazing victory, there was an attempt on the part of his people to make him a king with a hereditary succession (Judg. 8:22-23).

This he rejected. However, upon Gideon's death, his son Abimelech killed his brothers and claimed the kingship (Judg. 9:1-5).

Abimelech was crowned king by the people of Shechem and ruled over them three years (Judg. 9:6,22). However, the people of Shechem rebelled against Abimelech. In the conflict which followed, the city of Shechem was destroyed (Judg. 9:34-45). In the subsequent conflict, Abimelech himself was killed, ending this abortive attempt at Hebrew kingship (Judg. 9:50-55).

Archaeological excavations indicate that Shechem was destroyed, never to be rebuilt, about 1100 BC. If Gideon had presided over forty years of peace (Judg. 8:28), then the end of the Midianite oppression must be placed about 1143 BC. If, however, that period is to be understood as a round number referring to a generation, then the Midianite oppression would have ended about 1128 to 1130 BC. It would have begun some seven years earlier (Judg. 6:1).

Jephthah and the Ammonites.—Following the period of two other minor judges, Tola and Jair, there was an eighteen-year period of oppression brought about by the joint efforts of the Ammonites and the Philistines. This is a strange combination, for Ammon is east of Palestine and the Philistines were settled in the coastal plain on the west. A thorough reading of the episode brings to light that the major focus is upon Ammon while the Philistines appear to play only a very minor part. It would appear, therefore, that there was no coalition between the two peoples. Rather, it seems more likely that the Philistines were putting pressure on the western part of the central hill country at the same time that the Ammonites were doing the same on the eastern side.

Archaeological surface explorations and excavations make it appear that the Ammonites established themselves as a significant kingdom later than did the Edomites and the Moabites. This probably explains why Moses chose the Ammonites' region through which to make Israel's initial approach to Canaan. It seems that the Ammonites made a significant effort to establish their kingdom about 1100 BC. It may be at this time that they made their invasion from the Transjordan Plateau across the Jordan and into the central hill country. The Philistines were at the same time beginning to expand their foothold from the coastal plain into the Shephelah from the opposite direction. This made the people of Israel in that region feel the effect of a pincer movement upon them.

At this time, the people of the region turned to a man named Jephthah. This man, the son of a harlot, had been driven from his home by the self-righteous indignation of his people (Judg. 11:1-2,5-6). He had apparently gathered around himself other malcontents and had been leading a kind of Robin Hood existence. But the man who had not been good enough to live among his people in a time of peace was precisely the one to whom the people turned when things went wrong. That is quite an insight into human nature.

Jethro

Jephthah's victory over the Ammonites is generally remembered because of the vow he made to offer as a burnt offering the first living thing he saw upon his return home from the battle. Tragically, this happened to be his daughter (Judg. 11:30,34-35). While there is no way to condone Jephthah's sacrifice of his daughter, the event is a significant commentary upon the seriousness with which those ancients took a vow made to God.

Following Jephthah's victory, the people of the tribe of Ephraim expressed anger at having been left out of his battle, thus having no share in the victory spoils (Judg. 12:1). This resulted in a brief but bitter conflict between Jephthah and the Ephraimites (Judg. 12:4). A fascinating sidelight of this conflict is the dialectical difficulty the Ephraimites had in pronouncing "Shibboleth" (Judg. 12:5-6). There are numerous places in the Old Testament where it appears that one region or tribe of the country had a dialect which differed from others. This gives us a concrete example of that fact.

It is impossible to give anything more than an approximate date for the oppression by the Ammonites. It almost certainly was no earlier than 1100 BC and may have been

ISRAEL'S LAND

somewhat later than this. Jephthah's leadership drove the Ammonites back onto the Transjordan Plateau, but it apparently made no headway in pushing the Philistines back on the other side.

Samson and the Philistines.—It is quite likely that at the time Jephthah was attacking the Ammonites on the east, Samson was involved with the Philistines on the west. The Philistines were a very successful and warlike people. Part of their success can be attributed to their skill at war. But another part of their success was due to the fact that they had developed the ability to manufacture iron (Judg. 4:3; 1 Sam. 13:19-20). Their superiority in weapons gave them a significant advantage in any face-to-face conflict. Copper and bronze weapons just were not able to stand up to iron swords and spears.

Samson is significantly different from the other major judges. He never seems to have led an army but simply was a thorn-in-the-flesh to the Philistines due to his exceptional strength. He is portrayed throughout the Book of Judges as an earthy, headstrong young man whose only thought was to satisfy personal immediate urges. He was his own worst enemy, and his lust proved his ultimate downfall. Every major crisis in Samson's life involved his dalliance with a Philistine woman (Judg. 14:1-3; 15:1-2; 16:1-3,6-21). In his life, he killed numerous Philistines and was a constant problem to them. His death was apparently no different.

Samson's great gifts, however, ultimately were wasted. At his death, the Philistine threat to Israel was still real. The Philistines were still situated in the Shephelah and were still exerting pressure upon the central hill country.

In trying to date Samson's activities, we come face-to-face with another problem. Samson was a member of the tribe of Dan. The Danites had originally been assigned territory along the coast (Josh. 19:40-48). However, this is precisely where the Philistines settled, and the Philistines' pressure prevented the Danites from seizing their allotment. Thus, they set out to find a new territory (Judg. 18:1). They eventually moved to the northern borders of Canaan, seizing land there (Judg. 18:27-29). It appears that this occurred about 1150 BC, when the Philistines seized the coastland. But if Samson's judgeship is at all to be related with that of Jephthah, it should be after 1100 BC. There are two possible solutions to this problem. The first is that the two judgeships had no correlation in time. If this were true, then Samson must be dated prior to 1150 BC. On the other hand, it is also possible that not all of the people of Dan migrated when the main part of the tribe moved northward. At the present state of our knowledge, it is impossible to make either of these options look more probable than the other. It appears to me that it is slightly more likely that Samson and Jephthah are to be seen as living at approximately the same time and that, therefore, Samson's own family had remained behind when the main body of the tribe had moved northward.

Samuel: The End of an Era.—It is not often that a person gets to live through the transition between as many different dimensions of history as Samuel did and to have an influence upon those transitions. Samuel was the last of the judges. With him, that kind of charismatic leadership passed away and the Hebrew kingship began. But Samuel was also the person who brought about a major transition in the nature of the Hebrew prophetic movement, giving it that unique characteristic which no other ancient Near Eastern people ever developed but Israel. Samuel was also privileged to shape the formation of a nation. The kingship was established by Samuel, thus the Hebrew nation was never the same after him. He began to bind together the loosely organized tribes into a nation with a self-identity based upon a common faith.

Three major historical factors shaped Samuel's life. Historians sometimes debate whether the times make a man great or whether a great man makes his times great. With Samuel, the debate is needless. He was a great man who stepped upon the stage of history at a great time. In him, the times and the man came together.

The first of the factors which had such a significant part to play in Samuel's life was the Philistines. We have already seen the Philistine military genius and their arms superiority. They steadily exerted such pressure upon Israel as to make continued coexistence untenable. The Philistine pressure was on the verge of destroying Israel.

The second factor in shaping Samuel was the conditions which had arisen in the shrine at Shiloh under the old priest, Eli. After the destruction of Shechem by Abimelech (Judg. 9:34-45), Shiloh had apparently become the major worship center of premonarchical Israel. Eli, who was priest at Shiloh, had allowed his sons to become religious apostates—so much so that they were the talk of all Israel (1 Sam. 2:22-25). The situation which they had brought about at Shiloh was so bad that when Eli saw Hannah (Samuel's mother) praying, it never entered his mind that she was praying. He assumed that she was drunk (1 Sam. 1:13). Because of the influence from Shiloh, the whole spiritual nature of Israel had become quite decadent. We are told that "the word of the Lord was rare in those days; there was no frequent vision" (1 Sam. 3:1).

The third factor in shaping Samuel's life was his boyhood. He was aware that he was a special child to his parents. He also had been apprenticed to Eli to serve as an attendant (1 Sam. 1:27-28; 3:1-3). These two things touched a chord in Samuel, making him an extremely sensitive person in matters of religion. Coupled with this was Samuel's special sense of being appointed to a God-called ministry (1 Sam. 3:10-11). As he grew, Samuel matured and gained a reputation as God's prophet in Israel (1 Sam. 3:19-20).

Each of these factors played its part in the life and ministry of Samuel. When he arrived at manhood, Samuel's people were facing a new time of desperation before the onslaught of the Philistines (1 Sam. 4:2). Facing an utter rout, they determined to bring the ark of God to the battle (1 Sam. 4:3). In the ancient Near East, armies frequently brought the symbols or idols of their gods to battle, believing that this would guarantee that their gods would fight for them. By taking the ark, the Hebrews appear to have been succumbing to this idea. They were trying to manipulate God or to win by means of magic. The end result of this foolish enterprise was the capture of the ark and the death of Eli and Eli's sons (1 Sam. 4:11,16-18). It is clear that although Eli was a priest he was also in the line of the judges, for we are told "he had judged Israel forty years" (1 Sam. 4:18).

Following their capture of the ark, the Philistines brought it into Ashdod (1 Sam. 5:1). There was an outbreak of plague among the Philistines which they blamed upon the God of Israel. The ark was moved from Ashdod to Gath and from Gath to Ekron, seeking to avoid the plague (1 Sam. 5:5-10). Finally, in desperation, the ark was sent back to Israel along with an offering of "five golden tumors and five golden mice" (1 Sam. 6:4-5). The number was determined by the fact that there were five rulers from the five major Philistine city-states. The offerings were symbolic of the nature of the plague which they were undergoing. This plague of mice and tumors may indicate that there was an outbreak of bubonic plague in their midst.

When the ark was returned to Israel, Samuel called the people to a great convocation at Mizpah where there was apparently a covenant renewal celebration (1 Sam. 7:5-6). The Philistines attempted an ambush but were routed by a major storm, apparently in the same manner as the storm which routed Sisera before Deborah and Barak, for the "Lord thundered" against them (1 Sam. 7:10-11).

The experience with the plagues followed by the storm's destruction left the Philistines subdued for a while, but only for a while. As Samuel grew old, the people became aware that he had had no more success as a father than had Eli. Samuel's sons also became apostates. He himself had been a great leader, but he had failed as a father (1 Sam. 7:15 to 8:3). Facing the possibility of ultimate defeat before the Philistines after Samuel passed from the scene, the elders of Israel came asking for a king so that they could be "like all the nations" (1 Sam. 8:5). They believed that they needed more than charismatic leadership. They also believed that they needed more than a mere volunteer army whenever danger threatened.

With this cry, Israel's period of settlement in Canaan came to an end. They were in the land; but if they were going to remain there, something more had to happen than had happened in the past. The period of charismatic judges had ended. The period of the monarchy was about to begin.

In trying to establish a date for Samuel's ministry, we have two or three hints to help us. It obviously has to be at a time when the Philistines were at the height of their powers. It also has to be just before the rise of the Hebrew monarchy. As we shall note in the following chapter, Saul was apparently crowned king about 1020 BC. Such archaeological evidence as there is would indicate that the greatest pressure from the Philistines is probably to be dated as beginning about 1050 BC. This would establish Samuel's ministry as being from about 1050 BC to 1020 BC. This fits in well with the biblical narrative. It also gives us the final data for determining the overall period of the judges, which apparently extended from about 1200 to about 1020 BC.

The Significance of the Period

The history of the period between Moses' death and the beginning of Saul's kingship, as we have seen, was both quite eventful and quite involved. For Israel's developing faith, it was quite significant. In many ways, this period of conquest and settlement was one of the more formative of the entire Old Testament era.

A Time of Transition

Some of the more significant features of this era were all the transitions which Israel made. Like the first tottering steps of a child, a new world opened for Israel as a result of this period.

It was a time of transition from tribalism to nationhood.

It was a time of transition from a commitment to the divine kingship to the awareness of a need for a human king.

It was a time of transition from being freed slaves and wandering shepherds to being settled agriculturalists, beginning to become involved in business and trade.

It was a time of transition from the crushing awareness

of being a victim to the almost intoxicating feeling of being a victor, from being conquered to being a conqueror.

Now it is obvious that any period of history is a time of transition. For Israel, however, this period was a time of great transition. More significant changes took place in less time here than in any other era of Israel's pilgrimage of faith and history.

The Land as God's Gift

Throughout all the rest of Israel's history, one feature of this period was never forgotten: The land was God's special gift to Israel. Old Testament theologians often talk about the fact that Israel developed a land theology. This is quite true. They always felt a particular and peculiar relationship to the land because it had been God's gift to them.

This idea is still present and serves as the focus of much of the modern Arab-Israeli controversy. Like no other people on the face of the earth, Israel's ties with the land are a part of their heritage. This fact was seldom comprehended by anyone outside of Israel's own nation.

When King Ahab of Israel wanted the land which belonged to one of his peasants, Naboth, it was unavailable. He could not buy it or trade for it, and he apparently would not steal it (1 Kings 21:1-4). His queen, Jezebel, who had come from Phoenicia, could not understand this. In her land, no one had such ties to the land, and no king failed to take what he wanted, one way or another. So she did what Ahab would not have done. She stole the land by having Naboth murdered (1 Kings 21:8-10).

The same thing happened when the Assyrians laid siege to Jerusalem in 701 BC. The commander in chief of the Assyrian army just about had the starving Hebrews ready to surrender when he offered them abundant food and water (Isa. 36:16). But the foolish general destroyed the mood of the people when he announced that he was going to carry them away captive (Isa. 36:17). He just did not comprehend Israel's ties to the land.

This also offers an explanation for the Hebrews' desire

to be freed from the Babylonian Exile and allowed to return to the land. The land was God's gift to them. As such it was a trust and a stewardship, and they had to hold on to it. This tie to the land had its roots in the period of conquest and settlement. God had given it to them, and they were united with it in a unique way.

The Concept of "Called" Leaders

Another dimension of Israel's faith which underwent a major development in this period was the Hebrews' sense of God-called leaders. This sense that God gave certain "gifts" to men and women and then used those gifts in accomplishing His purposes for His people was always a major part of Israel's faith.

Theologians call such people charismatic leaders, for they have been specially prepared, according to the faith of the Bible, to meet the historical needs which God's people faced at any moment. The judges were especially seen to be of this nature and this served as the basis for Israel's future understanding of such people.

Admittedly, the Old Testament people were quite aware that God had "called" such people as Abraham and Moses. But there was no other period in Israel's history when there were so many "called" leaders on the scene as there were in this one.

Throughout the rest of Israel's history, whenever things got especially difficult, they looked for the one whom God had prepared to step into the position of leadership. Even throughout the period of the monarchy, there is abundant evidence that kings did not just step into the kingship because they were the eldest son of the king. The people expected such kings to show evidence that they had been especially "gifted" by God to meet the needs of the moment.

This has clearly made an impact upon subsequent Hebrew and Christian history. This sense that God prepares His leaders in advance to meet the historical crises of their present has been deeply rooted in the faith of the Judeo-Christian tradition.

The Cyclical View of History

Nowhere else in the Bible is the cyclical view of history as firmly rooted as it is in the period of Israel's settlement in Canaan. This, too, had a major impact upon all the rest of Israel's history and faith. They always saw temporal historical crises as being used by God to punish them for their apostasy. They also saw deliverance from such crises as being evidence of God's pity and mercy.

At the same time, even in this period, Israel never lost their sense that God was in control of history and that it was en route to a goal. Viewed in the short run, they saw it as cyclical. Viewed in the long run, they saw it as ever-moving toward God's ultimate purposes.

By their own sin, the people of Israel could thwart the immediate purposes of God, so they understood. This was a part of their freedom. But they always believed that humans could never ultimately thwart God's purposes. When one group sinned, God punished them and then raised up a new leader to accomplish His ultimate purposes.

It would be hard to believe at any single point in the history of this era that Israel would ever have gotten and maintained control of Palestine. But they did. They never saw this as the result of their own activity or intelligence, but it was seen simply as God's ultimate fulfillment of His purposes. To Israel, history might roll like a wheel, but it ultimately got where God wanted it.

The Need for Human Government

Out of this period of Israel's development came the conviction of the need for human government. They had become aware that, without some form of organization with a matching authority, the end result for them always appeared to be chaos. In spite of their commitment to the idea that God prepared and called His leaders, they found that even then such leaders often lacked the authority to accomplish all which they set out to do. Further, with the increasing pressures from outside, they found that their lack of organization was a severe handicap.

Now, as we shall see in the next chapter, some people in Israel also saw this need for a king as a lack of ultimate trust in God, yet they still felt its great need. I am not discussing here what was right or wrong but what they believed: Without a human government established and on the scene, they were helpless before their enemies.

Israel, after having gone through the chaotic period of the judges, basically believed that they needed some continuity in their leadership. The accomplishments of the judges were lost between the judges. Israel was seeking for a way to maintain what had been accomplished.

God's Sovereignty

Perhaps the most significant theological feature of this period for Israel was the undergirding of their absolute belief in God's sovereignty over both natural and historical forces. They believed that, even without the knowledge of foreign nations, God could use them to accomplish His purposes. He could also use natural forces, such as storms and floods, to do the same thing.

To Israel, God was in control. In no other nation of the ancient Near East was there ever a belief that the gods were in control when they suffered defeat. To those nations, a defeat meant that their gods were weaker than the gods of the nations with whom they warred. This was not so in Israel. They developed the idea in this period of their history that defeat for them was not a defeat for God. In fact, they became aware that a defeat for Israel might mean a victory for God's will and purposes.

This may be the most theologically significant aspect of the Hebrew faith which sprang from this era. From this root grew the idea of an "Exile theology" which allowed Israel to understand what happened to them in Assyria and in Babylon. If they had not had such a foundation, it is doubtful that their nation could have withstood such catastrophes.

Even more than this, out of this idea ultimately grew the belief in redemptive suffering. This concept was one of the most profound which Israel ever developed. It also served as the basis for the Christian understanding of the whole meaning of the crucifixion. The concept of the Suffering Servant of God, dying to redeem all people had its initial seed, at least in part, in the period of the settlement and conquest.

5
The Hebrew Kingdom: Union and Division

The period of the Hebrew settlement in Canaan left many marks upon Israel's subsequent history. Perhaps the most indelible was the growing awareness that, as things were, they would not long be able to maintain their hold upon the land. This was not a theological issue for Israel. Rather, it was a practical one. The growing external pressure from the Philistines coupled with the obvious divisions within the tribal confederation indicated the need for some kind of stronger government.

This awareness gave rise to Israel's plea for a "king to govern us like all the nations" (1 Sam. 8:5). Now it is quite obvious that such a plea had significant theological ramifications. But it also had major historical dimensions. It is impossible to say what Israel's history might have been if they had not developed into a monarchy. There is just no way of knowing. The fact is that they did develop a monarchy, and this shaped the subsequent path of their history. It is to these early days when the monarchy was developing that we must now direct our attention.

Sources for the Study

As is usually the case with each era of Hebrew history, a number of sources can add depth to our understanding of the history of this period; but by far, the most significant is the biblical material. We are essentially concerned here with the period which extends from the crowning of Saul through the death of Solomon. The biblical material dealing with this epoch and with the kings who reigned in it is identified in the following table.

The United Monarchy

King	Biblical Sources
Saul	1 Samuel 8:4 to 31:13; 1 Chronicles 10:1-14
David	2 Samuel 1:1 to 1 Kings 2:11; 1 Chronicles 3:1-9; 11:1 to 29:30
Solomon	1 Kings 2:12 to 11:43; 2 Chronicles 1:1 to 9:31

However, in addition to the biblical sources, several other ancient written sources add to our knowledge of the period. There are the Egyptian records and the ancient monuments upon which the pharaohs recorded some of their more significant achievements. To these, we must also add the Assyrian king lists. While these do not add a great deal of detail at this period, they at least offer such information as to make it possible to develop correlations with Egypt. This also adds some degree of understanding as to what was going on the in the geographical region between these two powers. We also have eponym lists from Assyria which record the major officials or events in each year of the Assyrian kings' reigns during this period. Further, we have some Babylonian king lists from this same era. These and the Assyrian lists are correlated with one another. While these ancient lists from Mesopotamia do not add great detail to our knowledge of Israel's history in the period, they do give a number of insights into what was going on in the ancient world into which the kingdom of Israel was born.

Archaeological excavations from Palestinian sites which cover this period of Palestinian history also add a great deal of detail to our knowledge. This is especially true of the time of Solomon since he was involved in so many building programs (see 2 Chron. 8:1-6). However, it is true of David and Saul as well.

It appears that we have actually uncovered the fortress which was built by Saul at Gibeah (see 1 Sam. 10:26; 11:4; 15:34). This was apparently destroyed when Saul was defeated at Gilboa and was reconstructed shortly thereafter in David's reign.

From David's reign, we may have recovered the water

shaft in the Jebusite city of Jerusalem up which Joab led his men to attack the city (2 Sam. 5:8). We have also apparently recovered the Millo terraces which David had constructed to strengthen the city (2 Sam. 5:9). Obviously, since Jerusalem is still a living city, only limited archaeological excavations can be done there.

This fact clearly limits any work which might be done to help us identify Solomonic construction in Jerusalem. However, this kind of limitation is not true of many other sites in Palestine. We have been able to discover from at least six scattered sites, as well as from a partial excavation of one spot in Jerusalem, that Solomon developed a new method of fortification in Israel. His fortress walls consisted of thick outer walls with a thinner inner wall some distance from it. The space between was filled with stone and rubble, making a very strong defensive position. Excavations also reveal that Solomon developed a technique of making the approaches to the gates of a city come at an angle so that attackers would be exposed for a significantly longer period to the defenders upon the walls. Solomon also characteristically strengthened or modernized the defensive water works of his fortresses so that defenders would have ample water supplies.

Furthermore, Solomon was famous for his sea trade (1 Kings 9:26; 2 Chron. 8:17-18). While no actual ships from this period have been unearthed, excavations near the modern Elath have shown a small fortress dating from this period with extensive storage houses adequate for warehousing commercial goods before they were shipped.

Thus the written records and the archaeological excavations have added significantly to our knowledge of the period of the united monarchy. Perhaps the greatest building achievement of the period was Solomon's Temple at Jerusalem. Although it was totally destroyed long before the time of Jesus, numerous modern attempts have been made to build models or make drawings of it. In general, these are based upon a study of the biblical descriptions and what we know of similar constructions from Solomon's time. We must always be aware that even the best of these reconstruction attempts is still the product of a significant amount of guesswork.

Major Problems for Consideration

As has been the case in dealing with other periods of Israel's history, there are several major problems with which the historian must deal before actually seeking to reconstruct the history of this era. In dealing with materials from such a great temporal and cultural difference, there are inevitably issues which are confusing. However, if we ignore these issues, our attempts at understanding this period of history are likely to go astray.

The Nature of the Biblical Sources

As I have already indicated, the basic biblical sources for this period are the Books of 1 and 2 Samuel, 1 Kings, and 1 and 2 Chronicles. The Books of 1 and 2 Chronicles appear to be a retelling of the material in Samuel and Kings with some differences. The question arises as to why we have such.

Students of the Old Testament generally agree that the Books of Samuel and Kings were originally one long work. It obviously could not have been completed until the end of the Hebrew monarchy, following the defeat of Judah by Babylon, since the history goes that far. Without going into all of the technical details of why and how this material was divided into four separate books, the basic reason was apparently twofold. In ancient times, books were written on scrolls rather than in bound volumes. The sheer limitation of size would have made it necessary to divide this work into separate books. It would have been impossible to handle one long scroll with all of this material upon it. Furthermore, in order to make it easier to refer to specific passages within such a book, even shorter scrolls would have been preferred.

Aside from such mundane matters, the material in the Books of Samuel and Kings has a peculiar outlook on the history of the Hebrew people. Scholars usually refer to this material as the Deuteronomic history work, or the Deuteronomic history. The reason for this identification rests in the fact that religious and theological evaluations of the acts of the kings and of the nation in the Books of Samuel and Kings appear to be based primarily upon the Book of Deuteronomy. Furthermore, these books are in that part of the Hebrew canon known as the Prophets. They are in the first part of that division and are usually identified as a part of the "the Former Prophets." As such a division might suggest, the prophets play a very important part in the history recorded by these books. The books, therefore, also have a decidedly prophetic outlook upon Hebrew history.

On the other hand, the Books of Chronicles are a wholly different matter. There are at least four major differences between them and the others. First, they begin their history by going all the way back to Adam (1 Chron. 1:1). Second, the chronicler, after the division of the kingdom at Solomon's death, follows only the history of Judah, the Southern Kingdom, rather than dealing with both Israel and Judah as Kings does. Third, the Books of Chronicles are found in the third and last section of the Hebrew canon, The Writings. Fourth, the author(s) seems to approach the history of the Hebrew nation from the standpoint of the Levitical priesthood. Now this does not mean that they created their history. But it does mean that the chronicler's interpretation of some events and interest in other events appear to be shaped by these interests. Thus the historian must keep these differences firmly in mind in dealing with these materials.

However, the problem of perspective is not the only issue involving the biblical sources which the historian must consider. There is another major issue which must be confronted. This is the nature of the material in the Samuel-Kings corpus itself. This problem first becomes obvious in the Books of Samuel where it appears that there are a significant number of duplicate accounts of events. Consider the following.

The sudden end of the house of Eli was announced twice (1 Sam. 2:31-36; 3:11-14).

Saul was annointed king privately and twice publicly (1 Sam. 9:27 to 10:1; 10:17-24; 11:15).

Saul was twice deposed from the throne but continued to rule until he died (1 Sam. 13:14; 15:26-29).

David was twice introduced to Saul (1 Sam. 16:14-23; 17:55-58).

David was three times offered a daughter of Saul in marriage (1 Sam. 18:17-19,20-21,22-26).

David twice escaped from Saul's court (1 Sam. 19:12; 20:42).

Saul was quickly aware of David's first flight, yet he later wondered why David was not present at dinner (1 Sam. 19:17; 20:25-29).

David twice had Saul in his power and spared his life (1 Sam. 24:3-7; 26:5-12).

David three times made a covenant with Jonathan (1 Sam. 18:3; 20:12-42; 23:18).

David twice sought refuge from Achish, king of Gath (1 Sam. 21:10-15; 27:3).

Goliath was slain by David and by Elhanan, one of David's heroes (1 Sam. 17:23,41-50; 21:9; 2 Sam. 21:19). This was later corrected by the chronicler (1 Chron. 20:5).

There are two accounts of the origin of the proverb, "Is Saul also among the prophets?" (1 Sam. 10:11; 19:24).

The treason of the Ziphites is twice recorded (1 Sam. 23:19-20; 26:1).

There also appears to be a question as to whether Absalom had sons (2 Sam. 14:27; 18:18).

There also appear to be two accounts of the circumstances surrounding Saul's death (1 Sam. 31:3-4; 2 Sam. 1:6-10).

Now it is quite obvious that, given the vagaries of life and the strange things which happen, there is not any one of these which might not be satisfactorily explained. However, the large number of these must make the historian question whether some of them are not duplicate accounts of the same event. If this is true, how can we explain it from a historical standpoint?

We must remember that, following the death of Solomon, the kingdom divided into two parts, Israel and Judah (1 Kings 12:16-20). When that happened, the two nations became enemies of one another. However, we know for a fact that they each preserved their own history, for this is clearly interwoven through the Books of Kings. It is at least possible, if not probable, that the traditions of the united kingdom under Saul, David, and Solomon were also preserved in each of the two kingdoms.

However, when the Northern Kingdom of Israel fell to the Assyrians in 722 BC, it came to an end as an independent entity. There is abundant evidence that, at that time, refugees from the north fled south to Judah, bringing with them both their oral and written records. From that time until the fall of Judah to Babylon in 587 BC, only one kingdom was preserving records and traditions. It is clearly obvious that the southern prophetic historians interwove the history of the two kingdoms dealing with the time they were separate. It is quite probable that they also interwove the traditions which each of the two kingdoms had preserved of the nation's earlier period of union.

This might raise the question as to why the same sort of things did not happen with the Levitical history of Chronicles. The answer may rest in the difference between the prophets and the priests. There were prophets of God in both kingdoms, and there was not any question as to whether at least some of them were rightly related to God. Thus the traditions which both groups preserved would have been believed to be valid and authentic. However, the same cannot be said of the priests. The priests who functioned in the Northern Kingdom served the golden calves at Dan and Bethel. They were never considered by the Jerusalem priests (the only ones who survived the double catastrophe) to have been loyal to the God of Israel. Any traditions which the northern priests preserved would not have been considered to be authentic.

Thus it appears that we have the double tradition of the kingdom preserved by the prophetic school, while we only have a single tradition preserved by the priestly school. If this is so, it leaves us not only with the witness of the prophets and the priests to add understanding to each other but also with the double tradition of the prophets to authenticate the history.

Admittedly, this is only a theory, a human attempt to explain known facts. For a more detailed study of the issue, I would refer you to any of the good biblical commentaries on 1 Samuel which seek to grapple with the problem. It is a complex question and demands the best of our thinking and studying to deal with it. The dual tradition of Kings and Chronicles is an obvious fact. The dual tradition of Israelite and Judean history in Kings is also an obvious fact. It appears that in these we may have the key to explain an apparent dual tradition as it relates to the united monarchy.

The Chronology

In trying to establish the chronology of the period of the united monarchy, we run into two basic problems. The first of these problems is the attempt to establish the relative chronology of each of the kingdoms involved (Egypt, Assyria, Israel, and others), while the second relates to the identification of the absolute chronology of the period (exactly when any specific event occured).

Within the Old Testament itself, there is no information from this era which can be specifically tied in with any other event outside of the Old Testament. We have noted that the excavations at Saul's capitol of Gibeah indicate the building of a crude fortress, presumably by Saul. It was subsequently destroyed, probably by the Philistines at the time of Saul's death. After that, it was rebuilt, possibly by David. This gives us a general synchronization but gives us no specific dates at all.

The only way by which we can establish a chronology of the period is by working backward from the time of the divided kingdoms to the time of the division. While scholars disagree slightly as to the precise date for the division, it is usually dated from 931 to 922 BC. For the moment, I shall use 931 BC as the date. (I will explain why in the next chapter.) Working from the direction of the Exodus, the conquest, and the settlement, it would appear that the beginning of the united monarchy should be placed about 1020 BC. This may vary by a factor of ten to fifteen years either way. We just cannot be more precise, given the present state of our knowledge. Basically, however, we shall assume that the period of the united monarchy extended from about 1020 BC to about 931 BC. Into this period, we must fit the reigns of Saul, David, and Solomon, if possible.

We immediately run into a problem with the reign of Saul. "Saul was . . . years old when he began to reign; and he reigned . . . and two years over Israel" (1 Sam. 13:1). It is obvious from the Hebrew that this traditional formula for the introduction of the reign of a king has some gaps left in it. Somewhere along the way, Saul's age and part of the number making up the length of his reign have been lost. (The very fact that the ancient scribes did not try to correct this obvious omission is an indication of just how carefully they sought to preserve the manuscripts passed on to them. It would have been quite easy to have inserted numbers here to make sense.) The sermon in Acts which attributed forty years of reign to Saul seems to have been a round number used as an approximation (Acts 13:21). The actual number would appear to have been "ten and two," "twenty and two," or some such number ending in "and two."

We run into a different problem at the other end of the period with the reign of Solomon. There we are told that Solomon reigned in Jerusalem for forty years (1 Kings 11:42; 2 Chron. 9:30). The question immediately arises as to whether this is to be understood as an actual figure, a large round number, or a generation. Any one of these can be easily defended as a common usage within the Old Testament. Depending upon the solution chosen, Solomon's reign would have begun anywhere from about 971 BC to about 956 BC.

David's reign is a different matter. He, too, is said to have reigned for forty years. However, this is said to be the sum of seven (or seven-and-a-half) years in Hebron and thirty-three years in Jerusalem (2 Sam. 2:11; 5:4-5; 1 Kings 2:11; 1 Chron. 29:27). Since this forty-year period is the sum of two very uneven numbers, there appears to be no reason at all to question it.

Now, if we accept the maximum years for Solomon (forty) and add this to the forty years for David, we have Solomon reigning from 971 to 931 BC and David reigning from about 1011 to about 971 BC. This would make Saul's reign most likely to have been from about 1023 to 1011 BC (ten and two, or twelve years). If we reduce Solomon's reign, then Saul's reign can be easily lengthened by another ten years to twenty-two years.

Given the present state of our knowledge, there is just no way to be more precise with these figures. However, it is clear that the chronological data do fit quite well into the period which we have.

The Nature of the Kingship

In dealing with the period in which Israel's monarchy arose, we must confront the nature of Israel's kingship. Here, we must be quite careful not to bring to the subject a view of kingship shaped by subsequent European history, for kingship in Israel was not exactly parallel to that in Europe. First, kingship among the Hebrews was always viewed as a mixed blessing. The biblical text makes it quite clear that kingship was generally evaluated from two very different standpoints. There was a significant belief that kingship was totally bad, for it represented a rejection of the kingship of God (1 Sam. 8:7). Furthermore, it was also seen as bad since the people surrendered a large degree of freedom (1 Sam. 8:11-18). On the other hand, there was also a strong feeling that kingship was absolutely necessary if Israel were going to survive the military threats with which they were faced (1 Sam. 8:19-22). This same sort of mixed reaction is also seen later in the messages of the prophets (see Hos. 8:4; 10:3; 13:10-11). While apparently condemning the failures and problems of kingship, the prophets also took the image of kingship and transformed it into their hope for a future King who would reign over Israel permanently (see Isa. 9:6-7; 11:1-9; 32:1-2). So kingship was seen as both good and bad.

Furthermore, kingship was not viewed by Israel as being automatically hereditary. Upon the death of Saul, the people clearly felt that they had the right to decide who would succeed him to reign over them (2 Sam. 2:10-11; 5:1-3). At the death of David, a similar thing happened with two of his sons contending as to which would become king. The younger son, Solomon, was clearly selected over the older son, Adonijah (1 Kings 1:5-6,32-34). When Solomon died, the people of the land obviously believed that they had the right to choose their king (1 Kings 12:1-4,16-17,20).

There are at least two features which stand out from all of this. The first is that the people obviously believed that they had the right to have a voice in who reigned over them. But there is also the clear implication that God also had a voice in who was to be king by the giving of special gifts or skills to the future king. Even though Israel had left the period of the judges behind, in the kingship as they observed it they were still being given charismatic leaders. Even before the people of Israel decided that they wanted Jeroboam to reign over them, the prophet Ahijah speaking for God had designated him as the future king (1 Kings 11:29-31). It was in this concept of succession that kingship in Israel differed from that of the surrounding nations. It was just not seen as automatic.

There was another factor in Israel's view of kingship which must also be considered. The king was not really seen as an absolute monarch. In fact, Saul is identified as a "king" (1 Sam. 10:1-2; here the term is translated as "prince"). At the very best, the king was seen in that time more as an exalted equal than as one who reigned because of his inherent right. Furthermore, the king was not seen to be in a special relationship to God or as semidivine as the kings of Egypt or Babylon were viewed. The king was a man who was responsible for keeping the laws of God and of the land. In no other ancient Near Eastern nation would any king have felt guilt or faced condemnation for commiting adultery. But Israel's kings were not above the law. David was held accountable for his sin with Bathsheba (2 Sam. 11:1 to 12:7). The great David was not only fearful of God and of God's prophet but was also fearful of public opinion. This, too, is a decided difference from our normal understanding of kingship.

The Nature of the Tribal Union

The last major problem with which we must deal in relation to this period is the nature of the tribal union. This is related both to the preceeding periods of Israel's history and to the Hebrew understanding of kingship. From Israel's earliest days, the people had been fiercely independent. There was always a much stronger sense of tribal commitments than there was of national commitment from the time of Moses all the way through the time of Samuel. As we have seen, tribes apparently responded to needs during the period of the settlement in direct proportion to the nearness of the crisis. There apparently was not a single instance where the entire nation responded to an oppression or to the leadership of a judge. In spite of the fact that the people themselves felt the need for a king to fight their battles, this deep seated tribal independence was not easily put by.

There also appears to have been a major difference between the common interests of the northern tribes and those of the south. Thus one of the first things the kings had to do was to try to win the overall allegiance of the entire nation. When Saul was crowned as Israel's first king, some viewed him with suspicion (1 Sam. 10:27). Saul did not try to force authority upon them but gently tried to win the people's commitment. Neither were Saul's own supporters allowed to try to force the disaffected to follow him (1 Sam. 11:12-13).

The same sort of thing can be seen in David's early reign in the period immediately following Saul's death. At that time, the northern tribes followed Saul's son while the southern tribes turned to David (2 Sam. 2:10). David made no attempt to force the northern tribes to follow him but eventually won them over by gentleness and examples of personal leadership. Through David's administration and later through that of his son Solomon, the attempt was made to break down the tribal loyalties while establishing national loyalties. This was only partially sucessful. At the death of Solomon, some of the old loyalties reappeared and the nation divided.

People have frequently talked about the divided kingdom as if it were some kind of new development in Israel. Actually, the reverse is true. The time of tribal union from Saul through Solomon was the new development. And it never worked very well.

During the united monarchy, the nation was never held together by any real sense of national goals or identity. When there was a united kingdom, it was united around the personality of a strong central figure or by the administrative strength of the leader. Both prior to and after the period of the united monarchy, we find abundant evidence that there was little national commitment. In fact, taking the long view of Hebrew history, we might say that the only thing which ever gave the Hebrews a real sense of identity was a common commitment to God. When this was lacking or grew weak, the nation disintegrated. Within this period, however, the stackpole around which the tribes came together was the strong personality of the leader. They were forced into union by the external dangers. They were held there primarily by the personal magnetism of their leaders. When that disappeared and the pressure was relieved, the nation once again fell apart.

The Background of the Period

It appears that each period of Hebrew history with which we have dealt was quite formative for their history, their faith, and their theology. Yet each of these periods has been formative in different ways. This process of formation was never more visible than in the period of the united monarchy. It can be seen with even greater clarity when viewed against the background of the era. Therefore, it is to that background that we must now turn.

International Weaknesses

The first background feature of significance from the period of about 1020 to 931 BC is the power vacuum which existed throughout the ancient Near East. Just prior to this period, Egypt had lost any control and political influence it had previously held in the region of Palestine, Asia Minor, and Assyria. Egypt's fortunes had waned. Thus, in this period, the Egyptians were able to exert no pressure on the Palestinian states. Neither were they able to offer any significant resistance to those peoples who wished to expand their territory into the Negeb or into the Sinai Peninsula.

The same sort of thing was true to the north and northeast of Palestine. The great Hittite kingdom of Mitanni had ceased to exist. Assyria was going through a major time of weakness, apparently caused by internal struggles for power. The Old Kingdom of Babylon had collapsed, and there was no new threat from that direction.

Thus, at the precise time that Israel was taking its first feeble steps toward nationhood, no major power was in existence or on the horizon to offer them any threat. This made a major impact upon the political and economic development in Israel. It also meant that their armies were not faced with extremely large and well-trained armies. This power vacuum among the major powers gave Israel the historical opportunity to move from tribalism to nationhood. But Israel was not the only small nation on the historical scene which sought to take advantage of this situation.

International Pressures

In the power vacuum created by the weakness of Egypt, Assyria, and the rest, at least four peoples or small nations were seeking to expand their holdings. The first of these was obviously Israel. The Hebrews had previously gotten a firm hold on the central hill country of Palestine. During this period, they sought to consolidate that hold and to expand the territory which they controlled. However, this desire on their part was threatened from three directions.

The major threat to Israel came from the Philistines. In fact, more than one interpreter has suggested that, from a human standpoint, the pressure from the Philistines was the primary force behind Israel's development of a monarchy. We have already seen that at the beginning of this era the Philistines had the ability to smelt iron and to forge iron weapons. This gave them a significant strategic advantage. Iron weapons are greatly superior to those made of bronze and copper. In addition, the Philistines also had chariots of iron, which gave them mobility and speed as well as protection from attack. However, this implement of war was only of value in plains and lowlands. It offered no advantage in the more rugged hill country.

By the middle of the lifetime of Samuel, the Philistines were pressing deeply into the heart of the southern Hebrew possessions. Saul at times slowed the Philistine advance from the coastal plain and occasionally reversed it. But Saul's own death was brought about by Philistine victories and by deep incursions into Israelite territory.

In addition to the Philistine pressures from the east, the beginnings of this period also saw a growing Ammonite pressure from the west (1 Sam. 11:1-2). It is obvious that at the beginning, the Ammonites did not feel that there was any leader or military force in Israel which could counter their invasion and attempted humiliation of the men of Jabesh-gilead. It is probable that if Saul had not already been on the scene, the Ammonites would have been right.

There also appears to have been a significant threat felt by the people of Israel from the Negeb, the regions to their south. This was the result of the wandering tribes of the Amalekites. They were clearly beginning to settle down in towns and cities (1 Sam. 15:1-7). Although the Amalekites were not an immediate threat to Israel, it is obvious that they had been a threat earlier. It was felt that, if their settlements were allowed to exist, it would not be long before they would again become a major southern threat.

These localized international pressures on the land of Palestine made this period very unsettled. With a major power vacuum, it was quite possible that one of these minor states would become an international power. It was this struggle for existence and supremacy which brought Israel's need for kingship to the fore. In the first place, their very existence seemed to be at stake. But even if they survived, their future appeared to be at stake as well.

The Nature of Warfare

In the wars which were fought in this period, several features need to be considered. Due to the fact that no major power was involved, there were no massive armies. Most of the battles were fought by small, guerrilla-type bands. In such battles, speed, mobility, surprise, and sheer audacity played a very major part. In addition, small bands of warriors might face one another over and over again, so soldiers of opposing armies might almost get to know one another and the ways in which they thought and fought. It was also not unheard of that the chosen champions of opposing sides might fight with the soldiers of both sides as onlookers. (The David-and-Goliath conflict was of this nature.)

In studying the battles which were fought in this era, we need to keep reminding ourselves that the numbers involved were not very large and that the casualties were usually rather limited. Battles would not normally last long, and the defeated armies would simply vanish, for a while, into the countryside. There was seldom a grand strategy. More often than not the battles appear to have been fought by almost semiindependent bands. Thus, the arising of a king to unite some of these bands under a common leader and with a common goal gave a significant advance to a nation's ability to wage war victoriously.

International Developments

There were three other developments on the international scene which were to have a significant impact upon the development of the Hebrew nation in this period. First, there was the burgeoning of the wisdom movements of the ancient Near East. Both Egypt and Babylon had long had a wisdom movement which was made up of counselors to kings, scribes, and what we might call philosophers and thinkers. These were people who studied life and made collections of wise sayings related to it or made wise observations upon it. With the transition occurring in Palestine, and with a time of more international stability, both Edom and Phoenicia also began to develop into major centers of wisdom. The time of relative peace following David's kingship allowed the same thing to happen in Israel. Solomon was given credit for founding the Hebrew wisdom movement, and he was always remembered as the Hebrew wise man par excellence (1 Kings 4:29-34). Although we do not often note it, the wise men of the later Hebrew monarchies are seen to be of almost equal importance to the prophet and priest (Jer. 18:18).

The second development of significance in this period was the growing technique of massive architecture, particularly among the Phoenicians. They were apparently the first of the small Palestinian states to arrive at a time of relative peace. This, when coupled with the skills which those peoples had brought with them from the Aegean regions, allowed them to develop other skills until they produced an architectural technique which was native to them. Thus when Israel reached a time of relative peace under Solomon, it was to the Phoenicians that Solomon turned for technical assistance in erecting the Temple of Jerusalem and his other major buildings (1 Kings 5:1-12). Prior to this time, building among the Hebrews had been strictly utilitarian. For the first time they had both the resources and the time to erect edifices which were beautiful as well.

Related to this, but independent from it, the weakness of major powers allowed the rise of international commerce on a grand scale. This was the third development which impacted on Hebrew history in a major way. We must remember that the Phoenicians had arrived in upper Palestine as a part of the Sea People. When the time of war passed, they were able to turn their seafaring abilities to ocean trade instead of conflict. With the close relationship which began to exist between Israel and Phoenicia, it was only natural that Israel also should get involved in sea trade (1 Kings 9:26-28; 2 Chron. 8:17).

In addition to Solomon's trade by sea, he also controlled every major highway which connected Mesopotamia with Egypt. Thus, Solomon's territory sat astride the only land bridge in the region. Caravans of all sorts had to pass through his land. This also offered abundant opportunity for Israel to become even more deeply engaged in international trade. It was this which brought a significant amount of international goods and products to Israel, adding to their prosperity in the period.

Internal Developments in Israel

A further dimension of the background of this period must be seen in several things which happened within Israel itself, even though these are related to the international features. Three are related to international developments, but two seem to be particularly Jewish.

First, by the middle of this period, a time of relative peace had settled over the land. At the beginning of Saul's reign, Israel was fighting for her very existence. By the end of the reign of David, every threat had been successfully dealt with, the land was expanded to its greatest historical dimensions, and peace had come. It is doubtful if David had not won for Israel this time of peace if any of the subsequent developments could have taken place.

The second development in Israel to which we have already alluded was the development of Hebrew arts and architecture. This could not have come if there had not been a time of relative peace when Israel could turn her resources to other tasks than war. The massive building projects of Solomon were a result of this. Further, the development of Israel's own wisdom movement came about in this period. But beyond this, in Solomon's reign, a major musical tradition developed in Israel (1 Kings 10:12).

Related to that development, the third internal development in Israel of significance was her international trade (1 Kings 10:21-29). The wealth which came into Jerusalem in that time was apparently greater than at any other time in Israel's history. The Hebrews were truly a major factor in international commerce.

Yet all three of these features of the historical background of the period came about in relationship to what was going on elsewhere. The other two features were not so related. The fourth internal development of significance in establishing the background of this period was the development of Israel's governmental administration. Governments require money, records, and personnel. In an attempt to furnish these, as well as to break down the old tribal allegiances, administrative divisions were set up in the land for the purpose of furnishing the kings with the resources which were needed. This would probably have been accepted by the people had they not become excessive under Solomon.

The Hebrew people had always been fiercely independent. When Solomon began conscripting people to work in his labor battalions, the seed of rebellion were planted. Originally, Solomon's labor had been supplied by foreign captives. But when his works exceeded their abilities, he was forced to begin conscripting Hebrews. This was where the trouble began.

The fifth major feature of the background of this period is found in the area of religion. With the centralization of religion in Jerusalem and with the building of the Temple there, a new dimension entered into Hebrew faith. No longer was the official faith to be found centered elsewhere. Further, the time of relative peace apparently allowed time for reflection and the development of the priesthood and the prophets in Israel. In addition, the very fact that the prophets felt that they had both the right and the responsibility to interfere in national matters brought a new development to religion.

The fact that David acknowledged Nathan's right to confront him made an impact that reverberated throughout all the rest of Hebrew history. The fact that prophets and priests were clearly involved in the selection of each of the kings of this period also made a permanent mark upon Israel's history.

The old tribal alliance was beginning to fade during

part of this period. But it raised its head again at the end. Throughout the entire period, there was never any question but that Israel was to be a theocracy. They might now have been given a king and have become a monarchy. Yet, there was never any question but that they were first and foremost a theocracy. God was supremely seen as their Head.

Let me offer one warning at this point. It is precisely the fact that the government of Israel was always considered to be subservient to Israel's faith which marks the major distinction between it and the government of the United States. In our land, church and state are separate. This was not so in Israel. There, they were coextensive. Thus the lessons of Israel's history cannot be merely lifted up and applied to our history. They must be translated and interpreted, for the forms of national life are wholly different.

The History of the Period

The biblical narratives of the period of Israel's united monarchy are among some of the best in the Old Testament. They are told with an energy that makes them both exciting and memorable. Even for a person who is neither interested in history nor in religion, these stories grip the imagination and hold the interest from beginning to end. Across the pages of the Old Testament which relate to this period move numerous peoples, but the action centers around the four central figures: Samuel, Saul, David, and Solomon.

Samuel and Saul: An Opportunity for Greatness

Other than Moses, there was probably no other person in all of Hebrew history who played as many roles as did Samuel. He was priest, prophet, seer, judge, and man of God. He seems also to have wanted to be king. In his older years, the people of Israel came to him with the request that he appoint a king to rule over them. The stated reason for this request was the evil lives of Samuel's sons (1 Sam. 8:4-5). But when pressed on the issue, the people finally admitted that they needed someone to lead them and to fight their battles (1 Sam. 8:19).

It is quite obvious that Samuel was greatly disturbed by this request for a king. He felt it was a personal rejection of his leadership and had to be encouraged by God that this was not so (1 Sam. 8:7). This sense of rejection which Samuel had appears to have colored all of his subsequent relations with Saul. His hostility to the kingship in general and to Saul in particular was seldom hidden. More often than not it was quite obvious. Before the actual search for a king was begun, Samuel warned the people in no uncertain terms what the consequences of the kingship would be (1 Sam. 8:10-18). As far as the people of Israel were concerned, the kingship would result in a serious loss of personal freedom. However, they were more concerned with the threat from the Philistines and others to their very existence. Greater security was of more concern than a limited loss of freedom. This is an issue with which people still have to deal.

Once the issue was basically decided for Samuel, the process of finding a king was set in order. This was where Saul came upon the stage of Israel's history.

Personally, Saul brought a great deal of outstanding characteristics to the throne of Israel. He was wealthy, handsome, young, and physically stood head and shoulders above any of his people (1 Sam. 9:1-2). From this standpoint, he was truly a man of leadership qualities. But there were some other dimensions to Saul's personality which were not so appropriate for the task with which he was faced. While Saul was a man of deep spirituality, he was also susceptible to excesses, occasionally falling into religious ecstasy or spells (1 Sam. 10:10-11; 11:7; 19:23-24). The nature of these spells is perhaps best described by the statement that when they happened, Saul would "be turned into another man" (1 Sam. 10:6).

To the kingship, Saul also brought both gentleness and harshness. He was gentle at first in dealing with those opposed to him (1 Sam. 10:27; 11:12-13). This seems to have eventually won both the hearts and the allegiance of those initially arrayed against him. At the same time, Saul's slaughter of the oxen and the subsequent sending of the pieces of the carcass throughout the land was both brutal and terrifying (1 Sam. 11:7). Coupled with this was either a deep sense of humility or of total inadequacy. At the dramatic moment of crowning, Saul was found "hidden . . . among the baggage" (1 Sam. 10:22). His nature was confused and confusing. These characteristics visible in his first introduction came back to haunt him and eventually to destroy him.

When Samuel crowned Saul privately, there was no question left in Saul's mind but that his kingship came to him directly from Samuel. Samuel gave God the credit, but it was Samuel who delivered the message (1 Sam. 10:1). Later, when Saul was to be crowned publicly, Samuel gathered the people together at Mizpah. After a further warning, Samuel began the dramatic selection of Saul as king (1 Sam. 10:17-21). The nature of the warning significantly undermined any basis the future king might have had for a successful reign. Samuel went through the whole rigmarole of choosing one of the tribes, a family from the tribe, and ultimately an individual from the family. You can almost feel the tension building. But the result was wholly unexpected. When Samuel called for Saul, the young man was nowhere to be found. He had hidden himself among the baggage (1 Sam. 10:22).

If Saul were smart enough, this might be interpreted as a game of one-upmanship. Samuel was seeking to capitalize upon the dramatic, but it was Saul who carried the day with drama. However, knowing the end of Saul's life, I think that he had been seized by an overwhelming sense of inadequacy. He seems always to have suffered from an inferiority complex. However, for whatever reason it was done, Samuel's great drama had been spoiled. This was but one more development in the hostility between the two men.

Sometime after Saul had been crowned king, the people of Jabesh-Gilead were beseiged by the Ammonites. That was the first major military crisis which Israel had faced following Saul's anointing. Acting with speed and energy, Saul mustered his troops and surprised the attacking Ammonites. The Ammonites were utterly defeated (1 Sam. 11:1-11).

At that point, the people were overwhelmed with the success of the kingship in accomplishing what they had wished. There was an immediate cry to execute all those who had opposed Saul's kingship. It was here that Saul showed his magnanimity by refusing (1 Sam. 11:12-13). He wisely realized that mercy would hold allegiance better than vengeance.

It is interesting to see that as preparations for the battle with the Ammonites began Saul's call to arms was issued in his name and the name of Samuel (1 Sam. 11:7). Either he was aware that his leadership of the nation depended upon his being associated with Samuel or he was afraid to face the enemy alone. This characteristic shows up again and again. It at the very least appears to continue to reflect Saul's sense of inferiority. Further solidifying this sense of dependence upon Samuel, Samuel again crowned Saul king, this time at Gilgal (1 Sam. 11:14-15). It is possible that this was done because Gilgal was a sacred site. It is also possible that this renewed anointing was intended to include more of the people than the first one. (We have already noted that this may also be evidence of duplicate sources in the Books of Samuel.)

Following this coronation at the shrine of Gilgal, Samuel issued a farewell address. At the beginning, the address was little more than a call to both the king and the people to be loyal to God. However, it was also an assertion that Samuel had in no way done anything wrong to Israel while he had led them (1 Sam. 12:3-4). Unfortunately, before Samuel finished, he launched into a tirade against the kingship declaring that "your wickedness is great, . . . in asking for yourselves a king" (1 Sam. 12:17). With this conclusion, Samuel just about destroyed any basis which Saul might have had for a successful kingship. The people can almost be seen to be cowering before Samuel. Sadly, Samuel's farewell address left Saul little chance for success.

At this point, Saul's attention was directed to the threat of the Philistines. We are told that they were camped at both Gebah and Michmash (1 Sam. 13:3,5). Both of these sites are on the eastern side of the central hill country, indicating that the Philistines were deep into the land and were about to take over all of this part of Israelite territory. At this point, Israel was holding on to their southern territories by the very barest of margins. So Saul prepared to confront the Philistines.

Before going into battle, Saul wanted the proper sacrifices offered, but Samuel delayed in coming. Saul's army, made up of volunteers, began to scatter because of the lack of activity (1 Sam. 13:8). In desperation, Saul himself offered sacrifices to prepare the people for battle. "As soon as he had finished . . . Samuel came" (1 Sam. 13:10). It almost seems as if Samuel were hiding nearby, waiting to see what Saul would do. Samuel condemned Saul for offering the sacrifice, but it was no less than David and Solomon later did without being condemned (2 Sam. 6:12-13; 1 Kings 8:5). Samuel publicly rejected Saul's kingship and abandoned him as he was about to go into battle (1 Sam. 13:13-15). This could not help but further enforce Saul's sense of inferiority. It is a tribute to Saul that he was able to go into battle at all.

In the ongoing conflict with the Philistines, we are told of the inadequacy of Israel's arms due to their inability to smelt or forge iron (1 Sam. 13:19-22). Furthermore, from the battle reports, it is obvious that Jonathan, Saul's son, was one of the leading warriors among the Israelites. It has been suggested that he later acquiesced in David's accession to the throne because he was no warrior. That just is not true. During one of the campaigns, when Saul foolishly made a vow that no one would eat until the battle was done, Jonathan was unaware of this and ate some honey (1 Sam. 14:27). Saul, like Jephthah before him, was about to fulfill his rash vow, but the people of Israel intervened on behalf of Jonathan, for the victory had been primarily of his doing (1 Sam. 14:45).

The end result of the Philistine campaign of Saul and Jonathan was that significant portions of the central hill country were retaken from the Philistines. The Philistines were at least driven back to the western side of the central hill country. But the end was not in sight, for there "was hard fighting against the Philistines all the days of Saul"

(1 Sam. 14:52). At the same time, Saul had apparently waged successful campaigns against several others of Israel's enemies, although these are not recorded in detail (1 Sam. 14:47-48). It appears that Saul had no real strategy but rather dealt with the enemies only as the problems arose.

Another major enemy arose to the south—the Amalekites. In Samuel's commission to Saul, Samuel demanded the same kinds of utter destruction which Joshua had wrought when he first came into the land (1 Sam. 15:3). The Amalekites were a group of tribes in the southern deserts who were apparently beginning to establish cities and thus were about to become a threat to Israel.

Saul again demonstrated his military abilities by the total destruction of the people of Amalek. Yet he sought to enrich himself with booty and also spared their king. He apparently felt that, by sparing the king, he would have a friend on his southern border. From Samuel's standpoint, Saul had simply failed to obey. This brought about one of the most memorable confrontations in the Bible between a prophet and a king. Samuel thundered at Saul, "Behold, to obey is better than sacrifice, and to hearken than the fat of rams" (1 Sam. 15:22). Saul had piously sought to appease Samuel by offering to sacrifice the choicest of the animals to God. For Samuel, that was not sufficient.

That was the ultimate confrontation for the two men. Each went home, never consciously to see one another again. Samuel went in bitterness and grief. Saul departed in defeat and embarassment. Saul's one source of strength had been taken from him. From this point onward, his weaknesses came more and more to the fore. Forced to be alone, he went from failure to chaos. Seeking to know what would have happened if . . . is a fruitless game. But it is easy to imagine that Saul might have been a better king if Samuel had offered encouragement and support at the beginning rather than always undercutting the young man who had had greatness thrust upon him. Saul just couldn't cope with the responsibilities of kingship. But things were to get worse.

Saul and David: Hostility and Dissolution

With the final separation between Samuel and Saul, David entered upon the scene. Samuel, heartbroken over Saul's failure (and perhaps feeling some guilt over his own part in it), was faced with the responsibility of anointing a replacement for Saul. Beginning with Samuel, the prophets of Israel freuqently (almost regularly) played a part in the process of selecting Israel's kings. Knowing the task had to be done, yet fearful of Saul's finding out, Samuel set out for Bethlehem. In order to have an excuse for going, Samuel let it be known that he was making a pilgrimage to offer sacrifice (1 Sam. 16:4-5). The open hostility between Samuel and the king apparently even made the elders of Bethlehem fearful when Samuel showed up in their midst.

In seeking for the new king, Samuel examined each of the sons of Jesse, finally calling David who was busy tending sheep. As soon as he had anointed David, he hurriedly departed (1 Sam. 16:13). David is introduced as handsome, with the ruddy complexion of an outdoorsman (1 Sam. 16:12).

An interesting theological observation is made at this point by the human author of 1 Samuel. We are told that "the Spirit of the Lord came mightily upon David from that day forward." We are also told that "the Spirit of the Lord departed from Saul" (1 Sam. 16:13-14). This is one more evidence of the fact that the Hebrews clearly sought a king who was obviously possessed by God. Although we have moved into the period of the monarchy, the sense of charismatic leadership is still present. The king, above all else, had to be God's man.

The observation that, from this point on, "an evil spirit from the Lord tormented" Saul causes some problems for modern interpreters (1 Sam. 16:14). We do not like to think of evil spirits coming from God. To the ancient Hebrews, however, this idea offered no real problem for they believed that God was ultimately responsible for all things. (This same problem gave difficulties to later Old Testament authors, as in seen in comparing 2 Sam. 24:1

with 1 Chron. 21:1.) Furthermore, the situation which gave rise to this theological diagnosis is quite similar to what we might term schizophrenia. Saul was beset by violent fits and depression. This tendency to excesses was visible in Saul from the beginning. It may also have been aggravated by insecurity and a sense of inferiority. In a strange twist of events, David was brought to Saul's court to soothe Saul with beautiful music (1 Sam. 16:21-23). In a further statement about the qualities of David, we are told that he was "skilful in playing, a man of valor, a man of war, prudent in speech, and a man of good presence; and the Lord is with him" (1 Sam. 16:18). Everything that Saul wasn't, David was. That became the basis of further problems for Saul.

Saul's final years as king were characterized by three major problems. Each of these has its roots in the early parts of Saul's ministry. First, there was the personal problem. His spiritual, emotional, and mental situation continued to deteriorate with an ever increasing speed. At times, he could hardly be classified as sane. Obviously, this seriously affected his personal relationships as well as his ability to govern.

The second major problem was clearly related to the first and that was Saul's relationship with David. In his saner moments, Saul recognized David as the greatest asset he had. Yet David's increasing successes aggravated Saul's fits of jealousy until he became obsessed with getting rid of the Bethlehemite. Furthermore, the very fact that Saul knew that the kingship was slipping away from him made his jealousy of David even more violent, for David was the most visible choice on the scene. When this was coupled with Jonathan's and Michal's obvious love for David, even choosing him over their father, Saul's desire to eliminate David knew no bounds (1 Sam. 19:1-17).

Saul's third major problem was the Philistines. Their threat had brought about Saul's kingship in the first place. In his early days, he had experienced some military success against them at least in the hill country. But he apparently became so obsessed with David that he neglected to deal with the Philistines. As their strength grew, they almost toppled the kingdom of Israel. They did finally destroy Saul and his son Jonathan.

These final years actually had their beginning in the confrontation between Israel and the Philistines in the Valley of Elah (1 Sam. 17:1-2). This was about halfway between Bethlehem and Libnah, in the heart of the Shephelah. There Goliath taunted the Hebrews, daring them to send a representative to fight with him (1 Sam. 17:8-11). Some of David's brothers were part of Saul's army, so David came down from Bethlehem to bring them supplies.

David was astounded that no one in Israel's army had the courage or the faith to face Goliath. This attitude on the part of David angered his older brothers. However, it was reported to Saul, and David was brought to him. At that point, Saul accepted David's offer to face Goliath, clothing him in his own armor (1 Sam. 17:38). This clearly indicates that David was of outstanding physique, for we must remember Saul's own exceptional size. If David could wear Saul's armor, he, too, must have been exceptionally large. It was put aside by the youth, not because it was too big but because he did not know how to use it (1 Sam. 17:39). He was a shepherd, not a warrior. Furthermore, when David approached Goliath without armor, the Philistine did not even bother to pull his visor down, thus leaving his face exposed to David's stone. The death of Goliath brought about the defeat of the Philistines (1 Sam. 17:50-52).

The celebrating women of Israel greeted the victorious army joyfully singing and dancing:

> Saul has slain his thousands,
> and David his ten thousands (1 Sam. 18:7).

This kind of greeting further intensified Saul's rage and his problems. Thus, "Saul eyed David from that time on" (1 Sam. 18:9).

Out of this astounding victory came two further developments. One was the friendship which began to develop between Jonathan and David (1 Sam. 18:1-4). It almost seems that the more Saul hated David, the more Jonathan loved him. Jonathan was truly an outstanding young man with no streak of envy within him. The other development was Saul's determination to destroy David by offering to marry one of his daughters to the youth (1 Sam. 18:17,20,25). By the subterfuge of sending David out against the Philistines for a bridal payment, Saul thought David would be killed. But David was wholly successful, and the marriage with Michal was consummated (1 Sam. 18:27).

With personality, good looks, abilities, and successes, David had won the hearts of Saul's children and was rapidly winning the hearts of the people of Israel. These very victories and his increasing popularity, however, were the basis for increasing hostility from Saul. Jonathan got Saul to agree not to kill David, but this deliverance was only temporary (1 Sam. 19:4-7). Saul's fits of rage and jealousy only intensified as David's successes continued. When Saul again tried to kill David, the young man fled with the help of his wife Michal, who deceived Saul's officers by placing a dummy in his bed (1 Sam. 19:13-16).

David temporarily fled to Samuel in Ramah (1 Sam. 19:18). When David shortly thereafter slipped back to the court of Saul, he sought out Jonathan for advice. At this point, Jonathan did not believe that Saul was still a threat to David. However, he quickly found out that David's fears were right. Jonathan then aided David in his final escape from the court of Saul (1 Sam. 20:2,35-42).

The friendship of David and Jonathan is one of the more beautiful episodes in the world's ancient literature. Jonathan had nothing to gain from it. In fact, he had everything to lose, for David's presence was certain to prevent Jonathan from becoming king. Yet Jonathan's love and loyalty toward David was greater than his ambition. It alienated him from his father, even to the point of endangering his own life (1 Sam. 20:30-34).

In David's final departure from the court of Saul, he went first to the sanctuary at Nob, which was southeast of Gibeah. There he obtained both food and a sword (1

Sam. 21:1,6,9). Another indication of the physical size and strength of David is seen in the fact that he could use the sword of Goliath without any apparent problem. David then fled to Gath, the very home of Goliath and one of the five major cities of the Philistines (1 Sam. 21:10)! The selection of Gath as a refuge from Saul was a stroke of genius. No one in Israel would ever have thought of David's going there in the first place. In the second place, there was no way by which Saul could reach him there even if he had known where he was. However, Gath was certainly a dangerous place for David. Beginning to fear for his life, David acted as if he were a madman thus escaping the wrath of Achish, king of Gath (1 Sam. 21:13). In the ancient world, madmen were feared and ocassionally ridiculed, but they were not oppressed.

When David felt it was safe to return to the land of Israel, he left Gath and established himself in a cave near Adullam, some ten miles southwest of Bethlehem (1 Sam. 22:1). He was clearly aware that his conflict with Saul was going to last for a long time. He began to gather a guerrilla band around him, made up of his own family and other disaffected people of the region (1 Sam. 22:1-2). It is intriguing that David immediately made provision for the safety of his parents, placing them in the care of the king of Moab (1 Sam. 22:3-4). This was clearly expedient for David, as he would not have to worry about protecting them from Saul's wrath. It was also expedient for Moab because it would have discomfited Saul since he would have been unable to vent his wrath toward David upon David's parents. The nature of Saul's wrath and instability at this point is clearly seen in his verbal attack against the people of Benjamin who had aided David and against the priests of Nob who had furnished him supplies. The priests were brutally slaughtered for this (1 Sam. 22:16-19).

The conflict between Saul and David raged on throughout the regions of the southern wilderness of Judah. It was a time of battle with the Philistines, who were certainly taking advantage of the civil war in Israel. It was also a time of treachery among those who supported one faction or the other. The only real scene of beauty in the entire narrative is found when Jonathan sought out David during this time and pleged his love and loyalty to David afresh (1 Sam. 23:16-18). It appears at one time as if Saul had just about captured David but was called away due to a fresh attack on the land by the Philistines (1 Sam. 23:26-28).

At this point, David moved his base of operations to the region of En-gedi (1 Sam. 23:29). This region was on the western shore of the Dead Sea. This barren region is extremely rough and rocky and is dotted with countless caves adequate for hiding. It was an ideal region for a fugitive band of warriors to hide almost indefinitely from a much larger army.

During that time, David had an opportunity to kill Saul, but he did not, saying, "The Lord forbid that I should do this thing to my lord, the Lord's anointed" (1 Sam. 24:6). By this act, David showed a magnanimous spirit toward his enemy. But he also showed respect toward whoever had been anointed king. This was politically astute, for if David had killed the reigning king, it might have suggested the same idea to others when he himself had become king. Furthermore, David's refusal to lift his hand against Saul reveals a willingness to wait for God to deliver the kingship to him. There was no lust for power on David's part.

The end result of that act of mercy on David's part was a temporary peace between himself and Saul. However, even though there was peace, there was no trust on David's part. He did not return to the court of Saul but remained in the safety of the wilderness (1 Sam. 24:16-22). Samuel died about this time (1 Sam. 25:1). The death of that great man apparently made David fear a renewed attack from Saul, so he briefly led his forces down to the wilderness of Paran, located deep in the Sinai Peninsula.

In some ways, it might have been better if David had stayed in Paran longer, but he shortly returned to the southern wilderness of Judah. There he apparently sustained his force of men by operating what might have been called a "protection racket." At the time of sheep shearing, he sent ten of his men to collect tribute from a man by the name of Nabal. This was to have been paid, according to David, because during the year Nabal's shepherds had received "no harm, and they missed nothing, all the time they were in Carmel" (1 Sam. 25:7). At the very least, David was asking for payment because his men had been honest and had stolen nothing from Nabal. As could have been expected, this demand incensed Nabal, and he refused (1 Sam. 25:10-11). David was narrowly prevented from attacking Nabal when Nabal's wife Abigail interceded and paid the tribute (1 Sam. 25:23-35). Hearing of what his wife had done, Nabal apparently had a stroke, dying a few days later. The end result was that David, who had been captivated by the beauty of Abigail, took her for his wife (1 Sam. 25:3,39-42). This is the first time that David's weakness for women has appeared. This would later return to haunt him.

Sometime thereafter, David's whereabouts were again betrayed by the residents of the region, and Saul came out after him (1 Sam. 26:1-2). David's skill in this type of warfare is seen by the fact that he was personally able to infiltrate Saul's camp. However, he once again refused to strike down the Lord's anointed (1 Sam. 26:9-10). It was an outstanding object lesson to his own followers: No one touches the man whom God has crowned king. When made aware of David's mercy, Saul was crestfallen and repentant and returned to his own home (1 Sam. 26:25).

David, however, realized that as long as Saul reigned and had sudden rages and fits, he would find no security in Israel. So David left Israel behind and again went down to Achish, king of Gath. This time, however, Achish was well aware that David was an outlaw in Israel and thus an enemy of Saul. David found welcome among the Philistines and a town to call his own (1 Sam. 27:1-2,5-6). It was certainly wise, from Achish's standpoint, to welcome an enemy of the king of Israel. This was particularly true when he was accompanied by an army of six hundred men experienced in wilderness warfare.

During David's stay in Ziklag, the town given him by the Philistines, David won the admiration of both the

Philistines and the people of Israel. David would make excursions against some of the southern marauders who had plagued Judah and then report to the Philistines that he had attacked the towns of Judah (1 Sam. 27:8-11). This made the Philistines trust him, believing him to be hated in Israel. But it also won the hearts of the people of Judah, for it delivered them from the pressure of these raiders on their southern borders.

An interesting development of this period of David's exile in the region of Philistia lies in the fact that a permanent relationship appears to have been established between the people of Gath and the royal line of David. Later in David's reign his personal bodyguard was made up of Gittites (people of Gath) and one of his three top military commanders was a Gittite (2 Sam. 18:2).

At this point, a critical series of events occurred which could have forever changed Israelite history. The Philistines amassed their forces for what was intended to be their final campaign in the subjugation of the land of Palestine. The king of Gath clearly planned for David and his troops to accompany him to battle, fighting for the Philistines (1 Sam. 28:1-2). However, when the other four Philistine lords gathered with their forces at Aphek (in the foothills of Ephraim), they refused to allow David to accompany them. Since he was a Hebrew, they just did not trust him in a battle against the Hebrew nation (1 Sam. 29:1-4). Obviously, there is no way of knowing what would have happened if this had not developed. However, it can be assumed that if David had fought with the Philistines in this battle, he would never have become the king of Israel. So it was that David was sent home from the battle before it began (1 Sam. 29:7).

When David and his troops returned to Ziklag, they discovered that their town had been plundered by raiding Amalekites (1 Sam. 30:1-2). Reacting with speed, David and his men raced into the southern wilderness to attempt a rescue. Part of his troops were too exhausted to keep up, so they were left behind along with the supplies which had slowed down the rest of his men (1 Sam. 30:9-10). So rapid was David's pursuit that he and his troops caught the Amalekites, who were totally surprised and quickly defeated (1 Sam. 30:16-17).

Following this victory, David instituted two policies which were innovative, generous, and politically wise. He shared the booty from his victory equally with those soldiers who had been left behind to guard the baggage (1 Sam. 30:24). This not only tied them even more tightly to him but also showed to all of his men that whatever their duty, each had a responsible part of play in battle. He also shared part of the booty with the men of Judah (1 Sam. 30:26-31). This bound the allegiance of those people more tightly to him. He was seen by all to be both fair and generous, attractive qualities which wins people's hearts.

In the meantime, however, the Philistine campaign against Israel was experiencing great success. The armies of Israel were defeated, and Saul and some of his sons were slain (1 Sam. 31:1-6). The victorious Philistines abused and exposed the body of Saul in one of those atrocities of warfare. In a daring rescue, the men of Jabesh-gilead expressed their final love for the man who had rescued them earlier (1 Sam. 11:9-11). They traveled all night and rescued the bodies of Saul and his sons in order to give them an honorable burial (1 Sam. 31:11-13).

Thus, the reign of Saul came to an end in defeat and tragedy. He was a great warrior who had found it easier to deal with enemies than with himself. Saul's own weaknesses had been the ultimate result of his downfall. At the end of his reign, as at the beginning, it appeared as if the Philistines were about ready to take over all of Palestine.

David's Kingship: The Best and the Worst

Rather than attempt to deal with David's reign by the process of recounting the overall sequence of events from the death of Saul to the death of David, I shall deal with this period of history topically. It appears that this is the most effective way for us to understand the man and his successes and failures.

David as King and Warrior. During the final days of Saul's reign, David is surely best known as a warrior. He was a leader of decision, quick to act, and an apparent military genius. These skills were all carried over into David's kingship.

Immediately following Saul's death, David was crowned king at Hebron by the men of Judah (2 Sam. 2:4). He was a popular hero in the region, a native of Bethlehem, and had won the hearts of the people of Judah by being generous while living in the Philistine city of Ziklag (1 Sam. 27:8-11; 30:26-31). At the same time, the northern tribes followed Saul's son, Ish-bosheth. (His name was originally Esh-baal, meaning "Man of Baal," but the author of Kings called him Ish-bosheth, meaning "Man of Shame." (See 2 Sam. 2:10; 1 Chron. 8:33; 9:31.) This divided loyalty among the people is just one more indication that the united monarchy was never tightly bound together except by allegiance to a specific individual. Just as he earlier did with Saul, David bided his time, making no overt action to eliminate Ish-bosheth and seize the kingdom.

For a period of time, there was civil war between the armies of David, under the command of Joab, and those of Ish-bosheth, under the command of Saul's former captain, Abner (2 Sam. 3:1). This war was apparently instigated by the northern armies with the purpose of subjugating David and Judah, but it was unsuccessful. Two assassinations brought this conflict to an end. Abner was assassinated by David's commander, Joab, and Ish-bosheth was assassinated by two traitors from among his own people (2 Sam. 3:27; 4:5-8). With the sudden loss of leadership in the north, those tribes came to David at Hebron and acclaimed him as their king (2 Sam. 5:1-3). Now he had it all. He had waited patiently, without raising a hand to seize the kingship, and it had finally been delivered to him.

David had reigned two-and-a-half years at Hebron over Judah alone. He reigned from there another five years over the entire nation. Finally, he moved his capitol to Jerusalem and reigned over the nation from that site for an additional thirty-three years. David's reign appears to have covered the period from about 1000 BC to 961 BC.

During David's reign, his primary accomplishments appear to have been in the area of warfare. After the civil war ended, David apparently had a period of about five years of peace in which he was able to consolidate the gains he had made. The question must be raised as to why the Philistines allowed this. They had been on the verge of capturing the whole nation when Saul was killed. Why did they not pursue this goal? We cannot give a definite answer, but there is a possibility to which we must give serious consideration. David had been the acknowledged vassal of Achish, king of Gath. It is quite possible that when David was crowned king at Hebron, the Philistines still considered him their man. If this were true, it would offer an explanation as to why they were not threatened by this. Further, the years of civil war would have been understood as one of their own men seeking to overthrow the nation, so the Philistines again could have simply stood aside and watched. According to this theory, it was only when David moved his capitol to Jerusalem that the Philistines began to realize that David was not their man. Be that as it may, it was only after David captured Jerusalem that the Philistines began to fight against David. Unfortunately for them, they had waited too long.

There is another feature of David's military successes which we must consider. Part of the reason for the Philistines' early successes over Israel in the time of the judges and of Saul had been due to their mastery of the techniques of smelting and forging iron. David, however, had lived among the Philistines for at least sixteen months (1 Sam. 27:7). During that time it is quite likely that David's men would have learned the techniques of ironmongery. This they would have brought back with them to the land of Israel. While this is pure theory, it is a fact that from this point on the Philistines did not enjoy the military superiority over Israel which they had in the past. It is also true that iron begins to show up in archaeological sites in Israel from about this time.

The factor which precipitated the Philistine attack on David was the moving of the capital to Jerusalem. Up to this point in time, Jerusalem still had not been captured by the Hebrews since their entrance into the land. This fact alone would indicate just how defensible it was. Still under Jebusite control and on the border between the northern and southern territories, it made an ideal site for a capitol for David. His attack was apparently made by the strategy of infiltrating the city by the process of climbing up the long water shaft through which the city got water in time of siege (2 Sam. 5:6-8; 1 Chron. 11:4-6).

As soon as David had moved the capitol to Jerusalem, the Philistines attacked. In a swift victory, David routed the Philistines' armies and captured their idols. After the initial assault, the battle was apparently carried on for a period of time, but the end result was a thorough defeat for the Philistines (2 Sam. 5:17-25; 1 Chron. 14:8-17). This marked the beginning of a long series of military successes for David. The ultimate result of this series of wars was that David expanded the borders of Israel northward into Syria and eastward into the Transjordan regions (2 Sam. 8:1-14; 10:1-19). The territory over which David then ruled was larger than Israel ever controlled again.

It is obvious that a major part of David's military successes sprang from his own military genius. But he had highly skilled officers serving under him, and they obviously led very loyal troops. As a warrior king, there was no one who ever reigned in Israel who came close to David's ability. At the same time, we must acknowledge that the introduction of iron at least gave Israel a parity in the ancient international arms race. Furthermore, the weakness of the major powers of the ancient Near East left a significant power vacuum on the scene. In David, both opportunity and ability met.

David as Politician and Administrator. Not only was David a military genius but he was also a very adept and astute politician, in the best sense of the word. He knew how to win and hold the loyalty of people. As we have noticed, some of these skills had shown up in the last days of King Saul. But they really become visible in David's own reign.

Beginning with the death of Saul, David quickly began to win the hearts of his enemies. His immediate execution of the Amalekite who claimed to have killed Saul would clearly have won the love or at least the respect of Saul's supporters (2 Sam. 1:14-16). David's obvious grief over the death of Saul and Jonathan, as well as the magnificient lament produced for the occasion, was also heartwarming (2 Sam. 1:11-12,19-27). Not only would this have impressed the followers of Saul but it would also provide a clear object lesson to his own followers that he whom the Lord had anointed as king was to be treated with special reverence and love. Bearing the same kind of testimony to both friend and foe was David's praise and reward to the men of Jabesh-gilead for giving proper burial to Saul and Saul's sons (2 Sam. 2:4*b*-7).

Equally as astute a move was David's show of grief over the death of Abner, the general of the northern armies. When Joab, David's cousin and the commander of David's army, treacherously assassinated Abner, David rebuked him and went into public mourning (2 Sam. 3:28-35). Regardless of David's motives for such actions, it was an act of political genius, for "all the people took notice of it, and it pleased them; as everything that the king did pleased all the people" (2 Sam. 3:36). Of the same nature was David's quick execution of the two men who assassinated Saul's son, Ish-bosheth (2 Sam. 4:8-12).

The results of these political moves was the fact that the elders of the northern tribes came to David and acclaimed him king (2 Sam. 5:1-3). This gave David the impetus for his next move of political genius. He was well aware that his capitol in Hebron was deep in the territory of Judah. This fact alone was likely to rankle the northern tribes. At the same time, if he had moved his capitol into the northern territories, it would clearly have alienated the people of Judah who had first supported him. So he chose Jerusalem, a city which belonged as yet to no tribe and which was approximately on the border between the two regions (2 Sam. 5:6-9). Another move of political genius was to bring the ark of God to Jerusalem, for establishing the center of worship there would even further weld the people's allegiance to him and to Jerusalem, the new capitol (2 Sam. 6:12-15).

However, as David's territory grew and as his responsibilities grew, it became obvious that the kingdom needed administering. He needed competent advisors and men to whom responsibility could be delegated. These were readily found (2 Sam. 8:15-18; 1 Chron. 16:4). Unfortunately, as David was forced to give more and more time to governing, he had to give less time to leading his armies. This development created problems for an active man like David.

David's Personal and Family Life. The saddest, most tragic developments in David's kingship are found in the area of his personal and family life. The roots of these developments have already been seen in the period of Saul's latter days.

Religion to David was real, and David's commitments to the God of Israel were deep. He determined to bring the ark of God to Jerusalem, as we have seen. When it was brought in, David did not act as a reserved, dignified king might have been expected to do but was the leader among the celebrants. He "danced before the Lord with all his might," and was not at all embarrassed to "make merry before the Lord" (2 Sam. 6:14,21).

A strange development followed this, for we are told that David's wife "Michal the daughter of Saul looked out of the window, and saw King David leaping and dancing before the Lord; and she despised him in her heart" (2 Sam. 6:16). Could it be that she was remembering the unrestrained nature of her father which had finally resulted in his fits and the loss of his kingdom? David's reaction to his wife's rebuke was to taunt her with her father's failure and to promise her that the other women of Israel would honor him (2 Sam. 6:21-22). Either of these statements would be likely to widen the crack developing in David's marriage. In point of fact, David and Michal were apparently separated from this time (2 Sam. 6:23). David's fascination with the women of Israel and his dissolving relation with Michal point to the future problem with sex which David was to have.

As far as his religion was concerned, David wished to honor God by building a temple in Jerusalem (2 Sam. 7:2).

An interesting sidelight here was the most human reaction of Nathan the prophet. The idea sounded great to him, and he immediately encouraged David in it. Unfortunately, upon reflection, he had to return to David and admit he was wrong (2 Sam. 7:3-14; 1 Chron. 17:2-4). Even the man of God can be wrong as to what the will of God is. However, Nathan did announce to David that the king was going to be the father of a royal dynasty (2 Sam. 7:11,16; 1 Chron. 17:10-14). Instead of honoring God, David had to accept God's honor of him.

As David's responsibility for governing grew, he had to remain behind in Jerusalem when his troops went forth to battle. This was obviously not pleasant to such a man of action. At such a time when he longed for the stimulus of action, David got involved with Bathsheba and committed adultery. When they discovered that she was pregnant, David panicked. He brought her husband Uriah home from battle and did his best to try to get him to sleep with his wife so the world might think that the child was Uriah's. The very fact that Uriah resisted this may indicate that he had already heard the palace gossip. If this is true, his love and loyalty to his king must be seen as almost boundless. When David's trickery did not work, he sent Uriah back to the battle, carrying his own death warrant in his hand. Relying on Uriah's own bravery, David ordered his troops to retreat leaving Uriah exposed to the enemy. And so it happened. Uriah was killed, and David and Bathsheba were married (2 Sam. 11:2-21).

It would appear that David had gotten away with sin. But he hadn't. Nathan the prophet confronted him with his sin, describing it in a matchless parable. David was so incensed by the obvious wrong which Nathan described that he cried out in anger, "As the Lord lives, the man who has done this deserves to die; and he shall restore the lamb fourfold" (2 Sam. 12:5-6). In response, the fearless prophet cried out, "You are the man" (2 Sam. 12:7). At that point, David caved in and confessed his sin. There are a number of features of great significance here. First, David, Bathsheba, Nathan, and all Israel expected the king to be obedient to the law. In no other kingdom of the ancient Near East would a king have given a second thought to taking whatever women he wanted. Second, in no other kingdom would a prophet of the royal household have dared confront a king over his sin. It is a mark of David's greatness that he did not execute Nathan but confessed his own wrong. Third, David's sin with Bathsheba was but the final step in a series of events which indicate that David already had some weaknesses in regard to his sexual appetites. He was human, and he had forgotten it. He had been able to control armies, but he had failed to control himself.

There is a strange quirk of history here in regard to David's judgment that the man of Nathan's parable must repay fourfold. David had murdered Uriah. The child which was born to Bathsheba died (2 Sam. 12:18). Then Amnon, another of David's sons, was murdered by Absalom following Amnon's rape of Tamar (2 Sam. 13:28-29). Next, Absalom was killed by Joab, following Absalom's rebellion against David (2 Sam. 18:14). Finally, Adonijah, another of David's sons was killed by Solomon (1 Kings 2:23-25). Fourfold, David had said. Fourfold, it was.

David's family problems went from bad to worse. Possibly incited by his father's own bad example, Amnon raped his half sister, Tamar (2 Sam. 13:1-19). David was angry at this but did nothing to try to deal with the situation (2 Sam. 13:21). The man who as a military commander had dealt decisively and swiftly with problems did neither as a father. The end result of his procrastination and indecisiveness was that Absalom took matters into his own hand and murdered Amnon (2 Sam. 13:28-29). As a consequence of this act, Absalom fled from the court.

David's heart went out to Absalom, but he did nothing to restore him (2 Sam. 13:39). However, through the intrigue of Joab, Absalom was finally allowed to return to Jerusalem. Yet even then, he was not allowed to come into the presence of David (2 Sam. 14:1-3,23-24). All of this brought about unrest in the land and in Absalom's heart.

This resulted in the rebellion which almost toppled David from the throne.

One of the interesting sidelights of Absalom's rebellion is the part played in it by Ahithophel, one of David's counselors (2 Sam. 15:12). It is obvious that David feared the wisdom of Ahithophel more than he did Absalom (2 Sam. 15:31). The question arises as to why a man who had been a trusted advisor of David should ally himself with Absalom. The answer probably lies in the fact that Ahithophel was Bathsheba's grandfather (2 Sam. 11:3; 23:34). Once again, David's sins were coming home to roost.

Absalom's rebellion was almost successful. It probably would have been if David had not effectively thwarted Ahithophel's advice by sending back another trusted friend to become an advisor to Absalom (2 Sam. 15:32-34; 17:1,5-14,23). The end result was the death of Absalom and the utter crushing of the rebellion. David's grief at the death of Absalom was overwhelming (2 Sam. 18:33). It took the rebuke of Joab to bring David back to the realities of life and to face the fact that, even though Absalom was dead, David could still lose the kingdom (2 Sam. 19:5-8).

As David grew old and death drew near, there arose in the palace a conflict as to which of his sons should succeed him. Both Adonijah and Solomon sought to claim the kingship. David's own counselors and advisors were divided, some supporting one and others, the other (1 Kings 1:5-27). It is both interesting and tragic at this point again to note David's failure as a father. We are told of Adonijah that David "had never at any time displeased him" (1 Kings 1:6). He had been spoiled by an indulgent father.

David finally settled the issue by declaring that Solomon should succeed to the throne (1 Kings 1:32-34). Thus it was that the long reign of David came to an end (1 Kings 2:10). It had begun in a shout of glory, but it ended more like a long, long whimper. The great David had failed his family. As a consequence, he had almost failed his people. He had certainly failed God by being less than he could have been.

Solomon's Kingship: Days of Success and Failure

If David's reign can be said to have been primarily one of territorial expansion, Solomon's can be described primarily as one of consolidation. He inherited from David a kingdom whose territory was extensive. But, administratively, the structure for governing that kingdom left a great deal to be desired.

Upon succeeding to the throne, Solomon set about to consolidate his position. Adonijah was still clearly a rival. When Adonijah requested that one of David's concubines be given to him, he was making an overt claim to the kingship (1 Kings 2:17). Solomon's immediate response was to execute Adonijah. He would allow no rival. To further strengthen his hold upon the throne, Solomon banished Abiathar, the priest who had supported Adonijah. He then executed Joab for the same reason (1 Kings 2:24-26,28-31). Not yet satisfied, Solomon also had Shimei executed as one who had been a threat to David and might possibly be one to him (1 Kings 2:8-9,36-46). By the time this bloodbath was over, Solomon was firmly in control of the land.

The reputation of King Solomon was established through his achievements in three major areas and in four minor ones. The first of Solomon's major achievements was in international relations. David had been a warrior; Solomon was a diplomat. He maintained his kingdom and its influence through a number of international treaties. It was common in those days for treaties to be sealed by marriages. The probability is very great that Solomon's famous harem came to him precisely in this way (1 Kings 3:1; 11:1-3). In addition to this, he also sealed his treaties with the Phoenicians by the gift of cities and payments of gold (1 Kings 9:10-14). Unfortunately, the latter days of Solomon were characterized by the failure of his policies. Further, although he had a significant army, it appears to have been primarily for show or for defense (1 Kings 4:26; 10:16-17). Near the end of Solomon's reign, many of the peoples whom David had conquered began to rebel and to win their freedom from Solomon, and he was unable to prevent this (1 Kings 11:14-25). As the beginning of David's reign had been characterized by expansion, the end of Solomon's was characterized by territorial contraction. Solomon simply let the kingdom slip through his fingers.

The second major achievement of Solomon rests in building projects. Solomon's fame for the building of the Temple in Jerusalem is well established (1 Kings 5:5; 6:37-38; 2 Chron. 2:1). But Solomon also built a royal palace in Jerusalem, along with palaces for many of his foreign wives (1 Kings 7:1-8). Furthermore, he also built shrines for the gods of his foreign wives (1 Kings 11:7-8). In addition to these royal buildings in Jerusalem, he also erected border fortresses for his troops (1 Kings 4:26; 9:17-19). A number of these have been excavated and show evidence of the affluence of Solomon's kingdom and the development of a typical Israelite style of architecture.

Solomon began massive building programs by importing artisans and materials from the region of Phoenicia. He also apparently trained workmen with those of Hiram, king of Tyre, and was able to complete most of the projects essentially without outside help.

As a third major achievement, Solomon gained a reputation as an administrator. Solomon's father, David, had been forced to become an administrator. But Solomon took over David's administration and throughly refined and developed it. In order to support his government, Solomon had to develop an effective means of collecting taxes. He also had to conscript laborers for his projects and soldiers for his army. At the beginning of his reign, Solomon only used Hebrews in his army, using foreigners for his building. But his building projects became so large that he was later forced to use Hebrew involuntary labor battalions in them (1 Kings 11:27-28). This clearly did not sit well with the highly independent Hebrew people and was the first major crack to occur in what later proved to be the division of the kingdom.

Solomon also used the assignment of tax burdens and the establishment of military districts to try to break down the old tribal alliances. The administrative districts which he set up did not at all follow the tribal regions of the land. It was an obvious attempt to weld the nation into a single unit. In this, he failed.

In addition to these major achievements, Solomon is also known as a patron of the arts. His basic request of God was that he would be a wise man (1 Kings 3:9). He certainly gained an international reputation for his wisdom (1 Kings 10:23). He was also remembered throughout all the rest of Israel's history as their wise man par excellance (Prov. 1:1; Eccl. 1:1,12-14). In addition to collecting wise sayings and establishing a group of wise men, Solomon also imported musical instruments and established music as a part of Israel's official culture (1 Kings 10:11; 2 Chron. 5:12). We might classify as one of the Hebrew art forms which Solomon developed or encouraged the classical style of architecture which emerged during Solomon's reign.

Closely related to all of Solomon's accomplishments is the establishment of Israel as a center of international commerce (1 Kings 9:26-28; 10:14-15,22,25,27-29). It is obvious that many of Solomon's other achievements were dependent upon the wealth which he ammassed through his commercial ventures.

This brings us to the third of Solomon's less significant accomplishments, his wealth. In the very early days of his kingdom, the wealth of his court was great (1 Kings 10:23). By the middle of his reign, he was known as one who "excelled all the kings of the earth in riches" (2 Chron. 9:22-28). He is also said to have "made silver as common in Jerusalem as stone" (2 Chron. 9:27). Again, it is obvious that he had to be quite wealthy in order to have engaged in the numerous and massive building projects of his reign. In every way, Solomon had become a rather typical oriental despot. Living in luxury, losing himself in every whim, King Solomon had lost touch with his people. He no longer sensed or felt their need. For him and for the united monarchy, that was the beginning of the end.

Solomon's last minor achievement is a negative one. He

became famous for his apostasy. His entanglements with the foreign wives of his harem led him into an entanglement with their gods (1 Kings 11:4-8). Solomon turned away from the God of Israel. That was the end.

Such apostasy caused the prophetic party of the land to begin to turn their allegiance to another. In Solomon's own labor battalions, they found the man for whom they sought. The prophet Ahijah sought out Jeroboam and announced to him that the kingdom would be torn away from Solomon and the major part given to the young labor leader (1 Kings 11:27-33). It is worthy of note that the projected division of the kingdom which Ahijah set forth was precisely the division which had been present at the beginning of the reign of David. The kingdom over which Saul and David had labored had fallen to pieces under Solomon. His own folly had sown the seed which was about to produce its bitter fruit.

The Significance of the Period

For the development of Old Testament faith and theology, as well as for the development of Israel's historiography, the period of the united monarchy was among the more significant. If we are to understand the real importance of this period, we must understand its fundamental meaning to Israel. It appears to me that this focuses itself primarily in four areas.

The Concept of Kingship

Obviously, all of Israel's future understanding of the kingship would have had its basis in this first attempt at kingship in Israel. As seen and expressed in the ambivalence of Samuel's attitude, the Hebrew kingship was always viewed from both a positive and a negative position. The kingship was always seen by some among Israel's people as being an open rejection of the kingship of God. Yet, at the same time, it was recognized that the historical situation had made a human king necessary. People being what they are, some form of government was apparently necessary in order for the nation to continue to exist.

Kings, however, were always seen as God's servants by the people of Israel. They were never above the law; they were always responsible to obey the commands of God just as any other person was. This was apparently a unique development in the ancient Near East. Nowhere else, at least as far as we have records, were kings held to be accountable to the same standards as the common people.

Furthermore, closely related to this, in Israel the kingship was always responsible to the organized religion. In modern terminology, the church and the state were not separate; in fact, the state was usually held to be subservient to and responsible to the church. At the very best, the church and state were coextensive and equal. To the Hebrews, whenever the state began to try to dominate the church, they ran into the problems of apostasy similar to that which Solomon brought upon the land. Also, there was a clear involvement of the religious leaders with the political ones. Not only did they view religion and politics as mixing but if they did not mix you would get bad politics and worse religion as well.

Also rooted and grounded in this period of Israel's history is the idea that a person who was the eldest son of a king did not automatically inherit the throne. Instead, he had to be designated by God and acclaimed by the people. Thus, Israel never really viewed the monarchy as automatically hereditary. It was hereditary only so long as it pleased God.

Change in the Concept of Nationhood

With the rise of the Hebrew monarchy, Israel went through a change in their identity as a nation. They were still the people of God. But instead of being a loosely organized group of tribes with a common faith in one God, they became a strongly organized nation with a deep sense of divine destiny.

After the conquests of David, the people of Israel always had a genuine sense of their importance as a nation among nations. With the wealth and positive accomplishments of Solomon, this was further undergirded. For Israel, the Temple in Jerusalem became the symbol of God's presence with them. The king in Jerusalem became the symbol of their national existence.

The Hebrews still knew that their basic commitment was to God. But the visible king gave them a human figure through whom that loyalty and commitment could be expressed. Further, whereas Israel had earlier merely reacted to national and international crises, after the advent of the kingship they at least had a sense of national policy.

In addition, prior to the rise of the monarchy, all Israel had to look back to was their days of slavery in Egypt. They had no sense of a grand or glorious past like so many nations. But after the reigns of David and Solomon at least, they could look back to a golden age of national history. This became so much a part of their heritage that centuries later Jesus could speak of "Solomon in all his glory" (Matt. 6:29).

The Awareness of Responsibility Before God

In a real sense, perhaps the most significant meaning of this period of Hebrew history was the deepening awareness that all people, including the king, are responsible to God. David had shown his awareness of this by the very fact that he tried to cover up his sin of adultery. He openly confessed such responsibility when confronted by the accusing prophet.

If the king had such responsibility to God, everyone else surely did. This was not only true in the case of individuals, but it was also the case for the nation as a whole. There was a clear sense of national morality set forth in the period of the monarchy. If the nation was to fulfill its purposes of service to God, it had to accept the fact that they were united in a national responsibility.

This had been seen in the time of the conquest in the fact that Achan's sin had brought about defeat for all of Israel (Josh. 7:1,11). But it was much more clearly underscored by the consequences of the sins of David and Solomon. Above everything else, Israel was to be righteous, and each citizen was to be righteous.

The Nature of the Hebrew Prophetic Movement

During the time of the united monarchy, a pattern was set for the Hebrew prophetic movement which was to be present throughout their entire history. When David acknowledged his guilt to Nathan, he established a pattern for all others. Yet when Nathan first confronted David, he was the real pattern setter. In no other kingdom of the ancient world could a prophet have confronted a monarch in the manner which Nathan did and expected to survive. At least from the time of Nathan, the prophets of Israel felt the authority and the responsibility to confront evil wherever they saw it. They did not hedge in approaching it but confronted evil directly and fearlessly. It is perhaps true that the Hebrew prophets feared no man because they feared God so much.

In addition to this, the fact that Samuel anointed both Saul and David and that he anointed David long before the youth actually assumed the kingship shows that the prophets felt that the kings, and thus all others, were in a sense to be subservient to the man of God. Prophets could establish and depose kings. This was further reflected when Ahijah made his announcement to Jeroboam. Ahijah was apparently content to wait for the working out of events. There appears to have been no disillusionment due to the fact that after their meeting, Jeroboam was forced to become a refugee in Egypt for a period of time.

Time and history were in the hands of God. The prophet intervened fearlessly. But he could also sit back and wait for God to accomplish His purposes in His own time.

The Future of the Hebrew Messianic Hope

If all we had in the Old Testament was the material related to the united monarchy, I could in no way suggest that Hebrew messianism had its basis here, for it is not mentioned. But, we have a great deal more in the Old Testament than that. Anyone who is familiar with the later development of Israel's messianic hope is quite aware that there is an aspect of it which is clearly rooted in this period.

Israel looked forward to a Messiah who would one day reign upon the throne of David. David, for all his human weaknesses, had established the golden age of the Hebrew monarchy. When Israel looked forward to that ultimate golden age of the future, it was regularly described in terms of the golden age under David. It was to be a time of national exaltation and the subservience of other nations to Israel. It was precisely this dimension of Israel's hope which caused many to reject any idea that Jesus could have been the Messiah, for he did not reinstitute the national glory which Israel had experienced under David. Be that as it may, from this time forward, Israel's hope for the future rested in great David's greater Son.

6
Division and Destruction: Judah and Israel to the Fall of Samaria

Following the death of Solomon, the entire kingdom appeared to collapse. The major territorial conquests of David's reign and the great administrative accomplishments of Solomon seemed about to disappear. The question immediately arises as to why this dissolution came and why it came so quickly.

In viewing the period of the united kingdom, four features stand out which appear to have a bearing on our answer to this question. Fundamental in importance is the fact that the kingdom was apparently never united by a truly common national allegiance among the people of Israel. The primary allegiance of the people always seemed to have been tribal or, at best, regional but not national. The only thing which had really held them together as a nation was a common enemy and the strong personality of the king. When this was lost, all else began to fall apart.

A second feature of significance is the attitude of David and Solomon toward the faith of Israel. David at least acknowledged that he was responsible to obey the will of God. He accepted the rebuke of the prophet Nathan with a simple confession of sin. Solomon, on the other hand, in turning to the worship of the gods of his wives, had begun to alienate the prophets. He appears to have felt above the law. The third feature is somewhat similar, for it is found in the differences of the attitudes of David and Solomon toward their people. David seems to have sought to serve the people fairly and with honor. Solomon, on the other hand, seems to have felt the people were little more than servants for himself. With the massive conscriptions of labor battalions to construct far-flung building projects, he seriously infringed upon the freedom of the people. This created major unrest among those who had no common tribal allegiance with him. Furthermore, in setting up the administrative districts of the land, Solomon sought to destroy the old tribal allegiances. This, too, was quite unpopular.

The fourth item which appears to have had a bearing upon the dissolution of the kingdom was the building of the Temple itself. For the first time, there was a major central sanctuary for the worship of Israel. This in itself drew the people of the land toward an ultimate allegiance to the city of David, for that was where the Temple was located. Tribal leaders of the north who sought to maintain tribal allegiances as primary in Israel knew that the attraction of the Temple would (or might) quickly destroy the more localized allegiances of the people. If this were going to be prevented, it had to be done quickly.

Those features, all coming together at a point following the death of Solomon, set the stage for the division of the kingdom that had apparently been firmly established by David. The unity of the kingdom was superficial only. With the death of Solomon, it all fell apart.

Sources for the Study

In comparison with the earlier periods of Hebrew history, when we get into the era of the divided kingdoms, we have an abundance of riches insofar as sources are concerned. As usual, however, the primary sources are still those of the Bible.

The basic biblical materials are found in 1 Kings 12:1 to 2 Kings 17:41 and in 2 Chronicles 10:1 to 28:27. We must be aware, however, that the material in Chronicles follows the history of Judah only, dealing with Israel only where they came in contact with Judah. In addition to these sources, the lives and ministries of Amos, Hosea, Isaiah, and Micah all came in the final years of this period. There is a great deal of information to be gleaned from the books bearing those names for understanding much of what was going on in both the north and south.

It is important to be aware that the authors of Kings and Chronicles were also using more basic sources. Many of these are cited by the authors. Among those used in Kings are "the Book of the Chronicles of the Kings of Israel" (1 Kings 14:19) and "the Book of the Chronicles of the Kings of Judah" (1 Kings 14:29). These are not to be confused with the biblical Books of Chronicles. Instead, they actually appear to have been the official court records of the two kingdoms. The chronicler also cited a source called "the Commentary on the Book of the Kings" (2 Chron. 24:27). In addition to the sources which these works cite, it is clear that both Kings and Chronicles used other ancient sources. Chronicles clearly quotes from numerous biblical books, and both appear to have used other materials which they do not cite. (If you are interested in pursuing this subject further, you may wish to refer to *The Broadman Bible Commentary*, 3, or any other good critical commentary.)

In addition to the biblical sources, there are numerous other records from the ancient Near East which are important. There are the usual types of written and monumental records from Egypt. By far the most significant records for the study of this period, however, are those from Assyria. The Assyrians kept what has come to be called an eponym list, a list of the major personages and events of each year of their national history. This, coupled with their king lists, allows a very detailed reconstruction of this era. Since the Assyrians were so involved with Hebrew history throughout this time, this material gives us a great deal of information to add to our knowledge. In addition, there are numerous monuments which record or depict events in which the people of the Hebrew kingdoms were involved. For example, the black obelisk of Shalmaneser III actually depicts King Jehu of Israel paying tribute to the Assyrian monarch. This not only gives us historical information but also portrays the clothing and hair styles of the day.

Furthermore, though not directly related to this period, we have the Babylonian Chronicle which correlates with the last days of Assyria. This allows a cross-check of the accuracy of the Assyrian records and establishes their chronological reliability beyond a reasonable doubt.

Beyond actual records and monuments, many archaeological excavations in Palestine give us visible records of the daily life in Israel and Judah. As an example, the excavations in Samaria show us abundant evidence of the daily life in Israel during its last half century. There is clear evidence of abundant wealth on the one hand and abysmal poverty on the other. There are also records (of a wine merchant?) showing the large quantities of wine being consumed. Further, the large number of personal names which have been found in that region which are made up of compounds with Baal show that the worship of Baal was extremely popular and widespread at the time. All of this, multiplied by the various sites which have been excavated add significant depth to our understanding of the day.

One last source which must be given thorough consideration, if we are to understand the history of the era, is the land itself. The geographical features, the ancient highways, and the location of the cities themselves all add to our understanding. We shall return to this in the next section, but it is extremely important to the understanding of this era of Hebrew history to have good maps at hand. You will miss a major source of help if you do not follow the biblical events on a map.

Major Problems for Consideration

As we have seen in each of the other periods of Hebrew history with which we have dealt, there are inevitably some problems of significance in trying to understand the period. This is just the nature of dealing with events from such a long time ago which occurred among people with such a different culture. In dealing with the period of the divided kingdoms, there are three such issues which must be considered. These are of varying degrees of importance relative to one another, but all must be dealt with if we are going to unravel the tangled webs of this part of the history of the Hebrew people.

The Chronological Data

By far the most significant problem of this part of Israel's history is that of the chronology. This is true of the relative chronology, relating different events in each of the kingdoms with one another and with those which occurred in other countries with whom the Hebrews came in contact. It is also true of the absolute chronology, determining the actual dates when some event occurred. I have already discussed how ancient dates are established. (See the section "Establishing an Absolute Chronology" in chapter 1, "Introduction to Old Testament History.")

The problem of unraveling the relative chronology of the period is quite another matter. Unfortunately, it is one which is all too frequently ignored by the nonspecialist in Old Testament studies. The reason that it is generally ignored appears to be that so much data are given that it would appear that everything ought to fit together smoothly. Sadly, this is not the case. So much data are given that everything quickly becomes chaotic when we try to make sense out of the available information. In order to demonstrate the nature of the problem to yourself, consider the following.

Both Rehoboam of Judah and Jeroboam of Israel began to reign at the death of Solomon. Let us call that point in Israel's history "year 0." In the Southern Kingdom of Judah, Rehoboam reigned seventeen years and was succeeded by his son Abijam (1 Kings 14:21). He in turn reigned three years and was succeeded by his son Asa (1 Kings 15:1-2). Asa had a long reign, ruling for forty-one years (1 Kings 15:9-10). At the same time, in the northern kingdom of Israel, Jeroboam reigned twenty-two years and was succeeded by his son Nadab, who in turn reigned two years (1 Kings 14:20; 15:25). Baasha assassinated Nadab and then reigned twenty-four years (1 Kings 15:27,33). He was followed on the throne by his son, Elah, who reigned two years (1 Kings 16:8). Elah was assassinated by Zimri who reigned only seven days before he was in turn defeated by Omri (1 Kings 16:10,15-19). Omri ruled twelve years and was followed on the throne by his son Ahab (1 Kings 16:23,28). Yet when Ahab came to the throne of Israel, we are told that this was "the thirty-eighth year of Asa king of Judah" (1 Kings 16:29).

Now Rehoboam had reigned seventeen years and Abijam three (a total of twenty), so the thirty-eighth year of Asa would have been the fifty-eighth year of Judah's existence (17+3+38=58). But if we add up the twenty-two years of Jeroboam, the two years of Nadab, the twenty-four years of Baasha, the two years of Elah and the twelve years of Omri which all preceeded Ahab's reign, we discover that there had been sixty-two years in Israel's history (22+2+24+2+12=62). Both kingdoms began at the same time, but in one it appears as if four more years have elapsed than in the other. How can we possibly make sense out of this problem?

Historians have grappled with this and similar problems over the years, and numerous solutions have been proposed. Some have suggested that the synchronisms from one kingdom to the other are completely inaccurate and are to be ignored; others have sought to accept the synchronisms while ignoring the actual lengths of reign. Still others have sought to accept some of each while ignoring other parts of the data. Yet still other interpreters have sought to reconstruct the history based solely on archaeological information and foreign records while essentially ignoring the biblical data. Each of these approaches had one thing in common: the basic assumption that the authors of the biblical material were not only in error in regard to their chronological data but also were essentially "nincompoops."

In the mid-twentieth century, Edwin R. Thiele made a major breakthrough in dealing with the problem. He began with the assumption that the biblical authors had basically accurate data and that they knew what they were doing as they handled it. But he also assumed that we had failed to grasp the methods of counting time which ancient peoples used.

Based on a study of methods of keeping ancient records, he discovered a number of different ways which had been used to count time. Some nations began their year in the spring while others began theirs in the fall. Furthermore, in some nations, a king's reign was counted only from the new year celebration following his accession while others counted that part of the year before the new year celebration as a whole year. (In this way, the year when one king died and another began to reign would actually be counted twice, once for each king, clearly adding an apparent error into the chronology.) Furthermore, Thiele recognized that there were numerous times when an aging father associated his son on the throne with him sometime before his death. At such a time both men sometimes counted the years of their coregency in their individual totals.

With this information as a background, Thiele assumed that during the time when one or both of the Hebrew kingdoms were under the influence of Assyria they were forced to use the Assyrian system of reckoning reigns. When they were relatively free of Assyrian domination, on the other hand, they may have expressed that freedom by rejecting the Assyrian system. Furthermore, based on a thorough study of the biblical text, he proposed a number of coregencies which appear to be indicated within the text. Finally, he also assumed that each of the Hebrew kingdoms would have stated the synchronisms with the other in terms of their own system of record keeping.

By applying these assumptions to the chronological data, he was able to make sense out of the data and to demonstrate that the major problem with understanding biblical chronology was not the inaccuracies of the ancient Hebrew recorders but our own ignorance. It appears, then, that the basic problem of the biblical chronology of the kings of Israel and Judah has been solved. Throughout my treatment of this period of Old Testament history, I shall essentially use the dates proposed by Thiele with a few minor modifications based upon my own analysis of the data.

The reader who is interested in pursuing this problem and its study in detail will find it fully set forth in Thiele's *The Mysterious Numbers of the Hebrew Kings* (rev. ed.). This has been simplified in his more recent *The Chronology of the Kings of Israel and Judah.* I must also acknowledge that whether you accept and use Thiele's dates, most histories of the Old Testament era have come up with comparatively similar dates. Considering the amount of time which has elapsed since those events, there is very little difference between the various dating systems proposed. However, it appears to me that Thiele does the best job of assimilating the biblical evidence into the ancient chronologies of other Near Eastern nations. With his approach, the apparent problem has yielded to a through-going scholarship coupled with a genuine respect for the biblical data.

The Nature of Baalism

It is quite apparent with just a cursory reading of the historical or prophetic books of the Old Testament which relate to this period that Baalism was a major problem of the times. This is especially true of the message of Hosea. The popularity of Baalism raises two questions with which the historian must deal. First, we must ask if the prophets were accurate in their description of the prevalence of Baal worship, or were they so incensed by any Baal worship that they actually exaggerated the magnitude of the problem? The second question, if the first is answered positively, is: Why was Baalism so attractive to the Hebrew people?

Both Amos and Hosea described the eighth century BC as an era when religion was thriving, but it was also being tragically debased by its assimilation with the Baal worship of Canaan (Amos 4:4-5; 5:21-24; Hos. 2:2-5,16-17; 4:6-14). A number of commentators have suggested that the situation could not have been as bad as the prophets described. Sadly, the archaeological excavations of Hebrew cities which existed in this period indicate that these prophets were almost certainly correct. It was common in the ancient Near East for people to give their children names compounded with the name (or an abbreviation of the name) of their god. This is quite obvious throughout the Old Testament. The name of the God of Israel was Yahweh (Jahweh), frequently shortened to Yah (Jah). It shows up in the names like Eli*jah,* Isa*iah* (-yah), or Jere*miah*

(-yah). Excavations of cities of the Northern Kingdom reveal that of the names compounded with the name of a god, more than one out of three are formed with Baal! This would indicate the tremendous popularity of Baalism in Israel. It is also quite interesting that the prophets of the Southern Kingdom do not indicate the same degree of problems with Baalism. Excavations of southern sites have yet to turn up a single name compounded with Baal. Thus, the excavations clearly indicate precisely what the prophetic messages had already indicated. Baalism, while present in Judah, was a far more minor problem than in Israel where such worship was apparently rampant.

This brings us to the question of why Baalism had been so readily assimilated into the Hebrew worship. It also raises the question as to why it was more readily assimilated in Israel than in Judah. The answers to these questions are closely related.

The ancient Canaanite literature from Ugarit has shown us the real nature of the Baalism of Canaan. Baalism was a fertility cult. The Baals of the land were supposed to ensure that the people, the flocks, and the land itself were fruitful. Because of this emphasis on fertility, the worship of the Baals and their female consorts, the Ashtaroth, was highly sexual in nature. In fact, the priests and priestesses were little more than "sacred prostitutes." The very nature of this worship appealed to the baser natures of the Hebrews. This alone, however, does not explain fully why this Canaanite worship was assimilated into Israel's worship.

Another reason for the fact that the Hebrews adopted the Baalism of Canaan probably lies in the ancient concept of localized gods. This idea suggested that a particular god had a particular land or region for which he or she was responsible. This is reflected by the request of Naaman of Syria that he be given "two mules' burden of earth" to take home with him so that he could worship the God of Israel (2 Kings 5:17). To Naaman's mind, the God of Israel was confined to the land of Israel. In this light, many Hebrews apparently believed that once they entered the land of Canaan, they had to worship the gods of Canaan.

Closely related to the concept of localized gods was the concept of functionalized gods. Many ancient peoples clearly believed that different gods had different functions. Thus, for example, in Egypt one goddess was responsible for keeping the land free from frogs while another was responsible for preserving the crops from locusts. In this light, many of the Hebrews apparently believed that God had shown himself to be able to deliver them from their enemies but that they needed another god to assure the abundance of crops and children. It is against this background that we must understand Hosea's promises that God would show Israel that He could grow crops by taking them back into the wilderness and doing it in that barren region (Hos. 2:3). The implication was that any god could produce crops in Canaan, but the God of Israel could produce crops in the desert!

At the same time, since much of their sacrificial system was similar to that of Canaan, many Hebrews also apparently assumed that God could be worshiped by all of the forms of worship which Canaan used. Thus they thought that Yahweh could be worshiped as Baal. There is some evidence that some of them even assumed that the two gods were identical (Hos. 2:16).

All of this may explain why some of the Hebrews got involved in Baal worship, but it does not explain why Israel got more involved than Judah. The answer to this part of the problem lies in a different direction. First, we must remember from our study of the conquest and settlement that there is significant evidence that many people were assimilated into Israel who had not gone through the Exodus experience. From a geographical standpoint, it appears that the overwhelming part of these were a part of the northern tribes. These people most likely were already involved in Baal worship and certainly did not have the vivid experience of the Exodus to tie them to the God of Israel. Their influence certainly made itself felt in the north. Furthermore, when the two kingdoms divided, Jeroboam of Israel established two sanctuaries at Dan and

Bethel with golden calves (1 Kings 12:28-29). From the archaeology of Canaan, we know that in many instances the Canaanites depicted Baal as riding upon the back of a calf or a bull. The very choice of images by Jeroboam may have influenced Israel's assimilation of Baal worship into the worship of Yahweh. These factors, then, probably explain why the Baal worship of Canaan became so much more of a problem in the Northern Kingdom than in the Southern.

The Geographical Influences

It is doubtful if there is any other period of Old Testament history where the geography of the land played as important a part in that history as it did in the time when the kingdoms of Israel and Judah existed side by side. It is quite important for anyone studying this era to keep a good set of biblical maps close at hand and to refer to them frequently.

In the early days of the two kingdoms, it is impossible to follow the border struggles between them without locating the sites referred to. Furthermore, the places fortified by Rehoboam (2 Chron. 11:5-12) make more sense when you know the locations of the valley routes by which attackers might have sought to gain entrance into the land. In addition, the whole era of King Ahab of Israel and the ministries of Elijah and Elisha become significantly more meaningful when the geographical references are identified and located. (In all honesty, however, these kinds of things can be said of any period of Hebrew history.)

On the other hand, there is one aspect of the history of this period which offers a major problem to the interpreter unless there is a thorough knowledge of ancient geography. Throughout this period, the Northern Kingdom was much more the object of foreign attack than was the Southern Kingdom. Furthermore, the Northern Kingdom had much greater ups and downs economically than did the Southern one. It is easy to offer a theological rationale for these things, but the historian must also seek for the human and historical factors.

The clues for the solution of this issue can be found in the study of a good map of Palestine and the ancient Near East which gives the locations of the major highways, as well as showing the major topographic features of the region. First, it is quickly obvious that Palestine itself served as a major land bridge between Egypt in the southwest and Mesopotamia in the north and northwest. During the period of history we are considering here, the world's major powers were Egypt and Assyria, which are located on the two ends of this land bridge. The reason, of course, Palestine was such an important bridge is that it is bounded on the west by the Mediterranean Sea and on the east by the great Arabian Desert. Any trade caravans which moved between the two major regions had to move through Palestine. It is just that simple. Thus whoever controlled Palestine controlled the major part of ancient Near Eastern trade. Even more important, no armies could move in the region without marching through Palestine. Thus any nation with either the wish or the will to conquer the ancient world must control Palestine. So the geography of the region makes it quite clear why the land of Palestine was both militarily and economically important to the ancient powers of the world.

But the necessity of controlling Palestine in order to dominate the world does not give us any solution to the problem of why Israel faced so many more crises than Judah. Here again, we must turn to our ancient maps. I have referred earlier to the importance of the major north-south highways for an understanding of Hebrew history. (See chapter 4.) There were four such routes. The most important route is known as the Way of the Sea or the Coastal Route. It descended from Damascus to Dan, cut down through the pass at Megiddo on to the coast at Joppa, and then went from Joppa through the Philistine Plain to Egypt. The other three routes are of much less importance. The second highway is known as the Water-Parting Route, or the Central Highlands Highway. It broke off from the Coastal Highway somewhere well north of Megiddo and came straight down through the mountainous backbone of the land, passing through Jez-

DIVISION AND DESTRUCTION 253

reel, Shechem, Jerusalem, Hebron, Beersheba, and then split with the major fork turning toward Egypt and a minor fork heading to the Gulf of Aqaba. The third and least significant highway descended from Dan on down the west side of the Jordan River. At the Dead Sea, the road forked with the major fork near Jericho ascending very steep mountains to Jerusalem. The minor fork forded the Jordan and ascended the steep Transjordan Plateau, going on southward. This basic route is called the Jordan Valley Highway.

The fourth highway of the region, second only in importance to the Way of the Sea, is known as the King's Highway. (It was given this name since it was the way followed by the four kings in Genesis 14.) It descended from Damascus and followed the edge of the Transjordan Plateau, always just a few miles east of the edge, staying in that small region between its edge and the Arabian Desert.

As I have noted, whoever controlled Palestine could control both the trade and the military movement through this region. We can now be more specific. Whoever controlled these four highways could control both the trade and the military movement throughout the region. Now, when we go back to our maps depicting this period, we discover an amazing fact. All four of these highways passed through the territory of the kingdom of Israel. However, only the Water-Parting Route passed through the territory of Judah. (The difficult fork of the Jordan Valley Route can be essentially discounted here.) Thus when either Egypt or Assyria wished to try to dominate their world, they had to attack Israel. The same is true when they wished to control the economy.

When both Egypt and Assyria were weak, Israel was able to exert significant military clout in the region because of the ease with which they could move troops. Also, at such times, Israel also gained extreme wealth by the fact that all trade of the region had to pass through their borders. The taxes imposed upon such caravans brought a steady flow of wealth into the land. Judah, on the other hand, was frequently bypassed by major armies just because their routes of travel did not lead them into the regions of Judah. An enemy had to plan to attack Judah to do so. For a major power to attack any other major enemy, however, Israel had to be attacked as well. Thus the geography of the region simply forced Israel into a major position on the stage of history in this era. Judah was frequently allowed to sit on the sidelines.

The Background of the Period

Having noted the geographical stage upon which and the religious influences among which Israel and Judah played their roles in this period of Old Testament history, we must also consider the other nations who had a significant role and exerted a major influence upon the history of the two Hebrew kingdoms. As we noted in the preceding chapter, Solomon's reign came to an end about 931 BC. Samaria fell to the Assyrian onslaught in 721 BC. These two dates form the chronological boundaries of our interest in the peoples who existed in parallel with the Hebrew kingdoms.

The Aramaean Kingdoms

Among the nations which exerted major influences upon the Hebrew history of this period were a number of small kingdoms to the north of Israel. These were frequently little more than city-states; but at two times during this period of Israel's history, two of these reached a degree of power and prominence that made a major impact upon that history.

The people who lived in the coastal regions to the north of Israel have come to be known to us as the Phoenicians. They had made quite an impact upon Solomon's reign. However, they never made as significant an impact as they did when the daughter of the king of Sidon married Ahab, king of Israel. Her name was Jezebel, a name which stands as the epitome of feminine evil in the world's history.

When Jezebel married Ahab, she imported the worship of the Phoenician gods, Baal and Asherah, to Israel. These are not to be confused with the Canaanite gods of the

DIVISION AND DESTRUCTION

same name. These two were the chief gods of Phoenicia. The importation of these foreign gods was nothing more than what many of Solomon's wives had done. The difference was that Jezebel appears to have had an almost evangelistic zeal for her gods. Furthermore, Jezebel came from a nation where the king had an absolute authority and was assumed to be above the law. Thus Jezebel's evil influence was felt in Israel by her assumption that her husband, King Ahab, could do what he pleased with no regard for any law. Both of these things precipitated the confrontation between Ahab and Elijah.

Jezebel's influence also made itself felt in Judah. This came about first simply because Judah was just about Israel's vassal at this time. It was further enhanced when the daughter of Jezebel, Athaliah, was married to Jehoram, king of Judah (2 Kings 8:18). Thus the idolatry and form of kingship of the Phoenicians began to be felt in Judah as well.

The major pressure upon the Hebrews from the Aramaean kingdoms, however, was brought to bear by the Syrians, whose center was at Damascus. Their pressures were a serious problem to the Hebrew kingdoms throughout the entire period, although the main force was felt by Israel due to the fact that they were nearer. From about 880 BC, the Syrians of Damascus began to make their influence felt in northern Palestine, actually beginning to gain the same kind of supremacy which David had held over the region. A monument from the reign of Ben-hadad I dated about 850 BC, shows that the Syrians at least claimed dominance over the entire region of northern Palestine, extending all the way to the upper reaches of Mesopotamia.

Particularly from the time of Ahab onward, Israel had major problems with the nation of Syria. This certainly confirms part of the claim of Ben-hadad's stela. During this time, there were some major conflicts between Israel and Syria, as well as alliances with one another against common enemies, such as Judah to the south and Assyria to the north and east.

The influence of Syria upon the Hebrew kingdoms apparently reached its zenith in the Syro-Ephraimitic crisis of 735 BC. There the kingdoms of Syria and Israel formed a coalition to overthrow the rising power of Assyria. When Judah refused to join them, they attacked Judah and planned to replace King Ahaz with a puppet who would join them (2 Kings 16:5; 2 Chron. 28:1-8; Isa. 7:1-9). Although initially successful, the attack ultimately failed when Assyria launched an attack upon both Syria and Israel. This was the beginning of the end for both Syria and Israel. Damascus fell to the powers of Assyria in 732 BC, effectively bringing to an end the Aramaean kingdoms.

Assyria

We have noted that at least part of the explanation for the military successes of David in the northern parts of the territories had been due to the extreme weakness of Assyria. With the decay and dissolution of the Hebrew nation, the opposite was taking place in Assyria. By the reign of Ashurnasirpal II (about 883-861 BC), the Assyrians were once again on the march. He made military atrocities an instrument of international diplomacy and began the systematic deportation of conquered peoples as a strategic part of military advance. By deporting large numbers of people from each conquered land and by the resettlement in those lands of diverse groups of other conquered peoples, Ashurnasirpal II sought to eliminate the effective ability of those lands and peoples to revolt against him. He conquered a large number of small Aramaean city-states. This served (or should have) as a warning to both Israel and Syria of events to come.

By the reign of Ahab of Israel, it became obvious that something had to be done by the Palestinian states to stop the expansive advance of Assyria. Although no mention is made of the coalition in the Old Testament, Ahab of Israel was part of a group which confronted Shalmaneser III of Assyria at Karkar in 853 BC. While the Assyrian records do not record a defeat there, the battle at least ended for a time the Assyrian advance into the region. However, this pause in the Assyrian advance was only brief. Shalmaneser resumed his advance into the region in 842 BC. The famous black obelisk of Shalmaneser bears a relief depicting Jehu, king of Israel, bringing tribute to the Assyrian king.

After the death of Jehu, Israel faced new incursions into their land by the Assyrians for the rest of the ninth century BC. However, from about 800 until around 745 BC, the Assyrians were ruled by a series of weak and ineffective kings. During this time of weakness, Israel under the reign of Jeroboam II was able once again to expand its borders until they almost reached the limits of the earlier Davidic kingdom. But in 745 BC, Tiglath-pileser III came to the throne of Assyria and started a new policy. Whereas Tiglath-pileser's predecessors had frequently been content with just collecting tribute as the result of their military conquests, Tiglath-pileser III was concerned primarily with territorial expansion.

At that point, Israel and Syria recognized the Assyrian threat and initiated the Syro-Ephraimitic crisis to which I referred in the preceding section. Ahaz of Judah, seeking relief from the forces of Israel and Syria, sent a tremendous gift to Tiglath-pileser, asking that he "come up, and rescue me from the hand of the king of Syria and from the hand of the king of Israel, who are attacking me" (2 Kings 16:7). It was a request which Tiglath-pileser could not refuse. To be paid for what he almost certainly was planning on doing anyway was more than any king could have expected. The Assyrians did begin to march, forcing the withdrawal of the Syrian and Israelite troops from Judah. This assault on the part of Assyria resulted ultimately in the final downfall of Syria with the fall of Damascus in 732 BC and the ultimate defeat of Israel with the fall of Samaria in 721 BC. Furthermore, because of the subservience of Ahaz, Judah itself became an Assyrian vassal for a period of time. To a very real extent, the fortunes of both Israel and Judah throughout this era were shaped by the waxing and waning of the Assyrian powers. It was this emerging empire which was the dominant force on the world scene.

Egypt

On the opposite end of the spectrum, both geographically and influentially, stood Egypt. In general, Egypt, which had been such a dominant factor in Hebrew history up to this point, almost ceased to have any major influence upon the Hebrew people throughout this era. However, there are three features of significance of which we must be aware.

First, we have already seen how the labor policies of Solomon gave rise to unrest among the people of Israel in general and among Joseph's tribes in particular. As a part of this, Jeroboam ben Nebat of Ephraim was designated as the one who would strip the northern tribes away from Solomon's son (1 Kings 11:29-37). Consequently, Jeroboam had been forced to flee from the territory of Israel and had been welcomed by Shishak, pharaoh of Egypt (1 Kings 11:40). It was obviously the policy of Egypt to do anything to create problems for the people of Israel. It is also quite probable that Shishak was hoping that, by offering refuge to Jeroboam, he would have him as a vassal if and when he should become king of part of the divided kingdom. However, when this occurred, it became immediately clear that Jeroboam had no intention of being anyone's vassal.

It was the fact that Jeroboam did not act as a vassal which precipitated an Egyptian crisis for the two Hebrew kingdoms. Pharaoh Shishak (variously known as Shoshenk and Sheshonk) recognized that, while Israel was weak and trying to gain strength and while Judah was faced with the problem of trying either to regain its lost tribes or to defend itself against them, Egypt had its best opportunity to make major inroads into the land.

It is obvious that Rehoboam had feared just this sort of thing, for the list of cities which he fortified for defense are located primarily in the south toward Egypt (2 Chron. 11:5-12). Further, it is also obvious that many of these fortresses were deep into Judah's territory, so Rehoboam apparently did not expect to be able to hold off an Egyptian onslaught at his borders. The biblical record of Shishak's invasion is corroborated by Shishak's own inscriptions on the wall of a temple in Karnak (1 Kings 14:25; 2 Chron. 12:2-12). The total defeat of Judah was apparently only averted by Rehoboam's payment of a massive tribute to Shishak.

The part of Shishak's military activity which was not recorded in the Bible was that he also invaded the Northern Kingdom. The long list of cities which he conquered appear to describe a major thrust deep into Israelite territory. Egypt's king was apparently seeking to assert (reassert) his authority over Jeroboam.

It is quite obvious that Shishak's invasion was of limited duration and influence. Shishak did not have the power at his command to occupy the territory of either kingdom. Furthermore, Shishak's record of cities captured in the Hebrew kingdom is the last such record we have from any Egyptian king. Following him, while occasionally it exerted some influence upon Hebrew policies, Egypt was never really a threat again either to Israel or Judah. This is the second feature of significance in the relationship between Egypt and the Hebrews. Although always was on the southern boundaries of Palestine, Egypt was seldom more than a passing shadow from this time onward. There were just no longer any real threats from Egypt.

This brings us to the third feature of the relationship between Israel and Egypt. While Egypt was no longer a threat to the Hebrew kingdoms, they were apparently frequently involved in intrigue, trying to keep both Judah and Israel strong enough to serve as a buffer between Egypt and the growing strength of Assyria. This is reflected in the last days of Israel, when the Assyrians discovered that Hoshea king of Israel was involved with Egypt in some such plot (2 Kings 17:3-4). Thus while too weak to be a threat to Israel or Judah, Egypt was shrewd enough to realize the value of the continued existence of the Hebrew nations. Unfortunately for Israel, the very intrigue with Egypt intended to preserve Israel's national existence was the event that ultimately brought about the final destruction of Israel by Assyria.

Other Peoples of Significance

During this time, there were some minor conflicts between the two Hebrew kingdoms and their three Transjordan neighbors: Ammon, Moab, and Edom (2 Kings 1:1; 2 Chron. 20:1-2). This is not unexpected, for we find conflict between them throughout the Old Testament period.

There are two things which are surprising, however, about the relationships between these nations. First, it is quite surprising to find the record of a coalition between Edom and the Hebrew nations (2 Kings 3:9). The hostility which is generally reflected between Edom and the Hebrews seems to allow little room for such coalitions. It was presumably brought about by the supremacy of Judah over Edom at the time, but we have no other mention of it in the Bible and no record of it outside the Bible.

The second feature of importance regarding Israel's relation with these nations is found in the repeated statement that "Moab rebelled" against Israel (2 Kings 1:1; 3:4-5). There is no record in the Old Testament of Israel ever having conquered Moab. However, archaeologists have recovered a stone monument from this period reflecting these events. It dates from about 840 BC and describes the successful rebellion of Mesha king of Moab against Israel. According to this, Moab had long been in subjection to Israel, following its conquest by Omri. Thus we gain another insight into the international relations of the period. It is just possible that the conquest of Moab was accompanied by some kind of subjugation of Edom. This might offer an explanation for Edom participating in a military campaign alongside the Hebrew kingdoms.

Be that as it may, it would appear that, while there were minor conflicts between Ammon, Moab, and Edom throughout this period, there was not any major threat to the independence of either Israel or Judah. Thus neither Israel nor Judah apparently had to devote a great deal of thought or energy to defending their eastern borders.

The History of the Period

In trying to summarize the history of the time when Israel and Judah existed side by side as separate kingdoms, the student of the period faces several distinct difficulties. First, although we are dealing with two distinct nations, their history is so intertwined as to make it necessary to try to tell both stories at the same time. However, by so doing, it tends to make the understanding of the developments in each kingdom a bit more difficult. Second, several of the kings were known by more than one name. Some of the names appear to be a nickname or a contraction of the basic name. At other times, it appears as if they had two names. Now this is not at all surprising, but it also makes it more difficult for the student. Third, there are occasions where different kings in different kingdoms have the same name. This is difficult enough; but when this occurs at the same time, it makes it even more necessary for care on the part of the student. Beyond this, some of the names, although different, are similiar enough to add even more confusion to the subject. Fourth, the chronology does offer major problems, as we have noted earlier in this chapter. In order to try to make this difficulty less of a problem, I will give a chronological summary at the beginning of each era of this period.

The Time of Separation and Conflict

With the death of Solomon, Rehoboam, Solomon's son, assumed the throne of Judah (1 Kings 11:43; 2 Chron. 9:31). It appears that there was no question who would succeed to the throne as there had been at the death of David. However, it would also appear that the succession to the throne of Israel was still not automatic, for a great convocation was held at Shechem (1 Kings 12:1-5; 2 Chron. 10:1-5). We must remember that Shechem had been a major shrine in the northern territory from the time of Joshua (Josh. 24:1). It should be noted that from all appearances Israel expected to crown Rehoboam, but they did wish to have their burdens of taxation and forced labor diminished.

Chronological Table

Judah		Israel	
Rehoboam	931-913	Jereboam ben Nebat	931-910
Abijah	913-911		
Asa	911-870	Nadab	910-909
		Baasha	909-886
		Elah	886-885
		Zimri	885

However, when the leaders of the northern tribes placed their demands before Rehoboam, he asked for an opportunity to take counsel with his advisors. At that time, the young king turned to the older councillors who had served Solomon over the years. These men, wise in the ways of politics, essentially advised the young king to promise anything in order to get the northerners' allegiance. Then, once he was king, he could do as he pleased (1 Kings 12:6-7; 2 Chron. 10:6-7). But Rehoboam's own youthful companions advised a policy of more straightforward honesty (1 Kings 12:8-11; 2 Chron. 10:8-11). The young king followed the advice of his companions with the result that he was totally rejected by the northern leaders (1 Kings 12:16; 2 Chron. 10:16).

When Rehoboam discovered that his claim to kingship had been rejected, he sent Adoram, director of forced labor, to deal with the Israelites, apparently with the intent of forcing them to acknowledge Rehoboam's claim to the throne. It was a foolish gesture, for the Israelites were in a violent mood and stoned Adoram to death (1 Kings 12:18). At that brutal turn of events, Rehoboam fled from the convocation, racing for the safety of Jerusalem.

Having rejected Rehoboam's kingship, the northern tribes were left without a king. However, Jeroboam, Solomon's exiled labor leader, had returned from Egypt. He had already been popular with his own people before he had been forced to flee from Solomon. Upon his return, he was the natural leader for the northern tribes to turn to as king (1 Kings 12:20). With this turn of events, the nation which had been held together primarily by the personality of the kings entered into that period of its history which we call the divided monarchy. This was not a new thing so much as it was a return to an earlier condition.

Upon the establishment of two separate kingdoms, both Rehoboam and Jeroboam were faced with the problems of consolidating their kingships. Rehoboam, who had suddenly lost the major portion of his kingdom and its resources, immediately turned to establishing a defensive perimeter. He had foolishly thought about attacking the much greater northern forces but was wisely dissuaded from that course of action (1 Kings 12:21-24; 2 Chron. 11:1-12). It would appear from the places which Rehoboam fortified that he feared an attack from Egypt. This may have been due to the fact that Jeroboam apparently had Egyptian support. Rehoboam may have feared that Egypt would try to annex his territory to that of Jeroboam, thus making Jeroboam king of the whole land.

Jeroboam, on the other hand, was faced with setting up a new administration and with making sure that the people did not turn back to the house of David. His primary fear at first appears to have been the attraction of the Temple in Jerusalem. Solomon had built a magnificient building to serve as the center of the Hebrew religion. Jeroboam was well aware that if his people regularly journeyed to Jerusalem to worship, they might soon wish to rejoin the southern part of the kingdom. To counteract that possibility, Jeroboam established the shrines which were at Dan and Bethel as the official sanctuaries of Israel. Dan was at the northern border of the land, and Bethel was just about at the southern border. These were ancient shrines which Jeroboam adapted to his purposes. In these shrines, Jeroboam set up two golden calves (1 Kings 12:26-29). It is possible that Jeroboam was adopting a Canaanite practice, for the Baals of Canaan are occasionally portrayed as riding upon the backs of calves. He may have been trying to portray Israel's invisible God as doing the same. If this was his intent, it certainly made it easier for the people of Israel to assimilate the worship of Baal into the worship of Yahweh. It is also clear that the calves themselves became objects of worship. Whatever Jeroboam's intent, the authors of the biblical narrative were absolutely clear that what he had done was wholly wrong.

Furthermore, it is at this point that we see again the rising influence of the prophets among the Hebrews, for one confronted Jeroboam about this sin (1 Kings 13:1-10). Unlike David, Jeroboam was not at first submissive to the prophetic message. However, he later tried to get the unknown prophet to become a part of his court.

Jeroboam's early years as king of Israel were also involved with a major struggle with Shishak of Egypt. The Egyptian pharaoh had sheltered Jeroboam when he was a fugitive from Solomon. Apparently, Shishak had expected Jeroboam to be a vassal to him when he came to the throne of Israel. However, this failed to materialize, so he seems to have set out to punish Jeroboam. Although this conflict is not recorded in the Bible, we have seen how Shishak's records describe his invasion of both Judah and Israel. The only biblical hint of this invasion of Israel may be found in the fact that Jeroboam first fortified Shechem as his capitol. From there he moved to Penuel and finally to Tirzah (1 Kings 12:25; 14:17). These moves might reflect his strategic retreats from the Egyptian attacks.

Rehoboam's reign in Judah was rather similar to that of Jeroboam in Israel. He, too, was forced to consolidate his kingdom and was also faced with a major invasion by Shishak of Egypt. Shishak apparently captured a large number of Rehoboam's cities, turning aside only when Rehoboam paid a massive tribute to him from the royal and Temple treasures (1 Kings 14:25-27).

Throughout the reigns of both Rehoboam and Jeroboam, there was an ongoing conflict between both Israel and Judah (2 Chron. 12:15). It does not appear that either kingdom made a significant impact upon the other at this time however. But they were using up their resources and their energies in the continual struggle.

Following the death of Rehoboam, Abijam his son came to the throne of Judah (1 Kings 14:31). He is also known as Abijah but he is not to be confused with the son of Jeroboam by the same name (1 Kings 14:1; 2 Chron. 12:16). The conflict between Israel and Judah continued. Even though Abijam is said to have been victorious, though outnumbered, Judah apparently was not able to make any major territorial inroads into Israel (2 Chron. 13:15-19). Only border sites were taken by Judah.

Following the brief reign of Abijam, the throne of Judah was occupied by Asa (1 Kings 15:8). At about the same time, Jeroboam of Israel was succeeded by his son Nadab (1 Kings 15:25). He was almost immediately assassinated by Baasha, who siezed the throne of Israel (1 Kings 15:27-28). This was to be only the first of nine different changes of dynasty in the Northern Kingdom. It would appear that the respect which David had shown for the reigning king continued to endure in Judah. Israel, on the other hand, having once rejected the house of David, apparently never felt the same respect for their reigning monarch.

The conflict between the two kingdoms continued during the reigns of Asa of Judah and Baasha of Israel (1 Kings 15:16). For the first time, however, international intrigue began to play a part. Asa sent a present of gold and silver to the king of Syria, asking him to attack Israel from the north (1 Kings 15:18-19). This was immediately done, forcing Baasha to cease fortifying the southern border and to fight against the Syrians. With the forces of Israel drawn off to the north, Asa was able to capture Israel's southern fortresses and to dismantle them. Adding insult to injury, Asa used the materials from Baasha's forts to strengthen his own defenses (1 Kings 15:22).

Also during Asa's reign, Judah was attacked by the army of "Zerah the Ethiopian" (2 Chron. 14:9). The Hebrew term used here could also allow the interpretation that Zerah was an Arabian, and some suggest this. The direction from which the attack came would support the interpretation that it was from Ethiopia. However, the booty which Asa obtained by his victory would sound more like a victory over Arabians. Since there is no other evidence available at the moment, we shall have to leave the question open.

Asa is also credited with instigating a major religious reform in Judah. This seems to have been significantly influenced by the prophets (2 Chron. 15:1-15). The influence of the prophets upon the governments of the two kingdoms was to be an ever-growing feature. Unfortunately for Asa, the prophetic support of earlier days turned against him later in his reign. When he was rebuked for having trusted more in international diplomacy than in the power of God (2 Chron. 16:7-10). The loss of prophetic support angered Asa. Unlike David, Asa began to oppress those who opposed him.

Meanwhile, in the Northern Kingdom, things become even more chaotic. There Baasha was succeeded by his son, Elah (1 Kings 16:6). Unfortunately, Zimri, one of the military commanders of Elah's army, conspired against him, killing him and seizing the throne (1 Kings 16:8-10). Although Zimri's overthrow of Elah was both thorough and brutal, he did not long enjoy the fruits of his rebellion. Just seven days later he was attacked by another of the military commanders of Israel, Omri. When the troops under Omri besieged Zimri in the palace at Tirzah, Zimri's brief rebellion was at an end. Recognizing the certainty of his defeat, Zimri set the palace on fire, burning himself to death within (1 Kings 16:17-18). Thus Omri became the king of Israel, and a new era dawned in the history of the two kingdoms.

The first fifty years of the history of the separated kingdoms were marked by major conflict. Both kingdoms had faced major invasions from without, and both had been involved throughout almost the entire period in conflict with each other on their common border. This time of conflict had certainly not given either kingdom an opportunity to develop a really effective government. With the major portion of their resources having been devoted to military conflict, both Israel and Judah came to the end of this period in a state of relative poverty. Weak, disillusioned, and generally ineffective, Israel and Judah were faced with either ultimate absorption by one of the kingdoms around them or their accomplishments had to take on a more positive direction. It was in that critical situation that Omri came to the throne in Israel. Shortly thereafter, Jehoshaphat came to the throne of Judah.

The Time of Israelite Supremacy

With the accession of Omri to the throne of Israel, it would appear that for the first time since Solomon an able administrator was in power in one of the two Hebrew kingdoms. This may not be quite fair to those who preceded Omri. But even if Omri were not a more able administrator, he at least altered the military situation between Israel and Judah so that he had the opportunity to exercise personal administrative skills.

Chronological Table

Judah		Israel	
[Asa	911-870]	Omri	885-874
Jehoshaphat	(873) 870-848	Ahab	874-853
Jehoram	(853) 848-841	Ahaziah	853-852
		Jehoram	852-841

(NOTE: *The information in brackets was included on the table in the preceding section. The dates in parentheses indicate the date when a coregency began. The date immediately following such a parenthetical date indicates when the independent reign began.*)

After the suicide of Zimri, the people of Israel were even further divided for a brief time, with one part following Omri and the other part following a rival by the name of Tibni. We have no way of knowing how the tribes were divided at the time, but it was not long until the armies of Omri were finally victorious. In one of the massive understatements of the Bible, we are told, "But the people who followed Omri overcame the people who followed Tibni . . . so Tibni died, and Omri became king" (1 Kings 16:22).

Although the biblical narrative tells us very little about the reign of Omri, we do know several facts about him which force upon us the conclusion that he was an able general and, more important, an able political leader. First, Omri relocated the capitol of Israel to the hill of Samaria (1 Kings 16:24). Samaria offered the same political advantages to Omri that Jerusalem had earlier offered to David. It did not actually belong to any tribe and, therefore, was not conducive to creating jealousy or partiality. Furthermore, it was highly defensible, situated at the top of a very steep hill. Archaeological excavations of the construction done by Omri show that it was both massive and effective, reflecting Omri's wisdom in such matters.

Second, Ahab, Omri's son, was married to Jezebel the daughter of Ethbaal, king of the Sidonians (1 Kings 16:31). Although this is told in the Bible in the biographical material related to Ahab, it was certainly arranged by Omri. This would indicate that the Phoenician (Aramaean) kingdom recognized Omri as a significant king. Such marriages were normally arranged to seal major treaties, and such treaties were not entered into this way by wholly unequal partners. Although this surely indicates Omri's importance, it was to have very tragic consequences for his kingdom following his death.

Third, although there is no mention of it in the Bible, the records of Mesha king of Moab record that Moab was conquered and subjugated by Israel during the reign of Omri. Furthermore, by the time Ahab became king, Israel and Judah were involved in a coalition of peace with Judah being very much the junior partner, essentially subservient to Israel. We do not know whether this was accomplished by Omri's military action, the threat of such action, or by international diplomacy. Regardless of how it had been accomplished, Omri had done it.

Fourth, although we have no record either in the Bible or in the Assyrian annals of the dealings between Omri and the Assyrians, we know that they certainly existed and that Omri was both impressive and successful in those relations. This is demonstrated by the fact that for as long as the Assyrian Empire existed they frequently referred to Israel as the land of Omri. For such a lasting impression to have been made, Omri must have struck them as being quite important.

All these things being considered, we must acknowledge the fact that Omri was a very successful ruler. He consolidated Israel, expanded Israel's influence, and brought it to a position of military and political stability and significance. By the end of Omri's reign, Israel was definitely in a position of supremacy with regard to Judah. Furthermore, by initiating a time of relative peace between the two nations, Omri had created a situation which allowed both kingdoms to turn their resources to things more constructive than fighting with one another.

Following the death of Omri, Omri's son Ahab assumed the throne of Israel. Shortly thereafter, it appears that Jehoshaphat began a coregency with his father, Asa, in Judah. During the reigns of these two men, there was relative peace between the two kingdoms. Both kings were apparently quite prominent in relation to their own neighbors. At the beginning, Judah may not have been wholly subservient to Israel; but by the end of Ahab's reign, he was certainly in essential leadership over Jehoshaphat of Judah, for he could require the Judean king to wear royal robes into battle while Ahab went in disguise (1 Kings 22:30; 2 Chron. 18:28). The purpose of this tactic was to make the king of Judah a more obvious target than Ahab. Such an act clearly demonstrates Ahab's authority over Jehoshaphat. Since Jehoshaphat is portrayed as being a very significant ruler of the region, Ahab's ultimate supremacy over Jehoshaphat would point up the power and political greatness of Israel in these days (2 Chron. 17:10-19).

Ahab is described by the biblical writers as a very mixed character. Politically and militarily, he had to be very competent. There were a number of wars in which he was engaged with great success. He was able, with the help of prophetic advisors, to survive a Syrian siege of Samaria and to ultimately drive the Syrians from the land (1 Kings 20:16-21,26-30). Furthermore, he concluded the wars with Ben-hadad of Syria by making a treaty which gave Israel a special trading quarter in Damascus, Syria's capitol city (1 Kings 20:34). This essentially put Syria into a vassal relationship with Israel. This relationship lasted at least long enough for the two nations to be a part of a coalition which was confronted by Shalmaneser III at the battle of Karkar in 853 BC. At that time, Ahab of Israel, according to the Assyrian records, furnished two thousand chariots and ten thousand foot soldiers to the alliance. The fact that Ahab furnished more chariots than any other king would further indicate Ahab's power and importance.

However, as soon as Assyria was defeated, the border warfare between Israel and Syria was resumed. The Syrians appear to have captured Ramoth-gilead which had been an important fortification of Solomon in the northern Transjordan region. Israel called upon Jehoshaphat and his troops from Judah to aid him in his attempt to recapture the city. Fearing his own death, Ahab went into battle dressed as an ordinary soldier, rather than as a king. However, a random arrow from a Syrian warrior struck him and he died (1 Kings 22:34-36). The death of Ahab brought the battle to an unsuccessful conclusion; and his troops, disheartened, returned home without having recaptured Ramoth-gilead. Furthermore, the fact that Judah also withdrew from the battle at this time would indicate that their presence there had been under duress all along.

Ahab's reign, however, is not so much known for his military and political accomplishments as it is for its religious failures. When Ahab had married Jezebel, daughter of the king of Sidon, she had imported the worship of Baal and Asherah of Phoenicia, along with a large number of prophets of her faith. Furthermore, Ahab had built a temple to her gods in Samaria. Baal and Asherah of Phoenicia are different from the many Baals which the Canaanites worshiped. The Phoenician Baal was the chief god of the Phoenicians, and Asherah was his female consort. Jezebel was apparently quite evangelistic about her faith, thus the worship of Yahweh in Israel appeared to be seriously threatened.

At this time, a major change occurred in the prophetic movement of Israel. Prior to this time the Hebrew prophets generally seem to have come on the scene only briefly, to have confronted one particular situation, and then to have disappeared. With the rise of Elijah to confront the idolatry and unrighteousness of Ahab, we find a prophet with an ongoing ministry. This was a major step toward what became the unique development of Hebrew prophecy. The ministry of Elijah made the reign of Ahab most significant for the biblical writers.

With no introduction, the prophet Elijah suddenly appeared on the scene to do battle for the God of Israel. Elijah confronted Ahab with the announcement, "As the Lord the God of Israel lives, before whom I stand, there shall be neither dew nor rain these years, except by my word" (1 Kings 17:1). Immediately thereafter, Elijah hid himself from the king. As the drought came and the crisis increased, the prophet went to Zarephath in the region of Sidon (1 Kings 17:9). The brilliance of that move is obvious when we remember that Sidon was Jezebel's home. Elijah's enemies would never have looked for him there.

The drought grew in intensity, and Elijah at last returned to face Ahab (1 Kings 18:17-18). At that time, Elijah announced that the real conflict was not between himself and Ahab but between Yahweh and Baal. The famous contest on Mount Carmel was held at this point to offer a testimony to the people of Israel as to which was the real God (1 Kings 18:21-24). Elijah's victory was accompanied by his slaughter of the prophets of Baal. Following Elijah's victory, he announced to Ahab that the drought was about to be broken and that rain was about to come (1 Kings 18:36-46).

Elijah was riding on the crest of that victory when Jezebel sent word to him that she was going to kill him within twenty-four hours (1 Kings 19:2-3). Suddenly Elijah caved in; turning and running, he left the territory of Israel behind. He fled on through Judah, eventually arriving at Sinai, the mount of Israel's beginnings. Two events along the way clearly portrayed Elijah's humanity. In the wilderness, he announced that he was ready to die (1 Kings 19:4). Those were just pious words; if he had really been ready to die, he could have stayed back in Israel where Jezebel would have accomplished that feat for him. Further, at Sinai, he declared that he was the only one left who was faithful to God and that he had fled with the purpose of preserving God's witness (1 Kings 19:10,14). He was wrong on all counts. He was not the only one left, having overestimated his own importance. Further, instead of trying to save his life, he needed to prepare someone to take his place. Finally, Elijah still had a ministry to perform (1 Kings 19:15-18).

It is important to note that a part of Elijah's remaining ministry had to do with a foreign ruler. Another dimension of the later Hebrew prophetic movement was their belief that their ministry was never necessarily confined to their own land and to their own people. This idea may have had its roots in this experience of Elijah.

Elijah's further ministry may be summed up in his confrontation of Ahab over Naboth's vineyard and in Elijah's call of Elisha to be his successor. As we have seen, the land of Israel was thought by them to be peculiarly God's gift. It was a stewardship which could not be abandoned. Ahab coveted the vineyard of Naboth but could not obtain it because of Naboth's commitment to his stewardship. Jezebel, on the other hand, did not understand Ahab's childish actions. In her land, a king did what he pleased. So she had Naboth killed and gave the vineyard to Ahab (1 Kings 21:1-16). At that point, Elijah stepped in again, pronouncing judgment upon Ahab and his house (1 Kings 21:20-24). Not long after this, Ahab was killed in the battle for Ramoth-gilead (1 Kings 22:34-35).

In addition to Elijah, at least two other prophets of similar nature ministered in Israel at that time. There was an unnamed prophet who confronted Ahab over the initial relations with Ben-hadad of Syria (1 Kings 20:13, 35-43). There was also Micaiah, the son of Imlah, who warned Ahab of impending doom (1 Kings 22:9,13-18).

However, we also note that Ahab had a group of court prophets who were supported by him, generally offering the king the kinds of advice which he wished to hear (1 Kings 22:5-6). At least from this time, the ongoing conflict between the true and the false prophets among the Hebrews had its beginning.

Ahab was succeeded briefly in Israel by his son, Ahaziah (1 Kings 22:51-53). He, too, had at least one conflict with Elijah because he sought the help of the god of Ekron (2 Kings 1:2-4). Following Ahaziah's death, his brother Jehoram became king (2 Kings 1:17; 3:1). During this period, Elijah passed off the scene and was succeeded by Elisha (2 Kings 2:9-12).

With the death of Ahab and the subsequent turmoil created by the brief reign of Ahaziah, the military strength of the Northern Kingdom began to wane. Immediately upon the accession of Jehoram of Israel, Mesha the king of Moab rebelled. However, Israel still appears to have been superior to Judah and to have led them in a coalition along with Edom in an unsuccessful attempt to bring Moab back into subjection (2 Kings 3:4-12,21-27). It was apparently almost successful but failed due to the superstitious fear which was engendered when the king of Moab sacrificed his own son. This victory of Moab is also commemorated on the Moabite stela, as we noted earlier.

During this period of history, as we have seen, Judah appears to have been pretty much at the beck and call of Israel. However, Jehoshaphat of Judah was not a nonentity. Jehoshaphat had been rather successful militarily in the region of Judah and was able to form a marriage alliance between his son Jehoram and Athaliah, the daughter of Ahab and Jezebel (2 Kings 8:18; 2 Chron. 21:6). Furthermore, Jehoshaphat tried to enter into the kind of deep-sea trade from Ezion-geber which Solomon had done. Unfortunately, this was unsuccessful, but it at least showed ambition and initiative, even though the alliance was condemned because of Jehoshaphat's spiritual insensitivity (2 Chron. 20:35-37).

Following the death of Jehoshaphat, Jehoram succeeded to the throne of Judah. This leaves us with the frustrating situation of having two kings by the same name ruling in the two separate kingdoms (2 Chron. 21:1). Perhaps urged on by the evil advice of Athaliah, Jehoram of Judah immediately slaughtered his own brothers who might have become rivals for the throne (2 Chron. 21:2-4). During his reign, Judah lost control of Edom, along with some of the Philistine territories (2 Chron. 21:8-10,16-17).

Meanwhile, in the Northern Kingdom, the conflict with the Syrians was renewed by the king of Syria with increased vigor. It would appear that, if it had not been for the aid and advice of the prophets, the Northern Kingdom might have been completely overrun (2 Kings 6:8 to 7:20). Furthermore, Elisha was also involved in a political coup in Syria itself (2 Kings 8:7-15).

The picture in both Israel and Judah during the reigns of the two Jehorams (sometimes shortened to Joram) is one of dissolution and decay again. This time, however, the political dissolution was accompanied by the growing idolatry of both kings, as well as by the injustice of the kings and their kingdoms. Furthermore, this time of difficulty found a growing dissatisfaction among the prophets of Yahweh who were on the scene. It was the sort of situation which could not long endure. It did not. The prophetic party intervened, taking the most active hand in governmental politics which they had ever had among the Hebrew people. It was the inevitable end of unrighteousness governments faced by men of faith who were inexorably comitted to personal and national allegiance to the God of Israel.

The Prophetic Revolution

The ongoing saga of the kingdoms of Israel and Judah next moved into a period which is regularly described by historians as the time of the prophetic revolution. The name itself can be misleading, for it was not the prophets themselves who actually overthrew their governments. However, it was through their influence and by their instigation that the revolution occurred.

Chronological Table

Judah		Israel	
Ahaziah	841	Jehu	841-814
Athaliah	841-835		
Joash	835-796	Jehoahaz	814-798
Amaziah	796-767	Joash	798-782

It will be recalled that Ahab of Israel received a fatal wound in the battle to retake Ramoth-gilead (1 Kings 22:29-35). Apparently the battle was unsuccessful and was not renewed by Israel for more than a decade. However, Ramoth-gilead was eventually assaulted again by Jehoram of Israel. During the assault, Jehoram was wounded and returned to the palace at Jezreel to recuperate (2 Kings 9:14b-15a). At that point, Elisha and his disciples took a hand in the monarchical succession of Israel. The commander of Israel's forces at Ramoth-gilead was Jehu, and Elisha sent a disciple to anoint Jehu as king (2 Kings 9:1-3). This anointing was carried out privately, and its effect was twofold. It assured Jehu of the support of the prophets, but its privacy allowed him, as the military strategist, to choose his own time for overthrowing the house of Omri.

As soon as the young prophet had departed, Jehu's followers wanted to know what had transpired. Jehu recounted the event as if it were insignificant and as if he believed that the prophet were a madman, apparently wishing to find out whether the other officers of the army would support him. Their reaction was immediate. Wholeheartedly, they proclaimed Jehu as king (2 Kings 9:11-13).

With the immediate support of the army, Jehu raced for Jezreel for a confrontation with Jehoram. When the king came out to meet his general, he was accused of sinfulness and idolatry and then was assassinated (2 Kings 9:21-24). Jehoram had been accompanied by Ahaziah of Judah, who was shot by Jehu (2 Kings 9:27-28; 2 Chron. 22:8-9). Jehu continued to purge the idolatrous leaders by executing all of the officials of Judah who had accompanied Ahaziah to Israel. Then he turned his attention back to the ruling party of Israel.

When Jehu reached Jezreel, his first act was to see to the execution of Jezebel (2 Kings 9:30-35). He apparently recognized that much of Israel's problems had come from her evil influence. Jehu next ordered the elders of the city of Samaria to execute all of Ahab's sons. This was brutally accomplished, and their heads were brought to Jehu at Jezreel (2 Kings 10:1-10). In a further purge, Jehu executed all of Ahab's counselors in Jezreel (2 Kings 10:11).

With all of this, Jehu's bloodbath was not yet over. He extended it to include a large party of the ruling family of Judah who had come to visit Samaria, unaware that a rebellion was in progress (2 Kings 10:12-14). Upon Jehu's arrival in Samaria, he allied himself with Jehonadab and then ordered the execution of anyone who was related to the evil Ahab (2 Kings 10:15-17).

Jehonadab was regarded as the founder of the Rechabites, who were named after one of Jehonadab's ancestors (Jer. 35:19). This ultraconservative group believed that Israel should live the simple life which their ancestors had lived in the desert. They appear to have basically been opposed to all of the advances of civilization. They were certainly utterly committed to the desert faith. This allegiance to Yahweh, Israel's God, made them an ideal group for Jehu to align himself with to carry out a policy of exterminating Ahab's family and the worship of the Phoenician Baal.

With Jehonadab's support, Jehu's final act in his purge of Israel was an attempt to eliminate the Baal worship from Israel. He ordered a great day of worship at the temple of Baal in Samaria, implying his own support of Baal. After the worshipers had arrived, he and his troops, accompanied by Jehonadab, sealed the temple and executed all of the Baal worshipers who were there (2 Kings 10:18-27).

As so often occurs in moments of religious zeal, Jehu allowed the purge to go to drastic excess. Almost a century later, the prophet Hosea was to announce judgment upon the dynasty of Jehu for his bloody deeds, proclaiming, "I will punish the house of Jehu for the blood of Jezreel, and I will put an end to the kingdom of the house of Israel. And on that day, I will break the bow of Israel in the valley of Jezreel" (Hos. 1:4-5).

It may be that while Jehu had devoted himself to the consolidation of power and to the extermination of the worship of the Phoenician Baal he neglected Israel's defenses. We are told that the Syrians began "to cut off parts of Israel" (2 Kings 10:32-33). This perhaps offers an explanation for Jehu's appearance on the black obelisk of Shalmaneser III of Assyria. There he is depicted as bringing massive tribute to the king of Assyria. This had to have occurred in the first year of Jehu's reign, but it is not recorded in the Bible. Either Jehu was paying tribute to keep Shalmaneser III from attacking him or he was paying tribute to get the Assyrian king to attack the Syrians, thus relieving their pressure on Israel. Although we cannot be certain, it was probably the former; for the Syrian pressure appears to have continued throughout Jehu's reign.

Jehu's rebellion in Israel had also created a problem for Judah with the death of Ahaziah of Judah. We must remember that Ahaziah's mother was Athaliah, the daughter of Ahab and Jezebel. She was apparently the same type of person as her mother. With the death of her son Ahaziah, Athaliah executed every member of the royal family who might have laid claim to the throne of Judah (2 Kings 11:1). This would have included both her own children and grandchildren! There was nothing of what we normally consider to be motherly love present in her at all. By this brutal act, Athaliah sought to eliminate any legitimate heir to the throne of Judah. Thus she was able to claim the throne for herself. This was the only time that a woman reigned over either of the Hebrew kingdoms. It was also the only time that anyone other than a member of the dynasty of David sat upon the throne of Judah. Her seizure of power appeared to be both successful and unchallenged. Athaliah apparently assumed that her claim to the throne was secure. She was wrong.

In an act of selfless bravery, "Jehosheba, the daughter of King Joram, sister of Ahaziah, took Joash the son of Ahaziah, and stole him away from among the king's sons who were about to be slain, and she put him and his nurse in a bedchamber. Thus she hid him . . . six years . . . in the house of the Lord" (2 Kings 11:2-3). Since "Jehoash was seven years old when he began to reign," he was about a year old at the time he was rescued (2 Kings 11:21; Jehoash is a variant spelling of Joash). The chronicler explains that Joash was able to be hidden in the Temple because Jehoshaeath (a variant spelling of Jehosheba) was "wife of Jehoiada the priest" (2 Chron. 22:11). The fact that Joash could have been rescued at all probably indicates that the slaughter of the royal family took place with such violence and brutality that no accounting of the slain was made. Further, the fact that the child could be hidden within the Temple precincts for six years probably indicates that neither Athaliah nor her closest followers ever frequented the Temple. Growing up in that holy place under the protection and guidance of Jehoiada also had to have made a significant impact upon the life of young Joash.

Finally, with the support of the Temple guards, Jehoiada had the seven-year-old Joash crowned king. When Athaliah heard of it, she raced for the Temple, but she was too late. She was seized, carried out of the Temple, and executed (2 Kings 11:4-14). It would appear that Athaliah's reign had been unpopular and that she had been able to maintain her position only through the force of her own troops. When she came to the Temple unaccompanied by them, all was lost.

As young Joash became king, he was obviously reigning under the regency of Jehoiada the priest. There was a renewal of the covenant and a refurbishing of the Temple (2 Kings 11:17; 12:4-16). The purifying of religion in Judah was much more gentle than it had been in Israel. Apparently as long as Jehoiada lived, Joash was loyal to the priest's teachings and to the faith of Yahweh.

However, upon Jehoiada's death, the situation changed. Joash apparently had resented the influence which the priest had had upon him and tried to show his independence of that influence when Jehoiada died. Joash turned away from the worship of the God of Israel. Rebuked for this by Jehoiada's son, Zechariah (not to be confused with the prophet by that same name), the king had the priest executed (2 Chron. 24:17-21).

Politically, everything fell apart in the latter years of Joash's reign. The Syrians had regained such strength that they were able to invade down the coastal plain as far as Gath. Following that success, they began to march toward Jerusalem. In the battle which followed, Joash was wounded, and Jerusalem was spared only by the payment of a major tribute (2 Kings 12:17-18; 2 Chron 24:23-25). In that weakened condition, Joash was assassinated by some of his servants (2 Kings 12:20; 2 Chron. 24:25). His is the sad, tragic story of a young man who started off well but turned aside from his earlier ways in his latter days. Such a policy brought devastation to his country and death to himself.

About midway through the reign of Joash of Judah, Jehu of Israel died and was succeeded by his son, Jehoahaz. The Syrians, who had made serious inroads into the border territories of Israel during Jehu's reign, continued their pressure upon Israel in the time of Jehoahaz (2 Kings 13:3). It was probably the continuing success of Hazael of Syria against Israel which encouraged the Syrians to make their invasion down the coastal plain and the assault upon Jerusalem near the end of the reign of Joash of Judah.

However, the Syrian pressure upon Jehoahaz of Israel brought about a strange result, at least at the first. Jehoahaz is said to have "besought the Lord" (2 Kings 13:4). We must remember that this was not the normal evaluation of the author of Kings concerning Israel's monarchs, for they were usually considered to be idolators. This religious attitude of Jehoahaz was probably influenced by the strength of the prophetic group in the Northern Kingdom. At this point, it almost sounds as if we were back in the period of the judges, for we are told that "the Lord gave Israel a savior, so that they escaped from the hand of the Syrians" (2 Kings 13:5). We are told nothing more about this unknown savior and the deliverance he wrought. Apparently, he was some sort of gifted leader similar to those found in the period of the judges. Unfortunately, the end result was just about the same. Once the deliverance had been wrought, the king and the people turned back to the same idolatrous ways which they had followed all along. The final decimation of the army of Jehoahaz bears mute testimony of the ultimate victory which the Syrians enjoyed. Remembering that even by Ahab's enemies' count, Ahab had massed two thousand chariots at the battle of Karkar in 853 BC, the fact that Jehoahaz was down to only ten chariots little more than fifty years later gives ample witness to Jehoahaz's weakness and establishes the basis for his ultimate defeat by the Syrians (2 Kings 13:7).

Following the death of Jehoahaz, the throne of Israel was filled by Joash, Jehoahaz's son. Once again, we are briefly faced by the confusion of a king of Israel having the same name as the king of Judah. Shortly after the accession of Joash in Israel, the old prophet Elisha fell sick. The king went to visit him, weeping and crying out, "My father, my father! The chariots of Israel and its horsemen!"—acknowledging that the real strength of the nation rested in its men of God (2 Kings 13:14). In a beautiful scene of prophetic symbolic action, Elisha predicted that Joash would be victorious for a while over the Syrians. Although some of the cities which the Syrians had earlier taken from Israel were recovered, we are unable to identify them with certainty and thus unable to say just how much territory was regained by Israel's king (2 Kings 13:25).

In the meantime, we had noted that Joash of Judah had been assassinated (2 Kings 12:19-21). Joash's son Amaziah succeeded to the throne (2 Kings 14:1). As soon as Amaziah had the reins of government firmly in hand, he had those who had assassinated Joash put to death (2 Kings 14:5). We must remind ourselves of the several bloodbaths which had accompanied recent accessions in both kingdoms. Unlike these, Amaziah showed both mercy and a reverence for the law of God by sparing the children of the assassins (2 Kings 14:6).

Perhaps seeing Joash of Israel beginning to retake some of the territories which had been lost to Syria inspired

Amaziah to try something of the same in Judah. Thus he set forth to retake the land of Edom which Judah had lost. In preparation he employed a large army of Israelite mercenaries. The very fact that he could adopt such a policy probably indicates that this was a time of relative peace between the two Hebrew kingdoms. However, Amaziah was rebuked by a prophet of Judah for the policy of utilizing Israelite mercenaries (2 Chron. 25:6-9). In obedient response, Amaziah discharged the mercenaries and sent them home. Amaziah's reaction reflects once again the earlier attitude of David toward the spokesmen of God. Unfortunately, his action incensed the Israelites. They felt that they had been insulted by their abrupt dismissal.

The war of Amaziah against the Edomites was successful, and Edom was again brought into subjection to Israel (2 Chron. 25:11-12). However, while Amaziah had been engaged in war with Edom, the army of Israel which he had sent home attacked Judah from the rear, meeting with significant victory (2 Chron. 25:13). This successful sneak attack apparently incensed Amaziah. He had sent the Israelites home at the command of God. Since he believed that God had not protected him, he brought home the Edomite gods to worship (2 Chron. 25:14). Once again a prophet confronted a king, but this time Amaziah refused to hear the prophet, actually threatening him with death (2 Chron. 25:15-16).

At this point, Amaziah sought to call King Joash of Israel to a conference. A weaker king does not call a stronger king to a conference, so Joash took this as an insult and refused to come. Amaziah, himself insulted at Joash's refusal, attacked Israel. The end result was catastrophic for Judah. Their army was defeated, their king was captured, the walls of Jerusalem were torn down over a large area, and a massive tribute was exacted (2 Chron. 25:21-24). Once again, Judah was brought under subjection to Israel. For the rest of the days of Joash of Israel and Amaziah of Judah, there was peace between the two kingdoms. However, it was a peace enforced by the defeat of Judah and the supremacy of the Northern Kingdom.

Israel's Revival as a World Power

The reign of Joash of Israel had set the stage for a period of great prosperity for the Northern Kingdom. With Joash's death and the accession of his son Jeroboam, we find several developments of major significance occurring in both kingdoms. In addition, changes on the international scene brought about the period of Israel's greatest prosperity. (NOTE: *For ease in identification, the new king of Israel is generally called Jeroboam II by historians in order to keep him from being confused with Israel's first king who was also named Jeroboam. He, of course, is usually called Jeroboam I.*)

Chronological Table

Judah	Israel	
Azariah (Uzziah) 767-740	Jeroboam II (793)	782-753
	Zechariah	753-752
	Shallum	752

Although very little is told by the author of Kings concerning Jeroboam II, we learn a great deal more from the messages of Amos and Hosea who began to minister in the last third of Jeroboam's reign. We also learn several things of significance about the period from the Assyrian annals and from archaeological excavations of sites in Israel.

First, Jeroboam II came to the throne at a time of great weakness on the part of the Assyrians. They had three rulers in a row who appear to have been quite ineffective. This eliminated Assyria as a threat to Israel, offering an opportunity to Israel to devote their energies to other matters without even having to consider Assyrian reactions and/or attitudes to the Hebrew policies. Furthermore, Jeroboam II had inherited the accomplishments of Joash who had brought Amaziah of Judah under complete subjection. Thus, Israel did not have to worry about any military threat from that direction. This also gave Israel the opportunity to turn their energies and interests into other directions. In addition, Jeroboam's father had also begun to defeat the Syrians, regaining territory which had been lost earlier. With no other military threat to distract him, Jeroboam II had been able to devote his full military attention to defeating the Syrians and to recapturing lost territories.

But opportunity and accomplishment are two different things. Jeroboam II obviously had the ability to seize the opportunity with vigor and to exploit it with effectiveness. "He restored the border of Israel from the entrance of Hamath as far as the Sea of the Arabah, . . . [and] he recovered for Israel Damascus and Hamath" (2 Kings 14:25-28). A quick look at a good map shows that Jeroboam II had conquered Syrian territory in the north and east and had also apparently conquered all of the Transjordan region which had once belonged to David's kingdom. The territory controlled by Israel and Judah at this time was almost as great, if not actually as great, as that which had been under their control in the days of David's greatest glory.

Military conquest alone, however, does not make a ruler great. Jeroboam II was also apparently able to exploit those conquests. The territory which he had conquered included every major highway which came through the region. That meant he and his people were in control of most commercial activity in the ancient Near East at that period. The opportunities for prosperity both through trade and through taxation upon those who passed through Israel's land stagger the imagination. According to the messages of Amos and Hosea, Jeroboam and the leaders were fully capable of seizing that opportunity as well. Amos particularly described the wealth which flowed into the Israelite capital, Samaria, speaking of "the notable men of the first of the nations, . . . beds of ivory, . . . lambs from the flock, . . . calves from the midst of the stall; . . . idle songs to the sound of the harp, . . . wine in bowls, . . . the finest oils" (Amos 6:1,4-6). As is often the case, such prosperity was shared by only a few in the nation of Israel. Prosperity bred greed and by the middle of the eighth century, the great middle class of Israel had virtually disappeared. The wealthy had exploited people, driving them into debt and then seizing the lands and even occasionally enslaving them. Furthermore, according to the prophets, that had all been accomplished through the bribing of judges and by the acquiescence of priests and prophets (Amos 8:4-6; Hos. 4:1-2,4-8; 5:1-2). Lest some accuse the prophets of excessive exaggeration at this point, the archaeological excavations give abundant support to this portrait of Israel's conditions. At that period in Samaria, one portion of the city had large houses while the rest was made up of very poor hovels. The lists of the wine merchants suggest an abundant flow of wine. Countless ivory inlays reflect the status of luxury enjoyed by some of the people.

In addition to the political and economic success of Jeroboam II, the religious shrines were thronged with people. Again, Amos and Hosea portray for us the great throngs who were worshiping. Unfortunately, the people of Israel had fully assimilated the worship of Baal with the worship of Yahweh. The fertility cult of Canaan with its sacred prostitutes had wholly captured the allegiance of Israel (Hos. 4:12-19; Amos 5:21-24).

To all outward appearances then, Jeroboam II had led the nation to its time of greatest achievement. Geographically, militarily, economically, politically, and religiously, Israel appeared to be thriving. The only voices which were raised in warning were those of Amos and Hosea. The people of Israel looked forward at that time to a coming day of the Lord when they would be vindicated upon all their enemies. To them Amos cried:

> Woe to you who desire the day of the Lord!
>   Why would you have the day of the Lord?
> It is darkness, and not light;
>   as if a man fled from a lion,
>   and a bear met him;
> or went into the house and leaned with his hand against the wall,
>   and a serpent bit him.
> Is not the day of the Lord darkness, and not light,
>   and gloom with no brightness in it? (Amos 5:18-20)

Hosea also added his words of warning:

> I will destroy you, O Israel;
> who can help you?
> Where now is your king, to save you;
> where all your princes, to defend you—
> ....
> The iniquity of Ephraim is bound up,
> his sin is kept in store (Hos. 13:9-12).

But no one heeded the prophets' warnings. Everything looked too good for anyone to pay any attention to those madmen. Amaziah, the priest of Bethel, warned Jeroboam about the preaching of Amos and then ordered the prophet to return home to Judah, saying, "O seer, go, flee away to the land of Judah, and eat bread there, and prophesy there; but never again prophesy at Bethel, for it is the king's sanctuary, and it is a temple of the kingdom" (Amos 7:12-13).

So the prosperity was only external. Tragically, it blinded the people of Israel to the real problems of their kingdom. The Israelite revival was a mere facade over a tottering structure which was about to fall.

Meanwhile, the situation in Judah was somewhat different. For some unknown reason, there was conspiracy against Amaziah. He fled to Lachish, seeking to avoid death, but was unsuccessful and was assassinated (2 Kings 14:19). It is possible that those who assassinated him were of the same group who had earlier assassinated his father Joash (2 Kings 12:20). Azariah (sometimes known as Uzziah) came to the throne of Judah upon the assassination of Amaziah, his father. Almost nothing is known of Azariah's reign, although he did become a leper in his last years and was forced to live "in a separate house," taking his son Jotham into a coregency with him (2 Kings 15:5). Azariah was apparently a very popular king. He is credited with expanding Judah's territories into the Philistine Plain and through the southern wilderness all the way to Eloth (Elath) on the Gulf of Aqaba (2 Chron. 26:2,6-8). Also, Azariah was remembered as a great builder (2 Chron. 26:9-10). The same sort of political situation which favored Jeroboam II of Israel also favored Azariah of Judah.

Azariah, however, was also remembered for having sought to take upon himself the function of a priest (2 Chron. 26:16-18). This was no more than either David or Solomon had done. However, the difference between them and Azariah seems to be found in the fact that Azariah acted from a motive of pride, not from a motive of honoring God.

However, the personal problems of Azariah aside, we must raise the questions as to why the obvious prosperity of Judah did not produce the same results as the prosperity of Israel. It is impossible for a historian to answer a negative question as to why something did not happen. However, we do have a few clues. Probably the basic reason lay in Judah's geography. They did not control the major highways as Israel did, so they did not have the opportunity for the excessive growth of wealth through trade and taxation which Israel enjoyed. Without that impetus, the greed of the leaders of Judah was not accelerated like that in Israel. Further, Baal worship never had the strength in Judah that it did in Israel. There has not yet been found a single name in any excavation in the territory of Judah which was compounded with Baal. Finally, we must remember that, for all of Azariah's success, Judah was apparently still subservient to Israel throughout this period. It is hard to grow too proud from a position of vassalage.

Back in Israel, however, the earlier warnings of Amos and Hosea were about to become reality. Jeroboam II died. Zechariah Jeroboam's son came to the throne (2 Kings 15:8). He had hardly become king, reigning for only six months, when Shallum assassinated him (2 Kings 15:10). We know of no reason for the assassination, but this kind of fact had almost become a pattern in Israel. It became more so, for Shallum only reigned one month when he was in turn assassinated by Menahem (2 Kings 15:13-14). The great prosperity and success which Israel appears to have achieved under Jeroboam II was about to be lost. Instability in government breeds instability in everything. This was the beginning of the end for Israel. The greatness of the kingdom of Jeroboam II was not only beginning to totter but also was to disappear totally within thirty years. Such was the shaky foundation upon which he had built his kingdom.

Before we pass on, however, we must note the most significant development of the reign of Jeroboam II: the rise of what has come to be known as the period of the classical prophets. A century earlier, we noticed that a major change in Hebrew prophetism had taken place with the ministry of Elijah, Elisha, Micaiah, and their followers. With the ministry of Amos and Hosea, yet another change took place. For the first time, the disciples or followers of a prophet collected the prophet's messages together, remembered them, and wrote them down in separate collection. It appears that, when the doom which Amos and Hosea had announced came to pass in the ultimate destruction of Israel, their messages were circulated as testimony both to the rightness of the prophets as well as to the power of God. In the ancient world, the defeat of a people was usually assumed to be a defeat for that people's god. By the circulation of the messages of Amos and Hosea, Israel and the world were being told that God had not been defeated when Israel was defeated. Rather, the contrary was true. With the defeat of Israel, God had been vindicated.

Amos had appeared upon the scene in Israel about 765 BC. He was a shepherd from Tekoa in Judah, who went north to warn Israel's people of the impending doom which their actions were inevitably bringing upon them. His message was concerned with the need for practical righteousness coupled with a deep sense of the awesome justice of God. The actions of the people of Israel were such as could not be ignored by anyone sensitive to the plight of the helpless poor.

Hosea, on the other hand, was a native Israelite preaching to his own people. He began his ministry shortly after Amos. Although concerned with the same injustices, Hosea's primary emphasis was upon the love of God. Amos had seen the sin of Israel as a violation of God's righteousness. Hosea saw their sin as a violation of God's love. For both of these men, the sins of Israel could have only one inevitable end. That end was about to come.

Israel's Ultimate Downfall

Upon Shallum's assassination, Menahem seized the throne of Israel. However, to possess the throne and to be secure on the throne are always two different things. With the six months reign of Zechariah and the one month reign of Shallum, accompanied by two assassinations within little more than a month, the situation in Israel could have been little more than chaotic. Although Menahem left a lot to be desired in matters of religion as far as the author of Kings was concerned (2 Kings 15:18), he must have been a fairly able ruler to be able to rule for ten years in such chaotic times.

Chronological Table

Judah		Israel	
Jotham	(750) 740-732	Menahem	752-742
		Pekahiah	742-740
Ahaz	(735) 732-716	Pekah	(752) 740-732
		Hoshea	732-722
Fall of Samaria			721

At the same time, we must acknowledge that Menahem was faced, for a few years at least, with a rather peaceful international situation. Judah was going through the trying period of having their reigning king, Azariah (Uzziah), living essentially in exile from leprosy and having Azariah's son serving as coregent. It appears that, during the period of Jotham's coregency, he accomplished little more than doing some repair work on the Temple and on some of Jerusalem's fortifications (2 Chron. 27:3a). At the very least, Judah offered no threat to Israel and took none of Menahem's time. It also appears that the Syrians and Transjordan peoples were nonaggressive during Menahem's early days. Further, the Assyrians were still in their period of weakness. (That, however, was about to change). Thus Menahem's early days gave him the opportunity to try to consolidate his authority in Israel.

In 745 BC, however, an event occurred which brought

trouble to Menahem and spelled ultimate destruction for Israel. That event was the coming of Tiglath-pileser III to the throne of Assyria. Tiglath-pileser III's accession marked the end of Assyrian weakness and the true beginning of Assyria's empire. He was a strong administrator and was able to establish an efficient administration in his own land. Further, Tiglath-pileser III was faced by no other major international power. Finally, he instituted the military policies for which Assyria came to be famous (or infamous). He established an organization within his army which kept it well equipped and prepared to march with almost no delay, a feat essentially unknown in ancient times. He also instituted the world's most efficient communication system up to that time. Further, he adopted policies of terrorism and cruelty toward conquered peoples which made them tremble at the very thought of the Assyrians. Then he reinstituted policies of deportation of captive peoples, resettling them in small groups in other places. This ensured that captured territories, due to their different racial, linguistic, and national groups, found it extremely difficult to organize any kind of rebellion. Ultimately, Tiglath-pileser III changed Assyria's policy toward conquest. His most successful predecessors had been interested primarily in tribute and booty. With Tiglath-pileser III, the Assyrians became interested in conquering territory and establishing an empire. This he set out to do with systematic purpose and with relative ease of accomplishment.

Upon accession to the throne of Assyria, Tiglath-pileser III defeated the decaying kingdom of Uartu to the north and the rising kingdom of Babylon to the south. Immediately thereafter, he marched into Palestine. The only way by which Menahem apparently was able to maintain a hold on the kingship, perhaps the only way by which he could preserve Israel's existence, was by the payment of a massive tribute to "Pul the king of Assyria" (2 Kings 15:19). (Pul was the Hebrew nickname of Tiglath-pileser.) In the official annals of the Assyrian king, the subjugation of Menahem and the payment of tribute are also recorded.

The payment of the massive tribute to Assyria, however, left Menahem with some major problems. The tribute money had to come from somewhere, and it could only come from taxation upon the wealthy. The poor had been so impoverished during the reign of Jeroboam II that there was no way a general tax could have raised that kind of money. Furthermore, we must remember that Jeroboam II had brought wealth into the country. Menahem's sending it out in such quantities had to bring about great unrest among the leaders of his land.

Thus Menahem came to the end of life as a vassal of Assyria with a great deal of hostility from the leaders of Israel. Pekahiah, Menahem's son, became king (2 Kings 15:22). The unrest which had begun under Menahem continued to grow until Pekahiah was assassinated by the captain of the guard, Pekah (2 Kings 15:25). This coup was accomplished with the support of the Gileadites, men from the Transjordan region. Their support may indicate that the policy of taxation had been more heavily enforced by Menahem and Pekahiah upon those furthest away from the capitol. Such a practice was not unknown in the Hebrew kingdoms.

Whatever the case, Pekah appears to have totally discounted the reigns of his two pro-Assyrian predecessors, apparently counting their years of reign as his own. Further, as soon as he was in power, he appears to have instituted an anti-Assyrian policy.

The first effects of this anti-Assyrian policy of Pekah are to be seen in the Syro-Ephraimitic crisis which began in 735 BC. Pekah was well aware that Tiglath-pileser III of Assyria was engaged in a policy of empire building. With Israel having already experienced some of the results of this policy, Pekah apparently decided that if Assyrian expansion into Palestine was going to be stopped it had to be done immediately. In order to try to stop Assyria, Pekah sought to form a coalition between Israel, Syria, and Judah. Pekah was right in assuming that he was faced with a now-or-never situation. He was wrong in ever believing that his dreamed of coalition had any hopes of stopping the Assyrians. Nonetheless, that was the policy upon which he embarked.

Meanwhile, Ahaz had come to the throne of Judah, apparently as a coregent during Jotham's last days. Pekah's hope for a coalition had met with success in Syria, for Rezin, king of Syria, joined. Judah, however, refused. Pekah dared not face Assyria with a nonaligned Judah to his rear. History had demonstrated that that was just inviting Judah to seize Israel's border fortresses. Further, Israel and Syria needed the economic and military support of Judah if they were to have any hope of dealing with the Assyrians. Thus Pekah and Rezin decided that they first had to attack Judah, depose its king, and place a puppet on the throne who would go along with the attack on Assyria. For their purposes, they selected a man known only as "the son of Tabeel" (Isa. 7:6). Since, at this point in time, the major part of Israel was made up of the territory which had once belonged to the tribe of Ephraim, and they were alligned with Syria, the whole conflict came to be known as the Syro-Ephraimitic crisis.

The plans for this attack were made while Jotham was still king, but it did not actually occur until after the accession of Ahaz (2 Kings 15:37; 16:5). Apparently, the initial invasion met with great success, for Ahaz is said to have lost a large number of troops and great spoil (2 Chron. 28:5-8). Furthermore, realizing Judah's weakness at this time, the Edomites recaptured the Edomite territory which Judah possessed in the regions south of the Dead Sea (2 Kings 16:6). All of this conflict terrified Ahaz. He apparently felt that the whole nation was about to be annihilated and that he would be killed. So he sent tribute to King Tiglath-Pileser, saying, "I am your servant and your son. Come up, and rescue me from the hand of the king of Syria and from the hand of the king of Israel, who are attacking me" (2 Kings 16:7). By this act, Ahaz had voluntarily made himself and Judah a vassal of Assyria.

At this point, Isaiah the prophet stepped on the scene. Isaiah's ministry had begun immediately following the death of Uzziah (Azariah; Isa. 6:1-13). At the time of the Syro-Ephraimitic crisis, Isaiah confronted Ahaz while the king was inspecting the waterworks of Jerusalem which were so necessary for defense (Isa. 7:3). Jerusalem's major source of water was outside the city wall. The city's ability to withstand a siege depended upon its water supply. For Isaiah, this was an obvious place to find the king when a siege was threatened. Isaiah was quite aware of Ahaz's submission to Assyria and was totally opposed to it. Upon being confronted by the prophet, the king pretended to be trusting God when in fact he was trusting intrigue with Assyria (Isa. 7:12). Isaiah was fully aware that Tiglath-pileser III could not possibly have ignored what was going on in Palestine. The Assyrian king was certain to attack both Syria and Israel. Thus there had been no need for Ahaz to have put himself and the people in submission to the Assyrians.

The policy, however, had already been adopted by Ahaz. The act of paying tribute had been performed. As far as the king of Judah was concerned, it was already too late. He had started on a path from which he could not, or would not, turn back.

The armies of Assyria had begun to march. By 732 BC the immediate crisis was totally over for Judah. In that year the Assyrians conquered Damascus, the capitol of Syria, and that Aramaean kingdom ceased to exist for all practical purposes. Its people were carried into exile, and others were resettled in Syria. Furthermore, major parts of northern and eastern Israel were captured and occupied by the Assyrian army. Also at that time Hoshea (not to be confused with Hosea the prophet) assassinated Pekah and seized the throne of Israel (2 Kings 15:30). His immediate submission to Assyria saved a small part of Israel for a brief while (2 Kings 17:3). Tiglath-pileser's own records confirm Hoshea's tribute and submission.

At the same time, Ahaz of Judah experienced the immediate relief and release from the pressures of the Syro-Ephraimitic coalition. However, that was to have serious consequences both for him and for Judah. With that coalition having been destroyed by the attacking Assyrians, the other small nations around Judah were also relieved from their anxieties about Israel and Syria. Thus, Judah began to be attacked from the south and east by the Edomites and from the west by the remnants of the Philistines (2 Chron. 28:17-18). Shortly thereafter, Tiglath-pileser III sent troops into Judah to collect yet more tribute from Ahaz (2 Chron. 28:20).

It clearly appeared to Ahaz that instead of getting better, everything had gotten worse. He must have decided that Yahweh, the God of Israel, was incapable of helping him. Searching for more powerful gods to worship, he immediately turned to the gods of the Syrians, saying, "Because the gods of the kings of Syria helped them, I will sacrifice to them that they may help me." In response to that action, the author of Chronicles added with bitterness, "But they were the ruin of him, and of all Israel" (2 Chron. 28:23).

For Ahaz, however, the end had not yet come. Apparently, shortly after Tiglath-pileser III had defeated Syria and gotten Hoshea safely settled as king of Israel, he called for Ahaz to come to Damascus (2 Kings 16:10). One of the ways by which conquerors in the ancient Near East showed their superiority over the vanquished was by forcing them to worship the conqueror's god(s). Ahaz, as a voluntary vassal was also apparently forced to adopt the gods of Assyria (2 Kings 16:10-18). It appears that Ahaz took to the Assyrian worship with vigor if not with evangelistic fervor. Thus his political policy decision to which Isaiah had objected had led him and the people into idolatrous apostasy.

Tiglath-pileser III died in 727 BC and was succeeded by his son, Shalmaneser V, a man of no less ability who was no less committed to terrorism and empire building than Tiglath-pileser. Frequently in the ancient East, the accession of a new king served as a time when vassals tried to break away from servitude. This was apparently what Hoshea tried to do at the accession of Shalmaneser V. This was quickly dealt with by the Assyrian king, and Hoshea immediately conceded, paying new tribute and again entering into vassalage (2 Kings 17:3). However, this situation did not last long.

As soon as it appeared that Shalmaneser's attentions

were directed elsewhere, Hoshea sent messengers to "So, king of Egypt" (2 Kings 17:4). The Hebrew king was apparently seeking military aid from the Egyptians and seems to have believed that it was forthcoming, for he again withheld tribute from the Assyrians. This was the kind of insult which no Assyrian king could ignore. Shalmaneser immediately marched upon the kingdom of Israel. It would appear that Hoshea went out to meet the Assyrian king, trying to appease him. This attempt was unsuccessful and Hoshea was taken prisoner. Shalmaneser V then occupied all that remained of Israel but the city of Samaria, laying siege to it. It is a measure of the strength of its defenses that Samaria was able to hold off the Assyrian siege for more than two years. In 722 BC, Shalmaneser died and was succeeded by Sargon II, to whom Samaria fell in 721 BC.

The Assyrians deported large numbers of Israelites to other conquered territories, importing other groups of captives who were settled in Israel. The nation of Israel had come to an end. Born in rebellion, it had died in violence. During Israel's history, there had been eight changes of dynasty, and nine of their kings had died violently. Five of those violent deaths had occurred in the final thirty years. The story of Israel is one of anarchy and rebellion. It is essentially a story of the lust for power and of the inability to use that power once it had been obtained. And so the warning words of the prophets Amos and Hosea had come to pass. When to all outward appearances, the kingdom of Israel had stood at its zenith in the reign of Jeroboam II, they had seen the cracks in its edifice. Israel's foundation was insecure; it tottered, collapsed, and fell into the ruins which those two men of God had foreseen. No one had heeded the warnings when there was time and opportunity. When the city of Samaria fell, it was too late.

The Significance of the Period

It is obvious that my attempt to reconstruct the history of this period of division and destruction has relied upon both the biblical narrative, contemporary ancient records and monuments, and information gathered from archaeological excavations. It is equally obvious that, even with the aid of these other materials, any attempt at reconstructing this history frequently must confess ignorance. Occasionally we may be able to make an educated guess toward filling in the details which just are not there. This brings us back to the fact that Old Testament history was not written as history. It was written as a message from the God of Israel through His spokesmen. Historical information was given primarily as the basis through which the God of Israel revealed His message. Thus to deal with this history without paying some attention to the theological message contained therein is at best to misuse the basic biblical material. At worst, such an approach is an abuse of the material.

In attempting to summarize the major teachings of this part of the biblical material, the theological historian is forced to do something which the original authors never did—systematize the material. These books proclaimed theology through the recitation of events. The content of faith was generally implicit rather than explicit. For modern students to attempt to deal with it, we collect the message of similar events under common headings. In so doing, however, we must always recognize that we are supplying the headings. The ancient material merely told the story. Therefore, since I am forced to supply the basic headings under which to organize the message of this part of Israel's history, it appears to me that there are at least five parts of this message with which the theological historian must deal.

The Insecurity of Faithlessness

The basic message which the biblical authors of the material related to the period of the two Hebrew kingdoms is that people who are in positions of both political and spiritual leadership must inevitably find that faithlessness to God offers an insecure foundation for life and work. I must note that each of the ancient Hebrew kingdoms were expected to be a theocracy. The God of Israel was actually considered to be the ruler of the land. To put that in more modern terms: There was no separation between church and state. Rather, these two were considered to be coextensive. It is obvious that there is a major and fundamental divergence between those kingdoms and our contemporary government.

The human authors who produced the Books of Kings and those who produced the Books of Chronicles consistently evaluated the kings of Israel and Judah on the basis of religion and the expression of religion. Of each of the kings of Israel we are told: "he walked in all the way of Jeroboam the son of Nebat, and in the sin which he made Israel to sin, provoking the Lord, the God of Israel, to anger by their idols," or some such similar statement (1 Kings 16:26). Of many of the kings of Judah we are told: "he walked in all the sins which his father did before him; and his heart was not wholly true to the Lord his God," or a similar kind of condemnation (1 Kings 15:3).

The point of this kind of evaluation is that each king was expected to be true to the faith of Israel. The king's success or failure as a ruler was not normally evaluated by his political or military achievements but by his loyalty to the God of Israel. To the biblical authors, a king could accomplish a great deal politically and economically, yet if he failed in his relationship to the God of Israel, he was a failure. It was just that simple.

Closely related to this idea of loyalty to God, but separate from it, was the idea that a king must worship and must lead the people to worship in honesty. There was a popular idea held with growing conviction throughout this period that as long as one followed the ritual of worship properly all was well. It was this, perhaps, which called forth prophetic wrath more than anything else.

To the Old Testament writers, worship which was not accompanied by practical, everyday righteousness was utterly meaningless. Thus the prophet Isaiah cried out near the end of this era:

> What to me is the multitude of your sacrifices?
> says the Lord;

I have had enough of burnt offerings of rams
and the fat of fed beasts;
I do not delight in the blood of bulls,
or of lambs, or of he-goats.
When you come to appear before me,
who requires of you
this trampling of my courts?
Bring no more vain offerings;
incense is an abomination to me.
New moon and sabbath and the calling of assemblies—
I cannot endure iniquity and solemn assembly (Isa. 1:11-13).

This dimension of the faith of Israel was not comprehended by outsiders. Jezebel in particular just could not grasp the fact that her husband, Ahab, felt that he had to obey the laws of righteousness. To the Old Testament messengers, ritual which was not backed up by righteousness was devoid of meaning. There is abundant evidence that many of the kings and people of the Hebrew kingdoms lost this idea. On many occasions, they seemed to have believed that merely worshiping God was all that was required. It was because of this foolish idea that the spokesmen of Israel and Judah were forced to call them back to a concept of goodness.

Also related to this idea of the insecurity of faithlessness is the idea that all positions of responsibility are a stewardship. King, priest, and/or prophet—they were all expected to be loyal to God and faithful to His will. Power was the gift of God. Ministry was the gift of God. Those who had such power and ministry had special responsibilities to God to use their power in accord with His will. Irresponsibility in the matter of the stewardship of authority could not and would not be ignored by God. This is still true.

The Flowering of Hebrew Prophecy

From the standpoint of Israel's faith, one of the more important developments of the period of the two Hebrew kingdoms was the flowering of Hebrew prophecy. As noted before, prophecy was not a phenomenon unique to Israel. Many of the ancient nations believed that there were people to whom one could go to find the will and/or word of gods. The point is that such prophets were usually paid for their message and that they usually only gave messages when asked. That kind of prophet was also present in Israel. We have earlier noted such prophets. In studying this particular era, we have seen the prophets who were kept as part of a king's court to give the king a message whenever he needed it.

Now, from the earliest days, we have seen people in Israel who spoke God's word to a specific situation without anyone asking for it. With the ministries of Elijah and Elisha, we came across men whose whole life was apparently devoted to such a task. With the rise of Amos, Hosea, Isaiah, and Micah, we found such men whose messages have been collected and placed in separate books.

It is interesting to note that with the advent of the first of these classical prophets, Amos, the high priest of Bethel still assumed that the prophet was expecting to be paid for his message. When Amaziah suggested that Amos should flee to Judah "and eat bread there," he was implying that only in Judah could Amos hope to be paid for his messages condemning Israel (Amos 7:12). Furthermore, Amos's denial that he was a prophet (Amos 7:14) was not a denial that he was speaking God's word but was a denial that he was the kind of a prophet which Amaziah thought he was. This was a clear statement that with him there was something new in prophecy.

That dimension in the development of prophecy is unique to Israel. No other ancient nation ever developed prophets who offered God's word unbidden and without hint of or hope for profit from such proclamation.

Furthermore, this development in Hebrew prophecy made a subsequent impact upon both Judaism and Christianity from which neither has ever escaped. The whole concept of human spokesmen through whom God proclaims His message to His people has its root here. Whether we consider the subsequent prophetic development in Israel or the rise of preaching among the early churches, for either or both we must come back to the model of the classical prophets of the separated kingdoms of Israel. The basic idea that God would proclaim His words through human spokesmen finds its most fruitful development in this era.

The Developing Concept of Judgment

Tied in with both the sense of the insecurity of faithlessness and the rise of classical Hebrew prophecy, the third major theological message of this period is the growing sense of divine judgment upon God's people. Faithlessness must be punished.

Israel had long had a sense that God was going to send judgment upon His enemies. It remained for Amos most pointedly to announce that by their faithlessness, Israel had made themselves an enemy of God (Amos 5:18-20). In all of the great eigth-century prophets is found the idea that because of their special relationship to God, there was going to be a special judgment upon them.

As a basic part of this prophetic sense of judgment, the author of Kings saw the ultimate downfall of Israel. He summed it up quite prosaically, saying,

> In the ninth year of Hoshea the king of Assyria captured Samaria, and he carried the Israelites away.... And this was so, because the people of Israel had sinned against the Lord their God, ... and had feared other gods and walked ... in the customs which the kings of Israel had introduced.... Therefore the Lord was very angry with Israel, and removed them out of his sight; none was left but the tribe of Judah only (2 Kings 17:6-18).

We must also note that the classical prophets developed the idea that God's judgment was frequently administered through historical forces. We often think of judgment in terms of supernatural or abnormal catastrophe. The prophets proclaimed to Israel that God used historical forces to execute His judgment. Shortly after the fall of Samaria, Isaiah announced to Jerusalem:

> Ah, Assyria, the rod of my anger,
> the staff of my fury!

> Against a godless nation I send him,
>   and against the people of my wrath I command him,
> to take spoil and seize plunder,
>   and to tread them down like the mire of the streets
> (Isa. 10:5-6).

That idea of God's use of historical forces in executing judgment did not eliminate the idea that natural and supernatural forces were also used in judgment. Instead, it was an added dimension. We can see that it was a natural outgrowth of the events of the period of the judges. Yet it was not so clearly proclaimed there as it was here.

The Developing Concept of Mercy

Closely allied with the developing sense of judgment is the prophetic spokesmen's sense of God's mercy. There are frequent announcements where judgment was withheld because of God's mercy. Furthermore, judgment was seen by Amos for the first time as an act of God's mercy. Five different times, Amos described a judgment of God which had befallen his people with the express purpose of turning them back to God (Amos 4:6,8,9,10,11). The purpose of that judgment had not been so much to punish as to offer mercy to Israel. That they had rejected God's offer of mercy did not negate the reality of the offer.

But Hosea most clearly came to understand God's love and mercy. He proclaimed this several ways, but none were more moving than the cry of the heartbroken Father.

> How can I give you up, O Ephraim!
> How can I hand you over, O Israel!
> How can I make you like Admah!
> How can I treat you like Zeboiim!
> My heart recoils within me,
>   my compassion grows warm and tender.
> I will not execute my fierce anger,
> I will not again destroy Ephraim;
> for I am God and not man,
>   the Holy One in your midst,
> and I will not come to destroy (Hos. 11:8-9).

To the prophetic historians of the Old Testament,

judgment was real. Yet by the end of this era, they were also certain that God's mercy was real. That, too, had its ultimate impact in the proclamation of mercy in the New Testament.

The Growing Sense of God's Sovereignty

Drawing all four of these basic messages together, the historical writers of the Old Testament were developing a richer sense of the absolute sovereignty of the God of Israel. Ultimately, whatever happened came from God. Nations were moved at God's will. Catastrophe came at His call. Deliverance from sickness and death as well as from foreign powers came from His mercy. It was that simple. God was in control.

Perhaps the most important part of this development was the people's attitude toward the final downfall of Israel. As we have noted, throughout the ancient Near East, whenever a nation was defeated, it was always considered to be a defeat for the gods of that nation. Israel alone developed what we may call a theology of exile. Because of the warning messages of the prophets, when the defeat and destruction of Israel came, the Hebrews saw it not as a defeat for God but as a victory for God. God's fortunes were not dependent upon Israel's fortunes. Instead, it was the other way around. Israel's defeat came because God was in control.

The kings of Israel, and of Judah also as we shall see, had established an insecure foundation through their faithlessness. In response to that, God had raised up His spokesmen to warn of an impending doom based upon the consequences of their actions. At the same time, mercy was offered from, through, and beyond the judgment. All of this was possible because God was sovereign. Men, nations, and nature were all under His control. This ultimately meant that history had become the story of His acts of punishment and deliverance, not the record of men's deeds.

Israel fell because God was in control. Judah was left for the same reason. It is to that nation, standing alone and lonely, that we must now turn our attention.

7
The Road to Judgment: Judah to the Fall of Jerusalem

For slightly more than two centuries, Judah and Israel existed side by side as separate kingdoms. Throughout that period, the two Hebrew kingdoms either had been engaged in actual conflict with one another or Judah had generally been in subservience to her northern sister, Israel. It is obvious, therefore, that for the entire period of coexistence Judah's policies had been fairly well shaped by having at least to consider the presence and concerns of Israel. Having to observe these kinds of policies for that length of time surely influenced the whole way of thinking among the political leaders in Jerusalem. With the swift and sudden demise of Israel, Judah was suddenly thrust out upon the seas of international diplomacy alone. For the first time in two centuries, Judah was independent of Israel's influence, either direct or indirect. This was clearly something for which the rulers of Judah had long wished.

Yet Judah's sudden independence from Israel was not an unmixed blessing. With Israel's demise, Judah faced two new problems. First, Israel had always been a buffer between Judah and the powerful enemies to the north. With the Assyrian conquest of Israel, Assyrian territory was suddenly in actual contact with Judah. This meant that Assyrian troops could move within a very few miles of Jerusalem before having to face any opposition. The second problem with which Judah was left was that they were the only major nation remaining in the Palestinian region. Prior to the demise of Israel, any major foreign power which coveted territory in Palestine would normally have turned toward Israel as the more desirable.

However, following the Assyrian conquest of Israel, Judah was left alone with a significant block of desirable territory. That meant that Judah had become a more attractive target. Yet Judah had to face the consequent assaults alone and with limited resources.

Sources for the Study

The primary sources for the study of this period of Hebrew history are not significantly different from those used in the preceding one. However, there is enough difference to make it worthwhile to reconsider them here.

As usual, the basic materials come from the Old Testament itself. The first to which we must give consideration are those found in 2 Kings 18:1 to 25:30 and 2 Chronicles 29:1 to 36:23. In addition to these sources, there is the material found in the books of the prophets who ministered during this era. Among these are materials in Isaiah 1 to 39 (especially the historical section in the final four chapters), Jeremiah, the first part of Ezekiel's ministry, and those brief glimpses of historical background found in the Books of Nahum, Habakkuk, Zephaniah, and possibly Obadiah.

In addition to the biblical materials, there are three other sets of written records to which the historian of this period must turn. Egypt played a significant role in the history of Judah during this period, so we must make careful use of the Egyptian records concerning the era. These records are much more important for Judah's time alone than they were for the period when both Hebrew kingdoms existed side by side. Further, we must continue to utilize the Assyrian records. With Assyria's border actually touching Judah throughout most of this period, their records can be expected to shed appreciable light upon Judah's history. Near the end of this era, we must also direct a searching look at the Babylonian Chronicle. For a long time, we had only very incomplete Babylonian records. However, this is no longer true. We now possess a relatively complete record of the history of Babylon beginning with the time just prior to their conquest and destruction of Assyria. Not only do the Babylonian records allow us to accurately correlate their history with that of Assyria, they also allow a thorough correlation between the latter history of Judah and that of Babylon's early days of empire.

To these ancient records, we must also add two ancient historians whose works shed some light upon this era. These are Herodotus, a Greek historian of the fifth century BC, and Josephus, a Jewish historian of the first century AD. In dealing with these, the modern historian must exercise extreme care; these men wrote long after the events with which we are concerned, and we do not generally know the quality of their sources. However, their materials can at least be used with caution.

Of course, the monumental and archaeological materials from this era are also extremely valuable. For example, the Assyrians made large friezes of their assault upon Lachish which portray for us many of the Assyrian practices of warfare. From almost a century later, we have a series of letters written upon pottery fragments which describe the situation and feelings of a soldier on a lonely outpost between Lachish and Azekah as the Babylonians advanced into the land of Judah. These were written to the soldiers' commander at Lachish and have come to be known as the Lachish letters.

In addition to the archaeological remains in Mesopotamia, Palestine, and Egypt which aid in our understanding of this era, there are excavations which have been carried out in the steppes of Russia which have added significantly to our knowledge of a people known as the Scythians. These people raided throughout the entire region during the early days of King Josiah of Judah.

Among the things which add detail to our knowledge of the period is the Siloam tunnel which was dug by King Hezekiah to bring water into the city of Jerusalem at a time of siege. We have actually found the inscription honoring King Hezekiah for its completion. Thus with this accomplishment the water problem which had confronted Jerusalem from its earliest days down to the reign of Ahaz was solved. It was this which allowed Jerusalem to hold out so long before the final onslaught of Babylon.

With all of the materials which are available to us, we are able to reconstruct the history of the period with a growing degree of confidence. While there are still numerous problems left for historians to grapple with, we seem to be standing on a firmer foundation for our historical summary of this period than for most others.

Major Problems for Consideration

There is no way by which the historian who deals with the ancient Near East in general and with the Old Testament era in particular can ever escape problems. The nature of our sources, the gaps in our information, the differences between our cultures, and the limitations of our knowledge all add to the problem. In dealing with the period when Judah existed alone as an independent Hebrew kingdom, it appears to me that there are three such major problems with which the historian must grapple.

The Chronological Difficulties

As is almost always the case, the first of the problems with which the historian must deal is that of the chronology. For this particular era, this problem centers around three issues. The historian must reconstruct the chronology of Judah itself. While we do not have the same difficulties here we had in the preceding era which were brought about by the synchronisms between Israel and Judah, we do have the same sort of questions. The synchronisms at least alerted us to the fact that chronological systems changed. Without these, we must assume that we have the same basic problems but do not know precisely when they occurred. This means that we must compare Judah's history with that of Assyria, Egypt, and Babylon with extreme care, being alert for any potential change in chronological system either in counting the years of reign or in the beginning of the official year. So our first chronological problem is in the general reconstruction of Judah's absolute chronology.

The second chronological problem has to do with the campaign of Sennacherib, king of Assyria, when he besieged Jerusalem in 701 BC (2 Kings 18:13 to 19:37; 2

Chron. 32:1-22; Isa. 36:1 to 37:38). This material appears to record the entire event as one invasion, and it has generally been so treated by historians. However, there is a problem created by the mention of the attack of "Tirhakah king of Ethiopia" who was apparently coming to the aid of Judah at that time (2 Kings 19:9; Isa. 37:9). Tirhakah was only nine years old in 701 BC and was living in Nubia. He did not come to Egypt, where he was associated as coregent with his brother, until at least 690 BC. There is just no way by which he could have been present eleven years earlier.

There are two different solutions which have been proposed to this problem. In general, most people ignore the problem, but that really offers no solution. Although the problem is quite complex, the two proposed solutions suggest either that Sennacherib made two campaigns into Judah and that the two accounts have been told as one or that the use of the name of Tirhakah is simply an anachronism (substituting a later name for an earlier ruler). Since anachronisms are fairly common in the records of the ancient Near East and of the Bible, it appears to me that this is the simplest solution to the problem and the one which I have adopted. (The student who may wish to grapple with this problem in detail will find a good starting point in John Bright's *A History of Israel,* 3rd ed.). I find it extremely difficult to propose a second campaign for Sennacherib more than a decade after the first when there is no other significant evidence for it.

The third major chronological problem of this period of Old Testament history has to do with the actual date of the fall of Jerusalem. It is difficult to determine with precision whether the city fell in 587 or in 586 BC. Various historians choose one date or the other. Some have even tried to solve the problem by dating the flight and capture of Zedekiah, Judah's last king, as being in 587 while maintaining that the city was not destroyed until a year later in 586 BC. Admittedly, from this distance, one year more or less makes little difference. However, since anyone trying to deal with this history should make a decision, I have accepted the date of 586 BC as the date for the capture of Zedekiah and for the destruction of Jerusalem. (The reasons for this decision are quite technical and beyond the concerns of this book. More technical histories will give guidance for a detailed study of the issues.)

The Scythians, Imaginary or Real?

In the Book of Jeremiah, a large number of messages warn of the impending assault of a foe from the north. The question of the identity of this unknown foe has puzzled Jeremiah commentators over the years. Given the fact that Jeremiah's ministry began about 626 BC and continued until some years after the fall of Jerusalem in 586 BC, it should not be surprising that Jeremiah's references to this foe from the north should be ambiguous. However, among those peoples sometimes suggested as the basis for some of his images depicting this foe are a group of raiders from north of the Black Sea and the Caspian Sea known as the Scythians.

The reason that this proposed identity for at least some of Jeremiah's references to a foe from the north has been a problem is that the only record that these people ever invaded Palestine comes from the writings of Herodotus, and Herodotus's writings are often suspect. Herodotus was thought to have invented history to cover those periods where he had no knowledge of what occurred. His descriptions of the Scythians were so unbelievable that many people just did not accept them as real people.

However, since World War II, Russian archaeologists excavating in the steppes of Russia have uncovered the ruins of these ancient peoples. What has been found has shown that they in fact did exist, that they did get at least as far south as Egypt, and that Herodotus did not exaggerate in his description of these brutal raiders. The Scythians were involved in worldwide raids and terrorism during the time in which Jeremiah's ministry began. While this does not prove that they actually invaded Palestine as Herodotus claimed, it at least makes his claim plausible; and some of Jeremiah's descriptions could easily have been of the real or potential threat of these terrifying tribesmen.

Josiah's Reform, Deuteronomy, and Jeremiah

The third major problem of this era relates to the reform of Josiah which found its greatest impetus with the discovery of the book of the law in the Temple in 622 BC (2 Kings 22:8-13). There are two problems which relate to this event with which the historian must deal. The first of these is the question of the identity of the book of the law which was found in the Temple. The second problem is why Jeremiah, whose ministry apparently covered this whole period, never mentioned Josiah's reform.

The question of the identity of the law book which furnished the authority for Josiah's reform is not as difficult as it might first seem. Admittedly, the book of the law is never named. However, the description of the things which Josiah did following the discovery of the law book is given in great detail (2 Kings 23:4-25). A number of the things which Josiah did can be found in several different places in the Old Testament in books which could conceivably be called a book of the law. However, everything listed in 2 Kings which Josiah did following the discovery of the book of the law is given in Deuteronomy. Thus, scholars have generally assumed that Deuteronomy was the book of the law which was found in the Temple and upon which Josiah based his ultimate reform.

The question as to why Jeremiah never appears to have mentioned Josiah's reform is more difficult. It has been suggested that Jeremiah did go out preaching Josiah's reform but that when the reform failed none of those messages were kept. Such a suggestion would imply an innate dishonesty on the part of Jeremiah in preserving only those messages where he was right. This, however, does not fit in with the picture which we are given in the Book of Jeremiah. He preserved many messages and particularly prayers which reveal him in a very unflattering light. Any man who would preserve some of the prayers which

Jeremiah prayed would surely have had no qualms about preserving sermons supporting Josiah's reform.

Others have suggested that we have no messages from Jeremiah dealing with Josiah's reform because Jeremiah was not preaching at that time. These people suggest that Jeremiah's ministry did not begin in 626 BC. Rather, they suggest that that was the year of his birth and that his ministry did not actually begin until after the death of Josiah. This might solve one problem, but it raises others far more difficult.

The best solution appears to be the suggestion that Jeremiah was wise enough not to get involved in a merely superficial, politically motivated reform movement. It seems that Jeremiah did not preach Josiah's reform but that he did preach Deuteronomy. Jeremiah referred to Deuteronomy on a number of occasions and appears to have dissociated himself from the reform of the politician while preaching the book upon which the reform was based. Jeremiah was looking for more than a simple reformation of religion, however much that was needed. He was looking for a real change of nature which could be accomplished not by reform but by a new commitment to the God of Israel.

The Background of the Period

If ever there was a period in Old Testament history where a knowledge of the background of the era is important, this is it. The history of Judah from the fall of Samaria to the end of the kingdom is so intimately bound up with the history of the surrounding peoples that it is virtually impossible to understand otherwise.

The Assyrians

We noted in the preceding chapter that Tiglath-pileser III (745-727 BC) was the virtual founder of the Assyrian empire. The road to Assyrian greatness was continued by Shalmaneser V (726-721 BC) and by Sargon II (721-705 BC) to whom Samaria finally fell. Sargon consolidated those gains and dealt with several rebellions. In 720 BC, he put down a rebellion in Hamath in Syria and in 711 BC quashed a revolt in Ashdod. This Philistine city had withheld tribute and apparently stirred up Edom, Moab, and Judah in an abortive rebellion. However, these interior kingdoms were seemingly able to appease Sargon, convincing him that they were not really rebellious.

Sennacherib, Sargon's son, became ruler after Sargon (705-681 BC). Frequently in the ancient Near East, the accession of a new king was a time when vassals rebelled, hoping to find the new king an ineffective ruler. This happened with Sennacherib. He was immediately faced with numerous uprisings, among them the Philistine cities of Askelon and Ekron and the Hebrew kingdom of Judah. The Assyrians turned their immediate attention to a rebellion in Babylon, which was far more serious than those in Palestine. It was not until 701 BC that Sennacherib was able to march into Palestine, dealing first with the more accessible Philistines and then directing an attack upon Judah. The details of that invasion are recorded both in the Bible and in the Assyrian chronicles. Additional insights may be given by Herodotus.

Sennacherib's attack on Judah was interrupted briefly by an army from Egypt, but that was quickly dispatched. According to his own records, Sennacherib captured forty-six walled cities in Judah and beseiged Hezekiah in Jerusalem. The reliefs of Sennacherib at Nineveh vividly depict his sack of Lachish. However, the Assyrian king did not capture Jerusalem and returned to his own land. (We shall return to this when we consider the history of the reign of King Hezekiah.) Sennacherib was murdered in 681 BC.

Just as the collapse of Israel came quickly after their days of greatness, the same was true of Assyria. Esarhaddon (681-669 BC) and Ashurbanipal (669-627 BC) maintained the supremacy of Assyria in their world, but the old vigor was gone, and there was no more expansion. Following the death of Ashurbanipal, everything began coming apart at the seams.

A coalition of the Babylonians and the Medes attacked and captured the Assyrian's capital at Nineveh in 612 BC. This forced the Assyrians to move their capital to the west at Haran. This was in turn attacked and destroyed in 610 BC, and the Assyrian army retreated further westward. In 609 BC, the Assyrians made an abortive attempt to retake Haran but were again defeated by the Babylonians.

The end was not long in coming. In 605 BC, a coalition of the Assyrians and the Egyptians marched against the Babylonians but were surprised by the Babylonians at Carchemish and sent reeling back in utter defeat. For all practical purposes, that marked the end of the Assyrians. They had been wholly eliminated as a world power and no longer exerted any influence over events in Judah.

The Egyptians

In the preceding era, Egypt had gone through two centuries of relative weakness. This was not quite the case in the time when Judah existed alone. An Ethiopian dynasty began to rule about 716 BC. It apparently sought to strengthen, or at least maintain, those small nations between Egypt and Assyria. The Egyptians were clearly involved in inciting the Ashdod rebellion (Isa. 20:1-6) and were probably involved in Hezekiah's rebellion in 705 BC. They at least sought to send help when Sennacherib was invading Judah, although that aid was fruitless, and they were defeated (2 Kings 18:20-21; 19:9). As we have noted, the use of the name Tirhakah in this connection is probably an anachronism since he was only nine years old at the time and was living in Nubia. He did not come to Egypt until 690 BC and, at that time, was made coregent with his brother.

In spite of attempts at political and military intervention, Egypt was still a relatively weak nation. Due to the continual intrigues between Egypt and the nations of southern Palestine, Assyria finally attempted to punish the Egyptians with an invasion in 663 BC. At that time, the Assyrians under Ashurbanipal drove as far south as Thebes, attacking and sacking that city. Although the Assyrians had been able to drive almost five hundred miles down the Nile, they did not long maintain a presence in Egypt because they themselves were growing weaker.

With the defeat of the Egyptians at Thebes, a new dynasty arose which was to exert even more influence in the regions of Syria and Palestine. Perhaps the most significant pharaoh of this dynasty (the twenty-sixth) was Neco II (610-594 BC). He came to the throne of Egypt precisely at the time when the Babylonians and the Medes were about to defeat the Assyrians. He was immediately aware of the growing threat of Babylon and realized that it was to Egypt's benefit to maintain a weak Assyria between Egypt and Babylon. He set out in 609 BC to aid the Assyrians in an attempt to retake Haran. Neco's march was delayed by an ambush at Megiddo by King Josiah of Judah. Although Josiah was killed in that battle, the ambush was apparently effective. Neco arrived at Haran too late to aid the Assyrians, for they had already been defeated.

Blaming the defeat upon the people of Judah, Neco turned homeward down the Water-Parting Route, deposing Jehoahaz of Judah who had succeeded Josiah. In Jehoahaz's place, Neco placed Jehoiakim upon the throne, forcing him into a pro-Egyptian policy.

Neco again sought to aid the Assyrians in 605 BC. The intent was to attack Babylon, but the Babylonians apparently struck first at Carchemish. There the Assyrians and the Egyptians were utterly defeated. Neco and the Egyptian army raced home in confusion. The Egyptians expected to be pursued by the Babylonians, but, as we shall see, this did not materialize.

The Egyptians, for a period of time, apparently were engaged with rebuilding their army and with dealing with internal problems. They were of no more significance in Judah until the accession of Pharaoh Hophra in 589 BC. Hophra, still following the Egyptian policy of keeping some sort of buffer between Egypt and Babylon, sought to aid King Zedekiah of Judah. He apparently instigated a revolt against Babylon among the small states of southern Palestine (Jer. 27:1-11). When the Babylonians invaded Judah and laid siege to Jerusalem, Hophra marched to the aid of Zedekiah. At that time, the Babylonians briefly lifted the siege, attacked and defeated the Egyptians, and returned to the siege (Jer. 37:11). The promised Egyptian aid had come, but it had been insufficient. Egypt had been as much of a problem for Judah in the things she did not do as she had been in the attacks she had made. To the end, Egypt's presence had been felt in Judah.

The Scythians

As noted in the preceding section, for a long time one of the historical problems of this period revolved around the question of the existence of the Scythians. Now we know that they did exist, clearly making raids into the territory of Assyria and Syria shortly after 630 BC. Almost certainly they came on down into Palestine, carrying out raids into Judah and going as far as Egypt. While they never seem to have been concerned with conquest of territory, they were concerned with booty and the sheer love of killing.

The women among them fought alongside the men, and they were not considered ready for marriage until after they had killed a man. They used the skulls of their victims to decorate their horses and used the tops of human skulls as dishes from which to eat. They frequently made quivers for their arrows out of human skin and occasionally made clothes out of tanned human skin.

The remains in their tombs show that they had captured goods from as far east as India (and perhaps even China), from as far west as the Aegean, and from as far south as Egypt. Even though they are not mentioned as such in the Bible, Jeremiah appears to reflect an awareness of their terrifying ways and the fact that the people were greatly frightened by their threat. Obviously, to see a horde of riders coming over the horizon clothed in human skin and with their saddles decorated with human skulls would have terrified even the staunchiest warriors. While they were not a threat for a long period, during the early days of Jeremiah's ministry their potential threat alone was enough to terrify the people of Judah. Furthermore, their very real incursions in the north distracted the attention of the Assyrians at a time which was very propitious for the Hebrews.

The Babylonians

As the Assyrians were the dominant influence in the early days of the period of Hebrew history, the Babylonians were clearly the dominant power of Judah's latter days. Nabopolassar came to the throne of Babylon in 626 BC. He made an immediate alliance with the Medians to the north and east of the Mesopotamian Valley. That coalition quickly became a threat to the Assyrians. The Medes apparently destroyed Assur, the old capital of Assyria, shortly thereafter.

The Babylonian-Median coalition attacked Assyria's capitol, Nineveh, capturing and destroying it in 612 BC. With that defeat, the death knell of Assyria had sounded. However, they still survived as a kingdom, transferring their capital to Haran. The Babylonian coalition defeated the Assyrians again in 610 BC, capturing Haran and driving the Assyrians on to the west.

The following year, 609 BC, the Assyrians, strengthened by promises of Egyptian aid, tried to retake Haran. But Egypt was delayed, as has been noted, and the Assyrians were again defeated. In 605 BC, the Assyrians, aided by the Egyptians, again tried to defeat the Babylonians through making a massive attack upon them. The Babylonians, led by a son of Nabopolassar by the name of Nebuchadnezzar, struck first. (Nebuchadnezzar is also known as Nebuchadrezzar.)The Assyrians and Egyptians were utterly routed at the Battle of Carchemish. The scattered remnants of the Assyrian army ceased to exist as a fighting force. Further, the defeated Egyptians fled for their own land, assuming that the victorious Babylonians would pursue them all the way to Egypt. That is precisely what they probably would have done if there had not been another event of major importance.

Exactly at that time, 605 BC, Nabopolassar died in Babylon. Nebuchadnezzar was faced with two choices. He could follow up the victory and pursue Egypt. If he had done so, however, one of his ambitious half brothers would almost certainly have seized the throne of Babylon, and Nebuchadnezzar would have found himself a victorious general but not king. The other choice was to allow the defeated and disillusioned Egyptians to flee unmolested while he marched back to Babylon with a victorious army. He chose to follow this latter course. When he arrived in Babylon, none of Nebuchadnezzar's rivals dared to resist him, so he succeeded to the throne of Babylon.

In the winter of 604/603 BC, Nebuchadnezzar marched into the region of Palestine. There he attacked and defeated Ashkelon. It was at that time Jehoiakim paid Nebuchadnezzar tribute and became a vassal (2 Kings 24:1). In the meantime, Nebuchadnezzar prepared for an attack upon Egypt. This was carried out in 601 BC. Amazingly, however, the Babylonians were defeated and driven back. The Egyptians must have also suffered heavy losses, for they made no attempt to follow up that victory in any way. Nebuchadnezzar's army was so decimated and demoralized by that defeat that it took him almost two years to get it reorganized into an effective instrument of warfare.

In the meantime, Judah had rebelled, so Nebuchadnezzar had been forced to use mercernaries to try to bring Judah back into line (2 Kings 24:2). By 598 BC, the Babylonian army had been refurbished, so Nebuchadnezzar marched upon Judah. When Nebuchadnezzar's armies actually arrived at Jerusalem in 597 BC, King Jehoiachin immediately surrendered and was carried prisoner to Babylon along with other captives.

After having installed Zedekiah as a puppet ruler on the throne of Judah, Nebuchadnezzar returned home. By installing his own choice upon the throne, Nebuchadnezzar intended to show his sovereignty over Judah. At the same time, following a rather enlightened policy for that day, Nebuchadnezzar's choice had been a man with a legitimate claim to the throne, being a descendent of David. Unfortunately, another one of Nebuchadnezzar's decisions at this time was to return later to haunt him. He took into Exile the leaders of Judah. His intent apparently was to destroy Judah's ability to wage war. However, he had also destroyed the new king's ability to govern effectively.

The next few years of Babylonian history are somewhat unclear. Apparently the Hebrews were at least considering a rebellion early in the reign of Zedekiah, for the Hebrew king was called to Babylon to give an account of himself (Jer. 51:59). What we do know is that Zedekiah did rebel in 588 BC. The army of Babylon was soon in the land, devastating the countryside and besieging Jerusalem. In a vain attempt to aid the Hebrew kingdom, the Egyptians sent forth an army under Pharaoh Hophra. However, it was quickly defeated by the Babylonians, and the siege was resumed.

In the summer of 586 BC, a breach was made in the walls of Jerusalem, and the city fell. Everything that would burn was burned. Zedekiah was brutally punished, for he had betrayed Nebuchadnezzar's own appointment. Having had enough of the problems created by the kingdom of Judah, Nebuchadnezzar brought it effectively to an end with the appointment of a governor instead of a king. Furthermore, the Babylonians took another group of the Hebrew people captive into Babylon. The Babylonian Exile had begun.

The History of the Period

The events of history never fit into the neat pigeon holes which historians might wish or novelists appear to imply. Insofar as Judah was concerned, the fall of Samaria was a momentous event. However, it did not actually coincide with a major turning point in Judah's history. The real turning point in Judah's history was not the fall of Samaria but the Syro-Ephraimitic crisis of 735 BC, for it was at that time that Judah voluntarily came under the suzerainty of the Assyrians. It is to that point which I turn in moving into the story of Judah's independent existence as a nation.

The Period of Assyrian Domination

With the fall of Samaria to the Assyrians under Sargon II, Ahaz was thrust to the center of Assyria's attention in Palestine. The full adoption of Assyrian worship most likely took place at this time. As far as we have any record, Ahaz remained a loyal vassal to the Assyrians for life. The religious life of Judah followed the syncretistic tendencies which King Ahaz had introduced. The worship of the foreign deities appears to have flourished due to the people's hope that those gods might be better able to deliver them than Yahweh had been able to deliver the Northern Kingdom. As might be expected, this kind of idolatrous apostasy brought forth the wrath of both Isaiah and Micah (Isa. 2:6-8; 8:19; Mic. 5:12-14). Even if Ahaz did not actually furnish the leadership in turning to these gods, he clearly did nothing to discourage it.

Chronological Table

Judah	
Ahaz	(735) 732-715
Hezekiah	715-687
Manasseh	(696) 687-642
Amon	642-640

Upon the death of Ahaz, the throne of Judah was filled by Hezekiah. He inherited a nation subservient to Assyria and in the midst of a major religious decay. There is a problem found in the assertion that Hezekiah began to reign in the "third year of Hoshea . . . king of Israel" (2 Kings 18:1). His father Ahaz had begun to reign at the age of twenty, in the seventeenth year of Pekah (2 Kings 16:1-2; 2 Chron. 28:1). Since Pekah reigned twenty years, Ahaz would have been twenty-three at the death of Pekah (2 Kings 15:27). Pekah was succeeded by Hoshea, and we have been told that Hezekiah began to reign in Hoshea's third year. At that time Ahaz would have been twenty-six. However, we are told that at that time Hezekiah, Ahaz's son, was twenty-five years old (2 Kings 18:2). There is no way by which Ahaz could be only one year older than Hezekiah. We are forced to admit that there are textual difficulties here and to hope for future developments which will shed light upon the problem.

During the early years of Hezekiah's reign, he is credited with a thorough-going program of purification of the religion of Judah (2 Kings 18:4-6; 2 Chron. 29:3 to 31:21). In that reform, there was a great celebration of the Passover which should have reminded the Hebrews of God's great acts of deliverance in the past and should have served as a basis for hope for such deliverance in the future. It is interesting that Hezekiah invited those of Israel who had survived the fall of their nation to come and share in the great celebration (2 Chron. 30:1). Unfortunately, only a few people responded to that gracious invitation (2 Chron. 30:11). The difficulties, of course, for those survivors to have traveled to Jerusalem would have been quite real. They were a defeated people under foreign domination.

We are also told that King Hezekiah was quite practical in that great celebration. They kept the Passover "in the second month" rather than in the first month as was commanded. The reason for this was that they had not begun the purification of the priests and Temple precincts soon enough. Further, the announcement to the people concerning the event had not been sent out soon enough (2 Chron. 30:2-4). It would have been easy for an extreme literalist to have postponed the celebration for an entire year, pleading that the Scriptures did not allow such a plan. Hezekiah clearly felt that for a people trying to come back to God the celebration itself was more important than the time of the celebration.

It would be interesting to know all of the factors behind Hezekiah's great reform. Clearly, the policies of his father, Ahaz, had angered both Isaiah and Micah. But it also appears that there was a large ground swell of support for the young king's reforms. The people of the land had obviously been incensed by the syncretism and apostasy of Ahaz. Furthermore, the feelings of these people had obviously been intensified by the messages of the prophets that the judgment which had befallen Israel had been the direct result of turning away from God. While we may never know precisely all that motivated Hezekiah, each of these factors probably played a part.

However, possibly some political motivations were at work in Hezekiah's reform as well. Shortly after Sargon II came to the throne, he was faced by the rebellion of Babylon led by Marduk-abal-iddina (the Merodach-baladan mentioned in 2 Kings 20:12 and in Isaiah 39:1). While Assyria's attention was turned toward Babylon, there were numerous other rebellions on the borders of his empire, not the least of which was that of the Philistines in Ashdod. These rebellions may have been encouraged by the success of Babylon in the east and by the rise of Egypt in the southwest. Hezekiah did not rebel militarily, but his religious reforms which included the elimination of the Assyrian worship imported by Ahaz was certainly a minor act of rebellion.

In 711 BC, the Assyrians assaulted and sacked Ashdod, putting the brief Ashdod rebellion to an end. Possibly due to the fact that Judah had not engaged in armed rebellion and due to other pressing needs, Sargon ignored Judah at this time. Egypt had apparently sought to involve Judah in that rebellion, but Hezekiah had heeded the graphic warning of Isaiah not to get involved (Isa. 20:1-6).

Sometime between the Ashdod rebellion in 711 BC and the invasion of Sennacherib in 701 BC, Hezekiah carried out several successful assaults upon the remaining Philistine territories which had not fallen into Assyrian hands (2 Kings 18:8).

A major turning point in the relations between Judah and Assyria came with the death of Sargon and the accession of Sennacherib to the Assyrian throne. He, too, was faced with numerous rebellions, the most significant of which was that of Babylon in 705-704 BC. It was apparently at this time that Merodach-baladan sent his envoys to visit Hezekiah. The public reason for that visit was to congratulate the Judean king upon his recovery from sickness (Isa. 39:1). However, it is quite likely that the Babylonian king was trying to create more problems for Assyria by getting Judah to join in the rising tide of rebellion. Ashkelon, Ekron, and Tyre were among those involved in the rebellions at the beginning of Sennacherib's reign. Hezekiah decided to act, joining in the rebellion.

Knowing that the Assyrians could not long ignore this state of affairs in Palestine, Hezekiah immediately began preparing for the Assyrian onslaught, paying particular attention to the problem of water supplies in Jerusalem (2 Chron. 32:2-6). Although not mentioned in the Bible, it is almost certain that Hezekiah's famous water tunnel was dug at Jerusalem at this time. Two teams of workers began digging the long, winding tunnel. One team worked from the Gihon Spring outside the city wall while the other worked from inside the wall at the spot later known as the Pool of Siloam. It is a measure of the engineering capabilities of those people that they dug a winding tunnel which met in the middle, covering a distance of several hundred meters, and when they met they were less than one-and-one-half inches off. (The inscription on the wall of the tunnel has been removed and is in the British Museum.)

The blow finally fell upon Judah when Sennacherib invaded the land in 701 BC. According to the Assyrian king's own records, it was an extensive campaign. He first defeated the king of Tyre. At that time, the revolt began to fall apart. Numerous kings from the smaller nations in the region brought tribute and made peace, but Judah, Ashkelon, and Ekron still held out. The Assyrians marched down the coastal plain and reduced the two Philistine cities. Then they turned inland toward Judah. The Egyptians came forth to help but were defeated near Ekron.

The attack on Judah was devastating. Sennacherib says that he captured forty-six fortified cities of Judah and shut up Hezekiah in Jerusalem "like a bird in a cage" before he returned home. The devastation must have been horrible. Excavations at Lachish have revealed a pit into which the remains of at least fifteen hundred human bodies were thrown. To add further insult, the bodies were covered with slaughtered pigs. According both to the Old Testament and to Sennacherib's own records,

Hezekiah sued for peace while Lachish was under attack, paying a very heavy tribute (2 Kings 18:14-16). At this point, however, we must face a difficult problem of interpretation. Why was it that Sennacherib accepted Hezekiah's tribute and still attacked Jerusalem? Furthermore, how do we deal with the Old Testament record which describes Hezekiah's miraculous victory over the Assyrians in the light of Sennacherib's claims (2 Kings 19:35-36)?

The first question may have its answer in the fact that the Assyrians had been faced with a continual series of problems from Hebrew kings. The acceptance of the tribute carried with it no overt agreement to end the assault. Sennacherib apparently was simply not satisfied by Hezekiah's offer. As far as the Assyrian was concerned, Jerusalem had to be destroyed and Judah rendered ineffective as a troublemaker. Thus the Assyrian Rabshakeh (chief commander and negotiator) was sent to speak to the citizens of Jerusalem (2 Kings 18:17; Isa. 36:2).

Here we find one of the more interesting bits of diplomatic by-play found in the entire Bible. Standing outside the walls of Jerusalem, with a large portion of the population looking on and listening, the Rabshakeh taunted the Hebrews with their helpnessness, reminding them that Egypt would be of no help and that they did not even have trained horsemen to fight for them (Isa. 36:4-10). He even offered to give them horses if they could furnish the riders. Further, he showed a knowledge of the internal affairs of Jerusalem, apparently reminding the Hebrews that Isaiah had proclaimed that Assyria was God's rod to punish His people (Isa. 10:5-6).

The words of the Assyrian were clearly demoralizing the people of Jerusalem, so the representatives of King Hezekiah pleaded with him to speak with them in the diplomatic language, Aramaic, which the common people could not understand. Then as now, much diplomatic language is used to keep the common people from really understanding what is going on. The Rabshakeh refused, saying, "Has my master sent me to speak these words to your master and to you, and not to the men sitting on the wall, who are doomed with you to eat their own dung and to drink their own urine?" (Isa. 36:12). Those terrifying words would have even further demoralized the Hebrews. In a final word, the Rabhsakeh almost settled the issue by urging surrender, promising that every one who did so would "eat of his own vine" and "drink the water of his own cistern" (Isa. 36:16). Such words, directed to a people who were feeling the results of a devastating siege and facing the fear of a hopeless situation, just about led the people to surrender. However, like so many people, the Rabshakeh talked too much. Instead of quitting, he went on to say that he would eventually come and take them away to Assyria (Isa. 36:17). To the Hebrew mind, that was unthinkable. God had given them the land, and they would not leave it voluntarily, under any condition. If the Rabshakeh had stopped sooner, Jerusalem might have surrendered.

But he did not quit, and they did not give in.

Even then, the Assyrian general was not aware of what he was doing. He went on to flaunt his power over the gods of other nations, taunting the God of Judah as having no power to defend His people (Isa. 36:19-20). That word brought forth a dramatic response from Isaiah the prophet: "Thus says the Lord, Do not be afraid because of the words that you have heard, with which the servants of the king of Assyria have reviled me. Behold, I will put a spirit in him, so that he shall hear a rumor, and return to his own land" (Isa. 37:6-7).

Again, an Egyptian army appeared on the scene, apparently intending to aid Judah, but they were quickly disposed of by the Assyrians (Isa. 37:9). As the siege intensified, the biblical account describes the sudden death of the major part of the Assyrian army and Sennacherib's abrupt departure for his homeland (Isa. 37:36-37; 2 Kings 19:35-36). This brings us back to the second question which we posed earlier: Can we reconcile this account with Sennacherib's own records?

A thorough study of the Assyrian records points up an interesting fact. They never recorded defeats as defeats. In comparing Assyrian records with those of Egypt or of

Babylon where they engaged in common conflicts, Assyrian defeats can only be seen by "reading between the lines." Now that is admittedly dangerous for the historian. But we must consider that, while Sennacherib claimed to have captured forty-six fortified cities of Judah, he never claimed to have captured Jerusalem. He only said that he shut up Hezekiah. Further, while he mentioned no great loss of troops, he never again moved the Assyrian army into Judah. That land was left unmolested for the remaining twenty years of Sennacherib's reign.

Furthermore, the Greek historian Herodotus described an Assyrian defeat before Egypt by the attack of an army of mice (rats) which ate the Assyrians' bowstrings, rendering them helpless. This raises the possibility that the plague which struck down the Assyrians was the bubonic plague, which is carried by the fleas on rats and mice. This suggestion may make more sense out of a puzzling series of events and conflicting reports.

Regardless of what happened, Hezekiah suffered great losses in Judah even though Jerusalem survived. However, Hezekiah's independence was maintained, and he reigned in apparent peace to the end of his days. He was remembered by his people as a good and effective king. There is no way of knowing how much of Hezekiah's goodness which was remembered was due to the influence of either Isaiah or Micah. Isaiah was clearly a counselor and confidant of the king (Isa. 37:2,5,21-29; 38:1-6; 39:3-7). Even if Micah had no direct impact upon the king, he certainly affected the temper of the people of the land, and that would have indirectly influenced the king.

As is all too often the case, good King Hezekiah was followed by a son known primarily for evil, Manasseh. Manasseh remained a loyal vassal of Assyria for the entire length of an extremely long reign. He quickly restored the worship of Assyrian gods, as well as of the old Canaanite gods (2 Chron. 33:3; the "host of heaven" refers to the astral deities of the Assyrians). He actually brought the Assyrian worship into the Temple itself and introduced human sacrifice, burning his sons as offerings (2

Kings 21:6; 2 Chron. 33:6). An ancient tradition says that Manasseh had Isaiah tied in the trunk of a hollow tree and sawn in two. This may be the basis for the reference in Hebrews to those who were "sawn asunder" (Heb. 11:37). Manasseh was also opposed by many people of Judah, being forced to put down the opposition with bloodshed (2 Kings 21:16).

Sometime while reigning, Manasseh was carried in chains before the king of Assyria (2 Chron. 33:11). This may have been at the time of an abortive revolt in Assyria about 650 BC. Whatever the reason, the Assyrians apparently were convinced of Manasseh's loyalty and restored him to his kingdom.

Manasseh is also said to have turned back to God late in life, engaging in a minor reform of religion (2 Chron. 33:12-16). However, Manasseh's reform was not very thorough (2 Chron. 33:17). He was ultimately remembered for his evil (2 Kings 21:17; 2 Chron. 33:19). Further, it was his evil which lived after him.

Amon succeeded Manasseh upon the throne, and it was said of Amon's two year reign that "he did what was evil in the sight of the Lord, as Manasseh his father had done. He walked in all the way in which his father walked, and served the idols that his father served, and worshiped them" (2 Kings 21:20-21). The opposition which Manasseh had tried to quell was still present, so Amon's own servants rose up against him to kill him (2 Kings 21:23). It is not known whether they were trying to establish a new dynasty. The assassins were immediately executed, and the royal line of David was maintained by the coronation of Amon's son Josiah (2 Kings 21:24).

Throughout the entire period from Ahaz to Amon, Judah had been under the influence, if not always the direct control, of Assyria. However, at the time of the death of Amon, that influence and control was about to end.

The Great Reform

There is no need for a chronological table for this section since the only king who reigned in Judah during this era was Josiah. He reigned from 640 to 609 BC. There is probably no other period in Hebrew history which appears to fit in so clearly with world events as this one does.

When Josiah came to the throne in 640 BC, he was but a child, being only eight years old (2 Kings 22:1; 2 Chron. 34:1). We do not know anything about these very early years, but we can surmise a number of things. He was too young to have been deeply influenced by the apostate policies of his grandfather Manasseh. Josiah's father, Amon, had ruled too briefly to have influenced him significant either. Further, the assassination of Amon would have made a deep imprint upon Josiah. The people of the land had obviously wished a change, and they surely would have tried to surround the boy king with advisors loyal to the God of the Hebrews. In addition, a priest by the name of Hilkiah clearly had an important impact upon Josiah slightly later (2 Kings 22:4,8,10,12,14; 23:4, 24). It is reasonable to suppose that this influence was exerted upon the young king from the beginning of his reign.

Regardless, however, of where the early influence upon the boy king came, Josiah sought to follow the teachings of Yahweh from his earliest days (2 Chron. 34:2). About the time he was sixteen (632 BC), Josiah let it be known that as official policy he was seeking the way of the Lord (2 Chron. 34:3*a*). If it had not occurred before, it was at least at this time that he would have begun consulting with the high priest at the Temple.

In 627 BC, an event occurred which gave Josiah the opportunity for which he had been looking. Ashurbanipal, king of Assyria, died. As we have noted, such an occasion generally signaled a time of rebellion among the vassals of a nation. For Josiah, the first step toward freedom was "to purge Judah" of the Assyrian worship, as well as of the other gods whose shrines had been rebuilt by Manasseh (2 Chron. 34:3*b*). But Josiah was not the only one who used this time as the opportunity for rebellion. One year later, in 626 BC, Nabopolassar became king of Babylon and rebelled. Further, at the same time, the Scythians from the steppes of Russia began making major raids into the very heart of the enfeebled Assyrian empire. With Assyria's attention totally devoted to these concerns in the north and east, their control of the western regions in Palestine began to slip badly. Josiah apparently used this as an opportunity to expand his reforms into the regions of northern Israel (2 Chron. 34:6-7). It is questionable as to whether this included a military expansion into those regions. At the most, this would have been little more than a raid.

These reforms on the part of Josiah clearly had the whole nation talking. There would have been excitement on the part of many just due to the throwing off of the Assyrian yoke. Others would have been excited by the return to Yahwism. Of course, those who had been involved in the idolatrous worship would also have been quite incensed by all of these developments. This certainly would have been true in the small town of Anathoth, about three to four miles north of Jerusalem. There, all of this talk about religion would have had its impact upon the mind and heart of a young man, opening his sensitive mind and heart to the coming of "the word of the Lord," for it was to the thirteenth year of Josiah that Jeremiah dated his call (Jer. 1:2).

Josiah had the great good fortune of being born at the right time. The period of Josiah's reign was the first time since the accession of Tiglath-pileser III in 745 BC that Assyria was too weak to take steps to deal with the kind of rebellion in which Judah was engaged.

As a part of the reform, Josiah next turned to the task of repairing and restoring the Temple. While doing this work, "the book of the law of the Lord given through Moses" was found (2 Chron. 34:8-15). This book was taken and read to the King, and Josiah's reaction was immediate. He was suddenly aware of just how deeply into sin his nation had fallen and tore his clothes in grief and repentance (2 Kings 22:11; 2 Chron. 34:19). We have already noted that this book was almost certainly the book we now know as Deuteronomy since everything which Josiah performed after this as a part of his reform is commanded in Deuteronomy.

There is a real question as to how such a book could have been lost in the first place. Although scholarship can by no means be certain of the chain of events which led to this point, it appears likely that during the time of the divided kingdoms the materials in Deuteronomy were preserved by pious followers of Yahweh in the Northern Kingdom of Israel. When that kingdom fell in 722-721, refugees would have fled south to Judah, carrying those materials with them. With the rise of the apostasy of wicked Manasseh, the scroll was apparently hidden in the Temple. However, the long reign of Manasseh makes it likely that those who hid the scroll in the Temple would have died and the scroll's location would have been lost. Regardless of whether this is the correct reconstruction, it is certain that the long, evil reign of Manasseh must be seen as the basis for the loss of the book.

With the finding of the book, Josiah immediately sought from Huldah, a prophetess, a word concerning the hopes for Judah (2 Kings 22:13-14). It is worthy of note that there was a woman prophet in Judah. Following her words of limited encouragement, the king had a ceremony of covenant renewal, a very thorough purging of the religion of Judah and the territories of Israel, and a great Passover celebration (2 Kings 23:3-23).

Perhaps the most significant thing from a historical standpoint is that this is the first time, insofar as we have any record, that a written scroll was accepted as the authoritative basis for a religious reform. This is the first great step on the part of the Hebrew people toward the identification and acceptance of a canon of Scripture.

The prophet Jeremiah was probably involved in the preaching of the covenant materials of Deuteronomy (Jer. 11:1-8), although he was apparently not directly involved in the Josianic reform itself. However, we must note that a major feature of the reform of Josiah was closing down the shrines scattered around the country and the centralization of worship in Jerusalem (2 Kings 23:8; 2 Chron. 34:32-33). This immediately put out of work the priests who were involved in such work. Since this action had been based upon Deuteronomy and since Jeremiah had been preaching Deuteronomy, a number of Jeremiah's priestly neighbors in Anathoth blamed the prophet for this and sought to kill him (Jer. 11:18-23).

The remaining years of Josiah's reign were apparently fairly peaceful, being filled with the further purification of the faith of Judah. Assyria was growing ever weaker, being engaged in a basic fight for survival with the Babylonian and Median coalition. Nineveh fell before the onslaught of that coalition in 612 BC and Haran in 610 BC.

The accession of Pharaoh Neco II to the throne of Egypt in 610 BC was a decisive event for Josiah of Judah. From Neco's standpoint, it was imperative to keep a weak Assyria in existence between the rising tide of the Babylonians and Egypt. Thus the Egyptian king set forth to the aid of Assyria in 609 in an attempt to maintain Assyria's very existence. However, this was the direct opposite of what Josiah and Judah would have desired. At that point, Assyrian territory still bordered on Judah, and Judah had suffered much, both politically and religiously, at the hands of the Assyrians. Josiah apparently felt very strongly that the Assyrians should be punished for all their deeds. There was no way by which Josiah could have hoped to defeat the armies of Egypt advancing up the Coastal Highway. On the other hand, he apparently felt that, if he could delay the Egyptian advance, perhaps the Babylonians would have already defeated the Assyrians. So Josiah marched with what forces he could muster and ambushed the overwhelmingly larger Egyptian forces at the pass at Megiddo. The geographic situation is such there that, for a while at least, a small force could hold off a much larger one. That is precisely what Josiah did. Although we are told that Josiah did this in opposition to the wishes of his godly advisors, he literally offered himself as a sacrifice, trying to maintain the independence of Judah. In the battle, Josiah was fatally wounded and the Egyptians finally won (2 Kings 23:29-30; 2 Chron. 35:20-24). However, Josiah's plan had been successful. The Egyptians had been sufficiently delayed. By the time they arrived at their destination, the Assyrians had already been beaten, and their forces scattered.

Josiah was remembered as the best of the kings of Judah. "Before him there was no king like him, who turned to the Lord with all his heart and with all his soul and with all his might, according to all the law of Moses; nor did any like him arise after him" (2 Kings 23:25). Josiah's religious and political reforms gave Judah its last real chance for survival. Unfortunately, his religion turned out to have been superficial only. His political policies passed away with his death. He was a great king and had an opportunity to be even greater. But that chance passed away with his own death. Truly, it could be said of him, "Greater love hath no man than this, that a man lay down his life for his friends" (John 15:13). That is precisely what Josiah did. We may fault his wisdom. We cannot fault his devotion to his people.

Judah's Last Days

When Josiah was killed at the battle of Megiddo, he was succeeded by his son Jehoahaz. There is no way of knowing what kind of a king he would actually have made, but the fact that he was chosen by "the people of the land" (2 Kings 23:30; 2 Chron. 36:1) over his older brother Eliakim may indicate that they at least thought that he would follow in the steps of Josiah his father. However, that was not to be. Pharaoh Neco had proceeded on northward after the defeat of Josiah. When he arrived too late to be of assistance to Assyria, he was certainly angered that all of Egypt's efforts had been thwarted by the puny little kingdom of Judah. He immediately turned back toward Judah in an extremely hostile mood.

Chronological Table

Jehoahaz	609 (3 months)
Jehoiakim	609-598
Jehoiachin	598-597 (3 months)
Zedekiah	597-586
Fall of Jerusalem	July, 586 BC

There was obviously nothing more that Neco could do to Josiah since he was already dead. However, there were two things which he could and did do. First, Neco deposed King Jehoahaz, carrying him captive to Egypt. This may be a further indication that everyone expected him to be the same kind of king Josiah had been. At the very least, it seems to indicate that Jehoahaz had a pro-Babylonian policy. As a part of deposing Jehoahaz, Neco placed another son of Josiah on the throne changing his name from Eliakim to Jehoiakim. The name change was an open proclamation that Neco had the power to control the new king. The fact that he chose Eliakim also means that the young king was able to convince Neco that he was and would continue to be pro-Egyptian.

The second thing which Neco did as punishment was to levy a very heavy tribute upon Judah (2 Kings 23:33). This was perhaps intended not only as punishment but also as repayment to Pharaoh Neco for his lost expenses in his fruitless expedition to the aid of the Assyrians. With the collection of his tribute, Neco departed for Egypt, carrying Jehoahaz with him. Nothing else is ever heard of the deposed king. He was most likely executed in Egypt.

The accession of Jehoiakim marked a significant change in the policies of Judah. Apparently, he and many of the people decided that Josiah's death was evidence that serving Yahweh and destroying all the pagan shrines had not paid off. Therefore, much of the paganism of Manasseh was brought back. Unfortunately, the ease with which this was done is evidence of the superficiality of Josiah's reform. Many of the people had gone along with it, but there obviously had been no real national commitment to the aims of Josiah. Furthermore, Jehoiakim clearly followed a pro-Egyptian policy. This may only indicate Jehoiakim's subservience to the Egyptian pharaoh. On the other hand, it may also be an indication that Jehoiakim was absolutely blind to the rising power of Babylon. Either way, that policy was to cost him dearly. The policies of Jehoiakim clearly brought forth some of Jeremiah's bitterest denunciations. It is also likely that Habakkuk's ministry fell in the first years of Jehoiakim's administration.

Things apparently moved along fairly smoothly in Judah for a while. However, the defeat of Egypt and Assyria at Carchemicsh in 605 BC, coupled with Nebuchadnezzar's hasty return to Babylon to claim the throne following his father's death, gave Jehoiakim the opportunity for which he had apparently been looking. He declared Judah's independence from Egypt. Egypt was too demoralized to do anything about it, and Babylon was too concerned with internal affairs to do anything about it. It was at that point that Jeremiah felt commanded to write down all the sermons which he had preached up to that point (Jer. 36:1-3). Jehoiakim's sudden independence might have been considered both by his people as well as by himself as a confirmation of the rightness of his policies. Jeremiah was trying to point out that, on the other hand, this was Judah's last chance. When Jeremiah's scroll was brought to the attention of King Jehoiakim, he cut it up and burned it in a cold fury (Jer. 36:23-24). Jeremiah, not to be outdone, did it all over again, "and many similar words were added to them" (Jer. 36:32). However, Jehoiakim continued upon his chosen path wholly undaunted.

In the winter of 604/603 BC, Nebuchadnezzar marched into the Philistine Plain defeating Ashkelon. It would appear that this was the time when Jehoiakim was brought before Nebuchadnezzar bound in fetters, becoming Nebuchadnezzar's vassal for three years (2 Chron. 36:6, 2 Kings 24:1*a*). Jehoiakim remained loyal to the Babylonians until their astonishing defeat by the Egyptians in 601 BC. That apparently marked the occasion of Jehoiakim's rebellion against Babylon (2 Kings 24:1*b*).

Babylon's defeat by the Egyptians left them with the task of rebuilding and reequipping an army. However, even though Nebuchadnezzar was unable for a time to march against Judah, he could not allow Jehoiakim's rebellion to go unpunished. The Babylonian king hired bands of mercenaries from among Judah's traditional enemies at least to prevent the Hebrew kingdom from enjoying a time of peace (2 Kings 24:2).

After a period of rebuilding, Nebuchadnezzar was at last ready to march upon Jehoiakim and Jerusalem. However, before the Babylonians arrived in the land, Jehoiakim died. It is possible, though by no means certain, that he was assassinated in an attempt to appease the wrath of Nebuchadnezzar. If King Jehoiakim were not assassinated, he at least chose a most propitious time to die, totally avoiding the vengeance of the Babylonians.

It is possible to date Jehoiakim's death with precision to December 7, 598 BC.

Jehoiakim was succeeded briefly by his eighteen-year-old son, Jehoiachin (2 Kings 24:6,8), who reigned for three months and ten days (2 Chron. 36:9). When the armies of Babylon reached Jerusalem, the young king surrendered in an attempt to spare Judah the desolation of war. According to the Babylonian Chronicle, Jerusalem surrendered to the Babylonians on March 16, 597 BC. However, that surrender only postponed the final destruction. Along with Jehoiachin, the palace officials also surrendered to the Babylonians. The Babylonian king carried away all of the leaders of the land, apparently trying to eliminate their potential for waging war (2 Kings 24:12-16). This is known to historians as the first deportation.

Nebuchadnezzar usually shows up as a very shrewd ruler. However, Nebuchadnezzar's decision to deport the leaders of Judah left the people without the ability to really maintain the peace. Those with experience in government were gone. This act on Nebuchadnezzar's part doomed Judah to ultimate destruction.

When Nebuchadnezzar carried Jehoiachin captive to Babylon, he and the people of Judah were allowed to live in relative peace. Some thirty-seven years later Jehoiachin was released from prison, still being recognized by the Babylonians as the king of Judah (Jer. 52:31-34).

However, having deposed the reigning king, Nebuchadnezzar still needed someone to rule in Judah. Therefore he placed Mattaniah, Jehoiachin's uncle, upon the throne. Mattaniah's name was changed to Zedekiah (2 Kings 24:17), apparently for the same reasons that Jehoiakim's name had earlier been changed by Neco of Egypt.

This time the new king had been chosen as a loyal vassal to Babylon. Unfortunately, there was still an apparently large pro-Egyptian group left in Jerusalem.

Little is known of Zedekiah's reign outside of the Book of Jeremiah. There Zedekiah is shown as a weak personality who perhaps wanted to do good but was unable to find the moral courage to do it. He is also shown on several occasions to have sought the advice of Jeremiah and then to have failed to follow it. During this period, Jeremiah had one major theme: submission to Babylon. He constantly insisted that Judah's only hope of continual existence rested in accepting the yoke of Babylon. He also communicated with the Exiles in Babylon, urging the same policy upon them. Unfortunately, there were those prophets in both Jerusalem and in Babylon urging the opposite (Jer. 27:12-15; 29:1-9).

It would appear that Zedekiah allowed himself to be controlled by pro-Egyptian advisors, sending to Egypt for aid (Ezek. 17:11-16). In 593 BC, Zedekiah was called to Babylon to give an account of his loyalty to Nebuchadnezzar (Jer. 51:59). It is possible that Zedekiah's policy had been influenced by the ambassadors from Edom, Moab, Ammon, Tyre, and Sidon (Jer. 27:3-7). Apparently, however, nothing resulted from these early meetings. There is no record of a revolt at this time either in the Bible or in the Babylonian records.

However, the revolt did come. In 588 BC Zedekiah rebelled, yielding to nationalistic and anti-Babylonian advisors. Nebuchadnezzar's reaction was swift and certain. By January 587 BC, his armies were surrounding Jerusalem. Nebuchadnezzar also began an assault upon the outlying cities of Judah. It was not long until the only cities which remained beside Jerusalem were Lachish and Azekah (Jer. 34:6). The Lachish letters clearly reflect this period. They were written from an outpost between Lachish and Azekah and describe the tragic fact that the signal lights of Azekah were no longer visible. It had apparently just fallen to Babylon. These letters also reflect the facts that all hope was pinned on Egypt and that a military commander had gone to Egypt for aid. It was possibly as a result of that journey that an army marched out of Egypt in an attempt to bring help to Zedekiah (Jer. 37:5).

The Babylonians lifted the seige of Jerusalem briefly, going to fight with the Egyptians. At this point Jeremiah sought to leave Jerusalem to visit Anathoth. However, due to Jeremiah's constant sermons urging submission to Babylon, the prophet was suspected of deserting to the enemy and was arrested and imprisoned (Jer. 37:11-15).

The Egyptians were quickly defeated and the armies of Babylon came back to the siege of Jerusalem. Even from prison, Jeremiah continued to proclaim that Judah's only hope of survival was submission to Babylon. Such messages were obviously demoralizing to the defenders of Jerusalem, so the advisors of Zedekiah urged Jeremiah's execution. The weak-willed Zedekiah agreed to the request, and Jeremiah was cast into one of the city's cesspools to die in the filth collected there (Jer. 38:1-6). Jeremiah would certainly have perished if it had not been for the compassionate concern of an Ethiopian slave in the king's court by the name of Ebed-melech (Jer. 38:7-13).

However, although spared, Jeremiah remained in prison until the city fell. In July 586 BC, just as the food supplies of Jerusalem were exhausted, Nebuchadnezzar's troops broke through the walls of the city. Zedekiah and his guard fled by night. Unfortunately, they were captured, probably as they tried to ford the Jordan near Jericho. They were brought to Nebuchadnezzar at Riblah, where Zedekiah's sons were executed and the king was blinded. The last thing he ever saw was the death of his sons, and he carried that vision of the price of his folly as long as he lived (2 Kings 25:2-7).

We have seen on numerous occasions how well informed the Babylonians were of events throughout their kingdom and throughout the territories of their enemies. Because of the messages of Jeremiah, Nebuchadnezzar had givens strict orders that Jeremiah was to be set free (Jer. 39:11-14). Unfortunately, in the confusion which follows any war, the prophet was later included in a group of Exiles being carried to Babylon. When he was recognized, he was given the choice of going to Babylon or returning home. Jeremiah showed deep love for those who had never heeded him by choosing to return and suffer with them (Jer. 40:1-6).

A month after Jerusalem had fallen, the Babylonian army moved in and burned everything in the city which would burn (2 Kings 25:8-9). When that was completed, the stone walls were all pulled down (2 Kings 25:10). Many of the people who survived the conflict were carried into Exile along with the treasures of the city. (This is known as the second Babylonian deportation.) The destruction of the city was so severe that where excavations had been made in Jerusalem, a very significant ash layer is found at this level.

With the fall of Jerusalem and the deportation of its king and people, the Hebrew kingdom came to an end. All of the great hopes which had surrounded the Hebrew's experiment at kingship appeared to have come to a tragic conclusion. It also appeared for them that there were no more tomorrows.

However, we do need to note one thing about the life and ministry of Jeremiah. From the time of Jeremiah's call in 626 BC until the Babylonian siege of Jerusalem, his message had been one of the certainty of punishment upon the idolatry and the social injustices of his people. Such sin as they had performed could not go unpunished. Yet when the Babylonians actually attacked the city and it appeared that all of his announcements of doom were about to be fulfilled, Jeremiah changed the theme of his message. Suddenly, just as it looked as if everything was hopeless, Jeremiah began offering hope to the people. He assured them that, even though punishment was certain, God still offered hope to His people. When all appeared to be gloom and destruction, Jeremiah saw light beyond (Jer. 31:31-34). According to the prophet of God, there was to be a new covenant between God and His people. Judah was to be defeated but not God. On that note, the end came.

The Significance of the Period

Given what we know of the rest of ancient Near Eastern society, the major collapse of a kingdom should have brought the literature of that kingdom to an end. Even more certainly, such a collapse should have brought the faith of that kingdom to an end. From a purely historical perspective, the very fact that neither of these things occured among the Hebrew people is extremely strange. It is so strange as to demand a thorough, critical investigation. However, the very nature of the Old Testament literature and of the message of the material with which we have been dealing may offer us some insights into the reasons why this did not happen. The message of the material from this era, found both in its historical formulations as well as in its prophetic spokesmen, seems to me to focus upon two points. It is this message which allowed the literature to be maintained and added to, its faith to grow and develop, and its people to continue to exist in the face of all odds.

An Enlarged Understanding of God

Throughout the earlier periods of Old Testament history, the people had been coming to grips with a growing understanding of God. That really blossomed in this era. The absolute sovereignty of God over people, nations, and nature had been visualized before this era. However, there is no period in Hebrew history where this idea developed the profundities which it did here. The Hebrew spokesmen and writers during this era developed what we call a theology of Exile. Instead of seeing Hebrew defeats as defeats for God, the prophetic voices of this time saw it as God's vindication. He was understood as a righteous God who could not and would not put up with evil, especially on the part of His people.

It has been obvious that the popular theology of this era did not agree. The people around Jehoiakim saw the defeat and death of good Josiah as a defeat for the God of Josiah. To this, the prophetic voices responded that God is not defeated by human defeat.

One of the more philosophical voices in the entire Old Testament, that of Habakkuk, was raised at this point. He pondered how God could put up with the sinfulness of the chosen people and with the sinfulness of others. Habakkuk's ultimate answer was quite simple. "The righteous one shall live (or 'begin to live' or 'go on living') in his faithfulness" (Hab. 2:4*b*, author's trans.). The prophet and the people were being told that God expects faithfulness from His people, regardless of what happens.

The message was quite clear. God expects His people to be faithful at all times, trusting the fact that history is in His hand. The point which the Hebrews discovered through the revelatory processes of their history was that God was not the subject of history. He is not its victim but its Author and its Sovereign.

This awareness, coupled with the idea that God could use the defeats of history to accomplish His purposes, truly set the foundation for the basic faith of the New Testament. What greater defeat was there than the Cross? What greater exile was there than the tomb? The message of Israel's spokesmen that God was greater than history established the basis for the church's proclamation following the resurrection event.

Israel's enlarged understanding of God gave them the foundation for the second major theme proclaimed from this era of their history. It is to this which we must now turn.

A New Hope

It would appear that there were not ever any more hopeless days in the history of the Old Testament than those last days of Judah's history. It is strange that out of those days of gloom sprang Israel's new hope. That new hope was expressed both by Jeremiah and by Ezekiel.

Everyone had seen that the Hebrew people had not been able to live within the terms of the covenant which had been established between them and God. In spite of great times of covenant renewal, such as that under Josiah, Israel had simply failed. To that failure, based upon their new understanding of God, Jeremiah addressed his greatest words.

> Behold, the days are coming, says the Lord, when I will make a new covenant with the house of Israel and the house of Judah, not like the covenant which I made with their fathers when I took them by the hand to bring them out of the land of Egypt, my covenant which they broke, though I was their husband, says the Lord. But this is the covenant which I will make with the house of Israel after those days, says the Lord: I will put my law within them, and I will write it upon their hearts; and I will be their God, and they shall be my people. And no longer shall each man teach his neighbor and each his brother, saying, "Know the Lord," for they shall all know me, from the least of them to the greatest, says the Lord; for I will forgive their iniquity, and I will remember their sin no more. (Jer. 31:31-34).

With these words, Jeremiah offered a hope that was both national and personal. God would overcome Israel's failure by establishing another covenant. The new covenant would be based upon God's forgiveness.

Ezekiel phrased this statement of the new hope somewhat differently. Promising a return from Exile, the prophet added:

> A new heart will I give you, and a new spirit I will put within you; and I will take out of your flesh the heart of stone and give you a heart of flesh. And I will put my spirit within you, and cause you to walk in my statutes and be careful to observe my ordinances. . . . you shall be my people, and I will be your God. . . . It is not for your sake that I will act, says the Lord God; let that be known to you (Ezek. 36:26-32).

Here again, the emphasis for the new hope is seen not to rest in Israel's righteousness but in God's sovereign acts. To the prophets of Israel and Judah, the collapse of their nations was not the end. There was a hope beyond the Exile. It was a new hope, but it was one which has endured the test of time. The nation had fallen, but God had not. Therefore, there was hope beyond the smoke and fire.

8
From the Fall of Jerusalem to Alexander's Conquest

The destruction of Jerusalem by the forces of Babylon marked the end of the Israelite experiment with kingship. By all rights, it should have marked the end of the Hebrew nation. Yet it did not. That it did not is a historical fact which needs investigation and explanation, if possible.

The continued existence of the Hebrews as a people and as a nation, following such a catastrophe, is a historical fact unique in the ancient Near East. No other nation ever survived such a defeat. Even more significant, no other people had a faith which survived as a living faith in the face of such a crisis.

It is easy to give simple (and simplistic) theological answers to the continued existence of Israel. It is simple to say that Israel was God's Chosen People. Yet that answer merely raises other questions. What do we mean by the expression *Chosen People?* In what way was Israel God's "Chosen People"? What made Israel believe such a thing? Each of these questions and others related to them must be investigated and answered, if possible, as the historian examines what happened to Israel in the years following their defeat. If there are any satisfactory answers to our questions, they must be found in the events which befell the Hebrew people and in what those events meant to the Hebrews.

Sources for the Study

In approaching the period of Hebrew history following the end of the kingship, we are in a wholly different situation insofar as biblical sources are concerned. There is no longer any basic book (or books) to which we can turn for a narrative of the era. Instead, there are only scattered biblical sources to which we can refer.

Jeremiah and Ezekiel both make only occasional references to the early part of the Babylonian Exile. The Book of Daniel appears to give us some information surrounding the final days of Babylon and the rise of the Medo-Persian Empire. The material in Isaiah 40—66 apparently reflects conditions just before and just after the end of the Babylonian Exile, around 539 BC. From each of these sources, we have to glean those items of information which are of interest to the historian.

In addition, Haggai and Zechariah give very precise references to the period surrounding the actual rebuilding of the Temple, from 520 to about 516 BC. However, there is another major gap in biblical sources, for almost a century elapsed before the ministries of Ezra and Nehemiah. A very brief era somewhere near the time of these two men appears to be reflected in Esther. Finally, Malachi seems to reflect the situation in Palestine as we draw near to the end of the Persian Empire, somewhere near 350 BC.

However, these books do not exhaust our biblical sources from this era. Although there are no more books of major historical interest, there are other scattered references in several different books which offer glimpses into some of the thinking among the Hebrews during this era.

In addition to the biblical sources, we do have some significant extrabiblical materials of value. The Babylonian Chronicles continue to be helpful up until the fall of Babylon. Furthermore, Persian records on monuments and in inscriptions prove invaluable. There are also countless materials of religious and cultural interest from the region of Mesopotamia. To these sources, we can also add Egyptian records which, although they were not of major significance, certainly recorded some vital historical events.

Of course, there are also some secondary written sources of varying degrees of value which relate to this period. The major ones are the works of Josephus and of Herodotus. To this we must certainly include the apocryphal book of 1 Esdras. Of some value are the papyrus fragments which have been found at the Jewish colony at Elephantine in Egypt.

Finally, archaeological excavations throughout the entire region of the ancient Near East add additional light to the social and cultural conditions of the era. This clearly gives depth to our understanding of the era.

However, in all honesty, the historian who deals with Hebrew history in this era must acknowledge that there are large gaps in our knowledge. Between certain fixed items of information, we can only offer occasional educated guesses to fill in the gaps. I shall try to be very careful to let you know of what we are sure, what we have good reason to believe, and what is at best a thoughtful guess.

Major Problems for Consideration

It is perhaps because our knowledge of this era has so many gaps, but there have been a large number of major problems for the historian in this period of Old Testament history. However, as I shall point out, some of these appear to have yielded to the slow growth of information regarding the era. We can only hope that this will continue to be the case in the future.

Chronology

Chronology is the backbone of history. Without an adequate and accurate chronology, we cannot begin to deal with any history. We have faced numerous problems with the chronology of Hebrew history in the earlier section of this book. Generally, all of these occurred because we had historical material in the Old Testament which had to be reconciled with other ancient records and with other records within the Bible. In the era following the fall of Jerusalem, we have major chronological problems, but they arise from a different reason.

The problems of Old Testament chronology as they relate to this era actually arise because we really do not have an ongoing narrative from this era. Thus, we are forced to the extremity of just studying the ancient Near

Eastern history and noting where Hebrew history appears to touch it. Beyond that, we can only guess where to plug in other events.

We know that the Babylonian Exile began in 586 BC. (Admittedly, some Hebrews were taken in exile to Babylon by Nebuchadnezzar in 597 BC, but the nation continued to exist for another decade. Thus we usually date the Exile from the actual end of the Kingdom of Judah.) We also know that Babylon fell before the Medo-Persians in 539 BC. Finally, the Persian Empire came to an end with the defeat of Persia by Alexander the Great at the battle of Issus (in Asia Minor) in 333 BC. Into this framework, we must fit what we know of the Hebrew people and what we can infer from the later books of the Old Testament. However, we should clearly understand that much of our Old Testament chronology from this period is only an approximation.

Problems Due to Geographical Location

There is another major problem for the historian of this period of Old Testament history which is unique to this period, and that is the problem of geography and its economic, religious, and cultural impact. For the first time in Hebrew history, the Hebrew people were not basically confined to a precise and limited area of the world. Following the debacle in 586 BC, a large number of Hebrews lived in foreign lands. Although there were certainly scattered refugees in many different places, there were at least three major centers of Hebrew population.

Of course, those Hebrews who had been carried captive to Babylon lived in that region. Although there appear to have been several settlements of the Hebrews in the vicinity of Babylon, basically the Hebrews there were in close contact with one another and this community can be considered to be a unit. Furthermore, there were some Hebrews who certainly fled to Egypt when the Babylonian onslaught of Jerusalem began. At the same time, we know of a large number who fled there following the assassination of Nebuchadrezzar's governor, Gedaliah (Jer. 41:2; 43:5-7). These apparently joined (or established?) a Jewish settlement at Elephantine in upper Egypt.

Finally, there were the very poor and impoverished people who survived the war, did not flee to Egypt, and were left behind in the Babylonian province of Judah. Now all of this serves as the background for a problem. We must take into account that conditions in any one place were certainly different from conditions in the others. Further, there was some degree of communication between each of these groups, and the writings of one group would thus find their way into the collections of the other. Thus, historians must be careful to recognize that we are dealing with three distinct groups who were facing three distinct sets of conditions. If we do not keep this straight, we shall find our historical reconstructions becoming hopelessly confused. The end result is that we shall be confused ourselves.

This problem is even further compounded when we remember that the people who were left behind following the fall of Samaria in 721 BC had long since intermarried with those whom the Assyrians had moved into the region. This gave rise to the group we know of as Samaritans. They, too, considered themselves to be Jews and followers of the God of Israel. This really leaves us with four groups of Hebrews which we must keep straight in our thinking.

The Last King of Babylon: A Nonproblem

The Old Testament clearly declares that the last king of Babylon was Belshazzar (Dan. 5:30-31). Yet the Babylonian Chronicle just as plainly indicates that the last king of Babylon was Nabonidus, for it was from him that the Medo-Persian Empire took over Babylon. Some historians have made many fruitless attempts to reconcile this problem while others have just ignored it, declaring that one source or the other was wrong. However, additional information has brought light to the subject, making a nonproblem out of the issue.

We now know that Nabonidus was the last official king of Babylon. However, he moved to Tema in Arabia and appointed his son, Belshazzar, to rule in his stead. Such was the situation when Babylon fell in 539 BC. To the Hebrew captives in Babylon, Belshazzar was the de facto king, for he actually ruled over them. However, the fact that he could only offer a reward of being "the third ruler in the kingdom" (Dan. 5:29) to one who could interpret the writing on the wall clearly demonstrates that this was the best he could do. He was the second ruler. Thus, our problem turned out to be one of ignorance.

The Nature of the Fall of Babylon

The events around the actual fall of Babylon also leave us with some problems. The biblical record reads: "That very night Belshazzar the Chaldean king was slain. And Darius the Mede received the kingdom, being about sixty-two years old" (Dan. 5:30-31). Both the Babylonian and the Persian records indicate that Babylon actually fell to the Medo-Persians on October 13, 539 BC *with no opposition.*

An ancient tradition has sought to explain this fact by describing a Persian diversion of the river which flowed under the walls of the city. This would have allowed the army to invade the city by marching under its walls, wholly catching its defenders by surprise. However, additional evidence indicates that its fall was a bit less exotic. The people of Babylon were so disenchanted with their king, Nabonidus, for staying away from the city that they apparently welcomed the armies of Persia as deliverers. The Babylonians had not been allowed to properly worship their chief god for a long period, as the presence of the king was necessary for the major festival. Compounding this problem, when the Persians threatened Babylon, Nabonidus had moved many different gods from the outlying provinces to Babylon, hoping to get help from them. This antagonized the people of those outlying areas who were deprived of their gods. It also antagonized the people of Babylon, for it implied that their god, Marduk, was not adequate. Thus Nabonidus's own people saw the Persians as delivering them from the whimsical folly of an absentee ruler.

However, this brings us to an even greater problem: Who was "Darius the Mede"? The Persian general who took the city was named Gobryas. The Persian king for whom he fought and who took possession of the city two weeks later was Cyrus (2 Chron. 36:22-23; Ezra 1:1-2). There just was no one by the name of Darius involved in the fall of Babylon.

However, in the original Aramaic of the Book of Daniel, what we know as 5:31 was actually 6:1. The fifth chapter of Daniel ended with the fall of the kingdom, but the conqueror was unnamed. Many years later, a king by the name of Darius did become king. (In fact, there were three kings named Darius.) Even here, however, some have suggested another problem. All three kings by the name of Darius were Persians. By no stretch of the imagination can they be called Medes. For all practical purposes however, the Medes ceased to exist as a separate nation about 550 BC, becoming a province in the Persian Empire. However, throughout the Old Testament, the nation continued to be called frequently by the combined title of the Medes and the Persians (Esther 1:19; Dan. 5:28; 6:8). Thus, to call Darius "the Mede" was probably never intended to be a racial or cultural identification. It was rather a title which was simply a common expression.

The Sequence of Ezra and Nehemiah

A major problem in trying to reconstruct the history of the Hebrew people during the time of Persian rule relates to the sequence of the ministries of Ezra and Nehemiah. For centuries, it was assumed that Ezra preceded Nehemiah and that the two men were contemporaries. However, since the end of the nineteenth century, scholarly opinion has changed; interpreters have generally assumed that Ezra followed Nehemiah and that almost fifty years separated their ministries. Obviously, the conclusion one draws here significantly affects the interpretation of the history of this era.

In order to deal with this problem, we need to get a few basic dates of the Persian period before us. Since both Ezra and Nehemiah served during the reign of a king by the name of Artaxerxes, we need to begin by identifying the possibilities. There were three Persian kings by that name, and their reigns are as follows: Artaxerxes I (Longimanus), 465-424 BC; Artaxerxes II (Mnemon) 404-358 BC; and Artaxerxes III (Ochus) 358-338 BC.

Ezra is said to have gone to Jerusalem in the "seventh year of Artaxerxes the king" (Ezra 7:1,7). Nehemiah began his ministry in the "twentieth year of King Artaxerxes" and continued until "the thirty-second year of Artaxerxes the king" (Neh. 2:1; 5:14). Since Artaxerxes III only ruled for twenty years, he could not have been king during Nehemiah's time. In trying to compare what we know about the reigns of the two earlier kings, scholars have almost wholly agreed that Nehemiah best fits into the period of Artaxerxes I. This would place Nehemiah's ministry as most likely occuring between 445 and 433 BC.

But what of Ezra? For many reasons, scholars of the past century have concluded that Ezra had to have followed Nehemiah, but not too long afterward. Thus they have generally dated Ezra to the reign of Artaxerxes II, with Ezra's ministry beginning in 398 BC. The major argument for this has rested upon our knowledge of the high priests in Jerusalem. Eliashib was high priest in Nehemiah's time (Neh. 3:1), but Jehohanan, Eliashib's grandson, appears to have been high priest during Ezra's time (Ezra 10:6; Neh. 12:10-11). However, a recent discovery of the lists of many of the high priests in Jerusalem during this era show that both names were quite common throughout. Thus the Jehohanan of Ezra's time may have preceded Eliashib rather than following him. The problem is quite complex and is not clearly settled as yet. However, it appears that there is not sufficient evidence at present to deny the traditional order as reflected in the two biblical books. Thus, I date Ezra's ministry as beginning in 458 BC. (For further study, you may wish to consult any of the major commentaries on the two books. However, be warned that the new work on the high priest list has been done since 1975, thus books before that time did not have that information readily available).

The Ten "Lost" Tribes

A minor problem in the history of this period with which we should deal has to do with the so-called ten "lost" tribes of Israel. It has long been popular in many circles to speak of those tribes of the Northern Kingdom of Israel which were carried captive by the Assyrians in 721 BC as having been lost forever. There have even been such fanciful suggestions that the early inhabitants of England, or even that the Iroquois Indians in North America, were these ten "lost" tribes. The question must be asked as to whether the tribes were in fact "lost."

Ezekiel, whose ministry overlapped the fall of Judah in 586 BC, expected those who had been carried captive from Israel in 721 BC to be reunited with those carried captive from Judah in 586 BC and returned to the land (Ezek. 37:15-23). This hope had been voiced only slightly earlier by Jeremiah (Jer. 3:18). Admittedly, to both of these prophets, this reunification was only a hope. However, we must admit that for them to have had this hope, they must have been aware that at least some of the exiles from the Northern Kingdom were still living in identifiable settlements. This should not be thought surprising, for the Jewish people throughout their history have generally maintained themselves in identifiable communities in times of crisis. Furthermore, even though there is uncertainty as to the full meaning of the census lists of those who returned from Exile (Ezra 2:1-70; Neh. 7:6-73*a*), some of the returnees were clearly associated with cities from the territory of Israel. This raises the distinct probability that members of the Northern Kingdom were among the returnees. Finally, if there had not been some representatives of the northerners among the returnees, a scribe would surely have been forced to offer some explanation as to why the hope of Jeremiah and Ezekiel was incorrect.

Thus we can say that the ten "lost" tribes are more a figment of contemporary imagination than an actual biblical fact. Representative descendants of all the Hebrew people came back to Jerusalem in the returns under Persia.

The Effect of Foreign Religions

One of the continuing problems for historians and theologians who deal with the Old Testament in general and with this period of Old Testament history in particular is the question of how much influence, if any, did the religions of Babylon and Persia have upon the Hebrews. The more that we learn about these religions makes the question even more pressing.

One of the reasons this question is raised is the fact that the Hebrew people always had a problem with pagan religions, even in their own land. How much more of a problem would they have had when they were forced to confront such religions on foreign soil where the Hebrew faith was the alien one? Even more basic to the issue is the distinct similarity which exists between the creation accounts of Genesis and those of Babylon or the similarity between the flood narrative of Noah in the Bible and that of Utanapistim in the Babylonian Gilgamesh Epic. Furthermore, there are numerous passages from the Book of Psalms which appear to parallel similar psalms from Babylon. Also, in the Persian era, Israel was certainly exposed to the dualism of Zoroastrianism, as well as to its highly developed angelology.

There are several distinct possibilities, and each of them finds its adherents. Some have suggested that Israel simply borrowed much of its religious thought from these pagan peoples. In a modification of this idea, others have suggested that Israel borrowed what was best from these faiths, translating it into the terminology and faith of Yahweh, the God of Israel.

On the other extreme, there are those who insist that the borrowing was all the other way. These believe that Babylon and Persia borrowed their thought from Israel. From a standpoint of chronology and in the light of what we now know about how these ideas developed, this position is hardly tenable any longer.

Between these two extremes, there are two other major positions. Some interpreters have suggested that Israel was exposed to these foreign ideas during the Exile and beyond. Having been exposed to these ideas, the most sensitive Hebrew minds and hearts pondered them in the light of their own faith. The ultimate suggestion here is that, while there was little direct borrowing, the general thought patterns did influence the revelatory processes in the minds of Israel's leading spokesmen. This basically claims that the foreign ideas forced Israel's theologians to respond with statements of their own theology.

Finally, there are those who see the relationship as one of missionary imperative. These see a similarity between Israel's experience in the Exile and beyond and that of Paul in Athens. There, Paul took the faith of the Athenians, began where they were in the worship of an "unknown God," and sought to evangelize them with the gospel of Jesus (Acts 17:22-31). The supporters of this view suggest that the Hebrew apologists or evangelists took the basic statements of faith of the Babylonians and the Persians and through that sought to introduce them to Yahweh, the God of Israel.

It is obvious that the problem is highly complex and will not be solved here. However, it appears to me to be beyond question that Israel was exposed to new ideas during this period. Further, it also appears to be beyond question that what they seem to have used has had its meaning signficantly altered from what it was in its pagan setting. I am convinced that the formers of Israel's faith in this period used these ideas as an evangelistic, missionary, and apologetic tool.

Now it goes without question that obviously many of the people of Israel and Judah did apostatize while they were in Exile. They had demonstrated this tendency before the Exile, and there is no reason to believe that they changed. Here again we are confronted with the fact that there is a difference between popular religion and true faith.

The Rise of Judaism

The final problem from this period of Hebrew history with which we must deal has to do with what happened to the means of expressing Israel's religion during this era.

At the time of the fall of Judah, the Israelites had a strongly centralized and throughly organized system of worship. Most of Israel's worship centered around the Temple of Jerusalem and its elaborate sacrificial system. By the end of this era, Israel's faith had become what we now know as Judaism, with a strong emphasis on synagogue worship and the decentralization which that implies.

Further, as we read the commentaries dealing with the books of the Bible produced during this period, we are likely to find someone introducing either Ezekiel or Ezra as the father of Judaism. The question immediately arises as to why Judaism arose here. What was its great impetus?

This is far too complex a question to be dealt with thoroughly in a survey such as this. However, the main part of the answer ought to be quite obvious. First, the Temple in Jerusalem had been destroyed. Further, at least two large groups of Hebrews were no longer in the land of Palestine. Some Hebrew refugees fled to Egypt and the captives in Babylon had been forcibly led away.

If worship were going to be continued in any way, it had to be continued without a sacrificial system and without the Temple. Further, when the Hebrews discovered that they could meet God on foreign soil, they needed some mechanism for structuring the continuation and propogation of their faith. The necessity of the times forced the creation of some kind of local congregations. Thus, the synagogues came into being. This also helped the people maintain their sense of identity, replacing the earlier tribal, clan, and village ties, at least to some extent. The rise of Judaism was Israel's response to the national crisis. It was forced upon them by the historical catastrophe and was developed and nurtured in a time of relative peace free from many major crises. In a very real sense, it may even have been the development of the synagogue which established the basis for Israel's continued existence as a people.

The Background of the Period

In this period of Old Testament history where we know so little of what actually happened to the people of Israel, the background becomes even more important. At least, as we know what was going on in the world of the ancient Near East, we are better able to make our educated guesses as to what was going on in Israel.

The Babylonians

With the capture of Jerusalem in 586 BC, Babylon under Nebuchadnezzar appeared to be at the zenith of power. Yet, as in so many other cases, the foundations were already beginning to crack. Part of the developing weakness in Babylon was due to the events just preceding this period. The Babylonian army had been called out to a major war twenty-one different times in the seventeen years prior to 594 BC. This constant drain upon Babylon's manpower and resources did not ease up appreciably in the next seventeen years. No matter how great a nation is or how successful her armies are, no nation will long endure that kind of strain.

Nebuchadnezzar was apparently unaware of the developing tensions within Babylon. He continued a policy of conflict and expansion by invading and subjugating, although not occupying, Egypt in 568 BC.

With the death of Nebuchadnezzar in 562 BC, the fortunes of Babylon swiftly declined. Nebuchadnezzar had made the city of Babylon into one of the wonders of the ancient world. With its mighty walls, its massive gates, and its magnificent architecture, the city attracted attention from all over the world. Its ruins still do. But victory abroad and magnificence at home are not sufficient to give a nation security.

Nebuchadnezzar was succeeded by his son, Evil-Merodach, who ruled for less than two years. Without Nebuchadnezzar's abilities at leadership, Evil-Merodach inherited the problems created by his father's policies. He was assassinated by Nergal-sharezer, his brother-in-law. That rebellion was doomed from the start, for Nergal-sharezer was surely too old to be an effective ruler. He had been one of the Babylonian generals who had been involved in the capture of Jerusalem more than a quarter of a century earlier (Jer. 39:3,13). Nergal-sharezer campaigned as far away as Cilicia to punish an attack on a Babylonian province, but he died within four years of becoming king.

Nergal-sharezer's son, Labashi-Marduk, succeeded to the throne but reigned less than a year when he was assassinated in a revolution led by Nabonidus from the Babylonian province of Haran. In less than seven years, the throne of Babylon had changed hands three times. Two of those times had been through revolution. This kind of torment and instability takes its toll upon any nation, no matter how great it has been.

Nabonidus ascended the throne about 556 BC and ruled until the fall of Babylon in 539 BC. A better ruler might have staved off the final overthrow of Babylon longer. Nabonidus actually added to the unrest which brought about the overthrow.

The mother of Nabonidus appears to have been a priestess of the moon god Sin in Haran. That is what lay behind Nabonidus's efforts to make the worship of Sin central throughout the Babylonian Empire and to make Sin the chief god of Babylon itself. This attempt to supplant Marduk, the chief god of Babylon, bred immediate opposition among the priests and the people of Babylon.

Nabonidus carried on at least three major campaigns, striking at Cilicia and Syria and moving deep into the Arabian Desert, apparently seeking to subdue the desert tribes. However, Nabonidus's major interests apparently were in the past. In Babylon itself, he excavated ruins of ancient temples, had their records translated, and sought to reinstitute much of the worship of ancient gods. This further alienated the followers of Marduk in Babylon itself. Apparently in order to escape from the growing hostility in Babylon, as well as to find the peace and quiet to pursue his studies of ancient records, Nabonidus moved his residence to Tema in Arabia. There he established a library and devoted himself to contemplation and study. At that time, he appointed Belshazzar to deal with matters of government. Unfortunately for Babylon, the departure of Nabonidus to Tema did not ease the unrest. The major religious festival of the Babylonian year was the annual new year celebration where the king was the central figure. Without the king in Babylon, those worship celebrations could not be held. The official Babylonian Chronicle of Nabonidus's reign over and over again begins the record for the year with the statement that the king remained in Tema and the festival of the new year was omitted. The city of Babylon was seething with unrest and dissatisfaction.

At this time, the Persian forces moved on Babylon as a plum ripe for the picking. The record of Babylon's fall is found both in the Babylonian records and in Cyprus's account recorded on the Cyrus Cylinder. It is quite precise, although leaving some questions unanswered. On October 10, 539 BC, the Persian forces took Sippar, a few miles to the north of Babylon. Two days later on October 12, the Persian army entered the city of Babylon without any battle. Seventeen days later, on October 29, Cyrus the Persian king entered Babylon and took official possession.

Babylon, with its massive walls, mighty gates, and mighty army, was one of the most strongly fortified and defended cities in the ancient Near East. But the real defenses of a city rest not in its walls or arms but in its people. They were totally disaffected by their own king and apparently welcomed the king of Persia as a deliverer. Cyrus was certainly so greeted by the large groups of captives which Babylon held. The taunt song predicted by Jeremiah had come to pass.

> O you who dwell by many waters,
> rich in treasures,
> your end has come,
> the thread of your life is cut.
> ....
> The broad wall of Babylon
> shall be leveled to the ground

and her high gates
shall be burned with fire (Jer. 51:13,58).

The Persians

One of the greatest and least known empires of the ancient world is that of the Persians. The homeland of that empire was the high, arid plateau which extended roughly from the mountains on the eastern side of the Tigris and Euphrates valley to the Indus River Valley in India. It was a massive region, sparsely populated and of little prior interest to the inhabitants of the Fertile Crescent. Although numerous tribes dwelt in this region, the two of most significance to us are the Medes and the Persians. The Medes originally inhabited the northwestern region of this area and the Persians were located farther to the south.

We have already come across the Medes, for they were involved with Babylon in the overthrow of Assyria. From that time until about the middle of the sixth century BC, the Persians had been an independent kingdom but clearly subservient to the Medes. That was to change with the accession of Cyrus the Great (also known as Cyrus II) to the throne of Persia around 550 BC. At that time, it immediately became clear to Astyages, king of Media, that the Persians were about to revolt against his rule. Astyages marched immediately against Cyrus. However, due to Astyages's harsh policies, his Median army revolted and followed Cyrus's victorious march to Ecbatana, the Median capital. From that time, the kingdom was clearly Persian with Media becoming only a province in the kingdom. Admittedly, it was still the province of second importance in the Persian Empire. Yet never again was there anything like the kingdom of the Medes. However, as we have noted, the biblical authors continued to speak of the empire as that of the Medes and the Persians (or of the Persians and the Medes; Esther 1:19; Dan. 5:28).

Cyrus, as ruler of the entire Iranian Plateau, immediately set his sights upon world conquest. He marched as far westward as Lydia, conquering that region by 546 BC. Then he moved southward, finally conquering Babylon itself in 539 BC. With that victory, Cyrus had established the empire in which the Hebrew people and the province of Judah were to be a part for at least two centuries. Cyrus established himself not only as a world conqueror but also as a deliverer of captive peoples and as a most humane ruler. The Jewish Exiles in Babylon viewed him as God's appointed deliverer (Isa. 45:1; 44:28). In conquering both the king of Media and the king of Lydia, Cyrus allowed the kings to live and to maintain royal courts. He also wrought as little destruction as possible upon the cities of the lands he conquered, seeking to win over the people with kindness. He allowed captives of nations he had conquered to go free and apparently even helped in rebuilding their capitals and their sanctuaries. He reestablished the worship of Marduk in Babylon and allowed the Jewish captives to return home and rebuild their Temple.

Cyrus was killed in 530 BC as he fought with enemies on the eastern edge of his empire. Upon Cyrus's death, his son Cambyses II (529-522 BC) succeed to the throne. Cambyses was apparently much like his father. He marched upon Egypt and added that land to the Persian empire in 525 BC, thus making it the greatest empire in the history of the world to that time. However, not long afterward, Cambyses went mad and committed suicide.

For a few months thereafter, the empire was in chaos. Gaumata claimed the throne, declaring himself to be Cambyses's younger brother Smerdis, who had actually been murdered. Further, numerous provinces which had been conquered by Cyrus sought to break away. However, Darius I (also known as Darius the Great) captured and executed Gaumata and seized the throne. He acted swiftly to put down the various revolts and quite literally saved the empire. The description of this victory was recorded in a pictorial relief and in inscriptions in three languages on the side of a mountain cliff at Behistun. The carving is several hundred feet above the great caravan route from Ectbatana to Babylon. It was this inscription which served as the basis for the ultimate decipherment of cuneiform writing. The text was recorded in the Persian, the Elamite, and the Akkadian languages. Darius I ruled over the Persian Empire from 521 to 486 BC and was a zealous follower of Ahura Mazda, the god of Zoroastrianism. Darius I basically made that faith the state religion of the empire, while allowing each province to serve its own god or gods in its own way.

Darius, however, demonstrated his greatest genius in the area of administration. To make the empire easier to rule, he divided it into twenty districts or satrapies with administrators or satraps distributed among them. This administrative setup is reflected in the Book of Daniel and significantly affected the ministries of Ezra and Nehemiah (Dan. 6:1-4; Ezra 7:21; Neh. 2:7). Darius was also known for great architectural works, such as the digging of a canal from the Nile River to the Red Sea. He also built a new capital for Persia, the fabulous city of Persepolis.

Darius was succeeded by his son, Xerxes I (485-465 BC), who was in turn followed on the throne by Artaxerxes I Longimanus (464-424 BC). From this period, a series of letters have come which are known as the Elephantine Papyri. Due to references in the Elephantine papyruses to persons apparently active in the time of Nehemiah, we normally date Ezra and Nehemiah to this reign. These papyruses give us a graphic picture of life in a remote province of the empire. We find reflected there the concern of the kings that the people freely worship their own gods in their own way. Furthermore, there was deep commitment to the fact that justice must be administered fairly. In addition, the Persians had introduced a system of taxation which allowed a significant amount of civil works, such as road building and maintenance, as well as the protection of life and property of the people. Further, the Persian kings apparently adhered to the same standards and laws which they applied to their people.

For almost a century following the death of Artaxerxes I Longimanus, the empire proceeded upon basically the same lines. In general, the populace made little effort to gain their full independence, for the Persian rule was quite beneficient.

However, late in the fourth century BC, the end of Persia came rapidly. Alexander the Great had made himself master of the eastern Mediterranean in a crusade to deliver the Greeks of Asia Minor from Persian rule. (This deliverance was apparently something which many of the Greeks did not want!) Alexander invaded in 334 BC, quickly overrunning all of Asia Minor. Following up on that victory, he met and devastated the main Persian forces in the Battle of Issus in 333 BC. Then Alexander turned southward, conquering Egypt in 332 BC. During this campaign, the provinces of Judah and Samaria came under Alexander's control, although we have no reliable record of how this occurred. As far as the Jews were concerned, the Persian era came to an end at this time. Persia, however, managed to hold out for a few more years. By the end of 327 BC, Alexander had campaigned victoriously all of the way to the Indus River. It was there that he wept because he had no more worlds to conquer, so legend has it.

Before its sudden fall, however, Persia had given the world of the ancient Near East almost two centuries of relative peace. It had been a time for the development of civilization in general and for the peaceful prosperity of the Hebrew peoples. As we shall see, its mark will always be upon the literature and faith of the Old Testament.

The History of the Period

Although, as we have noted, there is no ongoing biblical narrative of Old Testament history during the period which followed the Babylonian destruction of Jerusalem in 586 BC, we can reconstruct at least three significant parts of it. These begin with the Exile itself, particularly the early part of it. We can add to this the period of the return from Exile in 539 BC and the rebuilding of the Temple. Finally, we are able to describe with a reasonable amount of detail the period from 458 to 433 BC which encompasses the ministries of Ezra and Nehemiah.

The Era of the Babylonian Captivity

As is always the case following a military conquest, the days immediately after the Babylonian destruction of Jerusalem were quite chaotic. The land of Judah was obviously filled with refugees trying to escape and with troops of soldiers involved in mopping-up operations. It was in this kind of situation that King Zedekiah was captured and taken to Nebuchadnezzar (Jer. 39:4-5).

This time of chaos also explains what happened to Jeremiah in those first days of defeat. As we have noted, the king of Babylon had been aware of Jeremiah's preaching that Jerusalem's only hope had been to submit to Babylon. Wrongly assuming that Jeremiah was a Babylonian sympathizer, orders had been issued that Jeremiah was not to be made captive but was to be treated as a man of privilege (Jer. 39:11-14). In fulfillment of this order, the prophet had been freed from prison and released. However, sometime shortly thereafter, a band of Babylonian soldiers must have picked up Jeremiah in their mopping-up operations, failed to recognize him, and carried him off with other captives. However, the prophet was recognized by an officer at an encampment at Ramah and was again released. Fearing a repeat of the same sort of thing, the captain of the guard offered Jeremiah a choice of going as a free man to Babylon or remaining behind with the impoverished people of the land.

Obviously, if Jeremiah had gone to Babylon, he would have been honored and treated as some kind of hero by the Babylonians. The choice was really a choice of ending his life in honor and luxury or of ending it in deprivation coupled with a certain amount of distrust from his own people. The old prophet chose to remain with his people and to suffer whatever they suffered (Jer. 40:1-6). He had been called to serve his people, not to die in ease. His choice to remain with them was to be more costly than Jeremiah ever dreamed.

By the time of the fall of Jerusalem, the devastating war throughout the land of Judah must have left only a very small number of inhabitants in the land. The Babylonians are said to have carried away 832 people into captivity (Jer. 52:29). Although we cannot be sure, this number probably only included fighting men, and their families should be added to this. In addition, we know that some people who had deserted to the Babylonians during the conflict were also carried into Exile (2 Kings 25:11). They may not have been counted in the number of the captives. Furthermore, we also know that there were large-scale executions among the leaders of rebellious Judah (2 Kings 25:7,18-21). With the deportation and executions, apparently only the very poorest of the people were left behind. However, we are probably safe in suggesting that significant numbers of people fled from the onslaught and were able to find some sort of refuge in the wilderness and in surrounding countries (Jer. 40:7-8,11).

Nebuchadnezzar had apparently had enough of the rebellions of the kings of Judah. Thus he did not allow another king to assume the throne of Judah. Further, Nebuchadnezzar's destruction of the city and the Temple effectively ended its use as a center of administration. In an attempt to assimilate Judah into the Babylonian Empire, he appointed Gedaliah as governor of the land. Gedaliah was the son of Shaphan the scribe and the son of Ahikam. Both of these men had been involved in the official court of Judah. Thus it is probable that Gedaliah had also had some such experience. Further, Gedaliah's father had once saved Jeremiah's life (Jer. 26:24). This may suggest that there was already a certain degree of friendship between the new governor and the aged prophet.

Gedaliah was entrusted by the king of Babylon with the administration of the province of Judah. He managed to calm the fears of many of the refugees hiding in the wilderness and slowly began to restore some degree of normalcy to the devastated land. Gedaliah appears to have been a very open man, one who inspired trust because he trusted others. This, however, was his downfall.

Gedaliah was so trusting that he refused to believe that anyone could be plotting against him or Judah. The Ammonites, traditional enemies of Judah, were involved in a plot with a warrior by the name of Ishmael who had fled to their territory. They apparently just wanted to create more problems for Judah. Ishmael was probably incensed that any Jew would be involved with collaborating with the Babylonians. Their plot was discovered and reported to Gedaliah, yet he refused to believe that such treachery was possible (Jer. 40:13-16). So open was Gedaliah that he actually invited Ishmael to a state dinner at Mizpah. In an act of despicable treachery, Ishmael assassinated Gedaliah and killed all of his attendants, including the Babylonian garrison (Jer. 41:1-3). The bloodbath was brief but brutal.

Some of Gedaliah's supporters reacted quickly. They pursued Ishmael, rescuing his captives. Ishmael, however, escaped to the safety of Ammon (Jer. 41:11-15).

The people left in Judah who were in positions of responsibility were dismayed by this turn of events. They knew that Nebuchadnezzar could not and would not ignore the murder of his governor and his troops. It was decided that their only safe course of action was to flee to Egypt. With their minds already made up, they asked Jeremiah to inquire of the Lord "the way we should go, and the thing that we should do" (Jer. 42:3). When Jeremiah suggested that they should remain in the land, pleading for mercy from Nebuchadnezzar, they rejected Jeremiah's advice and fled to Egypt (Jer. 43:2). The prophet clearly warned them that seeking safety in Egypt was but to expose themselves to danger. However, they followed their predetermined course of action, fleeing to Egypt and carrying Jeremiah with them as a captive (Jer. 43:5-7).

There were two tragedies created by this action. First, Jeremiah, who had refused a life of ease and honor in Babylon in order to stay with his people, wound up in Egypt as a captive of his own people. There he died. The second tragedy is that in attempting to escape the wrath of Nebuchadnezzar, the Hebrew leaders failed. In 582 BC, the Babylonian armies invaded Egypt, wreaking great havoc and replacing one pharaoh with another.

There is no way by which we can date the assassination

of Gedaliah with any accuracy. It sounds as if it happened shortly after the fall of Jerusalem. Yet such an event would surely had brought an immediate response from the Babylonian king. The Book of Jeremiah records another deportation of Jews from Judah in 582 BC (Jer. 52:30). This would coincide with the time of the Babylonian invasion of Egypt. It seems likely that the overthrow of Gedaliah must be placed sometime just shortly before that invasion.

With the third deportation of people from the land of Judah, we are fully into the Exilic period. In this period, we are confronted with at least three major groups of Israelites whose plight must be considered. First, there were those who yet remained in the land, seeking to eke out some kind of of existence from their devastated country. Some kind of worship continued to be carried out among the blackened ruins of the Temple (Jer. 42:5). Even people from the long dead Northern Kingdom made pilgrimages there. Yet even though worship was carried on, no attempt was made to rebuild the ruins. The people were too poor and too crushed by the events of its destruction. There is no way of knowing what went on among the people left behind in Judah for the next several decades. Whatever happened, they obviously had a very difficult existence with no significant accomplishments being made by them. The situation in 539 BC in the land of Judah had changed little from that in 582 BC.

The second group of survivors whom we must consider are those who fled to Egypt. While many of them were probably slain in Nebuchadnezzar's attack in 582 BC, some of them apparently moved on up the Nile to join (establish?) the colony at Elephantine. There they built a temple and set up the worship of Yahweh. It appears, however, that the old Canaanite influence was still among them; for in the worship established there, they also worshiped a female consort of the God of Israel. For this group, their lot was neither extremely hard nor particularly easy. They, whose ancestors had fled from Egypt as slaves, had gone back as refugees. Some from that colony apparently drifted back to their homeland over the following years.

The major center of the Hebrews became Babylon where we find our third group of survivors. Those who were carried into Exile were the leaders of the land. This means that there were far more achievers there than anywhere else. Their lot was not particularly a hard one. Unlike the harsh slavery of earlier rulers, Nebuchadnezzar allowed captives to settle in their own communities, engage in their own activities, and generally do as they pleased in all aspects except their right to go home. Many of these Exiles were quite successful. This was so true that, when the time finally came in 539 BC that they were allowed to go home, many, if not most, of them did not care to go back to Judah. Furthermore, those who remained behind had been successful enough in the intervening years that they were able to send a significant offering back with the returnees for the rebuilding of the Temple. The Jewish colony in Babylon remained in existence for centuries.

The Exiles in Babylon were quite fruitful in many ways. It appears that the religious leaders there developed the idea of the synagogue in order to maintain their faith. Although their initial reaction in coming to Babylon was one of despair, it was there that some of the greatest masterpieces of their literature appear to have been put on paper. The Exiles were also fruitful in areas of government. They made a place for themselves in the government of their captors, as the books of Ezra, Nehemiah, Esther, and Daniel all suggest.

From 582 BC until the fall of Babylon in 539 BC, the three centers of Israelite life appear to have existed with little change. There was apparently some communication among the various groups. But each generally maintained its own existence relatively independent of the other. However, that all changed with the Persian conquest of the Babylonian Empire.

The Return from Exile and the Rebuilding of the Temple

When Cyrus moved into Babylon, taking over its empire in 539 BC, he immediately instituted two policies which were aimed at insuring the stability of the empire. The first of these was to leave the Babylonian administrative policies and procedures virtually intact. The second was to encourage captive peoples to go home and begin the rebuilding of their sanctuaries and temples, as well as their capital cities. This, of course, directly affected the Hebrews in Babylon.

There are two versions of this policy, as it affected the Hebrews, which are found in the Bible. Although the basic language of the Old Testament is Hebrew, there is a statement of the edict of Cyrus written in Aramaic, the official language of diplomacy in that day. This appears to be an excerpt from the official court records of Cyrus, which would have been written by the official recorder.

> A record. In the first year of Cyrus the king, Cyrus the king issued a decree: Concerning the house of God at Jerusalem, let the house be rebuilt, the place where sacrifices are offered and burnt offerings are brought; ... And also let the gold and silver vessels of the house of God, which Nebuchadnezzar took out of the temple that is in Jerusalem and brought to Babylon, be restored and brought back to the temple which is in Jerusalem, each to its place; you shall put them in the house of God (Ezra 6:2-5).

There is a slightly different version of this in Hebrew found in 2 Chronicles 36:23 and Ezra 1:2-4. This gives the appearance of being the kind of oral announcement which a king's messenger would make among the cities of the land. The messenger's announcement added two details which, while not spelled out in detail in the official decision, were certainly implied. The people were to be allowed to return to do the rebuilding. However, those who did not wish to return were to assist those who did go back by sending offerings to help in the rebuilding. This certainly implies that they had been successful enough in Babylon to be able to send offerings back. We should also recognize that the last Exiles had been brought to Babylon in 582 BC. Given the fact that forty-two years had passed since then and that between five and sixteen years additionally had passed since the Exile of most of the captives, it is obvious that most of the Hebrews living in Babylon at that time had never lived in Jerusalem. The eventual return to Jerusalem may have been a dream to the Exiles; but when the actual opportunity came, Babylon was the only home they knew.

It is obvious that Cyrus's policy in regard to the return of the Hebrew Exiles was directly in accord with his policy in regard to all of Babylon's captives as seen in the records found in the Cyrus Cylinder where a description of his major accomplishments are recorded. Cyrus was not specifically befriending the Israelites but was winning support from among all of the peoples of his empire. The release not only of captives but of Nebuchadnezzar's treasures captured from the sanctuaries of conquered peoples clearly shows that Cyrus's main concern was not the amassing of personal wealth but the building of a stable empire. It may also reflect his toleration of the faith of others and his desire to rule over happy, contented people.

The first return was led by "Shesh-bazzar the prince of Judah" (Ezra 1:8-11). Although we do not know for sure who this leader was, he is probably to be identified with Shenazzar, the fourth son of Jehoiachin (Jeconiah; 1 Chron. 3:18). Jehoiachin and his family had been carried into Exile in 597 BC. If this is correct, then Shesh-bazzar was of the royal line of David. This would have been an extremely pleasing thing to the Hebrew returnees. Shesh-bazzar would also have been quite old at the time of the return.

We do not know how long it was after the edict was issued before the Hebrews who wished to do so returned to Jerusalem, nor do we know how long the journey actually took. However, we are told that there was a great gathering in Jerusalem on the first day of the seventh month to dedicate the reconstructed altar to reinstitute the regular offering of sacrifices (Ezra 3:1-6). This was done under the administrative leadership of Joshua (Jeshua) the high priest and Zerubbabel the political leader (Ezra 3:2). This raises two problems. First, to what does the seventh month relate? and second, why was Zerubbabel the political leader? Although we cannot be certain, the seventh month probably refers to the seventh month (Sept.-Oct.) of the first year of Cyrus's reign. The second problem may be more complex. We know that Zerubbabel was political ruler in the period around 520 BC. The question arises as to whether this is an anachronism or whether he had taken over from Shesh-bazzar within the first few months of the return. It would appear that if the leader of the returnees had died so soon after the return, the despair of the people would have been overwhelming. However, there is the possibility that a party of returnees had come along right behind the first group and that Zerubbabel, being younger, had been entrusted with the task of leading in the restoration of the altar. (Zerubbabel was the nephew of Shesh-bazzar.) It is not impossible that Shesh-bazzar had died or had at least been incapacitated by illness or age and that his nephew had already been forced to assume the leadership. The people apparently immediately thereafter began to reclaim their family heritage, for the beginning of the laying of the foundation of the Temple did not take place until the second year of the return (Ezra 3:8-11). However, as we shall see later, this was simply begun with nothing further being done on the Temple until about 520 BC.

At this point, we are forced to take note of some problems which must have faced the returnees but to which the Old Testament hardly alludes. The people of the land of Judah who had lived there throughout the Exile would hardly have welcomed the returnees with exuberence. They had maintained some kind of official worship in the Temple ruins during the period (Jer. 41:5). They would certainly have viewed the labors of these newcomers with suspicion if not overt hostility. Further, those who had been left behind in Judah had regarded all of the land as theirs (Ezek. 33:24). Those who came back from Babylon would clearly have been seeking to take over their family heritages, necessitating the eviction of those who had been living there for one to two generations. This also would have generated great hostility.

In addition to these built-in problems, the inhabitants of Samaria, the Hebrews of the Northern Kingdom who had intermarried with those whom the Assyrians had settled there in 721 BC, also sought to help (Ezra 4:1-2). Their offer was immediately rejected. This would clearly have antagonized those who later came to be known as Samaritans.

The returnees and the people of the land faced other problems as well. The returnees had to find land and build homes, establish farms, vineyards, and businesses. Added to all of these problems, the land was devastated by a series of droughts and crop failures (Hag. 1:10-11; 2:16-17).

Faced with all of these difficulties, it is little wonder that work on the Temple came to a halt. This situation existed for almost two decades. In the meantime, there was a great upheaval in the empire, as we have noted, with the death of Cambyses and the accession to Darius I in 522 BC. There were numerous rebellions throughout the empire. It is possible that this served as an impetus among some of the people of Judah toward the reestablishment of the Davidic kingship under Zerubbabel (Hag. 2:23). If this were so, it may also explain why, shortly after Darius got everything under control, Zerubbabel seems to disappear from the biblical stories. He may have been recalled under suspicion of being a rebel.

Be that as it may, it is quite certain that a major push was made by the prophets Haggai and Zechariah to get the task of rebuilding of the Temple under way. Haggai's brief ministry is all dated to the second year of Darius the king (Hag. 1:1,15; 2:10). Haggai was apparently an old man who had actually seen the Temple of Solomon. His ministry was picked up and carried on by the younger Zechariah, who ministered for at least two years longer than Haggai (Zech. 7:1).

Under the leadership of these two men, the work on the Temple was begun again. This immediately aroused the suspicion of neighboring governors, who reported to

Darius what was going on in Judah (Ezra 5:3-17). It is interesting that the Cyrus decree had been forgotten and had to be found among the files of Darius (Ezra 6:1-5). However, with the finding of Cyrus's decree, Darius ordered that the work proceed without interference (Ezra 6:6-13). With that hurdle out of the way, the work proceeded and the Temple was finished in 515 BC (Ezra 6:15).

It is interesting to note that the work on the Temple was completed by "the elders of the Jews" (Ezra 6:14). This seems to imply that Zerubbabel was no longer on the scene. He had apparently become a victim of ambition and the encouragement of those who wished to establish an independent kingdom of Judah. Zechariah had tried to warn him of the folly of that ambition, saying, "This is the word of the Lord to Zerubbabel: Not by might, nor by power, but by my Spirit, says the Lord of hosts" (Zech. 4:6).

The new Temple was now available for Israel's worship. It was apparently much less ornate than that of Solomon and was somewhat disappointing to those few people who remembered the grandeur of that former place (Hag. 2:3). It did serve as a place where prayers were offered "for the life of the king and his sons" (Ezra 6:10). Whether that was a part of the original plan of Cyrus, an order by Darius I, or just something done for the peace of the empire is not known. The new Temple did serve as the center of Jewish faith, both for those who were in the land and for those dispersed throughout the empire.

Furthermore, with the disappearance of Zerubbabel, the leadership of Jerusalem appears to have fallen basically upon the shoulders of the priesthood. Thus, for the first time, the government of Judah seems to have become fully subservient to its religion. Israel was to become more a faith rather than a nation.

The Period of Ezra and Nehemiah

Following the rebuilding of the Temple, we enter into a long period of Hebrew history about which we know very little. Between the Temple dedication in 515 BC and the arrival of Ezra in 458 BC, there are only three Old Testament episodes which appear to fit. All of these seem to belong to the period following the reign of Darius I. He was succeeded by his son, Xerxes I (485-465 BC), who was in turn succeeded by Artaxerxes I Longimanus (464-424 BC).

A reasonably good case can be made for identifying Xerxes I with the Ahasu-erus of the Bible (Ezra 4:6; Esther 1:1). If this is so, then in the very early days of that reign, perhaps even in 485 BC, the Jewish people in Palestine were still facing opposition from some of the people of that land—"they wrote an accusation against the inhabitants of Judah and Jerusalem" (Ezra 4:6). We have no idea what situation aroused that accusation nor what Xerxes's reaction to it was. Life was obviously still far from easy for the Hebrews.

Some time later in Xerxes's reign we must put the story of Esther. Esther, a Jewess, became the favorite in the king's harem. A certain high official of the empire, Haman, persuaded the king to deliver the Jews of the empire to him for spoil and destruction. It is possible that Haman was in charge of tax gathering and paid the king large sums of money for the privilege of gathering taxes from the Jews, using this as a first step toward their ultimate destruction. However, Esther's uncle, Mordecai, thwarted the plan, bringing about the destruction of Haman and his followers. We have no Persian record which allows us to offer any suggestion to a more specific date than the reign of Xerxes I. However, there is enough detail given to reflect the situation of the Persian court at this time. Further, there does appear to have been a man serving as a high Persian official with a name quite similar to that of Mordecai.

The opposition within the empire which was directed toward the Jews did not die down. Probably quite early in the reign of Artaxerxes I, the opposition surfaced again. The people of Jerusalem were apparently beginning to rebuild the walls of Jerusalem (Ezra 4:12). To some of their enemies, this was seen as being a preliminary step toward rebellion; so a letter was addressed to the king, seeking to get him to stop this rebuilding (Ezra 4:7-16). When Artaxerxes searched the records, he discovered that the Jews had always been troublemakers to their rulers, so he ordered that the rebuilding of Jerusalem's fortifications be stopped. This rebuilding was the kind of threat which he believed no provincial city should be allowed to undertake outside of the king's purposes (Ezra 4:17-22). We must note that at a later time, Artaxerxes did authorize the rebuilding of Jerusalem's defenses under Nehemiah (Neh. 2:5-8).

When Artaxerxes's letter was received by the territorial governor, he and his forces stepped in and stopped the rebuilding by "force and power" (Ezra 4:23). They apparently at this time tore down whatever parts of the wall had already been built. It was the news of this destruction which seems to have served as the basis for Nehemiah's mission (Neh. 1:3).

At this point, we come to the mission of Ezra. He is described as being a priest (Ezra 7:11), "the scribe of the law of the God of heaven" (Ezra 7:12,21). This title may mean little more than that Ezra was an authority in the Hebrew law codes. However, it is more likely that it was an official title of the Persian court and that Ezra was an advisor to the Persian king in regard to Jewish legal matters. This appears to be more likely in that he was sent by Artazerxes to see that the people of Judah were living in accord with their laws (Ezra 7:14). It was Ezra's task to correct any abuses of the law there. Ezra was given quite broad powers in that regard and had authority to demand the help of the Persian officials in Samaria and Judah (Ezra 7:21-23). Ezra was also given the power and the responsibility of appointing judges in the land (Ezra 7:25-26). Although his responsibilities were primarily in the area of religious observance, he was given some political responsibilities. It seems surprising to us that Persia should be concerned with the religious observances of the Jewish people. However, this is not the case. The point was that persons who were classified as Jews must obey the laws of their religion. To enjoy the privileges, one must accept the obligations.

It appears that Ezra's first act upon returning to Jerusalem was the reading of the "book of the law of Moses" (Neh. 8:1-3). This was done in the seventh month (Neh. 7:73). This was at least two months after Ezra had arrived in Jerusalem (Ezra 7:9). The reason for the intervening two months was probably due to the time needed to plan for the great assembly of the people and to send notices throughout the region.

We have no way of knowing precisely what it was that Ezra read. However, the fact that it took half a day to read would make it probable that Ezra read the entire Pentateuch (Neh. 8:3). The reaction of the people to the hearing of the law was one of sorrow and contrition (Neh. 8:9). However, Ezra and the Levites encouraged the people to rejoice and to celebrate the fact that they had been able to receive the law of God. The Feast of Booths was celebrated immediately, as it was time for it (Neh. 8:13-18).

Later in the month a great day of prayer, fasting, and confession was scheduled. At that time, Ezra led the people in great ceremony of covenant renewal (Neh. 9:38). Following this, but as a part of it, the people pledged themselves to marriage and sabbath reforms, as well as to support adequately the finances of the Temple (Neh. 10:30-32). The end result, however, was that Ezra demanded that all the people of the land separate themselves from their foreign wives (Ezra 10:11). Although there was a general agreement to this, such an edict would certainly have been viewed with a great deal of hostility by those who had to send wives and children away. The end result was supposed to result in a purified community, but the cost in heartache to innocent wives and children was surely immeasurable. Ezra's extreme legalism must be viewed as the forerunner of the worst of the Pharisaic spirit of later Judaism. There is nothing else in Ezra's ministry which can with certainty be placed after this time.

The consequences of Ezra's work are difficult to assess, for we have no way of really knowing to what extent his actions were actually carried out. The one thing of which we can be reasonably certain is that his mission further widened the division between the racially mixed Samaritans and the people of Judah who had maintained their racial purity to some extent and who were urged to reinforce it so drastically. Although there is no way of knowing precisely when the final break between the Samaritans and the people of Judah took place, it is clear that only after the time of Ezra did the terms *Jew* and *Judaism* become common. Thus Ezra is frequently called the father of Judaism.

Sometime after the ministry of Ezra, Nehemiah appeared on the scene. He was "cupbearer to the king" (Neh. 1:11). This must be regarded as an extremely influential position. The office was one of great honor, for the cupbearer was a part of the king's innermost councils. When Nehemiah heard of the desolate condition of the people in Jerusalem and of the city itself, he was exteremely disturbed. Artaxerxes noticed Nehemiah's depression and inquired into it. It is a measure of Nehemiah's influence that his request to help his people rebuild their city walls was granted by the king (Neh. 2:3-6). This is all the more important since an earlier attempt to rebuild the walls had been stopped and whatever had been accomplished had been torn down (Ezra 4:23).

Nehemiah was sent to Jerusalem by the king and was granted rather extensive civil powers (Neh. 2:7-9). As should have been expected, Nehemiah faced major opposition, particularly from Sanballat, the Persian governor of Samaria (Neh. 2:10). Sanballat's opposition was probably due to the fact that he sensed that he was about to lose his authority over the province of Judah. The other opposition would have been due to the furtherance of the policies of segregation among the inhabitants of Judah (Neh. 2:19-20). Nehemiah did not inform the local people of his intent to rebuild the walls until he had thoroughly, but secretly, assessed the damage and the nature of the task which would be required (Neh. 2:11-16).

Finally, when Nehemiah had everything ready, he called the leaders together and informed them of his plans and of his authority. They responded with enthusiasm and the task was begun (Neh. 2:17-18). Nehemiah's enemies, however, plotted to overthrow him and his work. Fortunately, their plans became known to the Jewish leader, and he took immediate and adaquate defense measures (Neh. 4:6-8,13-23).

However, the problems were not solved. As is so often the case in major crises, there were those among the people of Judah whose sole concern was in making a profit through exploiting the situation. The workers on the wall were being taken advantage of by the money lenders. The wall which had not been prevented by outside opposition was about to be prevented by selfish exploitation of some within Judah's own people. However, Nehemiah again proved his leadership ability by confronting the money lenders and making them back down (Neh. 5:6-8,12).

At about the same time as this internal problem, Nehemiah faced a renewed attack from without. This time, however, instead of a threatened military action, Nehemiah's opponents accused him of treason and plotted to have him killed (Neh. 6:5-13). In neither case, however, were they successful. The wall was completed in fifty-two days (Neh. 6:15). That was quite an accomplishment. Nehemiah's journey from Susa and the entire task of rebuilding the wall had been accomplished in six months!

After the walls of the city were completed, Nehemiah held a great dedication service (Neh. 12:27-30). Further, recognizing that a wall in itself has little value, Nehemiah began to organize a defensive force to man the wall (Neh. 7:1-3).

Nehemiah spent some twelve years in Jerusalem as governor, returning to Artaxerxes in about 433 BC. We do not know if this were a special recall or just the conclusion of Nehemiah's period of appointment (Neh. 13:6). However, apparently after Nehemiah's return to Persia, new problems arose in Jerusalem.

The high priest of Jerusalem prepared a special chamber in the Temple itself for one of Nehemiah's enemies, Tobiah. Tobiah had some kind of involvement with a number of the leaders of Judah. Although clearly a Jew himself, he was governor of Ammon. He had sought to prevent the accomplishments of Nehemiah and had failed. He was apparently trying to ingratiate himself to the leaders of the land, perhaps with an aim to obtaining the governorship for himself. When Nehemiah became aware of what had happened, he asked for and received permission to go back to Jerusalem (Neh. 13:6-7). Some have suggested that this second visit of Nehemiah was as a private citizen, not a Persian governor. However, his actions upon arrival at the city seem to suggest that he came with the authority of the king behind him. That would imply that he had come in an official capacity.

Upon Nehemiah's return to Jerusalem, he immediately had Tobiah thrown out of the Temple precincts (Neh. 13:8-9). Furthermore, he discovered that the Temple finances were not being handled properly, so he took steps to rectify that situation (Neh. 13:10-14). He also joined in the task of trying to enforce the early programs of Ezra in regard to sabbath observance and in regard to the prohibition of mixed marriages (Neh. 13:15-21,23-25). The authority which he had been given and which he exercised was clearly both civil and religious. As with Ezra, Nehemiah passed off the scene with no notice.

At this point, our knowledge of the history of the Hebrew people fades for awhile. In this period of darkness, the final break came with the Samaritans. They withdrew wholly from Judah and Jerusalem and built their own temple on Mount Gerizim.

For all practical purposes, the history of Israel in the Old Testament period comes to an end with the reign of Artaxerxes I. There may be a few references to people or events following this time, but they are both uncertain and unclear. The Persian Empire endured for almost a century, leaving Judah and their people in relative peace. With Persia's defeat by Alexander the Great at the Battle of Issus, the empire came to an end, and the time of Greek domination began. The history of the Old Testament era had drawn to a close. With the rise of Greece, the stage began to be set for the era which gave birth to the New Testament world.

The Significance of the Period

In spite of the fact that this closing period of Israel's Old Testament history has so many gaps for the historian, it was an extremely important period for the development of Israel's faith. Furthermore, the message of the historical events which were recorded is quite significant. Our limited knowledge of the history of the era does not limit the messages proclaimed by the Old Testament authors through those events. It appears to me that there are five which we need to consider.

A Theology of Suffering

The first and most important message which the Old Testament writers proclaimed through the events of the Exile is what I have chosen to call a theology of suffering. However, any title which we might apply to this concept is too limiting. We have noted before that it was a common belief throughout the ancient Near East that a defeat for any people was at the same time a defeat for that people's god. Through the experience of the Exile, Israel was led to an understanding that Israel's suffering and defeat was not a defeat for God but God's victory.

Israel discovered that through the suffering of the Exile, a purification process was going on. The suffering which they underwent surely had a dimension of punishment, but it had a primary dimension of evangelism. The suffering was seen as a means whereby God was turning them away from their idolatry and their apostasy back to Himself. However, this was not the only dimension of their understanding here.

The great passages of the Suffering Servant (Isa. 42:1-7; 49:1-6; 50:4-9; 52:13 to 53:12) proclaim the concept of representative suffering or atoning suffering. This is the idea that one can suffer for another. Certainly, Christians believe that these ultimately point to the kind of suffering which Jesus endured for all people. But Israel in the Exilic period saw these as being descriptive of their suffering on behalf of others.

It was the development of this concept of suffering

with an evangelical and missionary purpose, of suffering in order to deliver others that laid the foundation for the New Testament. The whole experience of the crucifixion and the resurrection of Jesus took on a depth of meaning which would have been difficult for the Jewish people of the first century AD to comprehend if it had not been for the experience of the Exile. Further, much of the New Testament proclamation of those events had its basis in the Old Testament description of the Exile and the return.

The Decline of Prophecy

The second major message of the events of the Exile and beyond was that prophecy was on the way out. The prophets of the Exilic period were of an entirely different nature than those which preceded it. Instead of the great messages on social justice and ritual supported by righteousness proclaimed by men like Amos, Isaiah, Jeremiah, and others, we find the Temple rebuilders, Haggai and Zechariah, and the legalist, Malachi. Now this in no way implies that their ministries were not important, but they were of a wholly different nature.

There are many suggestions as to why prophecy declined. All of them are guesses, and not one of them has a great deal of support. The historical fact is that prophecy did decline and pass away. We do not know the real reason.

Two things began to take the place of Old Testament prophecy. The first of these was apocalyptic literature. The only fully developed Old Testament example of this is the Book of Daniel. Apocalyptic is highly visionary, filled with great portents and signs, peopled with angels and demons, and in general quite symbolic. Numerology plays a great part in its message, and there is a major use of numbers as theological symbols.

But the other thing which began to take the place of Old Testament prophecy was the Law, the Torah. In the post-Exilic period, particularly from the time of Ezra, there was a greater emphasis upon the law codes of Israel than there ever appears to have been earlier. With the rise of the scribes and the rabbis of the synagogues to interpret the Law to the people, there apparently became less need for the inspired prophet to proclaim the message of God.

The Rise of Judaism

Closely related to the foregoing, our third major message from this period of Israel's history was that the nature of religion and its expression was changing. As we have noted, prior to the Exile Israel's faith had been centered in worship. The sacrificial system, the sanctuary, and the shrines—all of these were the focal points of Israel's service to God. During the post-Exilic period, the local synagogue and the law began to be the center of Israel's expression of faith.

There is no question but that the religion which Jesus found in first-century Palestine was related to that of the main period of the Old Testament. But it was not very similar, really. The religion with which Jesus dealt was a Judaism which had been born in the period following the Exile. The emphasis upon law and synagogue were purely a post-Exilic development. Those groups with which Jesus had to content—the scribes, Pharisees, and Saducees—were all products of Judaism.

Now the development of Judaism was not necessarily bad. But we must recognize that it was different. The written law had, to a large extent, replaced the inspired spokesman. The emphasis led more and more to a legalism which replaced the free response of a people to their God with a code which regulated life and frequently seems to have replaced God in the allegiance of the people. It is an ever-present danger in religion, particularly in times of crisis.

The Beginning of Canonization

Most contemporary students of the Bible never really stop and think about how the Bible came to be the Bible. It is almost as if we assumed that it was handed down from heaven in exactly the form in which we now have it. A little thought will show that this just was not the case. Various books of the Bible were written at various times, probably with little, if any, self-conscious awareness that Scripture was being recorded. Yet, somehow, along the way individual books and groups of books came to be regarded by followers of Judaism (and ultimately, of Christianity) as authoritative Scripture.

We noted in the preceeding chapter that a book, probably Deuteronomy, was accepted as authoritative by Josiah in his great reform. This is the first time we have any historical record of a written book being accepted as authoritative over faith and its practice. With the mission of Ezra, "the book of the law of Moses" was accepted by the religious community in Jerusalem as authoritative (Neh. 8:1). We do not have any way of knowing precisely what this was, but it was quite likely the so-called five books of Moses, the Pentateuch. Shortly after Ezra's reform, the Samaritans and the Jews broke away from one another forever, and the Samaritans accepted these books as authoritative for them.

Regardless of what books Ezra read, we at least see a major step in the ongoing process of the development of a canon of authoritative Scripture. For all the subsequent history of both Judaism and Christianity, this was quite important. Furthermore, the message of this event is that God can be known through the written record of His dealings with people. This is the fourth message of significance from this period.

The Samaritan Schism

The fifth major message of this period focuses upon the final break between the Jews and those Hebrews from the old territory of northern Israel who had intermarried with other peoples over the years. This break was the ultimate result of the growing exclusivism of the Judaism of Jerusalem and Judah during the ministries of Ezra and Nehemiah.

The break between these peoples is the sad story, so often repeated in the world of religion, of peoples who believe so thoroughly that they are right while another closely related group is wrong. Such divisions are always charged with emotion, defended with righteous justification, yet seldom exhibit any spirit of love or compassion.

The Jews and the Samaritans had far more in common than the Jews and the Persians. Yet the community in Jerusalem got along far better with the Persian overlords than with their Samaritan neighbors. The point here is not that the division should not have happened. Rather, the point is that there was no excuse for the hostility and the bitterness engendered by both sides. To the Jews, the greatest insult was to be called a Samaritan. It remained for Jesus to transform the word into a compliment with His story of the good Samaritan (Luke 10:25-37).

So it was that the story of Israel in the Old Testament came to an end. The final note was one of division and hostility. Though the people of Israel were back in the land which God had promised to Abraham, yet, in all honesty, they had not yet found the country which they sought. The pilgrimage of faith was not yet over.

9
The Message of Israel's History

As the people of Israel passed from being a part of the Persian Empire to that of Greece, there was no great change in their political fortunes. For almost two centuries, they continued under the domination of one part or another of the Greek Empire, facing intense difficulties during the latter part of the Seleucid rule. Beginning with the Maccabean revolt in 167 BC and continuing until the Roman seizure of Palestine by Pompey in 63 BC, there was a renewed but futile attempt to reestablish an independent Judean state. With the victory of Rome, that hope was dashed to earth. Israel's history throughout this entire era sounds very much like that which had gone before, insofar as the actual events are concerned.

However, with the Greek defeat of the Persians, a major change did take place among the Jewish people. For all practical purposes, the Old Testament era came to an end. Admittedly, there is no clear-cut boundary where we can say that here is the line which clearly separates the Old Testament era from the interbiblical period. However, there are enough differences in what was happening to Israel and how they reacted to it for this to be adopted as the boundary. Admittedly, some books of the Old Testament were completed during this period, but they seem either to record earlier events and attitudes or to set the stage for the Judaism of the New Testament era. As such, they are better dealt with as background to the New Testament. Since a line has to be drawn, the fall of the Persian period is generally assumed to be the most appropriate.

Having said that, however, we are brought back to a

fact which was stated at the beginning of the book and which has been reemphasized throughout. Israel did not record its history in the books which we know as the Old Testament simply to be recording history. They already had history in the official annals of their kings or in the diaries, traditions, and memories of the past. The books of the Old Testament were written as a statement of faith. The so-called historians of the Old Testament were trying to answer the "So what?" of their history. What did it all mean? What was God saying to them through their history? What was He doing with them in those events? Above all, what was He saying to future generations through the experiences of the people of Israel?

In other words, the writers of biblical history were proclaiming a message. They recorded events as means to communicating divine truth. The very fact that the six major historical books, Joshua, Judges, 1 and 2 Samuel, and 1 and 2 Kings, are included among the books of the prophets in the Hebrew canon demonstrates this. Therefore, and this is of fundamental importance for either the theologian or the historian, to study Israel's history in the Old Testament without seeking to determine what its message was is to deal falsely with that history and with the people who recorded it. Regardless of whether one believes in the inspiration of the Old Testament—and I do firmly—anyone who seeks to understand Israel's history must do so from the standpoint of Israel's faith. To fail to do this is to totally distort both the history and the faith which came from it. In a very real sense, Israel's history in the Old Testament is both the product of their faith and the source of that faith. Therefore, we must give our final attention to that. We have not completed our survey of Israel's history until we have come to grips with the faith which is proclaimed therein.

In attempting to identify the basic truths which Israel's history writers proclaimed through their writings, it is abundantly clear they they never really said, and probably never even thought, "Now this is (or these are) the idea(s) which we are seeking to share." Rather, they reported their experiences and evaluated them in the light of their faith. Thus we do not in any way have a systematic proclamation of faith in the Old Testament. On the other hand, as we back off from our study of the history and try to take a long view at what was recorded and how it was recorded, we are able to identify several consistent themes which run throughout the history. I acknowledge that the following ideas are my own conclusions as to what the historians emphasized. But I do believe that I am being fair with those ancient historian-prophets. It appears to me that a brief survey of their proclamation through history can be gathered together under the following ideas or concepts.

The Sovereignty of God

Absolutely fundamental to all of Israel's history writing was the idea that God was the sovereign ruler of their world. Now we must plainly make a distinction here between the popular theology of the people and what the author of the biblical material was proclaiming. For example, throughout the history of the kingdom and even as far back as the sin with the golden calf during the Exodus experiences, there is no question but that many of the people of Israel turned to other gods (Ex. 32:4; 1 Kings 12:28). Yet the proclamation of the narratives themselves is always that God was in control. He may have been patient and merciful, but He was still sovereign.

This proclamation was first seen with the call of Abraham (Gen. 12:1-3). It was further underscored with the promise to the aged Abraham that he would yet be the father of many nations (Gen. 17:1-8). This concept continued and grew throughout the entire history. They saw the absolute sovereignty of God at work in the deliverance of the Hebrew slaves from the bondage of Egypt (Ex. 3:8). It was testified to in the divine sustenance throughout the entire period in the wilderness, where God fed them, watered them, and guided them (Ex. 15:23 to 16:5; Num. 9:15-23).

God's sovereignty was further proclaimed throughout the period of the Hebrew conquest and settlement of

Palestine, as well as during the time of the monarchy (Josh. 1:1-3; Jud. 2:11-23; 5:20-21). This concept of God's absolute control over the world of nature and over the affairs of men was further enlarged during the period of the kingdoms to show that God controlled the affairs of foreign kings and their nations, even when they did not even know it (Isa. 10:5-7). This divine sovereignty of God was further emphasized by the proclamation that foreign nations were also responsible to God for their actions (Amos 1:3 to 2:3).

The awareness that God was sovereign, however, was quite different from the concept of God which other ancient Near Eastern nations held of their gods. Even when they appeared to believe in the sovereignty of their gods, they were also terrified by the idea that their gods were unpredictable and capricious. This was never so in Israel. The history writers clearly saw God as being consistent and dependable. Thus they also became aware of the righteousness of God. His dependable actions and His dependable standards were seen as that against which all people were measured.

This concept of the righteousness of a sovereign God apparently lay behind Israel's growing understanding of judgment. Since God was righteous and made righteous demands upon the Chosen People, they were to be held accountable for their actions. Furthermore, that accountability meant that unrighteousness or infidelity must be punished. Israel had expected that God would one day punish the pagans. It came as a surprise to Israel that they had become God's enemies because of their unrighteousness (Amos 5:18-20).

The sovereignty of God was also seen in divine mercy. God's punishment had a redemptive purpose. He sought to bring His people back to Himself (through punishment, as the recurring refrain of Amos shows: "yet you did not return unto me" (Amos 4:6,8,9,10,11). Hosea, however, pointed out most clearly that mercy was a part of the divine sovereignty (Hos. 11:9). Yet there are abundant evidences of this throughout the historical materials where God did not punish but extended mercy. The Old

Testament clearly sees the divine purposes as unchanging and unchangable, but the historical writers just as clearly saw that God could accomplish His purposes in alternate ways when His people rebelled.

One of the more important parts of the historical writers' proclamation of the sovereignty of God is seen in the Hebrew experience of the Exile. First of all, there was still a popular belief that God was limited to the land of Palestine. Through the Exile, the people discovered that God was in Babylon and that He was sovereign there too. Further, they discovered that He could use even their defeat to accomplish His purposes. Such was His power and His sovereignty.

It is this concept of the sovereignty of God which seems to underlie everything else Israel's history writers proclaimed. God was unthreatened either by Israel or by Israel's enemies. He was further unthreatened by the gods of any nation. Both nature and nations were under His control. It was that simple. It was also that profound.

The Mission of Redemption

Closely related to Israel's proclamation of the divine sovereignty through their history is their proclamation of the redemptive purpose of God. Again, this is clearly seen from the beginning when Abraham was commissioned to be a blessing to all the peoples of the earth (Gen. 12:2). Israel, as Abraham's descendants, were to carry out that mission of being a blessing. Unfortunately, they appear to have become more concerned with receiving the blessings of being the children of Abraham than with sharing them (Matt. 3:9). Yet this failure on the part of the people in no way negated the proclamation of the prophetic historians of ancient Israel. God's purposes were redemptive.

Furthermore, the proclamation of Israel's history was that God's redemptive purposes sprang from His very nature. This may have been first seen clearly in the experience of Israel's deliverance from Egypt. God had delivered them from that bondage not because of any worth in themselves but because of His own nature (Deut. 7:7). This seems to imply that what He had done for Israel, He had done in order to bring them to Himself. His redeeming love had prompted their deliverance from slavery.

There is no question but that Israel basically failed to aid in fulfilling God's redemptive purposes for others. They did not seek to share their understanding of God with those round about them. This was true from their earliest days in the land, throughout the monarchy, through the Exile, and beyond. In fact, during and following the time of Ezra and Nehemiah, the people of Israel became so nationalistic, so turned inward upon themselves, that it appears that they had lost any concern for others at all. Instead of seeking to share their understanding of God with other nations, they actually drove others away. We must remember that this attitude, at least in part, was what lay at the foundation of their ultimate break with the Samaritans.

However, just because the people of Israel missed the understanding of God's redemptive mission in no way means that it was not proclaimed by their prophets and writers. They clearly sensed this in regard to themselves. At least from the time of Isaiah, they became aware that God would redeem a remnant of His people regardless of what catastrophes came upon them. Furthermore, God's concern that other peoples should share in His blessings was reflected in the fact that David, Israel's greatest king, was the great grandson of Ruth, a Moabitess (Ruth 4:21-22).

God's redemptive purpose for Israel was also clearly proclaimed through the experience of the Babylonian Exile. The people had not been ultimately cast off but were brought back to their land and to God.

As we have seen earlier, the greatest awareness of the redemptive purposes of God was proclaimed through the experience of the Suffering Servant of God (Isa. 42:1-7; 49:1-6; 50:4-9; 52:13 to 53:12). Although the Hebrews did not fully understand the concept of redemptive, atoning, suffering as it is proclaimed in the death of Jesus, yet they did become aware that suffering could be used by God for accomplishing His redemptive purposes.

Beyond this, throughout Israel's historical processes, the prophets did see that Israel was a part of God's redemptive plan (Isa. 2:1-4; Mic. 4:1-4). There was always that small group of people who perceived God's purpose to share His goodness with all nations. Thus we must face the fact that Israel's historians saw that God was not merely sovereign over all nations, He intended to bless all nations throughout Israel. Through Israel's spokesmen, the divine purposes were occasionally shared with foreign kings and their ambassadors (Jer. 27:1-11).

Finally, the whole concept of God's call of individuals (as well as of nations?) had a dimension of redemptive purpose. Amos was called to carry the message of God from his southern homeland to the Northern Kingdom of Israel (Amos 7:14-15). Hosea shared God's redemptive love with his own people in the north (Hos. 1:1; 3:1). Isaiah did the same in the south (Isa. 6:8). The roll call could go on. Jeremiah had the broadest of all comissions, being sent as a "prophet to the nations" (Jer. 1:5). This is the term normally used to refer to the Gentiles. Jeremiah's mission clearly had a major commitment to share God's message with others beyond his own countrymen.

The Old Testament historians clearly saw that God had a broader concern and love than just Israel. The popular idea may have been to limit that concern to themselves. But the Old Testament history plainly reveals that the concern was not so limited. The historians knew God is sovereign over the universe. As sovereign Lord, He loved and sought to redeem all of creation. Others might limit their concerns. God did not. Further, those who were faithful to Him did not limit their concerns either.

The Relationship Between Faith and History

One of the least noticed but more significant ideas which Israel's historians proclaimed was the relationship between faith and history. By this I mean that beliefs thoroughly affect life. This in no way means that faith determines what happens in history. Rather, what the history writers proclaimed was that an individual's or a nation's response to their history is determined by their understanding of and service to God.

For example, the difference between Jacob's early life and his later life was changed because his awareness of God had changed. At the beginning, Jacob was seeking solely what was good for himself, with no thought of its consequences for anyone around him. This is further illustrated by the recurring refrain of the historians in passing judgment upon the lives of the kings of Israel, for it is consistently said of them that they did not depart from "the sins of Jeroboam the son of Nebat" (1 Kings 16:31; 22:52; 2 Kings 3:3; 10:29; and others). Thus their lack of faithfulness to the God of Israel seriously affected the ultimate manner in which they ruled their land. The same sort of thing was also pointed out about the reigns of the kings of Judah.

Now it could easily be said that this kind of thing is obvious. Of course, faith affects what we do in and with the events of life. That is not the point. The point is that the biblical historians *said it.* They perceived that personal commitments had serious consequences.

It is quite popular in modern society to say that what I do does not hurt anyone but myself. But the Old Testament historians would not have said that. Recall the sin of Achan in stealing some of the goods from Jericho. It is said to have affected the outcome of Israel's attack on Ai and to have resulted in the death of family, servants, and flocks (Josh. 7:1-26). It is not my purpose to debate whether the punishment of all of Achan's family was justified. The point is that the author of the story was clearly proclaiming that Achan's faith affected both Israel's and his family's history.

Furthermore, David's sin with Bathsheba not only affected David, Bathsheba, and Uriah but also had significant consequences for David's children and his kingdom (2 Sam. 12:15-18; 13:1-14,28-29; 15:1-12; 18:9-17). On the other hand, David's submission to the confrontation by the prophet Nathan, his willingness to confess his sin, and his calm acceptance of the punishment and the mercy of God also affected the life of himself, his family, and his nation (2 Sam. 12:13-14).

The relationship between faith and history was not just proclaimed as it related to individuals. The historians clearly showed that the general faith of the nation could affect the life of that nation. This, too, is obvious. But it was proclaimed with fervor. The popular belief in Israel was that God's blessing should have been automatic because of who they were and from whom they descended. "Not so," said the history writers. Israel's faithfulness, or lack of it, affected those things which happened to them. Furthermore, their steady faithfulness to God in the midst of catastrophe or in the midst of prosperity was what was called for. Habakkuk raised this issue and settled it by proclaiming that "the just (the righteous) shall live in his faithfulness" (Hab. 2:4*b*, author's trans.). Regardless of what comes, those who were measuring up to God's standards were expected to go on being faithful.

To the Old Testament historian, history was shaped by faith. But the circle was completed by the fact that faith was also shaped by history. What a people experienced with God shaped their understanding of God. It was one thing to proclaim that God redeemed. It was another to have been redeemed. What the history writers proclaimed about God was what they had learned of Him in the practical, concrete affairs of life. To them, faith and history were so intertwined as to be inseparable. They knew nothing of an abstract set of beliefs or of some kind of nebulous commitment. What either a person or a nation did was a visible demonstration of their commitments, a visible acting out of their beliefs.

The Inadequacy of Empty Ritual

Insofar as we have any knowledge, all of the nations of the ancient Near East had highly developed religious rituals to govern and regulate every detail of their approach to their gods. Israel was certainly in the mainstream of the times, seemingly having neither significantly more nor less religious ritual. It appears that every feature of their approach to God was governed by ritual. This was true for the major festivals of the religious year, for the regular observances of sabbaths, for the family-centered worship of the new moons, for the private worship of thank offerings, peace offerings, or vow offerings, and for the great national Day of Atonement (Yom Kippur).

Israel's rituals are set forth in the regulations of the Pentateuch. But they are also demonstrated in the historical narratives of the Bible. To illustrate this, consider the covenant renewals of Joshua, Josiah, and Ezra (Josh. 24:1-28; 2 Kings 23:1-3; Neh. 8:1-18). The rituals are further seen in the new moon practices of David and Saul, as well as in the private sacrifice of Samuel when he anointed David as king (1 Sam. 16:1-3; 20:18-27). The point of this is that Israel's religion was rooted, grounded, and shaped by ritual.

There is no indication that any of the historians or prophets of Israel's faith ever thought that their rituals were wrong in and of themselves. However, there is ample evidence that these same spokesmen clearly believed that there was a great deal wrong with rituals which were observed without any kind of personal or national response to the God behind the ritual. In other words, if the ritual did not affect both the relationship between the worshiper and God and the worshiper and his fellows in a positive way, it was utterly worthless.

Micah clearly set forth the expectations of God in regard to worship.

> "With what shall I come before the Lord,
>   and bow myself before God on high?
> Shall I come before him with burnt offerings,
>   with calves a year old?
> Will the Lord be pleased with thousands of rams,
>   with ten thousands of rivers of oil?
> Shall I give my first-born for my transgression,
>   the fruit of my body for the sin of my soul?"
> He has showed you, O man, what is good;
>   and what does the Lord require of you
> But to do justice, and to love kindness,
>   and to walk humbly with your God (Mic. 6:6-8)?

THE MESSAGE OF ISRAEL'S HISTORY

Amos just as clearly proclaimed God's rejection of worship which is not based upon practical righteousness in daily living.

> I hate, I despise your feasts,
> and I take no delight in your solemn assemblies.
> Even though you offer me burnt offerings and cereal
>   offerings,
> I will not accept them,
> and the peace offerings of your fatted beasts
> I will not look upon.
> Take away from me the noise of your songs;
> to the melody of your harps I will not listen.
> But let justice roll down like waters,
> and righteousness like on ever-flowing stream
>   (Amos 5:21-24).

These memorable passages from the prophets are generally quite familiar. But we may be less familiar with the words of Samuel to Saul in relationship to the same sort of problem.

> Has the Lord as great delight in burnt offerings and
>   sacrifices,
> as in obeying the voice of the Lord?
> Behold, to obey is better than sacrifice,
> and to hearken as the fat of rams (1 Sam. 15:22).

Even if we are familiar with the words, we may be surprised to find them in a book of so-called history. This same kind of condemnation of meaningless ritual is reflected in much less memorable words as we see all of the steps which Josiah took to purify the ritual of his people in the great reform (2 Kings 23:4-25).

Admittedly, anything which is good can be prostituted and made bad. To the history writers of the Old Testament, this was what so frequently happened to their people's rituals. They carefully described what needed to be done with the empty rituals of their people.

We must be careful to note, however, that these writers never suggested that such rituals should be abandoned. To the contrary, some of these writers point out the importance of proper rituals when connected with a proper relationship between the worshiper and God and between the fellow worshipers. These writers proclaimed that it was not the ritual which was wrong; rather, it was ritual which was unrelated to life which was wrong. That is a lesson which may need to be learned by modern worshipers as well.

The Demand for Practical Righteousness

Closely related to the proclamation of the inadequacy of empty ritual was the Old Testament historians' demand for practical righteousness. A great deal has been written about the fact that the Old Testament's basic concern for righteousness related to matters of ritual. If all that is read is the Book of Leviticus, that may be true. But even there, it appears that the message is that if improper ritual is so wrong, improper ethics are even worse.

In the rest of the Old Testament, however, there is no question that the basic theme of righteousness relates to the way one person treats another. Even in those passages which focus upon the people's relation to God, this relationship is regularly made visible in the practical affairs of everyday life.

Consider for example, the case of Ahab. He was condemned for condoning, if not actually supporting, the worship of the Phoenician Baal. But Ahab's apostasy showed up in murder of Naboth and the theft of Naboth's home and land (1 Kings 21:1-26). Further, the kingdom of Israel revealed their apostasy from God by the frequent times of anarchy which they endured throughout their history.

It remained for the great prophets to examine the life of their nation and to come thundering down upon those who oppressed their neighbors. Isaiah demanded that the people "cease" doing evil and that they "learn to do good" (Isa. 1:17). He later spelled out precisely what he meant by listing the kinds of sin that needed to be given up. He condemned the greed that drove people to amass fortunes at the expense of their neighbors, the self-conceit which blurred all distinctions between good and evil, and the self-indulgence which made people devote their lives to becoming champions at drinking, thus losing control of themselves (Isa. 5:8,20-22).

Probably no one got so specific in denunciations of the abuse of neighbors as did Amos. But he also clearly pointed out that indifference to the plight of our neighbors is as much an abuse as outright oppression. (Amos 6:1). If the worship of God does not lead us to care about those round about us, then there is something wrong with that worship.

All of the great prophets clearly proclaimed that the mistreatment of the weak, the poor, and the helpless is an indication that a people is not right with God. But they also declared that such abuse or indifference will have historical consequences. The society which does not actively protect and care for its weakest members is doomed to destruction. There was just no other way.

The law of Israel showed that Israel's God had a particular concern for those who had no one to stand up for them. Israel's history showed all too often that they did not have such concern. Generally, they just do not appear to have cared for the helpless. Thus the society which they sought to establish was doomed to collapse.

Israel's history showed that there are inexorable demands placed upon God's people to care for others. If the relationship which they had with God did not produce practical righteousness, it was worthless. Further, if their faith did not produce practical deeds of goodness, it was worthless. The God of Israel was a demanding God. He still is. The history through which they lived showed that when the demands of practical righteousness were not met, there were inevitable historical consequences. Those consequences were variously called the judgment or the wrath of God. That was the price which had to be paid for a faith without ethics, for ritual without righteousness, and for a religion which had no effect upon their relationship with others.

It should be obvious that the ethics of the Old Testament were not the ethics of Jesus. If they had been, there would have been little need for Jesus' teachings. On the other hand, the ethics of the Old Testament made increasing demands upon Israel for the proper treatment of others. Israel's fault did not rest in the fact that their ethics were poor but in the fact that they did not measure up to the demands which their ethics made upon them.

The Covenant Community

One of the major factors which made Israel distinctive throughout the Old Testament period was their sense of being in a covenant relationship with God, of being a covenant community. We must acknowledge that, from the standpoint of the narrative, the specific covenant of relationship is first mentioned in connection with Abraham (Gen. 15:18). However, the covenant to which the nation of Israel turned again and again was that at Sinai (Ex. 19:5; 24:7). This is normally called the Mosaic covenant by interpreters since Moses was the representative figure involved in it.

The Mosaic covenant was periodically renewed in times of spiritual or national crises. This was the covenant which was renewed by Joshua at Shechem just before his death (Josh. 24:25). It was also the Mosaic covenant which was renewed by Solomon at the dedication of the Temple in Jerusalem (1 Kings 8:1-23). The Mosaic covenant was also renewed by Josiah after the discovery of Deuteronomy in the Temple during Josiah's reform (2 Kings 23:2-3). And it was still the Mosaic covenant which Ezra renewed with the returned community during the time of the Persian Empire (Neh. 9:38).

Yet it was not just the times of the covenant renewal when the Old Testament writers and spokesmen focused upon the covenant. The prophets regularly condemned their people for breaking the covenant, calling them back to the covenant (Isa. 24:5; Jer. 11:2-10; Ezek. 16:8,59). With all of this emphasis upon the covenant, it was obviously of major importance to the historians of the Old Testament. There are at least two reasons for this.

The first reason the covenant was so important to Israel may have to do with its form. As noted in chapter 3, in the ancient Near East there were two kinds of covenants. The first of these was a parity covenant, which was between parties of essential equality. On the other hand, the second kind of covenant was the suzerainty covenant, which was made by a great king (suzerain) and the king's vassals. Such a covenant had a fairly well-defined form and was not in the least negotiable. The Mosaic covenant seems clearly to be in such a form.

The point of the summary in chapter 3 was to note that it does appear that the Mosaic covenant was carefully presented to Israel in a form which was commonly known and used in their day. The form itself was a declaration that Yahweh was Israel's King. Furthermore, the form also communicated that Israel could not negotiate the covenant. They could (and frequently did) break it, but they could not change it. Once entered into, Israel had forever placed themselves as vassals of Yahweh.

Yet the content of the covenant communicated more than the form. The content of Israel's covenant with God established the pattern for their national and personal existence. Modern people see law as an abridgment of freedom. Israel's historians and prophets, on the other hand, were wise enough to recognize that the law of God made life livable. A game becomes unplayable without rules. The same is true of life. The rules had as their basis the establishment of a stable and ongoing community.

Furthermore, Israel also realized that the covenant truly made them into a community. Again, the modern world places a great premium upon individuality. Israel placed a far greater premium, probably as a result of their covenant, upon each person's part in the community. There was an interrelatedness which meant that each was responsible for everyone else. Upon this basis, many of the prophets' sermons thundered down upon Israel. Not everybody was necessarily guilty of any specific sin, but all were responsible for what went on among them. No Hebrew would ever, like Pilate, have tried to wash his hands of responsibility. They might have ignored their responsibility, but they knew that they had it. They were truly a covenant community.

The Expectation of Committed Leadership

Most people who read the Old Testament are familiar with the call of the prophets. We are aware that many of those spokemen of God reflect a deep sense of divine compulsion. They approached their task not of their own volition but because they believed that God had called them to it. Their own self-awareness of that divine call is reflected over and over again, both in the narratives of their calls (Amos 7:14-15; Isa. 6:1-12; Jer. 1:4-10) and in the recurring use of phrases such as, "the word of the Lord came to me" or "the hand of the Lord being strong upon me" (Jer. 2:1; Ezek. 3:14).

But one feature of the Old Testament's proclamation through history with which we are not so familiar was Israel's sense that their political and military leaders also ought to have some sense of divine commission. Moses' sense of call and commission is an excellent example of this (Ex. 3:1 to 4:17). The same is true of Joshua (Josh. 1:1-9). However, it might be said that these were primarily spiritual leaders. Admittedly, this was true of Moses. It was not nearly so true of Joshua. He was basically a fighting man and an administrator. Yet we must acknowledge that the Hebrews never separated political and religious leadership responsibilities as we do.

When we get into the period of the settlement, many of the judges were clearly acting under the sense of divine compulsion. Moving on into the period of the monarchy, we see that the people expected the same kind of leadership from their kings. Leaders in all areas of life were expected to be committed to the God of Israel and to be acting in response to God's call and commission.

In the last analysis, the authors of the Books of Kings and of Chronicles based their ultimate evaluation of their political leaders upon their faithfulness and loyalty to God. This was, to the Old Testament writers, infinitely more important than any other accomplishments which their reign might have made for their nation. To the Old Testament historian, it mattered not that Omri made a major impact upon the world. Rather, what did matter was that he was not faithful to God.

It is even more important from the standpoint of our comprehending the biblical message that we note that it is not significant whether or not we agree with the biblical basis for evaluating Israel's leaders. What is important is that this was their basis for evaluation. The proclamation of Israel's history is that all leaders should be committed to the God of the nation.

We must be reminded again that we cannot apply the biblical approach to political leadership directly to that of our nation today. Ancient Israel was a theocracy, not a democracy. Yet we can identify the underlying principle: God expects His people to carry their faith into whatever office they fill. Our political and business lives must be governed by our faith, by our commitments, and by our sense of call. To do any less is to wholly ignore this part of the message of the history of Israel in the Old Testament. God's people are responsible to God for all of life. There is no lesser way.

The Legacy of a Dynamic Faith

Not least in importance among the things proclaimed by Israel's historians was that faith is dynamic if it is anything. This is revealed first of all by the fact that Israel in the Old Testament era never really seems to have developed what we would call a theologian. The books of the Old Testament are not theological treatises about God; they are narratives about what God did. Israel proclaimed their faith not in a systematic philosophy but in a record of what God had done to, with, and through them. If we miss this fact, we have missed the very essence of both Israel's theology and her history.

Furthermore, Israel did not just discover God in history; they believed that He met them in history. Their relationship to God was active, not passive. Thus faith for them is best described as faithfulness. In fact, the Old Testament Hebrews really did not have any word for *faith*. Where it appears in our translations, we have usually forced our own concepts upon it. To Israel, their faith (or lack of it) was always made visible in their actions; thus, faith was seen in history. There was just no other way.

This is the primary legacy which Israel has left to us. It is one of the basic proclamations of their writings. To Israel, God was not thought about; He was met. God was never seen by them as an object to be turned this way and that for examination nor analyzed in order to describe. God was experienced in the affairs of life.

Beyond this, one's relation to God was seen as a relationship which was lived out. The historians of Israel thus proclaimed in the very writings which they produced that faith was a relationship which was lived. That was the whole basis for the recording of their history as a part of their sacred Scriptures. It was also the basis for preserving it and passing it on.

Setting the Stage for the New Testament

At this point, we are ready to draw our consideration of Israel's history in the Old Testament to a close. While Israel was not fully aware of it, their history had set the stage for the great drama of redemption which is proclaimed by the New Testament.

Israel's history had shown that the people of God had failed. They had failed to be what God had called them to be and what He had intended them to be. God had been faithful. Israel had been faithless. Israel's history had also shown that if humankind was finally to come to know God, humanity's basic sin problem had to be dealt with.

But Israel's history had prepared the way for the New Testament. The world had been prepared by what God had done through Israel. It had been given a vocabulary of sin and redemption. It had been given an awareness of God which no other ancient society had. Out of that crucible was to come God's great act of redemption.

Israel's history had also given them hope. Their past had little glory at which to look back. It was a rather consistent story of human failure. Their kings had never been what they expected nor what God had intended.

Out of that cradle, therefore, grew their great messianic hope. Thus, they looked forward as well as backward.

> The people who walk in darkness
>   Shall see a great light;
> Those who dwell in a land of deep darkness,
>   on them light shall shine.
> ....
> For to us a child shall be born,
>   to us a son shall be given;
> and the government shall be upon his shoulder,
>   and His name will be called
> "Wonderful, Counselor, Mighty God,
>   Everlasting Father, Prince of Peace"
>   (Isa. 9:2-6, author's trans.).

Not only did Israel's history make them look forward to a new King but they also looked forward to a new age established through a new covenant with God.

> Behold, the days are coming, says the Lord, when I will make a new covenant with the house of Israel and the house of Judah, not like the covenant which I made with their Fathers . . . But this is the covenant which I will make with the house of Israel . . . I will put my law within them, and I will write it upon their hearts; and I will be their God, and they shall be my people. . . . they shall all know me, from the least of them to the greatest, says the Lord; for I will forgive their iniquity, and I will remember their sin no more (Jer. 31:31-34).

Furthermore, the final stage of Israel's Old Testament pilgrimage was to give them a new language. The conquests by Greece was to make Greek the language of the world. When the divine drama was finally culminated in the life of Jesus, it could be proclaimed to the ends of the earth in one language. In addition, the many crises through which Israel had gone had sent refugees to almost every major city of the ancient Near East. There were people throughout the Roman Empire at the birth of the New Testament era who already knew the Old Testament background from which the apostles proclaimed God's new acts.

The last step in preparation had been wrought by the

emergence of the Roman Empire. It brought a rough peace to the world and a major system of roads and highways. Thus those who went out to carry the New Testament message had a background on which to draw, a language which was universally understood, roads upon which to travel, and the absence of national barriers to hinder their advance.

Beginning with Abraham, the people of Israel had set out to find a country in obedience to God. Their pilgrimage had led through Palestine, Egypt, Assyria, Babylon, and to the ends of the earth. These sought a country, but it was not to be found until Jesus Himself led the way.

Appendix: Chronological Table

2000 to 1700 BC	Patriarchal period, Abraham, Isaac, Jacob, and Joseph; wanderings in Canaan; descent into Egypt.		
1700 BC	Hyksos (Semitic) Dynasty rules in Egypt; primacy of Joseph		
1550 BC	Hyksos expelled from Egypt; Israel remains in Egypt		
1450 BC	Israel remained in Egypt, but some early migrations back to Canaan may have begun		
1300 BC	Seti pharaoh, ca. 1306-1290		
	Ramses pharaoh, ca. 1290-1228; the Exodus from Egypt ca. 1270		
	__EGYPT__	__CANAAN__	__MESPOTAMIA__
1250 BC	Ramses	Joshua, entrance into the land	Assyrian expansion
	Merneptah, ca. 1228-1121		
1200 BC		Sea People invade northern coastal plain	
	Ramses III, ca. 1185-1150	Othniel and Ehud, ca. 1200	
1150 BC		Philistines invade coastal plain	
		Deborah, ca. 1145	
		Gideon, ca. 1140	
1100 BC		Jephthah and Samson, ca. 1100	
		Eli	
1050 BC		Samuel, ca. 1050-1020	
		Saul, ca. 1020-1000	
1000 BC		David, ca. 1000-961	
950 BC		Solomon, ca. 961-931	

Appendix: Chronological Tables

	EGYPT	JUDAH	ISRAEL	SYRIA	ASSYRIA
	Shisak	Rehoboam, 931-913	Jeroboam I, 931-910		
		Abijam, 913-911	Nadab, 910-909		
900 BC		Asa, 911-870	Baasha, 909-886		
			Elah, 886-885		
			Zimri, 885		
		Jehoshapat,	Omri, 885-874	Ben-hadad II	Shalmaneser III
			Ahab, 874-853		(Battle of Karkar, 853)
			(Elijah)		
		Jehoram (853) 870-841	Ahaziah, 853-852		
			Jehoram, 854-841		
			(Elisha)		
		Ahaziah, 841	Jehu, 841-814	Hazael	
		Athaliah, 841-835			
		Joash, 835-796	Jehoahaz, 814-798	Ben-hadad	
800 BC		Amaziah, 796-767	Joash, 798-782		
		Azariah	Jeroboam II,		
		(791) 767-740	(793) 782-753		
			(Amos, Hosea)		
			Zechariah, 753-752		
			Shallum, 752		
		Jotham,	Menahem, 752-742		Tiglath-pileser III
750 BC		(750) 740-732			
		(Isaiah)	Pekahiah, 742-740		
		Ahaz, (735) 732-716	Pekah, (752) 740-732	Rezin	
		(Micah)			

	EGYPT	JUDAH	ASSYRIA	BABYLON
700 BC	Tirhakah	Hezekiah, 715-687 Manasseh, (696) 687-642	Sennacherib Esarhaddon Ashurbanipal	
650 BC		Amon, 642-640 Josiah, 640-609 (Jeremiah, Habakkuk) (Nahum)	(Fall of Nineveh to the Babylonians)	Nabopolassar
	Neco II	Jehoahaz, 609 Jehoiakim, 609-598 (Zephaniah)		
600 BC	Hophra	Jehoiakim, 598-597 Zedekiah, 597-586 (Fall of Jerusalem, 586)		Nehbuchadnezzar

		JUDAH		BABYLON	PERSIA
		Gedaliah, governor of Judah			
550 BC		(Daniel) Return to Judah, 539 Rebuilding of the Temple (520-515) (Haggai, Zechariah)		Nabonidus Belshazzar, regent Fall of Babylon to Persia, 539	Cyrus Cambyses Darius I
500 BC					
450 BC		Ezra, 458			Xerxes I (Esther)
350 BC		Samaritan schism			Artaxerxes I

Greece takes over the Persian Empire under the leadership of Alexander the Great, 333 BC.

Annotated Bibliography

The specialist in the field of Old Testament history will immediately recognize my indebtedness to a multiplicity of scholars whose works in the field are well known and readily available to such persons. However, since this book is not for the specialist, an exhaustive bibliography would not only be pointless but would only add to the problems of the nonspecialist in the field. What I am doing is suggesting sources for further study when the interest of the nonspecialist has been aroused. It is my hope that you will want to study one or more of these as you progress in your knowledge of the history of Israel in Old Testament times.

General Works

Cate, Robert L. *How to Interpret the Bible.* Nashville: Broadman Press, 1983.

A book designed to aid in the development of the techniques of biblical interpretation, it offers a step-by-step approach to the task of moving from a biblical text to an application in a sermon, devotional, or Bible lesson.

_____. *Old Testament Roots for New Testament Faith.* Nashville: Broadman Press, 1982.

This is a survey treatment of the basic themes of the faith of the Old Testament with an emphasis upon how the New Testament took these themes, developing and applying them.

Francisco, Clyde T. *Introducing the Old Testament.* Rev. ed. Nashville: Broadman Press, 1977.

This work is a classic introduction to the Old Testament written from the years of teaching experience of one of Southern Baptists' great biblical scholars. It is written from a conservative stance but treats all basic issues of introduction with fairness and clarity.

West, James King. *Introduction to the Old Testament.* 2nd ed.

Here is an excellent introduction to the Old Testament told in narrative form. It is clear, well written, and readable.

Archaeology and Geography

Baly, Dennis. *The Geography of the Bible.* New York: Harper and Brothers Publishers, 1957.

This is probably the best source for the study of biblical geography. It presents a detailed study of the climate, the geological features, and the geography of the land of Palestine as they affected the life and times of the peoples of the Bible.

Cornfeld, Gaalyah. *Archaeology of the Bible: Book by Book.* San Francisco: Harper and Row Publishers, 1976.

An outstanding survey of archaeology as it affects the study and interpretation of the Bible. The format is especially helpful for the nonspecialist in the field.

Frank, Harry Thomas, ed. *Atlas of the Bible Lands.* Nashville: Broadman Press, 1977.

This is one of the better collections of maps for the study of biblical geography. Its usefulness coupled with its inexpensiveness makes it extremely valuable.

May, Herbert G. *Oxford Bible Atlas.* London: Oxford University Press, 1976.

Here is absolutely the best set of biblical maps which are presently available. Both the text and the maps are outstanding, but their price takes them out of the range of most nonspecialists.

Wright, G. Ernest and Floyd V. Filson, eds. *Westminster Historical Maps of Bible Lands.* Philadelphia: The Westminster Press, 1952.

These were originally prepared for the *Westminster Historical Atlas of the Bible.* They are both outstanding and inexpensive. (NOTE: In addition to these, most Bibles have maps at the end of the text. These are all helpful and frequently quite good.)

Old Testament History

Bright, John. *A History of Israel.* 3rd ed. Philadelphia: The Westminster Press, 1981.

This is the best exhaustive study of the entire history of the Old Testament written from a generally conservative standpoint. There is a major emphasis placed upon the biblical text and upon the proven results of ancient Near Eastern archaeology.

Herrmann, Siegfried. *The History of Israel in Old Testament Times.* Translated by John Bowden. Philadelphia: Fortress Press, 1975.

An outstanding example of the best in contemporary German scholarship, this work will provide much fruitful thought for anyone who is seeking to become a specialist in Old Testament history.

Jagersma, Henk. *A History of Israel in the Old Testament Period.* Translated by John Bowden. Philadelphia: Fortress Press, 1983.

This is a briefer approach to the subject from an European standpoint, is well outlined, and generally quite thorough. It is a good book to go to for a first step beyond this present volume.

Thiele, Edwin R. *The Mysterious Numbers of the Hebrew Kings.* Rev. ed. Grand Rapids: Zondervan, 1983.

Here is the best solution which has been proposed to the difficulties of the chronology of the Hebrew kingdoms. It is based upon a thorough study of the chronological systems of the ancient Near East and an application of those systems to the Old Testament. While this work is quite technical and designed for someone devoted to a deep study of the issue, it has been summarized and popularized in Thiele's book *A Chronology of the Hebrew Kings* (Grand Rapids: Zondervan, 1977). This latter work should be sufficient for most students.

Wiseman, D. J. ed. *Peoples of Old Testament Times.* London: Oxford University Press, 1975.

Here is an excellent survey of the history and cultures of the significant peoples with whom Israel came in contact during her history. It is an outstanding reference book.

Scripture Index

Genesis
4:1	65
10:10	51
11:26,32	61
11:27	61
11:31	55,61
12—50	44,46
12	32
12:1-9	46
12:1-3	61,381
12:1	61
12:2	383
12:4	61
12:7a	61
12:7b	61
12:9	61
12:10	62
12:11-13	62
12:15-20	62
13:1-4	63
13:8-9	63
13:10-11	63
13:10,12	63
13:18	63
14	50,253
14:1-16	52
14:1-11	63
14:1-2	51
14:12	63
14:13	54
14:14-16	63
14:18-20	64
14:21-24	64
15:2-3	58
15:4-5	65,68
15:7-18a	64
15:13-16	94-95
15:13	49,50
15:16	49
15:17	64
15:18	392
16:1-3	58
16:3	65
16:7-9	65
16:13	65
17:1-14	64
17:1-8	381
17:5	61
17:17-19	68
17:17	48
18:9-15	68
18:12	66
18:16 to 19:29	46
18:23-33	65
19:1	63
19:5	65
19:24-25	51
19:37-38	156
20:1-18	62
20:2,11	48
21:1-6	66
21:1-3	68
21:5	48
21:8-14	69
21:12b	66
21:32	99
22:1-2	66
22:5b	67
22:7	66
22:8	67
22:9b	68
22:13	68
23:1	48
24:1-9,15,50-51	69
24:10	67
24:63	69
24:67a	69
25:2	111
25:7-8	48,67
25:9	69
25:20,26	48
25:26	70
25:27	71
25:28	69,71
25:29-34	59,71
25:29-30	156
26:1-11	62
26:1-9	69
26:12	57
26:28	99
27:1-40	46,59
27:1	69
27:3-17	69
27:5-29	71
27:20	72
27:22,27	72
27:27b-29	72
27:41	72
27:42-44	70
27:43	72
27:46 to 28:5	70,72
28:12-15	72
28:17	73
28:20-22	73
29:7	73
29:10	73
29:15-30	48
29:17a	74
29:18	73
29:20	73
29:22-25a	74
29:27-30	74
29:30	74
29:31 to 30:24	74

30:1-4,9 58	39:20-23 82	1:9-12 103
30:22-24 48	39:22-23 82	1:9-10 107
30:31-43 74	40:3 82	1:11 104,107
31:1-2 74	40:5-13,16-19 82	1:12 108
31:3 74-75	40:8 83	1:15-16 108
31:17-21 48,75	40:14-15 82	1:15 96
31:19,30 58	41:1-8 83	1:22 109
31:22-23 75	41:16 83	2:1-2 94,109
31:55 75	41:33 83	2:1,4 140
32:13-23 75	41:37-45 83	2:3-5 110
32:26-28 71	41:39-41, 46 48	2:4 109
32:26 75	41:46 83	2:10 110
32:28 75	41:47-49, 53-57 48	2:11-12 111
32:30 75	41:53-57 78	2:11 110
33:1 76	41:56 83	2:14-15 111
33:3 76	41:57 83	2:15 157
33:4 76	42:1-5 48,83	2:22 111
33:4,10 70	42:1-2 48,78	2:23 111
33:10 76	42:6-28 84	3:1 to 4:17
33:11 77	42:38 84	112,130,394
33:20 77	43:1-14 78	3:1 112
35:1-4 77	43:8-9 84	3:8 381
35:7 77	43:20-22 84	3:12 112,118
35:10 77	43:30 84	3:14 112
35:16-19 77	44:4-13 84	4:19 112
35:28-29 48,70,78	44:18-34 84	4:27 112
36:1,8,19 156	45:3-8 84	4:29-31 113
37:1-36 46	45:5 85	5:2 113
37:2-36 48	45:9-11 85	5:6-7,9 113
37:2,14 78	45:16-20 48	5:8 113
37:2b 80	45:26 to 46:7 79	5:10-11 113
37:3-4 80	47:1-12 85	5:21 113
37:3 78	47:6 106	6:7 128
37:5-11 80	47:9 79	6:13-26 95
37:5-7 57	47:9,28 48	7:1-2 130
37:10 80	47:14-21 92	7:3 113
37:11 80	47:15-21 83	7:5,16 128
37:14a 80	48:17-20 59	7:7 109,140
37:15-17 81	48:21 85	7:17 114
37:18 81	49:1-27 79	7:22 114
37:22,26-27 81	49:28-33 79	9:31-32 114
37:27-28 81	49:31 79	12:1-28 115
37:27,32-36 78	50:4-6 79	12:6 114
37:28b, 36 81	50:15-17 85	12:31-33 114
37:29 81	50:19-21 85	12:40 94
37:30-35 81	50:24-26 85	13:4 114
37:32 81	50:26 48	13:20 116
39:1-6a 81		14:2,6-7 116
39:1 82	**Exodus**	14:21 31,116
39:6 81	1:6-7 106	14:25,28 116
39:7-10 82	1:6 85	15:13-16 95
39:11-18 82	1:8 107	15:23 to 16:5 381

SCRIPTURE INDEX 407

15:25 117	14:44-45 124	8:30-35 139,169
16:1 117	20:14-21 93,125	8:30 163
16:4,12-14 117	21:4,13,21-23 93	8:32-35 163
17:8-13 117	21:21-24,33-35 125	9:3-6,15 165
17:9,13 159	21:23-24 175	9:3,15 142
18:2 118	21:26 174	10:1-27 139
18:7 118	22:4-5 125	10:3-5 165
18:17-24 118	25:1-3 126	10:9-11 166
19:1-6 43	25:1 126	10:9 165
19:1 118-119	26:59 109	10:9,43 169
19:5 392	27:18-23 159-160	10:28 166
19:18 64	27:18 126,160	10:28,29,31,34,35,38
20:1-17 101	32:1-5,33 126	139
20:2 99	32:6-7,16-18 126	10:29-30 166
20:3 100	32:33,37-38 175	10:31-32,34-35 166
20:4-17 100		10:36-37 166
21:1-11 105	**Deuteronomy** 27,308	10:38-39 166-167
23:20-33 101	1:2 122,123	10:43 169
24:1-18 119	1:26 123	11:1-13 176
24:5 119	1:26,43 124	11:1-11 168
24:7 392	1:41 124	11:1-9 139
24:9-10 120	1:45 124	11:10 139
25:21 100	2:9 125	11:23 138,168
32:1 121	3:29 126	12:1-24 139
32:3-5 121	4:37 127	13:1 138,140,168
32:4 381	5 100	13:7 to 19:51 168
32:15-18 159	7:7 127,383	14:6 169
32:25-34 122	7:17-24 96	19:40-48 181
33:11 159,160	27—28 101	21:43 138
34 100	31:1-6 126	24 100
40:38 64	34:5 126	24:1-28 139,170,388
	34:9 160	24:1 169,261
Leviticus	34:10 130	24:2-14 170
26 101		24:11 151-152
	Joshua 20,27,29	24:15 170
Numbers	1:1-9 394	24:22-27 170
1:2-3 122	1:1-3 382	24:22 101
1:17-46 95	1:1-2 126	24:25 392
9:1-3 122	1:1 160	
9:15-23 381	1:6,7,9,18 160	**Judges** 20,27,29
10:2 96	1:10-11 160	2:11-23 382
10:11-12 122	2:1 160	2:11 173
13:8,16 159,160	2:2-7,15-16 160	2:14 173
13:17-33 103	4:19-24 169	2:16 173
13:17-20 123	4:19 160	2:17 173
13:25 122	6:12-21 161	2:18 173
13:27-33 123	7:1-26 386	2:21 to 3:5 138
14:4 123	7:1,11 238	3:7-11 145,172,174
14:6-10 159	7:3-5 162	3:11 147
14:6-9 123	7:20-25 163	3:12-30 145
14:39 123	8:3-8 163	3:13 158
14:40 123	8:17 163	3:15-30 172

3:21   175
3:27-28   175
3:30   147
3:31   145,172
4:1 to 5:31   145
4:2   176
4:3   147,181
4:4 to 5:31   172
4:4   148,175
4:8   176
4:13   176
5:2-31   176
5:14-18   145,177
5:18   177
5:19   177
5:20-21   177,382
5:24   177
5:31   147
6:1 to 8:35   145
6:1-6   158,178
6:1   179
6:3   158
6:5   158
6:11 to 8:32   172
6:11   148,178
8:22-23   178
8:28   147,179
9:1-5   179
9:6,22   179
9:34-45   179,183
9:50-55   179
10:1-2   145,172
10:3-5   145,172
10:6 to 12:7   145
11:1 to 12:7   172
11:1-2,5-6   180
11:1   148
11:30,34-35   180
12:1   180
12:4   180
12:5-6   180
12:8-10   145,172
12:11-12   145,172
12:13-15   145,172
13:1 to 16:31   145
13:1   147
13:2 to 16:31   172
14:1-3   181
15:1-2   181
15:20   147
16:1-3,6-21   181
16:21-23   155

16:31   147
18:1   181
18:27-29   181

Ruth
4:21-22   384

Samuel   20,27,40,194
1:13   183
1:27-28   183
2:22-25   183
2:27-34   172
2:31-36   195
3:1 to 4:1*a*   172
3:1-3   183
3:1-3,20   148
3:1   183
3:10-11   183
3:11-14   195
3:19-20   183
4:2   183
4:3   183
4:11,16-18   183-184
4:12-18   172
4:18   184
5:1-2   155
5:1   184
5:5-10   184
6:4-5   184
7:3 to 8:22   172
7:5-6   184
7:10-11   184
7:15 to 8:3   184
8:4 to 31:13   192
8:4-5   210
8:5   184,191
8:7   200,211
8:10-18   211
8:11-18   200
8:19-22   200
8:19   210
9:1-2   211
9:27 to 10:1   195
10:1-2   201
10:1   212
10:6   211
10:10-11   211
10:11   196
10:17-24   195
10:17-21   212
10:22   212
10:26   192

10:27   202,211
11:1-11   212
11:1-2   205
11:1   99
11:4   192
11:7   211,212,213
11:9-11   224
11:12-13   202,211,213
11:14-15   213
11:15   195
12:3-4   213
12:17   213
13:1   199
13:3,5   213
13:8   214
13:10   214
13:13-15   214
13:14   196
13:19-22   155,214
13:19-20   181
14:27   214
14:45   214
14:47-48   215
14:52   214-215
15:1-7   205
15:3   215
15:22   215,389
15:26-29   196
15:34   192
16:1-3   388
16:4-5   216
16:12   216
16:13-14   216
16:13   216
16:14-23   196
16:14   216
16:18   217
16:21-23   217
17:1-2   218
17:8-11   218
17:23,41-50   196
17:38   218
17:39   218
17:50-52   218
17:55-58   196
18:1-4   218
18:3   196
18:7   218
18:9   218
18:17-19,20-21,22-26   196
18:17,20,25   219

SCRIPTURE INDEX

18:27 219	30:24 224	13:1-14,28-29 386
19:1-17 217	30:26-31 224,225	13:21 231
19:4-7 219	31:1-6 224	13:28-29 231
19:12 196	31:3-4 196	13:39 231
19:13-16 219	31:9-10 155	14:1-3,23-24 231
19:17 196	31:11-13 224	14:27 196
19:18 219		15:1-12 386
19:23-24 211	**2 Samuel** 20,27,40,194	15:12 232
19:24 196	1:1 to 1 Kings	15:31 232
20:2,35-42 219	2:11 192	15:32-34 232
20:12-42 196	1:6-10 196	17:1,5-14,23 232
20:18-27 388	1:11-12,19-27 228	18:2 223
20:25-29 196	1:14-16 228	18:9-17 386
20:30-34 219	2:4b-7 228	18:14 231
20:42 196	2:4 225	18:18 196
21:1,6,9 219-220	2:10-11 201	18:33 232
21:9 196	2:10 202,225	19:5-8 232
21:10-15 196	2:11 199	21:19 196
21:10 220	3:1 225	23:34 232
21:13 220	3:27 225	24:1 216
22:1-2 220	3:28-35 228	
22:1 220	3:36 228	**1 Kings** 20,27,
22:3-4 220	4:5-8 225	28,40,194
22:16-19 220	4:8-12 228	1:1 to 2:11 192
23:16-18 221	5:1-3 201,225,228	1:5-27 232
23:18 99,196	5:4-5 199	1:5-6,32-34 201
23:19-20 196	5:6-9 228	1:6 232
23:26-28 221	5:6-8 227	1:32-34 232
23:29 221	5:8 193	2:8-9,36-46 233
24:3-7 196	5:9 193	2:10 232
24:6 221	5:17-25 227	2:11 199
24:16-22 221	6:12-15 228	2:12 to 11:43 192
25:1 221	6:12-13 214	2:17 233
25:3,39-42 222	6:14,21 229	2:23-25 231
25:7 222	6:16 229	2:24-26,28-31 233
25:10-11 222	6:21-22 229	3:1 233
25:23-25 222	6:23 229	3:9 235
26:1-2 222	7:2 229	4:26 233,234
26:1 196	7:3-14 230	4:29-34 207
26:5-12 196	7:11,16 230	5:1-12 207
26:9-10 222	8:1-14 227	5:5 234
26:25 222	8:15-18 229	6:1 92
27:1-2,5-6 222	10:1-19 227	6:37-38 234
27:3 196	11:1 to 12:7 201	7:1-8 234
27:7 226	11:2-21 230	8:1-23 392
27:8-11 222,225	11:3 232	8:5 214
28:1-2 223	12:5-6 230	8:6-9 100
29:1-4 223	12:7 230	9:10-14 233
29:7 223	12:13-14 387	9:17-19 234
30:1-2 223	12:15-18 386	9:26-28 208,235
30:9-10 223	12:18 231	9:26 193
30:16-17 224	13:1-19 231	10:11 235

10:12 208	15:27,33 245	3:4-5 260
10:14-15,22,25,27-29 235	16:6 266	3:9 260
10:16-17 233	16:7 257	5:17 249
10:21-29 208	16:8-10 266	6:8 to 7:20 274
10:23 235	16:8 245	8:7-15 274
11:1-3 233	16:10,15-19 245	8:18 255,273
11:4-8 236	16:17-18 266	9:1-3 275
11:7-8 234	16:21-28 34	9:11-13 275
11:14-25 234	16:22 267	9:14b-15a 275
11:27-33 236	16:23,246 246	9:21-24 275
11:27-28 234	16:24 268	9:27-28 275
11:29-37 258	16:26 296	9:30-35 276
11:29-31 201	16:29 to 22:40 34	10:1-10 276
11:40 258	16:29 246	10:11 276
11:42 199	16:31 268,386	10:12-14 276
11:43 261	17:1 271	10:15-17 276
12:1 to 2 Kings 17:41 242	17:9 271	10:18-27 276
12:1-33 46	18:17-18 271	10:29 386
12:1-5 261	18:21-24 271	10:32-33 277
12:1-4,16-17,20 201	18:36-46 271	11:1 277
12:6-7 262	19:2-3 271	11:2-3 278
12:8-11 262	19:3-8 98	11:4-14 278
12:16-20 196	19:4 272	11:17 278
12:16 262	19:10,14 272	11:21 278
12:18 262	19:15-18 272	12:4-16 278
12:20 263	20:13,35-43 272	12:17-18 279
12:21-24 263	20:16-21,26-30 269	12:19-21 280
12:25 264	20:34 99,270	12:20 279,285
12:26-29 263	21:1-26 390	13:3 279
12:28-29 251	21:1-16 272	13:4 279
12:28 381	21:1-4 186	13:5 279
13:1-10 264	21:8-10 186	13:7 280
14:1 265	21:20-24 272	13:14 280
14:17 264	22:5-6 273	13:25 280
14:19 243	22:9,13-18 272	14:1 280
14:20 245	22:29-35 275	14:5 280
14:21 245	22:30 269	14:6 280
14:25-27 264	22:34-36 270	14:19 285
14:25 259	22:34-35 272	14:25-28 283
14:29 243	22:51-53 273	15:5 285
14:31 265	22:52 386	15:8 286
15:1-2 245		15:10 286
15:3 296	**2 Kings** 20,27, 28,40,308	15:13-14 286
15:8 265	1:1 260	15:18 288
15:9-10 245	1:2-4 273	15:19 289
15:16 265	1:2 155	15:22 290
15:18-19 265	1:17 273	15:25 290
15:22 265	2:9-12 273	15:27 317
15:25 245,265	3:1 273	15:30 292
15:27-28 265	3:3 386	15:37 291
	3:4-12,21-27 273	16:1-2 317
		16:5 256,291

16:6 291	25:2-7 334	20:1-2 260
16:7 257,291	25:7,18-21 359	20:35-37 273
16:10-18 293	25:8-9 335	21:1 274
16:10 293	25:10 335	21:2-4 274
17:3 292,293	25:11 359	21:6 273
17:3-4 259		21:8-10,16-17 274
17:4 294	**1 Chronicles** 28,40,194	22:8-9 275
17:6-18 299	1:1 195	22:11 278
17:6 42	3:1-9 192	24:17-21 279
18:1 to 25:30 303	3:18 364	24:23-25 279
18:1 317	7:20,27 160	24:25 279
18:2 317	8:33 225	24:27 243
18:4-6 318	9:31 225	25:6-9 281
18:8 319	10:1-14 192	25:11-12 281
18:13 to 19:37 305	11:1 to 29:30 192	25:13 281
18:14-16 321	11:4-6 227	25:14 281
18:17 321	14:8-17 227	25:15-16 281
18:20-21 311	16:4 229	25:21-24 281
19:9 306, 311	17:2-4 230	26:2,6-8 285
19:35-36 321,322	17:10-14 230	26:9-10 285
20:12 319	20:5 196	26:16-18 286
21:1-18 46	21:1 217	27:3*a* 288
21:6 323	29:27 199	28:1-8 256
21:16 324		28:1 317
21:17 324	**2 Chronicles** 28,40,194	28:5-8 291
21:20-21 324	1:1 to 9:31 192	28:17-18 293
21:23 324	2:1 234	28:20 293
21:24 324	3:1 68	28:23 293
22:1 325	5:12 235	29:1 to 36:23 303
22:4,8,10,12,14 325	8:1-6 192	29:3 to 31:21 318
22:8-13 308	8:17-18 193	30:1 318
22:11 278,326	8:17 208	30:2-4 318
22:13-14 327	9:22-28 235	30:11 318
23:1-3 388	9:27 235	32:1-22 306
23:2-3 392	9:30 199	32:2-6 320
23:3-23 327	9:31 261	33:3 323
23:4-25 308,389	10:1 to 28:27 242	33:6 323
23:4,24 325	10:1-5 261	33:11 324
23:8 327	10:6-7 262	33:12-16 324
23:25 329	10:8-11 262	33:17 324
23:29-30 328	10:16 262	33:19 324
23:29 41	11:1-2 263	34:1 325
23:30 329	11:5-12 251,258	34:2 325
23:33 330	12:2-12 259	34:3*a* 325
24:1 315	12:15 264	34:3*b* 325
24:1*a* 331	12:16 265	34:6-7 326
24:1*b* 331	13:15-19 265	34:8-15 326
24:2 315,331	14:9 265	34:19 326
24:6,8 332	15:1-15 266	34:32-33 327
24:12-16 332	16:7-10 266	35:20-24 42,328
24:17 332	17:10-19 269	36:1 329
25:1-7 42	18:28 269	36:6 331

36:9 332	6:5-13 372	9:2-6 397
36:22-23 345	6:15 372	9:6-7 200
36:23 363	7:1-3 372	10:5-7 382
	7:6-73a 347	10:5-6 299-300,321
Ezra	7:73 370	11:1-9 200
1:1-2 345	8:1-18 388	20:1-6 311,319
1:2-4 363	8:1-3 370	24:5 392
1:8-11 364	8:3 370	32:1-2 200
2:1-70 347	8:9 370	36:1 to 37:38 306
3:1-6 364	8:13-18 370	36:2 321
3:2 365	9:38 370,392	36:4-10 321
3:8-11 365	10:30-32 370	36:12 322
4:1-2 366	12:10-11 346	36:16 186,322
4:6 368	12:27-30 372	36:17 186,322
4:7-16 369	13:6-7 373	36:19-20 322
4:12 368	13:6 372	37:2,5,21-29 323
4:17-22 369	13:8-9 373	37:6-7 322
4:23 369,371	13:10-14 373	37:9 306,322
5:3-17 367	13:15-21,23-25 373	37:36-37 322
6:1-5 367		38:1-6 323
6:2-5 363	**Esther**	39:1 319
6:6-13 367	1:1 368	39:3-7 323
6:10 367	1:19 345,354	42:1-7 374,384
6:14 367		44:28 355
6:15 367	**Psalms**	45:1 355
7:1,7 346	78 89	49:1-6 374,384
7:9 370	105 89	50:4-9 374,384
7:11 369		52:13 to 53:12 374,384
7:12,21 369	**Proverbs**	
7:14 369	1:1 235	**Jeremiah** 308
7:21-23 369		1:2 326
7:21 356	**Ecclesiastes**	1:4-10 130,394
7:25-26 369	1:1,12-14 235	1:5 385
10:6 346	3:1-8 37	2:1 394
10:11 370	12:12 14	3:18 347
		11:1-8 327
Nehemiah	**Isaiah**	11:2-10 392
1:3 369	1—39 303	11:18-23 328
1:11 371	1:2-3 101	18:18 207
2:1 346	1:11-13 296-297	26:24 359
2:3-6 371	1:17 390	27:1-11 312,385
2:5-8 369	2:1-4 385	27:3-7 333
2:7-9 371	2:6-8 317	27:12-15 333
2:7 356	5:8,20-22 391	29:1-9 333
2:10 371	6:1-13 291	31:31-34 335,338,397
2:11-16 371	6:1-12 130,394	34:6 333
2:17-18 372	6:8 385	35:19 276
2:19-20 371	7:1-9 256	36:1-3 331
3:1 346	7:3 292	36:23-24 331
4:6-8,13-23 372	7:6 291	36:32 331
5:6-8,12 372	7:12 292	37:5 334
5:14 346	8:19 317	37:11-15 334

SCRIPTURE INDEX

37:11 313	**Hosea**	**Habakkuk** 303
38:1-6 334	1:1 385	2:4b 337,387
38:7-13 334	1:4-5 277	
39:3,13 352	2:2-5,16-17 248	**Zephaniah** 303
39:4-5 358	2:3 250	
39:11-14 334,358	2:16 250	**Haggai**
40:1-6 335,358	3:1 385	1:1,15 366
40:7-8,11 359	4:1-2,4-8 284	1:10-11 366
40:13-16 360	4:6-14 248	2:3 367
41:1-3 360	4:12-19 284	2:10 366
41:2 342	5:1-2 284	2:16-17 366
41:5 365	8:4 200	2:23 366
41:11-15 360	10:3 200	
42:3 360	11:8-9 300	**Zechariah**
42:5 361	11:9 382	4:6 367
43:2 360	13:9-12 284-285	7:1 366
43:5-7 342,360	13:10-11 200	
51:13,58 354		**Matthew**
51:59 316,333	**Amos**	1:5-16 160
52:29 359	1:3 to 2:3 382	3:9 65,383
52:30 361	4:4-5 248	5:17-18 13
52:31-34 332	4:6,8,9,10,11 300,382	6:29 238
	5:18-20 284,299,382	
Ezekiel	5:21-24 248,284,389	**Luke**
1:4 to 3:15 130	6:1 391	3:8 65
3:14 394	6:1,4-6 283	10:25-37 378
16:8,59 392	7:12-13 285	15:25-32 76
17:11-16 333	7:12 298	
21:21 13	7:14-15 385,394	**John**
33:24 365	7:14 298	8:33 65
36:26-32 338	8:4-6 284	15:13 329
37:15-23 347		
	Obadiah 303	**Acts**
Daniel		13:21 199
5:28 345,354	**Micah**	17:22-31 349
5:29 344	4:1-4 385	
5:30-31 343,344	5:12-14 317	**Galatians**
5:31 345	6:1-2 101	3:16-17 49
6:1-4 356	6:6-8 388	
6:1 345		**Hebrews**
6:8 345	**Nahum** 303	11:37 324